MAGILL'S SURVEY OF CINEMA

MAGILL'S SURVEY OF CINEMA

English Language Films

FIRST SERIES
VOLUME 4
SCA-Z

Edited by

FRANK N. MAGILL

Associate Editors

PATRICIA KING HANSON

STEPHEN L. HANSON

SALEM PRESS
Englewood Cliffs, N.J.

LIBRARY OF CONGRESS CATALOG CARD NUMBER: 80-52131

Complete Set: ISBN 0-89356-225-4
Volume 4: ISBN 0-89356-229-7

PRINTED IN THE UNITED STATES OF AMERICA

LIST OF TITLES IN VOLUME FOUR

LIST OF TITLES IN VOLUME FOUR

MAGILL'S SURVEY OF CINEMA

THE SCARLET PIMPERNEL

Released: 1934
Production: Alexander Korda for United Artists-London Film Productions
Direction: Howard Young
Screenplay: Robert E. Sherwood, Arthur Wimperis, Sam Berman, and Lajos Biro; based on Robert E. Sherwood's and Arthur Wimperis' adaptation of the novel of the same name by Baroness Orczy
Cinematography: Harold Rosson
Editing: William Hornbeck
Running time: 98 minutes

Principal characters:
Sir Percy Blakeney .... Leslie Howard
Lady Marguerite Blakeney .... Merle Oberon
Chauvelin .... Raymond Massey
Prince of Wales .... Nigel Bruce
Comte de Tournay .... O. B. Clarence
Suzanne de Tournay .... Joan Gardner
Armand St. Just .... Walter Rilla

Sir Percy Blakeney (Leslie Howard) is one of England's richest men and is newly married to the most beautiful woman in Europe, *une française* named Lady Marguerite Blakeney (Merle Oberon), *née* St. Just. As the sole repository of the Blakeney fortune and lineage, only Sir Percy knows of a certain symbol on the family crest—a modest English primrose of a deep red hue. He has taken this scarlet pimpernel as his personal emblem. Its simple outline is carved on a signet ring he wears but the decoration is concealed by a large stone which clasps over it.

The time is 1792, and France is bathed in the blood of the Revolution at the hands of Robespierre and the Reign of Terror. The Prince of Wales (Nigel Bruce) and all of English nobility are outraged at the daily slaughter of the aristocratic French, many of whom have been their friends. Sir Percy is particularly horrified by the death of the Marquis de St. Cyr and his family, whom his wife had unintentionally betrayed to a Revolutionary tribunal in a fit of misdirected, republican goodwill, extracted from her by the French ambassador to England, Monsieur Chauvelin (Raymond Massey). In vicarious expiation for Lady Blakeney's ghastly *faux pas*, Sir Percy has organized a small band of conspirators engaged in smuggling death-bound aristocrats and royalists from French prisons to the safe shores of England. The deeds of these men are widely known throughout France and England but their identity and that of their leader remain hidden behind the mysterious appellation, the "Scarlet Pimpernel." Imprisoned nobility receive news of their impending liberation at the sight of the pimpernel signet impressed upon a scrap of paper which finds its way into their cell, and each time France is delivered of a group of aristocrats, Robespierre is brought a note bearing their names and signed only with a floral design rendered in red wax.

Despite his great love for his bride of one year, Sir Percy cannot reveal himself to her for fear of endangering her. She might also unwittingly divulge her husband's mission, thereby endangering his life and those of the élite still to be rescued. His long absences from her, however, have severely undermined their marriage, as have the silly manners he has assumed of late in order to elude her suspicion. Leslie Howard is required to play a demanding dual role, since the greater part of his screen time is devoted to the extravagantly attired *poseur* concerned with little else beyond the cut of his cuff. The slender, fair-complexioned Howard beautifully enacts the simpering affectations of the vapid, self-amused Sir Percy whose aching expression discloses in private the suffering to which he is also subjecting his beloved wife.

Merle Oberon, at the height of her beauty, plays Lady Blakeney. In her second leading-lady role, she is possibly too exotic in facial features for the drawing-room setting, but her dark loveliness provides a striking chiaroscuro to the pale Howard. Lady Blakeney is at a loss to understand the foppish, limp-wristed ways her husband has recently adopted. Relieved at his departure under yet another pretext, she nevertheless longs for the return of the man she formerly loved so well.

Enduring the humiliation of being thought an indolent dandy, Sir Percy continues to plot further expeditions to Paris with his compatriots, one of whom is his wife's brother, Armand St. Just (Walter Rilla). The first feat of daring the audience sees is Howard disguised as an old hag driving a hay wagon about the prison and guillotine platform, cackling pro-Revolutionary harangues amid the teeming throng. Atop his whip are the tendrils of several noble heads, lately relieved of their bodies by an obliging "Madame Guillotine." Brandishing his trophy, he confides to the sentry of the suspiciously guarded Porte St. Denis that the boy at his side is afflicted with the plague. The sentry immediately ceases the search of his wagon and demands that the city gate be raised for his riddance. Only too late does he realize that the Scarlet Pimpernel has escaped with the Comtesse de Tournay and her daughter under a load of hay. According to plan, a coach and four, driven by men in the uniforms of the Revolutionary Army, awaits the refugees in the countryside north of Paris and the ladies are escorted to England.

Enraged at the mockery made of the Revolution by the Pimpernel, Robespierre demands that the Englishman be found at once. He dispatches the tale's quintessential villain, Chauvelin (Raymond Massey), to Dover where he and his spies discover a note identifying Armand St. Just as a member of the Pimpernel underground. In London, he gains entrée to the home of Lady Blakeney and preys upon her love for her brother to again trick her into betraying the identity of his quarry, the Scarlet Pimpernel. As a woman of wealth, beauty, and position, she knows everyone in English society and through wit and guile can surely learn for Chauvelin the name of the République's arch enemy. To assure her cooperation, Chauvelin threatens death to her brother in the event of her failure. Lady Blakeney is now torn between saving Armand, whom she believes has been captured by French spies, and shielding from discovery the Scarlet Pimpernel, whom she greatly admires. At Lord Glenville's ball she cleverly aquires a note meant for a Pimpernel comrade and, to the waiting Chauvelin who is also a guest, she reveals a midnight meeting in Glenville's library. Triumphantly expectant of the Pimpernel's imminent discovery, he enters the library only to find the sartorially splendid fool, Sir Percy Blakeney, who is snoring loudly, sleeping on the settee. When Chauvelin succumbs to sleep while waiting, the wary Sir Percy slips away, again eluding his grasp.

Sad and lonely at her husband's latest departure, Lady Blakeney wanders into his private study where by chance she glimpses an intricately carved ring on the finger of a Blakeney ancestor in a huge portrait over the fireplace; the portrait bears a ribbon of faintly readable words: ". . . the Scarlet Pimpernel . . . ." Distraught at thus learning the truth of the Pimpernel's identity, she hastens to join him at the Calais rendezvous where she has learned he is bound. Knowing that Chauvelin, too, will soon be aware of his destination, she vows to save her husband or die with him. Lady Blakeney arrives at the seaside meeting place, the Lion d'Or, ahead of her husband, as has Chauvelin. In a garret there she sees a dressing table strewn with the disguises used by the Pimpernel; she is forced by Chauvelin to wave an "all clear" signal at its window, knowing that she beckons her husband to doom. During the suspenseful confrontation scene, the personalities of Sir Percy and the Scarlet Pimpernel merge. Outsmarting the clever Chauvelin at every turn, Blakeney envelops the scoundrel in a trap of his own making, and as the defeated Chauvelin is carried off, the Blakeneys bear homeward across the Channel, united by their love for England and for each other.

The Scarlet Pimpernel was made during producer Alexander Korda's "golden years," and it achieved such success that it financed the foundations of the studio complex at Denham, England. For this lighthearted adventure, Korda drew upon a novel he had read and loved as a boy in Hungary. The book, published in 1905, was written by the daughter of a Hungarian aristocrat who defected in the mid-1800's. Its popular reception, together with the successful play based upon it (also appearing in 1905), guaranteed Korda a box-office hit.

The film was reissued in 1942 and 1947; a 1950 remake starring David Niven, entitled *The Elusive Pimpernel*, did not compare favorably with its predecessor, which owes much of its success to the casting of Leslie Howard. Charles Laughton had originally been planned for the part, but in an unprecedented move, Korda responded to the letters of Laughton fans by removing him from the cast.

All performances in the film are first-rate and are surpassed only by the exquisite period costumes and interiors. Raymond Massey plays the hateful villain with much zest. Equal in excitement to his role are the early scenes of rowdy peasants who scream with delight each time an aristocrat is beheaded. More footage might well have been devoted to the adventures of the rather extravagantly clothed Pimpernel than to the elegant salons of English society. The pace slows a bit, and is only slightly relieved by mincing Sir Percy's overdone "Sink me!," "Wot!," and his inane doggerel.

The denouement comes too abruptly in a story dwelling overlong on Regency repartee as the end is thrust suddenly upon the viewer still caught up in the unravelings of the late-developing plot. The book is better structured, since surprises and secrets are adroitly revealed at spaced intervals rather than disclosed almost together as in the last several scenes of the film. Nevertheless, *The Scarlet Pimpernel* is an exciting drama of international intrigue set in a dramatic, tumultuous period; and it is little wonder that it has endured as another of Korda's cinema classics.

Nancy S. Kinney

THE SEA HAWK

Released: 1940
Production: Hal B. Wallis for Warner Bros.
Direction: Michael Curtiz
Screenplay: Howard Koch and Seton I. Miller; based on the novel of the same name by Rafael Sabatini
Cinematography: Sol Polito
Editing: George Amy
Music: Erich W. Korngold
Running time: 124 minutes

Principal characters:

Geoffrey Thorpe	Errol Flynn
Doña Maria	Brenda Marshall
Don Jose Alvarez de Cordoba	Claude Rains
Queen Elizabeth	Flora Robson
Carl Pitt	Alan Hale

With *The Sea Hawk* Michael Curtiz established himself as the most flamboyant director of Hollywood swashbucklers. His expressionistic style coupled with Errol Flynn's dashing screen personality was evident in films such as *Captain Blood* (1935), *The Adventures of Robin Hood* (1938), *The Charge of the Light Brigade* (1936), and the ultimate swashbuckling escapism of *The Sea Hawk*.

Errol Flynn plays Geoffrey Thorpe, a privateer serving Queen Elizabeth I (Flora Robson), who plunders Spanish ships on the high seas. His most recent catch is the ship carrying the Spanish Ambassador to the English court. Realizing the irony of the situation, Thorpe agrees to escort the diplomat and his niece safely to England. It is obvious that the Queen privately sanctions the efforts of her "sea hawks," but must, in public, criticize and censure those who make themselves too visible. Thorpe falls into this latter category.

Through the course of his stay on English soil, Thorpe falls in love with Doña Maria (Brenda Marshall), the Spanish Ambassador's niece. Realizing the impossibility of their love, they keep their feelings a secret while Thorpe convinces the Queen to allow him to make a secret raid on the Central American gold route used by the Spanish. What better idea, muses Thorpe, than to have a pirate raid in the heart of the jungle. He leaves his sweetheart, unaware that his plans have been discovered and an ambush awaits him and his men. Thorpe's raiding party is ambushed and almost totally wiped out. The few survivors make their way into the impenetrable jungle in a desperate attempt to avoid capture, and most of them die as they try to hack their way back to the ocean and freedom. A handful find their way to their ship at anchor only to encounter a company of Spanish soldiers awaiting them.

Thorpe and the remaining crew are captured and sentenced to live out the rest of their lives as galley slaves. After several months of rowing the Spanish gentry through battles and intrigues, they overhear a plot to invade England which is to be conveyed to a "fifth columnist" in the English court. The sailors manage to free themselves and return to England with evidence incriminating the traitor. After sneaking into the palace and fighting a number of guards, Thorpe confronts his enemy. Fighting at swordpoint, Thorpe eventually kills the high-ranking traitor and proves to the Queen the existence of the Spanish plot. He is reunited with Doña Maria and once again England rules the waves.

Errol Flynn was one of the leading male film stars of the 1930's and 1940's. His career began suddenly when he rose from obscurity to replace an ailing Robert Donat in the picture *Captain Blood*. During the period between 1935 and 1945, Flynn starred in nearly twenty feature films. His remarkable range as an actor took him from Westerns and drawing room comedies to exciting swashbucklers and patriotic war films. Yet along with *The Adventures of Robin Hood*, *The Sea Hawk* remains the consummate Flynn vehicle. It contains all the ingredients of a classic swashbuckler: romance, adventure, intrigue, and almost continuous action. The sea battle which opens the film is a brilliantly staged piece of filmmaking. The final sword duel is outrageous in its opulence yet able to generate a high level of believability and suspense.

Michael Curtiz directed *The Sea Hawk* with his characteristic expressionism. He had directed many Flynn films, and he left his unmistakable brand of gigantic shadows and unusual camera angles on *The Sea Hawk*. He was able to suggest the splendor of the English court and the exoticism of the Central American jungle with a directorial economy that is remarkable.

Beyond the basic adventure plot in *The Sea Hawk*, there are obvious references to the coming of World War II. The screenplay by Seton I. Miller and Howard W. Koch (who wrote *Casablanca*) hints at the Nazi takeover of Europe, except that in *The Sea Hawk* the Nazi is transposed into the imperialistic Spaniard whose singular purpose is to conquer the world. There is even reference to fifth columnists infiltrating the English court. The instigation of a planned invasion of England is the final and most convincing association between the Spanish court and Nazi Germany. This reference to World War II did not go unnoticed at the time; several reviewers were quick to point out the similarities, although through the intervening years these similarities have become more obscure. *The Sea Hawk* nevertheless remains a classic swashbuckler and a superb vehicle for the dashing Errol Flynn.

Carl F. Macek

THE SEARCH

Released: 1948
Production: Lazar Wechsler for Praesens Film; released by Metro-Goldwyn-Mayer
Direction: Fred Zinnemann
Screenplay: Richard Schweizer and David Wechsler (AA), with additional dialogue by Paul Jarrico
Cinematography: Emil Berna
Editing: Hermann Haller
Running time: 105 minutes

Principal characters:
Ralph Stevenson .... Montgomery Clift
Karel Malik .... Ivan Jandl
(AA Special Award)
Mrs. Malik .... Jarmila Novotna
Mrs. Murray .... Aline MacMahon
Jerry Fisher .... Wendell Corey
Mrs. Fisher .... Mary Patton
Tom Fisher .... William Rogers

Although the initial premise of *The Search* may have simply been to illustrate the then-current topic of the plight of European refugees, it transcended any melodramatic limitations this premise might have imposed because of its overall high quality of documentary realism, particularly achieved in the performance of Montgomery Clift. Technically speaking this was Clift's second film, but because *Red River* (1952) was delayed in postproduction, *The Search* became the first Clift film ever seen in general release. The film's plot was very timely in 1948: ten-year-old Karel Malik (Ivan Jandl) escapes from a United Nations Relief center to which he has been taken in the aftermath of surviving Auschwitz since he considers the center to be another concentration camp, and after what might be weeks of wandering, he is taken in by a charitable American soldier (Montgomery Clift). Although the boy's mother (Jarmila Novotna) is still alive, he does not know this, and in the wake of surviving Auschwitz herself, she now travels on foot from place to place looking for him.

Both mother's and son's paths are on the constant verge of crossing. The mother arrives at the same United Nations camp from which her son has escaped only to be told that he has died; the authorities believe that he has drowned during his escape attempt. Upon hearing the news, she suffers a collapse. Meanwhile, after a rough start to the relationship, the soldier has befriended the boy and is gradually restoring him to health. He notifies United Nations Relief, providing the boy's Auschwitz number as identification, and receives the reply that most of the women identified by that series were killed, the mother almost certainly being among them. Since the adoption process represents an abysmal labyrinth of time and red tape, he makes reckless plans to smuggle the boy to the United States.

The climax of the film comes when the paths of mother and son nearly miss crossing the final time. The mother has befriended the British woman in charge of the camp, a Mrs. Murray (Aline MacMahon), whom she has helped with the vast numbers of orphans in her charge. Mrs. Malik has shown such a passionate talent for her work that she is offered a job with United Nations Relief, but she turns it down. She will not accept the fact that her son is dead since no body was ever recovered from the "drowning," and she desires to go on searching. Having realized that he should leave the boy with the authorities until he can send for him, the soldier drives into the camp less than a minute after the mother has left by another entrance. She, nevertheless, has a change of heart; while seated in her railway coach, she observes the trainloads of even more ragged children being brought in and decides to stay and work after all, caring for whomever she can. It is significant that her final deliverance comes out of this sacrifice: she presents herself to Mrs. Murray, who, along with the soldier, has just realized what is about to happen, and, as she is given her first group of children, she discovers her son among the others. This moment, with mother and child first staring at each other in a paralysis of recognition and then bursting into each other's arms, must stand as one of the most overpowering reunions in the history of cinema.

What brings about this denouement without becoming overly dramatic are Fred Zinnemann's consummately authentic and cinematic creation of the world of postwar Europe; the fact that the desire for realism extended to the casting of actors whose nationality matched that of their roles; and finally, the presence of Montgomery Clift, as unique now as it was unprecedented then. The film was shot on location in Munich, and the burnt-out ruins were real, as were the factories, squalid night cafes, and miraculously preserved prewar houses. As the film opens, a trainload of ragged children arrives in cattle cars by night at a depot of bomb-shattered walls and broken windows. Because of filming on location and the film's close proximity to the actual events of war, there is virtually no way to discern which props are genuine and which have been reconstructed, where reality begins or leaves off, and the film's slow style reinforces the uncertainty by allowing the images to sink in. This good effect is occasionally marred, however, by a female voice-over narration that comments on things the audience is already seeing. Although the narration adds to the matriarchal feel and theme of the film, Zinnemann's direction is more than enough to communicate, nonverbally, the ideas it desires to manifest, and a modern viewer often wishes it had been deleted.

The performances are excellent, particularly those of Ivan Jandl, Jarmila Novotna, and Aline MacMahon; Wendell Corey, Mary Patton, and William Rogers, as the American family that shares the soldier's house and causes a crisis by awakening the boy's memory of his mother, succeed to a lesser extent, although this may have been the fault of the screenplay. Their concept of reality, at least in comparison to the other characters and elements in the film, is too idealized and saccharine. The filmmakers obviously felt safer dealing authentically with Europeans than they did with Americans.

Whatever qualities the remainder of the cast present, *The Search* belongs to Montgomery Clift. Much has been written about Clift, but it is difficult to isolate in words the exact quality that made him so striking as an actor. For audiences in 1948, it was his physical beauty, but there was also a subconscious magnetism at work. During the making of *The Search*, Clift battled with screenwriters in order to make his soldier more real and less of a "boy scout." He worked long hours at night rewriting sections of the script with this in mind, and carefully rehearsed his versions with Ivan Jandl between takes. Lazar and David Wechsler, producer and writer, respectively, were outraged by the revisions, charging that his distillations of the script's speeches and reworkings of scenes were killing the "message," and that what he was substituting was sloppy and awkward. Yet it is through Clift's scenes that the film comes most to life. For example, in the scene directly following his capture of the boy, the soldier locks him up in the dining room until he can figure out a plan. The terrified boy smashes the fishtank and every other glass fixture in the room, and the soldier threatens to quiet him with an injection until he realizes what a horrible mistake he has made upon seeing, for the first time, the Auschwitz tattoo on the boy's inner arm. His reaction, and the dialogue, are sparse and asymmetrical, but oddly vivid and natural. It is not difficult to empathize with a producer, particularly a message-oriented one, receiving such changes from a publicly untried film star. In any case, it is Clift's scenes alone with Ivan Jandl that best withstand the test of time; other parts of the film possess much less vitality by comparison. In the end, Fred Zinnemann settled the conflict simply by showing the rushes, whereupon the Wechslers relented to the changes; and ironically, one of the film's two Academy Awards was for Best Screenplay, the other being a Special Award to Ivan Jandi.

The film was a huge success in its time. It saw enormous returns at the box office, and lives on through prolific showings in revival houses and on television. Montgomery Clift was rocketed to overnight stardom: he went on to make eighteen films altogether, including Fred Zinnemann's *From Here to Eternity* (1953). Although it would seem that audiences were responding at their most conscious level to the purity of his good looks, it is also clear that they were responding, deeply and for the first time, to a hero who was both masculine and sensitive, an actor who was both a movie star and a serious artist.

F. X. Feeney

THE SEARCHERS

Released: 1956
Production: Merian C. Cooper and Patrick Ford for C. V. Whitney Pictures; released by Warner Bros.
Direction: John Ford
Screenplay: Frank S. Nugent; based on the novel of the same name by Alan LeMay
Cinematography: Winton C. Hoch
Editing: Jack Murray
Running time: 119 minutes

Principal characters:
Ethan Edwards .... John Wayne
Martin Pawley .... Jeffrey Hunter
Laurie Jorgensen .... Vera Miles
Captain Reverend Clayton .... Ward Bond
Debbie Edwards (older) .... Natalie Wood
Debbie Edwards (younger) .... Lana Wood
Lars Jorgensen .... John Qualen
Mrs. Jorgensen .... Olive Carey
Chief Scar .... Henry Brandon
Aaron Edwards .... Walter Coy
Martha Edwards .... Dorothy Jordan
Look .... Beulah Archuletta
Lucy Edwards .... Pippa Scott

The Searchers is unquestionably the masterpiece of America's foremost director, John Ford. Ostensibly a conventional Western, *The Searchers* brings together themes that concerned Ford in his fifty-year film career, and illuminates them anew with the power and vigor of the mature artist working at the peak of his creativity. Full of the action typical of the genre, the film is also a subtle study of psychological torment. Finally it becomes an epic of the American experience which parallels Melville's *Moby Dick* in its concern with the fundamental tensions at the heart of that experience.

The plot of the film is relatively simple. A cabin door opens onto a desolate wilderness and Ethan Edwards (John Wayne) is seen approaching his brother's homestead after a long absence fighting in the Civil War. His brother Aaron (Walter Coy), his sister-in-law Martha (Dorothy Jordan), his nephew, and his nieces Debbie (Lana Wood) and Lucy (Pippa Scott) greet him and lead him into the cabin. Ford quickly establishes a tension between the brothers that resides in a long-suppressed love between Martha and Ethan. Perhaps for this reason Ethan has remained away long past the end of the war. Martin Pawley (Jeffrey Hunter), the adopted son of the Edwardses, is introduced, and we learn that Ethan rescued him as a child after his parents were killed in an Indian raid.

The Edwards' breakfast the next morning is interrupted by their neighbor Mr. Jorgensen (John Qualen), Captain Clayton (Ward Bond), and a posse of Texas Rangers pursuing cattle rustlers. Captain Clayton deputizes Ethan and Martin, and the posse rides off in pursuit. They find the cattle forty miles away killed with Comanche lances. Ethan realizes that the cattle have been driven off to lure the men away from the ranchers so that a war party can attack the settlers left behind. Ethan and Martin return to the cabin to find Aaron, Martha, and their son dead, and the girls kidnaped by the Comanches. The effort to find and ransom the girls motivates what is to become a five-year search.

Ethan and Martin soon learn that Lucy has been killed but they continue to search for Debbie. During this period, Ethan's desire for vengeance is transformed into a monomaniacal obsession. Coupled with the knowledge that Debbie has been adopted by the Indians and undoubtedly married to one of the warriors, Ethan's obsession and racial hatred approaches madness. Martin stays with the search because of his concern for Debbie and because he is fearful of what Ethan will do when he finds her.

After an encounter with a treacherous trader, a comical "marriage" between Martin and the Indian woman he calls Look (Beulah Archuletta), and a Cavalry massacre of an Indian village, the searchers at last catch up with the Comanche chief Scar (Henry Brandon) and his band. The dramatic encounter between Ethan and Scar emphasizes the similarities of pursuer and pursued. Debbie (Natalie Wood) is a member of the tribe and Scar's wife. Ethan and Martin attempt to rescue her, but when they do, Ethan wants to kill her. Martin stops him, but Ethan is wounded in the fight with the Indians and the men must return to the Jorgensens' without Debbie.

When they arrive at the Jorgensen homestead, Martin discovers that his fiancée, Laurie Jorgensen (Vera Miles), has grown tired of waiting for him and intends to marry a Texas Ranger that very evening. Martin fights his rival for the right to marry Laurie, but before the matter is resolved, a Cavalry Lieutenant arrives with the news that Scar's band has been located once more.

Ethan, Martin, Captain Clayton, and his Rangers surround the camp and prepare for the attack. Martin is permitted to attempt Debbie's rescue before the attack begins. He finds her but must kill Scar in order to effect their escape. In the ensuing battle, Ethan finds Scar's body and scalps it. He then rides down Debbie; but instead of killing her, he sweeps her into his arms. The searchers return to the Jorgensens', where Debbie is welcomed back, and Martin claims Laurie for his bride. All enter the house but Ethan. The last shot reverses the first shot of the film, showing Ethan returning alone to his wilderness as the door of civilization closes.

The Searchers is a superb example of the Western film. It draws upon the familiar conventions of the genre to present multidimensional characters in surprising and unpredictable fashion. The film transcends those conventions, however, in its subtle exploration of racial prejudice and psychological turmoil. Ethan Edwards is a man obsessed with the desire for revenge and hatred for the man who violated and killed the woman he loved. As such he is not the typical Western hero concerned with clear-cut issues, but is rather a man with very human qualities forced to deal with his surroundings in a superhuman manner.

At its most profound, *The Searchers* is an archetype of the American experience. Ethan Edwards embodies the conflicts experienced by the European settlers confronting the American wilderness and its native inhabitants. Ethan is more competent in the wilderness than his fellow settlers and more akin than even he suspects to his Indian adversary. The freedom that attracts him to the wilderness also carries with it an implicit alienation from the civilization represented by his sister-in-law and by the Jorgensens. This conflict between the freedom of the wilderness and the comfort of civilization with its attendant responsibilities, is a major conflict in American history and literature. Ethan Edwards joins Daniel Boone, Leatherstocking, Huck Finn, and Ahab in the pantheon of American heroes personifying these opposing attractions.

The theme of the wilderness in opposition to civilization in the American experience is also a major concern of John Ford which he explores in the several Westerns he made during his long career. In Ethan Edwards he creates a character whose neurotic intensity and consuming obsessions render him quite unlike any other character in a Ford film. He is a tragic hero who suffers from the conflicting attractions of the vast and empty American landscape and the need for civilized order. Committed to that wilderness, he loses his beloved Martha, first to his brother and then to the savage wilderness itself as embodied by Scar.

John Wayne described the role of Ethan as his favorite among all his roles, and he brings to it a depth of feeling and range of expression that marks it as the outstanding performance of his long career. Believable as the thoroughly authoritative frontiersman, he subtly and with economy of gesture conveys the anguish and increasing madness of a character tormented by pressures he cannot control. Ford employs many of his stock company of actors in the other roles. Ward Bond as Captain Clayton and Olive Carey and John Qualen as the Jorgensens are especially effective in small but extremely important roles.

The concern with the dynamics of racism and the more violent aspects of the American experience makes *The Searchers* all the more remarkable for a film produced in 1956. Although a financial success, the film was largely ignored by the critics and it did not receive any Academy nominations. By 1972, however, *The Searchers* had increased in critical stature to the point where, in a poll of international film critics conducted by *Sight and Sound*, it was included in the list of the top twenty films of all time. It is the only Ford film on the list. Recently film directors have consciously paid homage to the film by patterning their films on *The Searchers*. Martin Scorsese's *Taxi Driver* (1976) and Paul Schrader's *Hardcore* (1979) are two examples of this trend. *The Searchers* will stand as John Ford's masterpiece and a cinematic achievement that can serve as an example to all future filmmakers of the possibilities of the art form.

Don K Thompson

SEPARATE TABLES

Released: 1958
Production: Harold Hecht for Clifton/Joanna Productions; released by United Artists
Direction: Delbert Mann
Screenplay: Terence Rattigan and John Gay; based on the play of the same name by Terence Rattigan
Cinematography: Charles Lang
Editing: Marjorie Fowler and Charles Ennis
Music: David Raksin
Running time: 98 minutes

Principal characters:
Ann Shankland .... Rita Hayworth
Sibyl Railton-Bell .... Deborah Kerr
Major Pollock ....David Niven (AA)
John Malcolm .... Burt Lancaster
Miss Cooper ....Wendy Hiller (AA)
Mrs. Railton-Bell .... Gladys Cooper
Lady Matheson ....Cathleen Nesbitt
Mr. Fowler ....Felix Aylmer
Charles .... Rod Taylor
Jean .... Audrey Dalton

During the 1950's, Terence Rattigan's play *Separate Tables* had been a hit both on the West Side of London and on Broadway in New York. It dealt largely with the problems of two couples residing at Bournemouth, an English seaside resort, during the off-season. Both couples were portrayed by two players, Margaret Leighton and Eric Portman, in *tour de force* performances. The play was actually two playlets having as a unifying force the setting of the residential hotel in Bournemouth, where the principal characters meet to dine at separate tables.

Hecht, Hill, and Lancaster acquired the rights to film *Separate Tables* and engaged Terence Rattigan and John Gay to combine the two playlets and to provide four big roles for four stars. Their efforts were remarkably successful, and the film version became one of the few instances of a movie which is actually better than the play from which it was adapted. Terence Rattigan had wanted it that way. When he sold the rights to *Separate Tables*, he did so with the stipulation that the story could not be presented as it had been on the stage, for the entire dramatic continuity would have to be reconstructed in order to unify the narrative content. He himself wished to be hired to alter the story's form, but he was agreeable to working with a collaborator. Thus, Hecht, Hill, and Lancaster teamed him with John Gay, and their screenplay, as based upon Rattigan's play, became a model for clarity in adaptation from one medium to another.

In revising the screenplay, the producers lost Laurence Olivier, who had originally been signed to direct and costar in it with his then-wife, Vivien Leigh; but they indubitably gained a tighter, more filmable screenplay. Under the circumstances, Delbert Mann was a better choice for director, and the cast he assembled could not have been improved upon. David Niven won the Oscar for Best Actor for his role as the bogus Major Pollock, with his phony Sandhurst background and his fictitious World War II conquests. Niven also won the New York Film Acting Award as Best Actor of the year. Wendy Hiller as Miss Cooper, the manager of the hotel, was likewise awarded an Oscar for Best Supporting Actress. Besides these two winners, *Separate Tables* gained nominations in five other catagories, including Best Picture and Best Screenplay, and was recognized as one of the most prestigious films of 1958.

All the characters residing in the story's seaside hotel are lonely and frustrated people. Major Pollock is a pathetic, blustering windbag whose nervous lying and petty fabrications cover up his fears and inadequacies. Sibyl Railton-Bell (Deborah Kerr), a modest spinster entirely dominated by her tyrannical mother (Gladys Cooper), is drawn to him. The major is kind to her, and she in turn listens to his fictitious exploits. It is the major who gives her the courage to rebel against her mother when the time comes, and it is Sibyl who comforts him when he is exposed as a molester of women in the local movie house and faces humiliation and complete disgrace.

John Malcolm (Burt Lancaster) is a writer who at first finds encouragement and understanding in the hotel's manager, Miss Cooper, and leads her to believe that the two of them can build a relationship together. John's ex-wife Ann Shankland (Rita Hayworth), however, turns up at the hotel. She is a handsome woman who loves herself more devotedly than she has ever loved any man. Her marriage to John had been fraught with bitterness, for he had never been one to cater to and flatter a woman's ego. They are nevertheless drawn to each other again, because sexually, at least, the old fire is more than a dying ember. Ann deliberately teases and leads her former husband on, building him up to such a frenzy of thwarted passion that he attempts to kill her. Only through his attempted violence does she come to her senses, as he does to his, and they both realize that there might be a new future for them together.

Separate Tables thus becomes a series of dramatic vignettes, with the players gathering under one roof to bare their loves and hates, establishing and reestablishing new and old unions. The mood is beautifully built and sustained by director Delbert Mann, who contrasts the two larger stories admirably and also deals sympathetically with other characters who are assigned separate tables in the dining-room; for example, the old teacher (Felix Aylmer) who has nothing to live for but memories of his past, and an earnest young medical student (Rod Taylor) who has problems with his girl friend (Audrey Dalton), a girl from another class and walk of life. Mann builds his two main stories so that they are intensely dramatic, one balancing the other, and so that the characters are completely believable.

In his role as Major Pollock, David Niven is at his best. An expert comedian in most of his screen appearances, he invests the aging Pollock with a tragic sense of pity, gaining a sympathy that makes the character warm and unforgettably real. Likewise, Deborah Kerr as the ugly ducking Sibyl, cursed with a mother who is a cruel and possessive virago, becomes a thoroughly admirable heroine. When she finally turns on her mother, no longer willing to submit to the woman's outrageous demands, she plays the scene with so much honesty and fire that the audience wants to applaud her heroics. Gladys Cooper as the mother is as hateful and insensitive as she was playing the mother in *Now, Voyager* (1942).

The other story, a completely different triangle, is equally well-helmed. Burt Lancaster, too often an underrated actor, plays with quiet intelligence the unhappy writer who gets a second chance to win the wife who had divorced him. He is a man who has been hurt once to the quick, but he is ready to believe that the wife who had mistreated and left him has changed and wants to resume life with him as much as he does with her.

Rita Hayworth had been the glamour girl and sex goddess of the 1940's and early 1950's, starring in such memorable films as *Cover Girl* (1944), *Blood and Sand* (1941), and *Gilda* (1946). By the end of the 1950's, she was playing in several movies of a different nature, the first of which was *Separate Tables*, in which she was not only mature but middle-aged. As Ann Shankland, she is vain and selfish, a woman who scarcely deserves another try at the man she had once denigrated and divorced. She is always beautifully groomed, but she is no longer really glamorous. John Malcolm is Ann's last refuge from ultimate loneliness, for it is obvious that the men in her life after her divorce soon saw through her petty vanities and abandoned her.

During the 1950's, Delbert Mann was one of the best of the many directors who migrated from top work in early television to a series of very fine and sensitive feature films. Starting with *Marty* in 1955, for which he won an Academy Award, he went on to interpret other homely stories such as *The Bachelor Party* (1957); but *Separate Tables* presents him at his best, weaving an intricate pattern, going from one story line to another with consummate ease. His talent grew in the 1950's, but by the 1970's he had returned to television and such network specials as *David Copperfield* and *Jane Eyre*, neither of which were as distinguished as the versions directed by George Cukor or Robert Stevenson.

DeWitt Bodeen

SERGEANT YORK

Released: 1941
Production: Jesse L. Lasky and Hal B. Wallis for Warner Bros.
Direction: Howard Hawks
Screenplay: Howard Koch, John Huston, Abem Finkel, and Harry Chandlee; based on the diary of Sergeant Alvin C. York as edited by Tom Skeyhill
Cinematography: Sol Polito
Editing: William Holmes (AA)
Music: Max Steiner
Running time: 134 minutes

Principal characters:

Alvin C. York .... Gary Cooper (AA)
Pastor Rosier Pile .... Walter Brennan
Gracie Williams .... Joan Leslie
Michael T. "Pusher" Ross .... George Tobias
Ike Botkin .... Ward Bond

Sergeant York is the story of Alvin C. York (Gary Cooper), a simple farmer trying to live his own life in the Tennessee Valley in the years prior to World War I. He lives with his family, working hard to build a place of his own someday. His needs are simple. He meets and falls in love with a local girl named Gracie (Joan Leslie) and plans to marry her eventually. He gets pleasure out of winning the annual turkey shoot, and he never allows anyone to get the better of him. He has an emotional experience which gives him "religion." It is this intense yet simple religious philosophy which causes him to register as a conscientious objector when he is inducted for service in the army during World War I. It is at this point that York first becomes aware of the real issues behind this so-called "Great War." Unschooled, and unsophisticated about the issues of the war, York's point of view is simple: he does not hate the Germans and he sees no reason to fight them. Eventually, however, he comes to believe that sometimes violence is needed in order to ensure freedom.

York is sent to France, where, in the Argonne Forest, his best friend "Pusher" Ross (George Tobias) is killed by enemy soldiers. York passionately vows vengeance; driven by anger and fueled by hate for the killer of his friend, he single-handedly kills twenty-five enemy soldiers and captures an additional 132 prisoners. This feat of unbelievable courage causes General John J. Pershing, leader of the American Expeditionary Forces, to cite York as the greatest civilian soldier of the war. He is also honored with numerous medals from both France and the United States.

On his return to America, York's fame causes him to be bombarded by promoters and merchandizers eager to have him endorse or promote their products. For a time, he appears to be swayed by all the glamour and attention; however, reflecting upon his roots and upon the girl he left behind, he soon rejects the limelight and returns to the Tennessee Valley and the life he has always known.

Gary Cooper won his first Oscar for Best Actor for his performance in *Sergeant York*. *Sergeant York* is a tribute to the solid, down-home philosophy which characterizes much of middle America, and Cooper portrays York with a sensitivity and naturalness that is captivating. The film was also nominated for eleven Academy Awards, including Best Picture, Best Screenplay, Best Musical Score, and Best Supporting Actor and Actress. Besides Cooper's award as Best Actor, the film received an Adademy Award for Best Film Editing by William Holmes.

Sergeant York is interesting for its political attitudes as well as for its historical content. The early portions of the film characterize York as an individual who sees things in his own unique way. As the lengthy prelude to his involvement in the war develops, bits and pieces of his philosophy filter through his dialogue and that of his fellow Tennesseeans. However, once the film begins to focus on the real dilemma of a pacifist forced to bear arms in a war that does not affect his immediate life-style, the tone becomes more direct. Howard Koch, one of the four credited screenwriters, was a master at infusing a script with spirit, which he does splendidly in *Sergeant York* and did a year later in *Casablanca*. Without being preachy or too obvious, the tone of *Sergeant York* becomes political. The film foreshadows America's involvement in World War II while presenting a highly romanticized vision of army life and combat.

Much of the directness of the film can be attributed to the influence of veteran filmmaker Howard Hawks, whose direction seems effortless and completely natural. The Tennessee sequence was filmed primarily inside a studio. It is here, with the ability to control even the smallest detail, that Hawks creates the proper atmosphere to present York's story. His eventual acceptance of "religion," although preposterous in implication, is presented with such simplicity and directness that it is truly believable.

The ending in which York is sought after by numerous manipulators and merchandizers was relatively controversial for the time; many critics felt that it detracted from the film's authenticity. However, what this conclusion actually did was to reestablish York's set of values. *Sergeant York* can be seen as two different movies: the Tennessee prelude and the war section. The final confrontation with wealth and fame is York's ultimate battle. He recognizes his simple origins as a farmer, and he is also aware of the reasons for which he fought in the war. York is lured temporarily by the possibility of "life at the top." The voice of reason which snaps him out of his newfound "stardom" back to reality comes from back home; he realizes his place in the structure of things and returns to Tennessee.

There is a humility which surrounds this film. Gary Cooper, fresh from his unusual role in Frank Capra's provocative *Meet John Doe* (1941), replaces energy with common sense. Cooper embodied the spirit of the American soldier in World War I; it was a role he played in several films prior to *Sergeant York*, and he returned to it once again in *The Court-Martial of Billy Mitchell* (1955). In all these roles Cooper infuses a quality of dignity. As Cooper is attributed to have said, "Sergeant York and I had a few things in common . . . . I liked the role because of the background of the picture and because I was portraying a good, sound American character."

Carl Macek

SERPICO

Released: 1973
Production: Dino de Laurentiis and Martin Bregman for Paramount
Direction: Sidney Lumet
Screenplay: Waldo Salt and Norman Wexler; based on the book of the same name by Peter Maas
Cinematography: Arthur J. Ornitz
Editing: Dede Allen
Production design: Charles Bailey
Running time: 130 minutes

Principal characters:

Frank Serpico	Al Pacino
Sidney Green	John Randolph
Tom Keough	Jack Kehoe
Inspector McClain	Biff McGuire
Laurie	Barbara Eda-Young
Leslie Lane	Cornelia Sharpe
Bob Blair	Tony Roberts
Lombardo	Ed Grover
Rubello	Norman Ornellas
Pasquale	John Medici
District Attorney Tauber	Allan Rich

Serpico was part of a wave of 1970's police films that included *Dirty Harry* (1971) and *The French Connection* (1971) (cops as crusaders), *The Seven-Ups* (1973) (cops as acrobats), *Cops and Robbers* (1973) (cops as robbers), and *The Laughing Policeman* (1974) (cops as jaundiced observers of a crooked world). But *Serpico* was different; it was about a real-life police detective appalled at the corruption within the system in which he worked, a cop at war with his professional brothers, alone and vulnerable. It also arrived during the Watergate crisis at a time when people wanted to believe that *somebody* was honest, that every public official was not venal, immoral, or a fool.

Serpico is told entirely from its hero's point of view. It begins at the end, with Frank Serpico (Al Pacino) in the hospital with a wound that may have been inflicted by his fellow officers. The film then flashes back to explain how he arrived at this deplorable position, beginning with plainsclothesman Serpico's growing awareness that much of the New York City police force seems to be on the take. Serpico talks the situation over with a fellow officer, Bob Blair (Tony Roberts), who, being more politically astute, thinks he knows whom they should tell. The two work their way from the investigative department to the Police Commissioner and a man in the mayor's office. Each time, they are told action will be taken, and each time nothing happens. Meanwhile Serpico is being moved from precinct to precinct; at one point his partner is the bagman for the area. Serpico's refusal to take money turns him into a pariah, and eventually he finds himself completely isolated within the force. His growing obsession with corruption is paralleled by his romance with a nurse, Laurie (Barbara Eda-Young), which breaks up because she cannot bear his pain and frustration.

Serpico has repeatedly refused to testify before the Department's internal investigative body to protect himself, but when he and Blair go the the *New York Times* and the story breaks, he agrees to appear before the newly created Knapp Commission. Assigned to a Brooklyn drug squad, Serpico and three detectives break into a suspected pusher's home. The others fail to cover him, and Serpico is shot in the head. Serpico gets both threatening mail in the hospital and a gold shield which he rejects bitterly. He has lost the hearing in his left ear and still has shell fragments in his skull. An end title tells the audience that he resigned in June, 1972, and received the "medal of honor for conspicuous bravery in action," and is now living "somewhere in Switzerland."

Serpico focuses exclusively on Al Pacino. We never see any action of which he is not part, with the result that the performances of several very good supporting players (John Randolph, Jack Kehoe, Tony Roberts, and Ed Grover among others) get lost in the shuffle. But Pacino's performance makes up for this defect. Although we are never told how he came by his moral outrage and reformer's zeal, Pacino carries us along with such waves of vitality that it is not until the film is over that we realize crucial information has been withheld. Pacino does a great deal to convince us he is Serpico; he affects a shambling walk, nasal voice, and, in the course of developing various disguises to use in his undercover work, he goes from clean shaven to a full beard and flowing hair. And Pacino *does* convince us. His performance (nominated for an Academy Award) is galvanizing; you believe this man can succeed in his crusade simply by virtue of Pacino's energy.

The most important thing about Serpico is his obsessiveness. In the eyes of director Sidney Lumet and scenarists Waldo Salt and Norman Excler, Serpico is a hippie saint, a self-made martyr and a holy fool who did it all alone and whose only mistake lay in not knowing that the job of policing the police was impossible. Of course, the real Serpico did not do it alone; he had help from David Durks (here disguised as Blair), the honest inspector represented here as Lombardo (Ed Grover), and others. The film does not tell us what Peter Maas' book does: that when he was wounded, thirty-five policemen volunteered to give blood and that several told Serpico that they would prefer to be honest.

The film also implies that nothing happened, that when it was all over, the crooked business resumed as usual. This is not true. The Knapp Commission was formed, and the result of its investigation was a massive shakeup in the police department. Ultimately, *Serpico* undermines its own hero; it says that the effort he expended was worthless, that he was a fool, and that anyone who goes as far as he did can expect to be killed.

The Lumet/Salt/Wexler Serpico is an extrovert; if he were not in the opposite camp, his fellow cops would love him. He is funny and high-spirited, but he is also such a monomaniacal loner that he eventually manages to alienate everyone but Blair and Lombardo. An early, very funny scene shows Serpico at a party where everyone is on their way to being something else; they are all would-be poets, novelists, and writers working in advertising, insurance, and photography. Only Serpico has reached his goal; he is already what he wanted to be. He charms the guests with his silly dancing, talking to everyone about everything. It is an effective sequence, one that goes a long way toward establishing reasons for us to care about Serpico.

Lumet's most telling contribution to *Serpico* is his use of New York—its slums, parks, and warehouse districts—as a location. He creates an ambiance that is the physical equivalent of the grubby moral atmosphere Serpico struggles against.

Serpico gratuitously denigrates the entire police force by seeing its protagonists as either black or white, good or bad. Only Serpico, Blair, and Lombardo are "good"; the other detectives are vengeful, mercenary, and vicious. Without excusing their behavior, surely it is not asking too much to wish that the movie had presented another side to their characters, made them more fully rounded, complex individuals. But that might have made them people and vitiated the impact of Serpico's crusade. The film does allow Lombardo into its tiny circle of saints by showing him at home. "This man has a family, therefore he's OK," the movie seems to say.

The film is understandably reluctant to name real names, presumably for fear of libel suits. John V. Lindsay was mayor at the time, but the film only mentions "the mayor's office." David Burnham, the *New York Times* reporter whose articles led to the creation of the Knapp Commission, is the only other person other than Serpico to be called by his actual name.

Judith M. Kass

SEVEN BRIDES FOR SEVEN BROTHERS

Released: 1954
Production: Jack Cummings for Metro-Goldwyn-Mayer
Direction: Stanley Donen
Screenplay: Albert Hackett, Frances Goodrich, and Dorothy Kingsley; based on the short story "The Sobbin' Women" by Stephen Vincent Benet
Cinematography: George J. Folsey
Editing: Ralph E. Winters
Choreography: Michael Kidd (AA Special Award)
Music: Saul Chaplin and Adolph Deutsch (AA)
Song: Gene de Paul and Johnny Mercer
Running time: 103 minutes

Principal characters:

Adam	Howard Keel
Benjamin	Jeff Richards
Caleb	Matt Mattox
Daniel	Marc Platt
Ephraim	Jacques d'Amboise
Frank	Tommy Rall
Gideon	Russ Tamblyn
Milly	Jane Powell
Dorcas	Julie Newmeyer (Newmar)
Alice	Nancy Kilgas
Sarah	Betty Carr
Liza	Virginia Gibson
Ruth	Ruta Kilmonis (Lee)
Martha	Norma Doggett

Seven Brides for Seven Brothers is a fanciful romp which succeeds because of its perfect blending of story, dance, and music. The songs and dances not only complement the story, but they also actually move it along. The story is set in Oregon in the 1850's, and the title states the theme. It is about the seven Pontipee brothers—Adam (Howard Keel), Benjamin (Jeff Richards), Caleb (Matt Mattox), Daniel (Marc Platt), Ephraim (Jacques d'Amboise), Frank (short for Frankincense) (Tommy Rall), and Gideon (Russ Tamblyn)—and how they get their wives. It is no ordinary method. Neither the seven backwoodsmen nor their house have known a woman's touch in years. The eldest, Adam, decides to find a wife to clean up things when he goes to town to purchase supplies for the winter. After looking over the women of the town and delineating his wifely requirements in the song "Bless Your Beautiful Hide," he sees Milly (Jane Powell) as she chops wood and serves her home-made stew to the hungry customers of an inn. Impressed by her capacity for work, he decides that she is the one. Milly is also impressed with the handsome backwoodsman, and agrees to marry him—after she finishes her chores.

On the way to the farm, Milly speaks of her hopes for their future and rejoices that she will now have to take care of only one man. As she sings "Wonderful, Wonderful Day," Adam listens in guilty silence. Milly's optimism is dashed when she is met by Adam's unkempt and fractious brothers. She sees the mess in the house and realizes that Adam has married her for her housekeeping abilities. Since she is in love with him, she is hurt; but she spunkily goes about putting the house and all seven brothers in order. She explains her disappointment to Adam, but forgives him as she sings the film's love ballad, "When You're in Love."

Adam's six brothers are very impressed with Milly and are open to her advice on manners and courting. Adam does not feel that he needs any advice as he got his wife without any courting at all, and he avoids all the lessons. Milly's description of the fun of courting is done to a polka tune, "Goin' Courtin'." The singing and dancing that accompany the tune grow energetically as the brothers change from interested skeptics to boisterous enthusiasts on the subject. They get to test their new manners at a barn raising to which all the town and country folk are invited. Since one foray into town with a few of the brothers concluded in a brawl between them and the young men of the town, Milly has made her six brothers promise that they will not fight. The seven handsome, redheaded backwoodsmen are immediately noticed by the girls of the town who flock to help Milly unload the wagon. As each girl picks something up, one of the brothers politely offers to help her carry it. Even Adam is impressed.

The barn dance ballet is the choreographic highpoint of the film. It begins with a square dance not unlike the social dancing of the 1850's and soon turns into a jaunty modern dance, but one which never loses its period flavor. During the dance, friction develops once again between the brothers and the young men of the town as they vie for the attention of the girls. When the girls make it clear that they prefer the brothers, a contest of acrobatic skills develops between the rivals, and again the brothers emerge the winners. This entire dance sequence is so humorously and infectiously exuberant that it has emerged as one of the most memorable dance sequences on film.

The energy continues as the young men provoke the brothers into a fight during the barn raising. Mindful of their promise to Milly, they try to resist, but eventually they are pushed too far. In the ensuing free-for-all between them and the townsfolk, the seven brothers not only knock out all comers, but destroy the barn as well. Filled with flying objects and falling wooden beams, this episode is as precisely choreographed as any of the dances.

The brothers return to the farm, disgraced in their victory since neither the girls nor their parents want anything more to do with them. What makes their situation worse is that all six are now in love with the girls they have met. An underlying theme of the story is Milly's desire for Adam to love her as she loves him. As Gideon, the youngest, struggles with his love pangs, Adam counsels him by reprising "When You're in Love." Milly, hoping that Adam's attitude toward her has changed, is touched as she overhears his song, but Adam dashes her hopes when he tells Gideon that he is sure to find another girl as all women are pretty much alike.

The brothers collectively express their longings in the dirgelike "Lament" (I'm a lonesome polecat). While not really a dance, the song is rhythmically punctuated with axe blows and saw strokes as the brothers plod through their chores. Adam comes upon the brothers wallowing in lovesickness. Still having no comprehension of the proprieties of courting, Adam suggests that they force the girls to marry them by abducting them, and gustily tells the story of the Sabine women. The Sabines were kidnaped for wives by Roman soldiers, and when their former husbands came to rescue them, the women refused to go, preferring instead to stay with their captors. The story is sung in lusty fashion by Adam in the song "Sobbin' Women." In a matter of minutes he has the brothers fired up and on their way to town to grab the girls. They abduct them, and as the outraged fathers and beaux chase them, a snowslide conveniently seals the only pass leading to the Pontipee farm. The townsfolk grimly return to town to await spring when the pass will reopen.

Milly is equally outraged when confronted with the six sobbing girls. Since the brothers forgot to abduct a preacher, she prohibits courting of any kind. She banishes the brothers to the barn for the winter, and then turns her fury against Adam for thinking that since he had gained a wife so easily, all each of his brothers had to do was grab one for himself. Adam, stung by Milly's anger, goes into the mountains for the winter, leaving her to cope with the situation. Milly rallies the girls to her side with the news that she will be having a baby in the spring. In a series of short scenes that indicate the passing months, the girls make it clear to the men that they are not to be trifled with; at least not until spring. When the girls sing "June Bride" it signifies the end of their resistance, and the six couples finally get around to a tuneful courting with "Spring, Spring, Spring."

With spring, Milly has her baby, a girl. Fatherhood gives Adam a sense of family responsibility, and he returns to the farm realizing the enormity of his error in abducting the girls. He also realizes that he loves Milly. He informs everyone that the pass is open and the girls must return to town before the fathers come to the farm and get ahold of the brothers. But it is too late. As the brothers try to round up the reluctant girls, the fathers arrive with a preacher in tow and round up everyone. As the girls are herded together, the crying of Milly's baby is heard above the sobbing of the girls. When the preacher asks whose baby it is, they all see a way of getting what they want, and they all claim it. The story ends happily with a six-way shotgun wedding taking place with the reunited Milly and Adam looking on.

The film has one major defect; this outdoor tale was filmed mainly on a soundstage. The backdrop scenes which represent the Oregon countryside are beautiful, but it is obvious that they are backdrops. However, the cast is excellent. Howard Keel's rugged good looks and rich baritone are perfectly suited to Adam Pontipee. In addition to a lovely voice, Jane Powell as Milly conveys a true pioneer spirit as she copes with the unruly brothers. An excellent group of dancers performs Michael Kidd's exuberant choreography, and the entire cast ably sings the original songs and music which capture the robust humor of the story.

The film was both a critical and financial success, much to the surprise of M-G-M which had given more attention to less successful musicals that year. Critical praise went to choreographer Kidd and to director Stanley Donen, who maintained a light and lyric style throughout. Critics hailed the film as a new-style motion picture musical, pointing out that in its integration of music and dance it resembled a Rodgers and Hammerstein musical play rather than a standard Hollywood musical. *Seven Brides for Seven Brothers* was nominated for an Oscar in the Best Picture category but lost to the heavyweight of the year, *On the Waterfront*. However, Saul Chaplin and Adolph Deutsch won Oscars for musical scoring, and Michael Kidd received a special award for his choreography.

The rather farfetched story and historical setting of the film resist dating, and it has come to be recognized as a classic musical because of its blending of cast, dancing, music, and story.

Ellen J. Snyder

THE SEVEN YEAR ITCH

Released: 1955
Production: Charles K. Feldman and Billy Wilder for Twentieth Century-Fox
Direction: Billy Wilder
Screenplay: Billy Wilder and George Axelrod; based on the play of the same name by George Axelrod
Cinematography: Milton Krasner
Editing: Hugh S. Fowler
Running time: 105 minutes

Principal characters:

The Girl	Marilyn Monroe
Richard Sherman	Tom Ewell
Helen Sherman	Evelyn Keyes
Ricky Sherman	Butch Bernard

A delightful and witty farce, *The Seven Year Itch* combines the talents of Marilyn Monroe and Tom Ewell with hilarious results. Adapted by George Axelrod and Billy Wilder from Axelrod's Broadway play, it is essentially the extended reverie of a plain, middle-aged publisher of paperback books concerning his amorous fantasies. Ewell's deft comic timing, Wilder's brisk direction, and the radiant presence of Marilyn Monroe give luster to this sophisticated comedy.

The script sets up situations bound to have many comic possibilities, then explores most of them inventively and at a rapid pace, and quickly finishes before we tire of the gags. New Yorker Richard Sherman (Tom Ewell) sends his wife, Helen (Evelyn Keyes), and son, Ricky (Butch Bernard), to Maine for the summer so they can escape the city's heat and humidity. Although he has a vivid sexual imagination continually kept sharp through its exercise, he is determined to lead a sensible life during the summer and not be like the other men he knows who start playing around as soon as their wives leave town. The very first night he is alone, however, he finds his good resolutions severely tested by The Girl upstairs (Marilyn Monroe)—she is never given a name—a summer tenant in the building where he lives.

Having decided not to smoke, drink (following the orders of Helen and his doctor), or give in to other forms of temptation, he goes to a vegetarian restaurant for dinner. All the other diners are elderly. Even the waitress is plain and middle-aged and does not accept tips; she does, however, solicit a contribution for the nudist fund, explaining that without clothes there would be no wars: soldiers would not be able to tell enemies from friends. Depressed by this experience, Sherman returns to his comfortably cluttered apartment, stepping on one of Ricky's roller skates in the process, and then prepares to read a manuscript his firm is planning to publish.

At this point he meets the new summer tenant in the apartment above his—a shapely, wide-eyed blonde in a tight dress. The meeting triggers his always active imagination, and instead of reading the manuscript which he has brought home, he begins to fantasize. Written by a psychiatrist, the manuscript is about the repressed urges of middle-aged men. Sherman thinks it will be boring, but when he later reads it, he finds it describes a condition particularly applicable to himself—the tendency of men married for seven years to seek extramarital adventures. The psychiatrist calls it the seven-year itch. In his fantasy, Sherman tells his wife he has an "animal thing" which arouses something in the women he meets. He tells her of the attempts of his secretary, a beautiful nurse, and finally her best friend to seduce him (the scene with her best friend taking place on a deserted beach with waves crashing on the shore in a parody of the famous love scene in *From Here to Eternity*, 1953). His wife, however, refuses to take him seriously and just laughs at his stories.

Soon after he returns to reality from this fantasy, he meets The Girl again when she knocks a tomato plant off her balcony onto his—in fact, onto the chair he has just vacated. He invites her down for a drink, unlocks the drawer where he keeps his cigarettes, turns down the lights, and plumps up the pillows before he realizes what he is doing. As he turns up the lights, he begins another fantasy in which The Girl appears in a slinky strapless evening gown and black gloves, flourishing a long cigarette holder. Sherman is at the piano in an elegant dressing gown, silk scarf wound about his throat, distinguishedly gray at the temples, lighted candelabra on the piano, playing Rachmaninoff's *Second Piano Concerto*. The Girl is overwhelmed, swept away by the music. As they embrace on the piano bench (in a manner reminiscent of the famous Tabu perfume advertisement), the doorbell rings, and he awakens from his fantasy. It is only the slovenly janitor who wants to pick up the rugs for cleaning. Sherman gets rid of him just before The Girl arrives in tight slacks and matching pale pink blouse. He tells her that he is not married and has no children, explaining away the roller skate he is holding (on which he has once again slipped as he rushed to answer the door) by telling her he likes to rollerskate.

The Girl does not know what a martini is but lets him make her one while she stands in front of the air conditioner, raising her blouse to let the cool air blow on her midriff. New York is in the middle of a heat wave, and her apartment is not air conditioned. She tells Sherman she tried to sleep in a bathtub full of cold water but had to call in the plumber because her toe got stuck in the faucet. It was embarrassing, she says, because the man was a stranger and she had not polished her toenails. She also discloses that she has posed for an "artistic" picture in *U.S. Camera* and does Dazzledent toothpaste commercials for television. "More people see me than saw Sarah Bernhardt," she muses.

The Girl's artless conversation establishes her character; she is the empty-headed but beautiful and desirable blonde, the natural object of a quiet middle-aged man's fantasies. She is so amiably childlike and innocent that she cannot be considered immoral. When she accidentally discovers that Sherman is married, she is relieved because nothing can get "drastic" with married men. "No matter what happens he can't ask you to marry him," she says.

When Sherman plays a recording of the Rachmaninoff Piano Concerto, she is not swept away as he had fantasized, but exclaims that it must be classical music because there is no vocal. "I have this big thing for Eddie Fisher," she informs him, dipping her potato chip in champagne. The Girl's favorite expression of approval is "delicate," which she uses to describe drinking champagne with a married man in an air-conditioned apartment. She is trusting, too, not suspecting or looking for hidden motives in Sherman's actions. He is able very easily to trick her into kissing him by saying that he doubts the truth of the Dazzledent commercials. Like a child, she is pleased by the cool breeze that escapes from the ducts of the subway when a train whishes through, and squealing delightedly, she allows her full skirt to billow up.

The Girl is presented as more than merely an object. Although she is not sophisticated, she is kind and smart enough to realize that Sherman's self-confidence needs bolstering. In a scene that demonstrates her kindness and gives some individuality to her character, she reassures Sherman, telling him that not every girl wants a man who looks like Gregory Peck. What is really exciting, she tells him, is the nervous, shy man sitting in a corner at a party. At first he may be overlooked, but a woman can sense that he is gentle, kind, and sweet, and will be tender with her. She ends by assuring Sherman that if she were his wife she would be very jealous of him and awards him her ultimate accolade: "You're just delicate."

In the play Sherman spends one night with The Girl, but in the film he merely lets her use his air-conditioned bedroom while he sleeps on the living room couch. His conscience having become as active as his libido, he then flees to Maine to spend two weeks with his wife and son. The Girl kisses him good-bye and tells him not to wipe off the lipstick, implying that a little jealousy on Helen's part will make her more aware of his appeal to other women.

Under the direction of Billy Wilder, Marilyn Monroe and Tom Ewell give remarkable performances which are funny and entertaining while keeping the lighthearted eroticism of the film from becoming vulgar. Evelyn Keyes is good as the wife, particularly in the fantasy scene in which she discovers The Girl with her husband and shoots him, saying, "The wives of America will give me a medal." Indeed, the fantasy scenes are well handled throughout to show us the workings of Sherman's hyperactive imagination.

It is not difficult to see why *The Seven Year Itch* was the most popular film released by Twentieth Century-Fox that year, and remains one of Marilyn Monroe's most noteworthy films.

Julia Johnson

THE SEVENTH VEIL

Released: 1946
Production: Sydney Box for Sydney Box-Ortus; distributed by Theatrecraft
Direction: Compton Bennett
Screenplay: Muriel Box and Sydney Box (AA)
Cinematography: Reginald H. Wyer
Editing: Gordon Hales
Running time: 95 minutes

Principal characters:
Nicholas .... James Mason
Francesca Cunningham .... Ann Todd
Dr. Larsen ....Herbert Lom
Peter Gay .... Hugh McDermott
Maxwell Leyden .... Albert Lieven

The Seventh Veil has a devoted audience who seek out the film whenever it appears on television or at revival houses. Extremely popular upon its release, it has continued to exert a hold on those who remember it. It is not hard to understand why, for it is one of the strangest films to come out of Britain. Made in 1945, it was the second production of the new film unit formed by producer Sydney Box, who had been associated with Denham Studios. Although made in a matter of weeks for a modest budget, the film comes across as a polished work with sumptuous settings and an unforgettable performance by James Mason in one of his most puzzling and ambiguous roles.

The film provides much enjoyment for music lovers. The heroine, admirably portrayed by Ann Todd, is a concert pianist who plays a score of famous pieces by Mozart, Beethoven, Grieg, and Chopin. The film greatly capitalizes on the 1940's craze for Viennese psychiatrists: much of the action takes place on the doctor's couch. Oddly enough, another success of 1945 was Hitchcock's *Spellbound*, made in America, which also dealt with psychoanalysis. Perhaps the Western world was going through a collective trauma as a reaction to the war. Whatever the reason, *The Seventh Veil* was certainly one of the more interesting postwar films to come out of Britain. Its bizarre combination of masochism, music, and melodrama proved both satisfying and stimulating to its audiences.

The film begins as a young woman, Francesca Cunningham (Ann Todd), attempts to drown herself in the Thames. She is rescued and placed in a nursing home where she maintains an obstinate silence about the cause of her acute depression. Dr. Larsen (Herbert Lom), an eminent psychiatrist, is called in and decides to place Francesca under narcohypnosis to discover the reason for her mental unrest. The film then flashes back to Francesca as a fourteen-year-old schoolgirl studying music. When late for chapel one day, she is caned on the hands by her headmistress; it is the afternoon of a serious musical examination. She fails her examination and is heartbroken: music is her consuming passion in life. Francesca's hands become a recurrent theme throughout her treatment, as she keeps wringing them during her trance.

Later left an orphan, Francesca goes to live with Nicholas (James Mason), a distant cousin of her father who becomes her guardian. Nicholas is a dark, handsome, brooding man. An apparent misogynist, he refuses even to have female servants, which adds to his mystery. He very soon discovers Francesca's talent for music, which he cultivates and encourages. Eventually, she is sent to the Royal Academy of Music to study, and there she meets and falls in love with Peter Gay (Hugh McDermott), a popular band leader from the United States. Nicholas, however, disapproves of the romance and takes Francesca to Paris to continue her studies. After years of intensive training, she makes a triumphant debut in Venice as a concert pianist. Returning to London, she accepts an offer to play at the Royal Albert Hall, where she scores a great success. She attempts to pick up her romance with Peter but finds that he has already married. She becomes depressed until she meets Maxwell Leyden (Albert Lieven), a famous artist and charming *bon vivant*, and falls in love with him.

Leyden persuades Francesca to spend a few weeks with him at his Italian villa. However, when Nicholas learns that she intends to leave he is infuriated, and in one of the most startling scenes in the film, he takes his cane and attempts to break her fingers. Nicholas becomes a demon in the scene as he raps his ward across the knuckles, damaging her most precious possession. Previous scenes foreshadow this event, such as when Nicholas strikes the keyboard soundly with his cane when angered or agitated. But the viewer remains unprepared for this act of aggression. Francesca recoils from her guardian in horror and runs to Max, who is waiting outside in his car. They drive off hastily, have an accident, and the car catches fire. Rescuing Max from the flames, Francesca burns her hands and is sure that she will never play the piano again. Her despair over the loss of the use of her hands causes her to jump into the Thames, thus bringing the story back to the present.

After hearing her story, Dr. Larsen has Francesca thoroughly examined and finds that the burns on her hands are merely superficial, a fact that she was told at the time of the accident. Her scars are psychological rather than physical. Larsen works with Francesca and manages to cure her with the help of Peter, Max, and Nicholas, convincing her that she is as talented as ever. At the end of the film, Larsen reunites Francesca with the one man she has always really loved: Nicholas, whom she no longer fears.

The ending of the film received much comment from British critics, often in very humorous terms. One critic remarked that at the end of the film, James Mason should have broken his cane across his knee, taken his ward into his arms, and listened to her play a triumphant symphony as the finale. The ending notwithstanding, most reviewers praised Mason's performance.

The Seventh Veil was a huge box-office hit in England, and also did well in the United States. Its modest budget and short shooting schedule proved to the British film industry that success need not be equated with wild and enormous spending.

Joan Cohen

SHADOW OF A DOUBT

Released: 1943
Production: Jack H. Skirball for Universal
Direction: Alfred Hitchcock
Screenplay: Thornton Wilder, Alma Reville, and Sally Benson; based on a screen story by Gordon McDonell
Cinematography: Joseph A. Valentine
Editing: Milton Carruth
Running time: 108 minutes

Principal characters:

Charlie Oakley .... Joseph Cotten
Young Charlie .... Teresa Wright
Jack Graham .... Macdonald Carey
Emma Newton .... Patricia Collinge
Joseph Newton .... Henry Travers
Herbie Hawkins .... Hume Cronyn

Regarded by many critics as Alfred Hitchcock's best American film, *Shadow of a Doubt* certainly displays the master of suspense thrillers in top form. Mixing doubt and fear with ordinary small-town life, Hitchcock keeps his audience off balance throughout the film. The story is set in the town of Santa Rosa, California, and the film was largely shot there. Such use of location shooting was not a usual practice in the 1940's, but in *Shadow of a Doubt* the contrast between the placid, conventional life in the town and the twisted mind of Uncle Charlie Oakley (Joseph Cotten) is definitely aided by the real setting.

The film portrays throughout the theme of the affinity between Uncle Charlie and his niece Charlie (Teresa Wright), who is named after him. The niece feels that the presence of her uncle is what the family needs to get it out of its rut, and she decides to telegraph him, only to find that he has just telegraphed the family himself. Young Charlie is delighted with this example of what she sees as telepathy and keeps stressing to her uncle that they are closer than uncle and niece. As the plot progresses, however, she begins to fear their closeness. At first she gleefully tells him that he cannot hide anything from her, but by the middle of the film she wishes he could. Instead of being kindred spirits, the two Charlies turn out to be opposites—the good and evil parts of the same personality.

There is, of course, suspense and mystery in *Shadow of a Doubt*. The mystery is not, however, who committed the crime but rather what crime was committed. As the first half of the film progresses, we grow more and more certain that Uncle Charlie is a criminal, but we have no idea what his crime is. It is not until a suspenseful scene in which the niece rushes to the library to find a newspaper article that she learns that her uncle is the so-called Merry Widow murderer, a man who has been murdering rich widows for their money. Before this is discovered, however, we have reason to become increasingly suspicious of him. The first time he appears he is in a furnished room with a great deal of money lying about, and when his landlady tells him two men want to see him, he decides to escape from them by visiting his sister and her family in Santa Rosa.

In Santa Rosa, Uncle Charlie at first seems to be a personable, successful individual, but he becomes unreasonably upset when he thinks people are trying to find out about him. After the library scene, the mystery and suspense change. Now the questions center on what Uncle Charlie will do (he has already met a rich widow in Santa Rosa), whether the detectives will find him out, and what young Charlie will do with her information. Young Charlie does not feel she can turn in her own uncle, especially since she believes that it would kill her mother to find out that her younger brother is a murderer. Once Uncle Charlie realizes that she knows of his guilt and even has a ring which connects him with the murders, young Charlie's life is in danger.

When the detectives drop the case because they think another man is the murderer, the danger to young Charlie increases, since she is now the only threat to her uncle. After surviving two "accidents" which are clearly murder attempts by Uncle Charlie, she finally persuades him to leave town by threatening to turn her evidence over to the police. When she boards the train to see him off, he again tries to kill her; they struggle, and finally he falls into the path of a speeding train. The film ends with Uncle Charlie's funeral. He is eulogized, and only young Charlie and Detective Jack Graham (Macdonald Carey), with whom she has fallen in love, know the true story.

Hitchcock makes a point of contrasting the large city with the small town. Before we see Uncle Charlie, we see establishing shots of the city in which he lives; then, as we hear him say "Santa Rosa" on the telephone, we see establishing shots of that quiet town. Indeed, Hitchcock chose Thornton Wilder as the principal screenwriter for the film because of his splendid evocation of small-town life in his play *Our Town*. It is ironic, then, that in finding something to lift the family out of its rut, young Charlie gets more than she bargains for. It is almost as if the film is suggesting that to have excitement you have to have danger or decadence also. In fact, Uncle Charlie himself, though he is part of the problem, decries cities and modern life.

Under the opening credits we see couples in old-fashioned dress waltzing to "The Merry Widow." This scene is inserted or superimposed several times during the film, but it is not until we see it immediately after young Charlie finds the article about the Merry Widow murderer that we realize its significance. In a sense, the music has a dual meaning which reflects the distorted mind of Uncle Charlie. He frequently says that the modern world is corrupt, a "foul city" he calls it, and contrasts it with his romanticized idea of the past.

Thus the "Merry Widow" dancers represent both the idealized past and the grotesque situation of the present.

The film is filled with other deft Hitchcock touches besides the motif of the dancers. The affinity of the uncle and niece is brought out by the fact that each is first shown in profile lying on a bed. The scene in which Uncle Charlie tries to kill young Charlie by shutting her in a garage where a car's motor is running is ironically set up by a previous scene in which Graham proposes to young Charlie in the same garage. The pace of the film is also carefully controlled, with some scenes being deliberately slowed down. After the telegraph office calls the family about Uncle Charlie's message, for example, it takes them an inordinately long time to find out what the message is. When young Charlie decides to go to the library, however, the pace accelerates and the tension increases; she has only a few minutes to reach the library before closing time, and we see shots of her rushing through the streets heedless of the traffic; of the town clock showing the time; and of the library lights being turned out just as she arrives. After she manages to get in—despite the protestations of a stereotyped old-maid librarian—and finds the damning information, the camera pulls back for a long shot from above which dissolves into the shot of the "Merry Widow" dancers. After the quick and exciting editing of the scene on the train in which uncle and niece struggle until the uncle falls in front of a speeding locomotive, Hitchcock slows down the pace for the ironic ending at the funeral. Graham and young Charlie, who are the only ones who know the truth, listen to the service as Uncle Charlie is eulogized. The last words in the film are "the sweetness of their characters live on forever."

Joseph Cotten and Teresa Wright as the uncle and niece contribute excellent performances which give vitality to the conception of their like but opposite personalities. Cotten is able to convey the surface charm which almost covers the menace within, and Wright convincingly shows us a naïve young woman who finds herself in a situation she could not imagine, much less suspect. The others in the cast are adequate, including Henry Travers and Hume Cronyn as Charlie's father and his friend, who both read pulp mystery stories and continually talk about murder while they are unaware that a real murderer is right under their noses.

Shadow of a Doubt is vintage Hitchcock. From the overall conception to the smallest detail, the imprint of this master filmmaker is evident.

Timothy W. Johnson

SHALL WE DANCE

Released: 1937
Production: Pandro S. Berman for RKO/Radio
Direction: Mark Sandrich
Screenplay: Allan Scott and Ernest Pagano; based on P. J. Wolfson's adaptation of the story, "Watch Your Step" by Lee Loeb and Harold Buchman
Cinematography: David Abel
Editing: William Hamilton
Art direction: Van Nest Polglase
Choreography: Hermes Pan and Harry Losee
Music: George Gershwin and Ira Gershwin
Running time: 116 minutes

Principal characters:

Peter P. Peters (Petrov)	Fred Astaire
Linda Keene	Ginger Rogers
Jeffrey Baird	Edward Everett Horton
Arthur Miller	Jerome Cowan
Lady Tarrington	Ketti Gallian
Cecil Flintridge	Eric Blore
Jim Montgomery	William Brisbane

Shall We Dance is a film which made use of the excitement and glamour of ballet—an art form which by 1937 had gained greatly in popularity—in the same manner that an earlier Fred Astaire and Ginger Rogers film, *Follow the Fleet* (1936), had tried to catch the atmosphere of the Big Band era. Indeed, the theme of *Shall We Dance* is popular art or musical comedy *versus* highbrow art or ballet, and the attempted synthesis of the two by the character played by Fred Astaire. *Shall We Dance* was released third from the end of the series of films that Fred Astaire and Ginger Rogers were to make for RKO in the 1930's, and it is representative of these films after the series had reached its peak in 1936. Although it lacks some of the buoyancy and spontaneity of their earlier efforts, it is nevertheless a charming film with some wonderful dance sequences and an outstanding musical score by George and Ira Gershwin.

As is usual in an Astaire-Rogers film, the Astaire character immediately falls in love with the Rogers character, but it takes her longer to reciprocate. Indeed, in *Shall We Dance*, Peter P. Peters of Philadelphia (Fred Astaire) falls in love with Linda Keene (Ginger Rogers) before he even meets her. Peter is a ballet star using the professional name of Petrov, and, while appearing in Paris, he sees a flip book of Linda, an American musical comedy star who is also in Paris. The book consists of pictures of Linda, and thumbing or flipping the pages gives the impression of Linda dancing. The director of the ballet, Jeffrey Baird (Edward Everett Horton), already horrified because he has found Peter practicing tap dancing rather than ballet, is even more upset to hear him say that, although he has not met Linda, he wants to marry her. "Think I will," Peter tells the startled Jeffrey as he leaves for Linda's apartment.

Peter, however, has not picked an opportune time to visit Linda; she is upset because of the amorous advances of her dancing partners, and has just announced to her manager, Arthur Miller (Jerome Cowan), that she is finished with show business. When Peter sends in his card of introduction, she is puzzled and unimpressed. "What's a Petrov?" she asks Arthur, adding that he is probably a simpering toe dancer who has seen her picture and fallen in love with her. Peter overhears Linda's tirade while waiting outside the door and decides to put on an act for her benefit. He bursts into the room and, in a fake Russian accent, announces that he is Petrov. Having been told that Linda wants to dance with him, he has come to inspect her. Linda is surprised by his sudden appearance and pompous manner, and when he commands her to "tweest" for him, she does so, but ends up falling on the keyboard of her piano. Peter departs as abruptly as he has entered, leaving Linda with the impression that he is dangerously unbalanced. She expresses her delight that she is sailing back to the United States in the morning. Peter, who has stopped outside to find out her reaction, naturally overhears this comment, and immediately decides to sail on the same boat.

Although Peter and Linda do sail on the same ship, all does not go well. Linda has found out that he is not Petrov from Moscow but rather Peter P. Peters from Philadelphia; also, a small lie Jeffrey has told becomes a source of conflict and confusion throughout the remainder of the film: to discourage a persistent admirer of Peter, Lady Tarrington (Ketti Gallian), Jeffrey had told her that Peter was married, and in no time the rumor spreads through the ship that Peter and Linda were secretly married. Before Linda hears the rumor, the two do share a few moments together while Linda is walking her dog, but she finally becomes so upset by the situation that she persuades the pilot of the mail plane to take her with him on his return flight to New York.

Once in New York, Linda ignores Arthur's pleas to return to show business and decides to marry an old admirer, Jim Montgomery (William Brisbane). Arthur, however, thinking that he can still convince Linda to change her mind, arranges to give her and Jim a farewell dinner at his rooftop nightclub where, with the help of the orchestra leader, he tricks her into dancing with Peter. Although the two dance beautifully together to the appreciative applause of the crowd, Linda is still determined to marry Montgomery. Arthur now decides that keeping the marriage rumors about Linda and Petrov alive will prevent Linda's marriage and retirement. In order to keep the story alive, he uses a life-sized model of Linda to stage a photograph which is supposed to prove that Linda and Peter are actually married.

When Linda sees the picture in the newspapers the next morning, she is naturally furious and is soon besieged by reporters wanting confirmation of her marriage to Petrov. In order to escape the reporters, she and Peter hide out in Central Park where they go rowing and rollerskating. Exhausted from dodging the reporters, Linda finally decides on a solution to the problem: Peter has to marry her so that she can divorce him, thus putting all the rumors to rest. They go to New Jersey for a quick marriage ceremony; on the ferry back to New York, however, Linda tells Peter that she did not realize getting married would be so depressing, and Peter then sings to her the lovely ballad, "They Can't Take That Away from Me," in which he extols all the little but meaningful things he will always remember about her to console himself after he loses her.

Back at their hotel there are further complications when Lady Tarrington arrives to cause trouble just as Linda is beginning to reciprocate Peter's affections. Peter gets rids of Lady Tarrington, but not before Linda has packed her bag and left. A disconsolate Peter, whose engagement at the Metropolitan has been canceled because of the scandal, accepts Arthur's offer to appear at his nightclub. For the show he decides to combine ballet and musical comedy and as a final inspiration has Linda Keene masks made for the chorus. He tells Arthur that if he cannot dance with the real Linda, he will dance with images of her.

In the big production number that climaxes the film, all the innovative elements of the plot are neatly resolved in the song and dance to the film's title song "Shall We Dance." First comes a section devoted to ballet, in which Astaire as Petrov dances with a ballerina and the corps du ballet to a reprise of "They Can't Take That Away from Me." The ballet dancers then dance off and a chorus wearing the Linda masks dances onstage. At this point the real Linda enters the club, having decided to serve Peter personally with the divorce summons. But when she sees the dancers wearing masks of her face and realizes that Peter really loves her, she asks to be taken backstage where she changes into a matching costume and, unknown to Peter, joins the chorus onstage. She dances with the chorus, briefly removing her mask and speaking to him before again hiding behind it. Realizing that the real Linda is onstage, Peter stops and frantically begins searching for her among the chorus, pulling off their masks until he finds Linda. He then leads her to the center of the stage, where they dance together as the film ends, singing "They all said we'd never get together, They laughed at us and how. But ho, ho, ho—who's got the last laugh now?"

The music for every Astaire-Rogers film is notable, but the Gershwin score for *Shall We Dance* is particularly outstanding. Nearly all the songs written for the film have become standards: "They All Laughed," "They Can't Take That Away from Me," "Beginner's Luck," and "Let's Call the Whole Thing Off." George Gershwin and his brother Ira had written the music for two

Broadway revues in which Astaire had appeared with his sister Adele—*Lady Be Good* and *Funny Face*—and had also written the score for *Girl Crazy*, Ginger Rogers' last Broadway show before she was sent to Hollywood. However, this was the first film score they had written for either Astaire or Rogers.

"Beginner's Luck" is sung by Peter to Linda on board the ocean liner traveling from Paris to New York. Peter tries to ingratiate himself with Linda, who is distant and reserved, and in song, he tells her that he has beginner's luck because the first time he has fallen in love, it is with her. He sings to her on the kennel deck of the ship, and at the end of the song, all the dogs howl mournfully. Peter also sings "They Can't Take That Away from Me," a lovely, romantic ballad, in a scene on the ferry from New Jersey to New York City. Linda is depressed and he sings to cheer her up; then, he proceeds affectionately to recall all the things he will never forget about her, such as the way she sips her tea, holds her knife, and wears her hat. The mood of the song and Astaire's low-key delivery are perfectly suited to the atmosphere of the scene.

The most imaginatively staged dance number in the film is Astaire's solo dance to "Slap That Bass," performed in the ship's gleaming, white, modernistic engine room. Peter listens to a black jazz band composed of crew members, then jumps up to sing a chorus of the song before taking off his coat and beginning to tap to the chugging, thumping, and pounding of the ship's machinery. As he taps, he adapts his steps to both mimic and counterpoint the rhythm of the machine.

"They All Laughed" is the only real Astaire-Rogers dance duet in the film. After Linda sings the lyric, she is tricked into dancing with Peter and watches him apprehensively as he swoops grandly about her in exaggerated balletlike movements. Finally, he holds out his hand and she puts hers into it, asking what she is supposed to do now. He tells her to "tweest," recalling their first meeting; and she responds with a burst of taps. After a few more nonsensical balletlike turns, Astaire finishes with a brisk salvo of taps to match hers. She then relaxes, and they begin dancing side by side. Rather than any deep emotion or poignant mood, the dance conveys the basic fun of two dancers performing together; it is as varied and as inventive as any of their duets and uses shifts in the music's tempo to signal changes in the style and tempo of the dance. The dance successfully mingles the two styles of tap dance and ballet, and at the number's climax, the two jump onto white pianos to the cheers and applause of the audience.

The film's novelty number takes place in Central Park where Peter and Linda have gone rollerskating to avoid inquisitive reporters. They argue amiably, their difference culminating musically in "Let's Call the Whole Thing Off." After finishing the song, the two begin tapping with their skates and spinning their wheels before suddenly rising to dance on their skates.

The only screen credit for dance direction or choreography in *Shall We*

Dance is give to Hermes Pan and Harry Losee for staging the ballet segments, but, as usual, Fred Astaire was closely associated with every aspect of the dances—from choreography through camera placement to the final editing of the sound and picture. His technique was to film a dance in one continuous shot, keeping the full length of the dancer or dancers in the camera frame and the flow of the dance uninterrupted. He did not use close-ups because he believed that in any dance, even tap, the movement of the rest of the body was as important as that of the feet, and he avoided reaction shots, those showing someone observing the dancers, because they broke up the flow of the dance. He also avoided unusual camera angles, such as overhead shots, because they called attention to the camera, and Astaire wanted the audience to be aware only of the dance. He did have to make a slight concession in filming "Let's Call the Whole Thing Off," danced on roller skates, since it was so difficult that it had to be filmed in two segments.

The exquisite Gershwin score and the charm, buoyancy, and talent of Fred Astaire and Ginger Rogers earned *Shall We Dance* almost universal critical acclaim and great success at the box office.

Julia Johnson

SHANE

Released: 1953
Production: George Stevens for Paramount
Direction: George Stevens
Screenplay: A. B. Guthrie, Jr., with additional dialogue by Jack Sher; based on the novel of the same name by Jack Schaefer
Cinematography: Loyal Griggs (AA)
Editing: William Hornbeck and Tom McAdoo
Running time: 118 minutes

Principal characters:

Shane	Alan Ladd
Marian Starrett	Jean Arthur
Joe Starrett	Van Heflin
Joey Starrett	Brandon De Wilde
Wilson	Jack Palance

Of the countless Westerns produced in Hollywood, *Shane* is among the most familiar and highly regarded. Its significance can be measured in terms of Hollywood's Western past, since *Shane* is a film that reflects upon the Westerns preceding it. It draws on the residue of this most enduring of film genres and abstracts its standard conventions, transforming them into myth. Given that many of the film's narrative events are seen through the eyes of a small boy, *Shane* further underscores the mythic status of the genre, suggesting its function as an outlet for the dreams and fantasies of youngsters.

The film's plot is deceptively simple. Shane (Alan Ladd), a mysterious, buckskin-clad loner, rides into a Wyoming valley during the late 1860's. He soon becomes a hired hand on the fledgling homestead of the Starrett family: Joe (Van Heflin), Marian (Jean Arthur), and young Joey (Brandon De Wilde). Shane is in fact a gunfighter who wants to change his ways; he hopes to settle down and start his own homestead. But Ryker, a cattle baron, intends to drive Starrett and the other homesteaders out of the valley, and Shane finds that he is being gradually drawn back into his past way of life. Because of Starrett's determined leadership, Ryker is unable to harass the homesteaders into leaving, so he hires Wilson (Jack Palance), a cold-blooded hired gun, to scare them out. After Wilson taunts, then easily kills one of the homesteaders in a one-sided gunfight, Starrett decides to put on his guns and stand up to Wilson and the Ryker bunch. Shane, however, knows that Starrett does not stand a chance against these seasoned killers, so he straps on his gun again. When Starrett insists on going, he and Shane wage a furious fistfight; Shane emerges victorious and rides off to meet the killers. In the town saloon, Shane outdraws and kills Wilson, as well as the Rykers. Though wounded, Shane rides out of the valley after indicating to Joey that he will never return.

Crucial to an understanding of *Shane* is its depiction of a mythic genre figure who tries to adapt to changing times by divesting himself of his heroic stature. The difficulty in making this transformation is first suggested when Shane trades in his buckskins for an outfit of drab workclothes. In these clothes, Shane enters a saloon, where he orders not the traditional shot of whiskey, but a bottle of soda pop. In the garb of a homesteader, Shane is taunted by one of the Ryker bunch. Since Shane wants to avoid trouble, he backs down from a fight, which leads the homesteaders to think him a coward. Wearing the same outfit, Shane eventually returns to the saloon, and with Starrett's help, bests the Rykers in a fistfight. The change of clothes allows Shane to initially "become" like a homesteader, but unlike them, Shane ultimately cannot back down from a fight.

Shane's relationship to the Starretts also points to him as one outside the locus of family/community/progress which they embody. While Joe likes Shane, and Joey worships him, Shane is nevertheless positioned as an outsider to the family unit. This is underscored by the unspoken love that he shares with Marian. Marian represents the nonheroic life style Shane can never attain, and their relationship is an idealized one. She is an insider while Shane is an outsider. The inside/outside duality is pointed up during a scene in which Shane stands outside in the rain while Marian is inside the Starrett house. The cross-cutting between the two emphasizes the inside/outside relationship, just as the gentle rendition of "Beautiful Dreamer" on the soundtrack at this point emphasizes the impossibility of Shane's transformation. When Shane finally goes to his quarters—which are, appropriately enough, away from the main house—Marian implies her love for Shane to Joey, telling him, "He'll be moving along one day and you'll be upset if you get to liking him too much." She then blows out a candle, causing the room to go dark. This suggests that her own attraction to Shane is as unattainable as his desire for her.

While Shane can never be a part of this family, he performs a heroic deed so that they—and the other homesteaders—can thrive in the valley. Before Shane rides off to meet Wilson, Marian asks, "Are you doing this just for me?" Shane replies, "For you—and Joe—and little Joey." As Shane rides off to the gunfight, he is again clad in his buckskins and, of course, is wearing a gun. Once again, his outsider status in relation to the family unit is suggested by editing: the Starretts are seen together in a single frame, while Shane rides off alone. Moreover, the ensuing long shots of Shane framed against the sky and mountains reaffirm his status as mythic figure.

Shane's relationship with Joey points to the Western genre as a source of preadolescent wish-fulfillment. This relationship is delineated in a number of ways. The lengthy fight in the saloon contains several cut-ins of Joey watching in fascination, as does the final gunfight. During the gunfight, Joey gets to realize his wish of participating in Shane's heroic actions, since he warns Shane that one of the Rykers is about to ambush him from upstairs, enabling Shane to kill the man. Prior to the climax, Joey gets to "be like" Shane be means of cutting on sound. During the saloon fight, after Shane lands a punch on the jaw of a Ryker henchman, a cut to Joey shows him biting hard on a candy stick. Here, the snapping sound of the bite replaces the sound of the punch.

Also crucial to an understanding of the film is the structuring opposition of civilization *versus* savagery that is a vital part of the generic structure of the Western. The valley town is not a thriving community but a few spread-out buildings and some tents. We see a disparate group of settlers (including an immigrant family and a family headed by a man who fought for the Confederacy), and the film posits that this cross-section holds the promise for a future—the transformation of a wilderness into a garden. The settlers are shown as nonviolent, and they are further ennobled by their harmonious relationship with the earth. During the scene in which they ride into town as a group, they are framed against the majestic mountains, the morning mist, and a sparkling brook. Moreover, the settlers clearly represent progress. This is suggested when Joe looks at a store catalogue from the East, and from his point of view we see the pages, full of appliances, dress suits, and so forth. The settlers, however, lack the ability to bring law to the savage land; they are ill-equipped to stop Ryker from transgressing nature. One homesteader notes that there is not a marshal within a hundred miles. The law, then, belongs to whomever has the fastest gun.

Within this opposition, Ryker and Shane, both of whom represent savagery, have no place in the advent of civilization. While Ryker is a villain, there are shades of gray to his character. He is the man who tamed the valley with his own sweat and blood. As he tells Starrett at one point, "We made this country. We found it and we made it." But Ryker's frontier dream has been perverted by his capitalistic greed, and Starrett's reply to his remark, "That ain't the way the government sees it," suggests the homesteaders are sanctioned by culture and law. The film closely equates Starrett with democratic populism. This is especially suggested during the Independence Day celebration—the day honoring the establishment of the United States is also the anniversary date of the Starretts. During the celebration, the American flag is featured prominently.

While *Shane* clearly champions the populism represented by Starrett and the settlers, it also sadly concludes that there is no place for the rugged individualist within this new system. Finally, the film demonstrates that Ryker's kind of capitalist individualism violates law and community, while Shane's individualism enforces the principals of collective life. When Shane tells the cattle baron, "Your kind of days are over," Ryker replies, "My days? What about yours, gunfighter?" But Shane's next line, "The difference is I know it," stresses his own awareness of what he is. Shane, then, is the noble outlaw/savage who cannot be accommodated by civilization. It is he alone who is equipped to take effective action when words have proved to be inadequate.

In recent years, many revisionist critics have sought to devalue *Shane* because of its rigorous classicism. These critics argue that the "real" Hollywood Westerns have been made by once-slighted directors such as John Ford, Howard Hawks, Anthony Mann, and Budd Boetticher. While the great contribution made to the genre by these directors is incontestable, George Stevens' brief foray into a genre in which he had never worked (and never again worked) can be equated with the writers who came from the East to write about the frontier. Stevens takes the most familiar conventions of the West and stylizes them considerably. For him, the generic material becomes a means of glamorizing this most durable of Hollywood forms. This material also becomes a means of self-expression, and *Shane*'s greatness is due in no small measure to Stevens' pictorial style and personal vision. Stevens himself has been devalued by revisionist critics, but he represents the best of the classical Hollywood cinema. Few directors used the close-up as effectively as Stevens, and the editing patterns linking close-ups of Shane, Marian, and Joey serve to make the film genuinely touching and dramatically potent. This kind of editing recalls Stevens' great love stories, including *Swing Time* (1936), *Woman of the Year* (1942), *The More the Merrier* (1943), and *A Place in the Sun* (1951). After *Shane*, Stevens was weighted down by several elephantine spectacles which contain only flashes of his early brilliance. *Shane* is perhaps his last fully realized work. It is like those Stevens films in which a social misfit/outcast helps to make life better for someone who has a position within the social order, but who has certain problems which only the misfit/outsider can resolve. Notable among these films are *Vigil in the Night* (1940) and *The Talk of the Town* (1942). Other Stevens films detail the trials and tribulations of the social misfit/outcast in general, especially *Alice Adams* (1935), *A Damsel in Distress* (1937), *A Place in the Sun*, and *The Diary of Anne Frank* (1959).

Shane was made during the peak of Stevens' career, when the release of any film from him was considered an event (in this sense, Stevens was like Capra, Wilder, and Hitchcock). At the time of its release, *Shane* earned as much acclaim as any film of the 1950's. It was nominated for Academy Awards for Best Picture, Best Director, and Best Writing (screenplay). De Wilde's poignant performance was nominated for Best Supporting Actor, as was Palance's menacing Wilson. Loyal Griggs received an Oscar for his breathtaking color cinematography. Stevens won the National Board of Review's Best Director award, and was also honored by the Director's Guild for quarterly directorial achievement. *Shane* was included on the ten best films of the year lists of the National Board of Review, *Time* magazine, and the *New York Times*. The film's box-office gross of eight million dollars made it the third biggest moneymaker of 1953, and even today, it is one of the most financially successful Westerns of all time.

Charles Albright, Jr.

SHE DONE HIM WRONG

Released: 1933
Production: Paramount
Direction: Lowell Sherman
Screenplay: Harvey Thew and John Bright; based on the play *Diamond Lil* by Mae West
Cinematography: Charles Lang
Editing: Alexander Hall
Costume design: Edith Head
Running time: 66 minutes

Principal characters:
Lady Lou .... Mae West
Captain Cummings .... Cary Grant
Gus Jordan .... Noah Beery
Russian Rita .... Rafaela Ottiano
Dan Flynn .... David Landau
Sally .... Rochelle Hudson
Chick Clark .... Owen Moore

The spicy humor and sexual double entendres that characterized Mae West's career were brought to the nation's attention in the 1933 film *She Done Him Wrong*, with a screenplay, based on the play, *Diamond Lil*, written by West. After opening in New York in 1928, *Diamond Lil* had received critical acclaim and box-office success, both in New York and on the road, and with this taste of success, Hollywood became West's next challenge. After her screen debut with George Raft in *Night After Night* (1932) was a hit, she concentrated on transferring *Diamond Lil* to the screen. *She Done Him Wrong* made the transition well, and Mae West's risque humor and sexiness soon became known across the country.

The film proved to be important to the industry in that the financial condition of Paramount Studios received a boost from West's overnight success. It was the content of the film, however, that created the greater impact; since it was found to be objectionable to some, it forced the motion picture industry to impose its Motion Picture Production Code, administered by the Hays Office. Although this restrictive code had been adopted in 1930, it had been largely ignored by its creators. Then, under pressure primarily from the League of Decency, self-censorship was imposed by the filmmakers on their own productions. The popular burlesque humor of Mae West would be visible in her next film, *I'm No Angel* (1933), but by 1934, her films would be sanitized by the Code until they lacked the distinctive West flair, and although popular thereafter, they did not match her early works.

In *She Done Him Wrong*, Lady Lou (Mae West) is the main attraction of the story; although the supporting cast and other actors are talented, they seem incidental to the film's main interest. The film is notable as one of the early works in the great film career of Cary Grant, who as Captain Cummings of the Salvation Army, is pitted against Lady Lou. The resulting match of wits and charm is one of the most enjoyable parts of the movie. The story is set in the New York Bowery in the 1890's, and the audience's first view of Lady Lou occurs when a large picture of a naked lady over the bar in the establishment of Gus Jordan (Noah Beery) appears on the screen. In a conversation with Dan Flynn (David Landau), it becomes apparent that Flynn and Jordan are engaged in a power struggle—for control of the Bowery as well as a personal battle for the affections of Lou, who is living over the bar in a lavish apartment, complete with maid and, of course, all her diamonds.

The soft-hearted nature of Lady Lou is seen in an early episode in which a young pregnant woman, Sally (Rochelle Hudson), chooses the bar as the location for a suicide attempt. Failing in this attempt, she is befriended by Lou, who takes her upstairs and buoys her spirits with a recitation of her philosophy of life. Heartened by this display of friendship, both she and Lou are pleased when Russian Rita (Rafaela Ottiano) offers Sally a job on the Barbary Coast. Sally, who believes that she is embarking on a new career of song and dance, takes the job with Lou's blessing.

We learn a little of Lou's past when word is received from her former boyfriend, Chick Clark (Owen Moore), who is doing time on a "bum rap" set up by Dan Flynn. As well as indicating his belief that she has been faithful in his absence, the message also requests that she visits Chick in prison, and when she does, he threatens her life if he discovers that she has not been true to him, declaring that he does not intend to stay imprisoned any longer. It is obvious that Lou has not remained faithful to Chick since she is not the type of woman who lets opportunity pass her by. However, her real challenge comes when she is smitten by the good Captain Cummings, who runs the mission next to the bar. While rescuing a young offender from the police, he catches Lou's fancy, and it is here that the famous lines, "Why don't you come up sometime, see me. Come up, I'll tell your fortune" are spoken. To this, Cummings replies that perhaps she should come to meet him, and, in a gesture of warm-heartedness and also as a lure to get Cummings to her room, Lou purchases the mission for $12,000 in diamonds, and then turns the deed over to Cummings.

However, Lou's life of tranquility is soon coming to an end. First she learns that Chick has indeed escaped and is in town; there are also rumors circulating that a detective called the Hawk is closing in on Gus's counterfeiting ring. Then, Lou learns from Cummings that Sally had been sold by her "benefactress." The film's pacing quickens at this point as Chick returns, and is told by Lou to get out of her life. She has a teasing encounter with Cummings, although neither of them emerges victorious, and then is finally approached by Rita's boyfriend. Rita appears on the scene and, in the ensuing struggle, is stabbed with one of Lou's diamond stick pins.

In the conclusion, as Lou is onstage singing her version of "Frankie and Johnny," shots ring out. Flynn is killed, and Gus, Chick, and Lou are arrested by the Hawk, who turns out to be Captain Cummings. Although the men are taken away in a police van, Lou and Cummings leave in his car, and instead of handcuffs, he puts a ring on her finger, telling her that she is going to do time for a long time.

She Done Him Wrong is a most enjoyable vehicle for Mae West's comedic talents. Her timing, inflection, and phrases are pure fun, and her demeanor and carriage bring to the screen the playful sexiness with which she was so integrally associated. West's musical talents are also displayed in several numbers, including "I Wonder Where My Easy Rider's Gone."

The direction by former stage actor Lowell Sherman is excellent, but it is obvious that West carried the movie where she desired it to be led. Grant's portrayal is well done and believable, and his transition from missionary to detective is accepted because he had presented Captain Cummings as an individual who, in retrospect, manifested shades of the Hawk even in his own character. One of the early period films in the history of talking motion pictures, *She Done Him Wrong* was costumed by Edith Head. Although nominated, the film did not receive the Academy Award for Best Picture, but *She Done Him Wrong* should be considered a classic of comedy films, and remembered as one of the few uncensored film presentations of Mae West's humor and style.

Elaine Raines

THE SHOOTIST

Released: 1976
Production: M. J. Frankovich and William Self for Dino de Laurentis and Paramount
Direction: Don Siegel
Screenplay: Miles Hood Swarthout and Scott Hale; based on the novel of the same name by Glendon Swarthout
Cinematography: Bruce Surtees
Editing: Douglas Stewart
Running time: 100 minutes

Principal characters:

J. B. Books .... John Wayne
Bond Rogers .... Lauren Bacall
Dr. Hostetler .... James Stewart
Gillom Rogers .... Ron Howard
Sweeney .... Richard Boone

The Shootist opens with a black-and-white montage of scenes from old John Wayne movies. Over each episode a date is superimposed, and the last years of the nineteenth century slip away as Wayne fights out a series of gun duels. Color begins to seep into the picture with a scene of a bleak winter landscape through which an older Wayne is riding. It is, perhaps, a self-conscious starting point for a film which deals not only with the Western myth, but also with that myth's best-known representative.

Although Wayne's range as an actor is limited and his manner somewhat wooden, he is in a sense the movie actor *par excellence*. Unwilling to attempt "uncharacteristic" roles, Wayne the actor is Wayne the man. The politics of the people he portrays (obedient soldiers, cattlemen, peace officers, rugged individuals one and all) are Wayne's politics; and although his view of America may not be widely accepted by a generation which has witnessed race riots, assassinations, imperialistic war, and Watergate, his championship of the cowboy code is integral to the motion picture industry's most enduring genre. Wayne does not embody the freshly laundered, guitar-strumming serial hero, for it is the texture of flaws below the surface of his character which gives his roles their vitality and enables even those who disagree with his politics to respect the man he plays.

Two-fisted chivalry and love of home and family are no longer solutions to all human ills, and John Wayne's reaction to the anomalies of a complex and compromised society has been the pivot of his most successful films. In *The Searchers* (1956), Wayne's prolonged quest for vengeance and redemption leaves him drained and purposeless, an obsessive outcast. In *The Man Who Shot Liberty Valance* (1962), he fights a losing battle against the encroachment of Eastern values, only to hasten the death of the Old West when he kills its foremost exponent, the vicious outlaw played by Lee Marvin. In *The Shootist*, Wayne is an aging gunfighter who knows he will shortly die from cancer. Ironically, Wayne died of cancer himself within three years of the filming of *The Shootist*, his last picture.

The dawn of the twentieth century is at hand, and "shootists" of J. B. Books's caliber are in short supply. The opening montage depicts highlights from Books's long career, and shortly afterwards we see Books outwit an inept ambusher with practiced ease. Arriving in a thriving township which is no longer part of the "frontier," he seeks out his old friend Dr. Hostetler (James Stewart) and learns that he has only a few months to live. For most of the time that remains to him, the doctor relates, he will be incapacitated and in great pain. For the average Westerner, the way out would be swift and certain, but Books is not average even by Western standards. Well aware of what he is doing, he sets up residence in a boardinghouse and waits for the challenges which will inevitably come. Shortly they do in the form of glory-seekers, bullies with imagined grudges, and even an immaculate derringer-and-brocade gambler. The essential confrontation is similar to the one faced by Gregory Peck in *The Gunfighter* (1950). Wayne's character, like Peck's, is a quiet professional hounded by ambitious gunmen who want to wear his "crown." However, Books is not sustained by the prospect of a new life in another town. He chooses to attract attention, knowing what the inevitable result will be.

Ironically, Books reckons without his prowess, and emerges wounded but very much alive from a showdown with the three most deadly gunfighters available. No one ever bested John Wayne in a fair fight, and *The Shootist* could hardly break the mold. Instead Wayne dies as Peck died—from a bullet in the back. His assassin, a minor character of no importance, is immediately gunned down by Wayne's youthful protégé Gillom Rogers (Ron Howard)—a rather feeble resolution compared to that of *The Gunfighter*, where the assassin is allowed to live, in terror at the prospect of more glory-hunters coming after *him*. The poor ending aside, Wayne could hardly have had a more appropriate screen departure, and despite qualms about the film, the press was unanimous in its praise for Wayne.

The Shootist was directed by Don Siegel, a veteran director of low-budget action features including *Riot in Cell Block 11* (1954) and the highly regarded science fiction thriller *Invasion of the Body Snatchers* (1956). A gifted editor (he began his career as a studio montage artist), Siegel has always relied on actors with presence rather than performers, a legitimate approach, given the genres in which he works, but one which normally demands strong original material. John Milius' script for *Dirty Harry* (1971) is an obvious example. Unfortunately, although its premise is unique, *The Shootist*'s treatment is often mundane. A subplot involving the landlady's naïve son (a plodding Ron Howard, who tags after Wayne and "learns to respect him") lends no depth or originality to the film, and to have the son execute Books's cowardly killer is simply an excuse for more bloodshed at the cost of grossly mismanaging the myth.

The most stylized aspect of *The Shootist*'s structure actually fits the theme extremely well: short sequences reel rapidly away, linked by titles reading "First Day," "Second Day," and finally "Last Day." The titles inevitably underscore the recurring theme of this and many other Westerns of the 1970's—Sam Peckinpah's in particular—namely, that the Western hero's day is over. The audience had grown too sophisticated for the old brand of heroics: the heroism of the New Western is born out of desperation and, in a way, surrender and the inability to change.

Siegel's cast is for the most part excellent. Lauren Bacall, in particular, turns her stereotypal character Bond Rogers, into something considerably finer, and the villains, led by Richard Boone as Sweeney, are a suitably unsavory bunch. One of the script's major shortcomings is its failure to give the "Badmen" more to do. Obviously the focus of the story is J. B. Books, but this is all the more reason to provide him with a set of worthy adversaries. The villains of *The Shootist* are gun-crazy suburbanites, sketchily drawn. To paint them more fully would not be to abandon the irony of Books's battle against unworthy men, but instead would enhance the conflict.

Bruce Surtees' cinematography contrasts the barren exteriors with a make-shift opulence in the saloons and houses. Much of the film was shot in a preserved settlement in Colorado, and Surtees' sensitive use of natural light enhances the existing beauty of the location. The art direction pays close attention to a burgeoning technology: Books rides a streetcar to his final destination. All other considerations aside, *The Shootist* is John Wayne's film, and, regardless of its imperfections, it is an achievement of interpretation on his part, and no small tribute to the legend he helped to create.

V. I. Huxner

SHOW BOAT

Released: 1936
Production: Carl Laemmle, Jr., for Universal
Direction: James Whale
Screenplay: Oscar Hammerstein II; based on the novel of the same name by Edna Ferber
Cinematography: John J. Mescall
Editing: Ted Kent and Bernard W. Burton
Music: Jerome Kern and Oscar Hammerstein II
Running time: 110 minutes

Principal characters:
Magnolia Hawks Ravenal .... Irene Dunne
Gaylord Ravenal .... Allan Jones
Captain Andy Hawks .... Charles Winniger
Joe .... Paul Robeson
Julie LaVerne .... Helen Morgan
Steve .... Donald Cook
Kim (younger) .... Marilyn Knowlden
Kim (older) .... Sunnie O'Dea

Show Boat was a successful novel; a broadway musical that enjoyed a long run, a European tour, and frequent revivals; and a film which was produced no less than three times. Universal Films acquired the rights to the Edna Ferber novel and made a silent film with talking sequences in the 1920's; it was remade in 1936 as a big-budget musical with many of the theater stars in the roles they had created on stage (Charles Winniger as Captain Andy, Helen Morgan as Julie LaVerne, and Paul Robeson as Joe). In 1951, George Sidney directed the most recent film musical version, with Kathryn Grayson and Howard Keel as the romantic leads and Ava Gardner in the poignant role of Julie LaVerne. Although this last remake is generally admired and has its staunch advocates, the 1936 version is generally considered to be the superior effort.

Show Boat of 1936 was a big-budget picture. Irene Dunne was an important star; the recent Broadway run had been a success; and the music of Oscar Hammerstein and Jerome Kern was popular. These factors combined virtually to insure success; the film was an audience favorite and a critical success, in spite of director James Whale's "filmed theater" visuals. The problems Whale faced in filming *Show Boat* are ever-present dangers for directors who make movies from stage plays, whether they are musicals, dramas, or comedies. Whale inserted some very expressionistic montage sequences of dramatically lit blacks during Paul Robeson's "Ole Man River" number, and used montage again to span quickly the years between Magnolia's successful theatrical career and her daughter's quick rise to fame in the theater, but generally the film's scenes are static and the camera moves only follow action.

Show Boat, set in the 1900's, begins on Captain Andy Hawks's riverboat *Cotton Blossom*, which travels the Mississippi stopping at towns to give theater performances. Magnolia (Nola) Hawks (Irene Dunne) is the daughter of Captain Andy (Charles Winniger); his wife is determined to protect Nola from the cheerful casualness of "show people." Nola, however, meets a handsome stranger with whom she sings "Make Believe." On down the river, Captain Andy's show runs into trouble when a formerly spurned suitor of leading lady Julie LaVerne (Helen Morgan) informs a local sheriff that she is a Negress married to a white man—a crime in the South. Steve (Donald Cook), Julie's husband and the show's leading man, cuts her hand and swallows her blood so he can tell the sheriff that he too has Negro blood; they escape jail but must leave the riverboat. Nola is heartsick; she and Julie were like sisters. Captain Andy solves his problem of losing his leading cast members by putting Nola in Julie's role and the handsome stranger Nola has already met in Steve's. The stranger is Gaylord Ravenal (Allan Jones), a gambler who asks passage on the riverboat because he must leave town. Nola and Gaylord fall in love and marry, but the future is foreshadowed when he is off gambling on the stormy night their daughter Kim is born. It is "lazy" Joe (Paul Robeson) who brings the reluctant doctor back through the high waves. The little family goes to Chicago, where Nola writes letters to her parents of wealth and high living, but eventually Gaylord's luck runs out and he leaves Nola to spare her further pain and humiliation. She goes back to work in the theater, landing her first job when Julie, remaining hidden, quits her position so that Nola will be hired. Nola becomes a star, and Kim (Sunnie O'Dea) follows in her footsteps. When Nola is retired, she goes to Kim's debut and finds that Gaylord is the doorman at the theater. They are united in a final song.

Show Boat uses many typical musical genre elements interestingly. Like many classic musicals, it is a "back stage" story, in which theater acts as a metaphor for life. The tension between life and theater is particularly rich in *Show Boat*, since Gaylord and Nola's real life is sordid and tragic, whereas their love is as much a function of theater as it is reality. They sing "Make Believe" before they are even introduced, and we see their courtship onstage through the roles they play when they are the romantic leads in Captain Andy's shows. Both of their lives—his as a gambler and hers as an actress—are based on fantasy, and when Gaylord leaves his family, he tells young Kim to "make believe" when she is sad. Clearly this make-believe fails them in the real world, but the strength of *Show Boat* is that it insists upon the fragile beauty of fantasy, which sustains their love over the years and allows them a bittersweet reunion. When Captain Andy finds Nola supporting herself singing in a club on New Year's Eve—a very different picture from the happy, wealthy family he and his wife were expecting to spend the holidays with—he encourages her to give her all to her life and work, and helps her see the beauty through the pain. Unlike musicals in which everything comes together in an upbeat musical ending, *Show Boat* does not avoid depicting either the joy of make-believe (the basis of the theater) or its heartbreak.

Julie LaVerne is as compelling a character as Nola, if not more so. The 1951 version of the story ends with Julie, her face prematurely ravaged, watching unseen as Nola and Kim and Gaylord are reconciled on the show-boat. Julie has lost her husband and her career, but the sight of the young family seems to make it all worthwhile. Julie's suffering is the heart of the 1951 film; in the 1936 version, however, she and Nola both suffer; they are the kind of women who will "love one man 'till they die," no matter what he does. Julie then sings "Can't Help Loving That Man of Mine," although Queenie, the black comic character played by Hattie McDaniel, says that only blacks sing that song. Indeed, suffering becomes the ennobling connection not only between Julie and Nola, but among the black characters who provide the background of the film.

The role of the blacks in *Show Boat* is one of its most interesting elements. When Jerome Kern composed "Ole Man River" (with lyrics by Oscar Hammerstein) for the Broadway musical, he wanted Paul Robeson to play the role of Joe, who sings the song. Robeson was prevented by other commitments, but he was able to accept the role in London, Europe, and later in the film. Robeson is an important figure in American theater, and his incredible voice and commanding, dignified presence stopped the show many times during its performance as the audience demanded that he repeat "Ole Man River." Nevertheless, the character of Joe was criticized by many as being a demeaning racist stereotype. Indeed, *Show Boat* contributed to Robeson's pessimism over the treatment of black characterizations both in American theater and in cinema.

Although the blacks in *Show Boat* are comic stereotypes, they also provide the film with its depth and its ennobling view of suffering. Julie's "Negro blood" in no way diminishes her; on the contrary, she is mourned by both blacks and whites when she must leave the show boat. Julie gives Nola the warmth and training she needs for her life, and there are ample implications that she is capable of such giving because of her link to the blacks. This neither excuses nor eliminates the damage done by racist portrayals, but *Show Boat* is a fine example of the dual, and often contradictory, nature of such portrayals.

Two of the best songs in the film are about women loving worthless men—"Bill" and "Can't Help Loving That Man of Mine,"—and the two most appealing characters in the movie suffer from such hopeless love. Also, the warmest, most meaningful relationship occurs between these women; Nola and Julie are like sisters who defend each other and sacrifice for each other, and their interactions onscreen are among the high points of the film. *Show Boat* is filled with this kind of dichotomy, and it is a clue to the continuing high regard in which the film is held that there is a significant substructure which does not entirely conform to the surface narrative.

Janey Place

SHOW BOAT

Released: 1951
Production: Arthur Freed for Metro-Goldwyn-Mayer
Direction: George Sidney
Screenplay: John Lee Mahin; based on the musical play of the same name by Jerome Kern and Oscar Hammerstein II, adapted from the novel of the same name by Edna Ferber
Cinematography: Charles Rosher
Editing: John D. Dunning
Music: Adolph Deutsch and Conrad Salinger
Running time: 107 minutes

Principal characters:

Magnolia Hawks	Kathryn Grayson
Julie Laverne	Ava Gardner
Gaylord Ravenal	Howard Keel
Captain Andy Hawks	Joe E. Brown
Ellie May Shipley	Marge Champion
Frank Schulz	Gower Champion
Stephen Baker	Robert Sterling
Parthy Hawks	Agnes Moorehead
Joe	William Warfield

Universal first acquired the rights to film Edna Ferber's best-selling novel *Show Boat*, and that production was released in 1929. It was silent, with a sound and music track, and it featured a prologue of variety entertainment mostly from the Kern/Hammerstein musical version of *Show Boat* which Ziegfeld had produced on Broadway with enormous success. Ferber only leased the rights to her book for seven years, so before that period was up, Universal made a splendid second version, directed by James Whale and starring Irene Dunne and Allan Jones, which has come to be considered definitive.

Eventually M-G-M acquired the rights to make yet a third version, this time in Technicolor, and it was released in 1951. Color admittedly should have been a positive addition to the story of *Show Boat*, but the Technicolor used was often too garish. The best of the three versions remains the second one, in simple black-and-white, with its flawless cast and its direction by an Englishman who had a genuine flair for the theatrical.

The basic story line remains the same in all three productions. Edna Ferber has told in her autobiography, *A Peculiar Treasure*, of how she first heard the term "show boat." When she learned what a show boat was, she was absolutely fascinated by the idea of a boat sailing the Mississippi and Ohio Rivers, stopping at certain designated river ports where the actors living on board the boat put on a show attended by the townspeople. The show consisted of a melodrama designed to the popular taste of the day, followed by an olio, in which those same actors performed vaudeville stunts to entertain their eager audiences. It was authentic Americana, and it stirred Ferber's imagination.

Ferber's show boat, the *Cotton Blossom*, is owned and run by Captain Andy Hawks (Joe E. Brown). He selects and directs his shows and picks the company, which must meet the approval of his dominating, tight-lipped wife, Parthy (Agnes Moorehead). Early in their married life, Andy and Parthy have a daughter, whom they name Magnolia (Kathryn Grayson). As Magnolia grows up, Parthy's protection of the child is fierce. Magnolia is not allowed to associate with the actors, and, of course, there is no thought of Magnolia's appearing in any of Captain Andy's productions, although Parthy does, for she is the leading character actress in the company.

Magnolia, however, is a true romantic, a charming, fresh, teen-aged beauty, and she sings like a lark. She knows all of the lines and all of the songs and dances from the programmed shows. Her chance comes early. The leading lady of the *Cotton Blossom* is a beautiful, dark-haired, talented young woman of black heritage named Julie Laverne (Ava Gardner) who is in love with her leading man, Stephen Baker (Robert Sterling). Unfortunately, a no-good suitor whom Julie has repulsed has done some detective work and has learned that Julie is undeniably an octoroon. The sheriff boards the boat. Julie's lover, Stephen, knowing what is about to happen, draws a knife, cuts his own hand and Julie's, and mingles their blood, so that he too has more than a drop of black blood in him. Although miscegenation can no longer be proved, they are dismissed from the boat by Captain Andy. This hurts Magnolia for Julie was like a sister to her, and they loved each other dearly.

Captain Andy is left in a quandary, with his two lead performers gone and a show to give to the river towns. There is only one person who knows Julie's part and her songs. Although Parthy protests, Captain Andy makes Magnolia the *Cotton Blossom*'s new leading lady. With Stephen also gone, however, they do not have a proper leading man. By chance, the right man comes along, a Southern gentleman and adventurer named Gaylord Ravenal (Howard Keel), who has an excellent voice and looks like a hero out of a romantic storybook.

At first, Ravenal is not too interested in being enlisted as the *Cotton Blossom*'s leading man, but then he sees the youthful Magnolia and loses his heart to her. She helps him learn his words and songs, and, thrown together as they are, much to Parthy's consternation, they fall in love. They are the hit of all the riverboats sailing the Mississippi. Parthy notices what is happening. She cannot object to audiences taking them as lovers, but she fears that the two will become lovers in reality. They do, and Ravenal persuades Magnolia to elope with him; the two run off to Chicago, where Ravenal has connections.

Af first Magnolia is divinely happy, and it is not long after they are married that she knows she is going to have a baby. Ravenal, however, is too often not at hand to help her. He has gambling blood in his veins and frequents the famed gambling and sporting houses of the city. Magnolia for the first time in her life knows want and is frightened. She goes looking for Ravenal, tracing him to a fashionable brothel, where she is horrified to find that the woman whose favors he is enjoying is her own beloved childhood companion, Julie Laverne.

Magnolia finds out where the *Cotton Blossom* is and manages to get back there, where she gives birth to her daughter, Kim, and eventually returns to acting. This M-G-M version of the story departs from previous ones in that the Chicago Fair episodes are softened, and Ravenal returns to Magnolia while his daughter is still a young child. There is a happy ending in this version; a reconciliation takes place and all is forgiven.

The element that always makes stage productions of *Show Boat* memorable is the score written by Jerome Kern and Oscar Hammerstein II. Their melodies pour forth from the sound track just as they had once brightened the magic of the theater. They are wonderful, unforgettable songs that are absolutely right for the *Cotton Blossom*'s characters—songs such as Magnolia and Ravenal's "Make Believe," "You Are Love," and "Why Do I Love You?" Julie has two wonderful blues songs— "Can't Help Lovin' That Man" and "My Bill." Julie is one of Ava Gardner's most moving cinema portrayals, and she is not only believable but devastatingly beautiful as the unfortunate Julie. Gardner had wanted to sing her own songs, and she studied hard to present them as they should be. If one listens to the show record of the movie production, the real voice of Ava Gardner will be heard singing her two songs. At the last moment, however, she was dubbed by another voice for the released picture. Julie's songs are professionally done, but at no time is there the sob behind the blues as Helen Morgan had sung them onstage or in the second movie version in which she played Julie. (Morgan also sang Julie's songs in the prologue of the initial silent version of *Show Boat* starring Alma Rubens as Julie.) Gardner has always lamented not being allowed to sing her own songs, for she tried to present them much after the inimitable style of Helen Morgan.

Joe E. Brown is an animated and amusing Captain Andy, and Agnes Moorehead is sharp, but she seems more spinsterish than maternally repressed the way Helen Westley had been in the James Whale film version and Edna May Oliver had been onstage in the Ziegfeld production. William Warfield sings the now-classic "Ol' Man River" with genuine feeling. The pleasant surprise of the movie is the team of Marge and Gower Champion, who play the roles of Ellie May Shipley and Frank Schultz, the show boat's youthful dance team, the soubrette and the juvenile. They have three numbers that bring down the house—"Ballyhoo," "I Fall Back on You," and "Life upon the Wicked Stage." Howard Keel, as Ravenal, has an effective solo, "Gambling," and Kathryn Grayson warbles part of "After the Ball," which does not fit in with all the other fresh, lovely Kern/Hammerstein songs.

Remakes of a big hit can be fatal, and while this big splashy Technicolor version of *Show Boat* can hardly be called a fatality, neither does it have the endearing magic that made the second film version a movie to remember. One misses the sheer joy that illuminated that early production. It was a story of a kind of theater directly out of the American past, and it had people who were young, talented, and believable. This attempt by M-G-M to outdo the second Universal production fails to achieve its goal.

DeWitt Bodeen

SILK STOCKINGS

Released: 1957
Production: Arthur Freed for Metro-Goldwyn-Mayer
Direction: Rouben Mamoulian
Screenplay: Leonard Gershe and Leonard Spigelgass; based on the play of the same name by George S. Kaufman, Leueen McGrath, and Abe Burrows, adapted from the film *Ninotchka*
Cinematography: Robert Bronner
Editing: Harold F. Kress
Choreography: Hermes Pan and Eugene Loring
Music: Cole Porter
Running time: 117 minutes

Principal characters:

Steve Canfield	Fred Astaire
Ninotchka	Cyd Charisse (sung by Carol Richards)
Peggy Dayton	Janis Paige
Vassili Markovitch	George Tobias
Brankov	Peter Lorre
Bibinski	Jules Munshin
Ivanov	Joseph Buloff
Peter Ilyitch Boroff	Wim Sonneveld

A Cold War commentary on Soviet-American relations, Rouben Mamoulian's *Silk Stockings* also develops the theme of an individual's emotional awakening and lightly satirizes the popular entertainment of the 1950's. Based on the film *Ninotchka* (1939) by way of the 1955 stage play *Silk Stockings*, the film not only serves as a showcase for the dancing of Fred Astaire and Cyd Charisse, but also reflects the political, social, and cultural values of the times. Politically, the film captures the stereotypes of Communist and capitalist ideologies that pervaded much of American culture. Socially, *Silk Stockings* celebrates an American view of warm femininity contrasted with the cold, brusque manner attributed to Russian women. Culturally, it reacts to the trend in motion pictures toward extravaganza and to a new musical form, rock and roll. Throughout, the musical numbers choreographed by Hermes Pan and Eugene Loring effectively provide continuity in plot, underscore the film's thematic import, and graphically portray the awakening experience.

Although the film mirrors American values, the setting is elegant Paris, whose luxuriant decadence provides an antithesis to bleak Soviet life. During a concert tour in the French city, acclaimed Soviet composer-pianist Peter Ilyitch Boroff (Wim Sonneveld) is persuaded by American film producer Steve Canfield (Fred Astaire) to write the music for his new film, supposedly a version of *War and Peace*. This production will inaugurate the serious film career of Peggy Dayton (Janis Paige), already well-known to moviegoers as "America's swimming sweetheart." The Soviet government, upset by Boroff's impending defection, sends Brankov (Peter Lorre), Bibinski (Jules Munshin), and Ivanov (Joseph Buloff) to effect his return to Moscow. But Canfield introduces the three to the pleasures of wine, women, and song in capitalistic Paris, and they forget their mission. Meanwhile, back in Moscow, Vassili Markovitch (George Tobias) has become Minister of Culture in one of the characteristically abrupt changes in regime said to define Soviet politics. Reflecting the hypocrisy of the Communist system, the minister's businesslike exterior is belied by his less than businesslike interest in one of the ballerinas under his charge. But now he faces the task of sending someone to retrieve the wayward Boroff and the three errant emissaries. The assignment falls to Ninotchka (Cyd Charisse), who appears before him in the drab garb of Soviet officialdom named Yoshenko, spouting Communist and antiindividualist rhetoric and exhibiting an impressive portfolio of credentials.

After Yoshenko arrives in Paris, Canfield tries to convince her by means of a falsified affidavit that Boroff's father was a French traveling salesman, thus making Boroff a French citizen. A day's tour of Paris with Canfield makes no dent in the comrade's severity. Although Canfield emphasizes the romantic beauty of Paris, she is interested only in mills and factories. However, later that evening in his hotel room, Canfield introduces Comrade Yoshenko to emotional warmth. Though she asserts that love is merely a chemical reaction, Canfield proves her wrong with the concrete illustrations of dance, kiss, and the song "All of You." Under his spell, Comrade Yoshenko begins to awaken and to doff Soviet impersonality and conformity for Western individuality. She becomes Ninotchka.

The activities of the couple are interrupted by the intrusion of Peggy Dayton, who reveals Canfield's plan to have Boroff compose music for his film. Her Soviet dignity and pride offended, Ninotchka leaves. Canfield then convinces Peggy to use her considerable charms to enlist Boroff himself in their cause; that is, to allow his music to be converted into tunes appropriate for the hit parade. For Canfield's plan is not to produce a version of *War and Peace* at all, but a spicy account of the life of Josephine in "glorious technicolor, breathtaking CinemaScope, and stereophonic sound"—features of the Hollywood spectacular which earlier provided a rousing, satiric musical number for Canfield and Peggy.

The next morning, Ninotchka is so starry-eyed from Canfield's dancing, singing, and kissing that she cannot seriously deal with the matter which has brought her to Paris. As her three colleagues discuss Boroff with her, she dreamily picks at the typewriter. Her hair, softened into waves which contrast with the austere style of the previous day, signals the feminizing process inherent in her awakening experience.

In the meantime, Peggy has lured Boroff to her fashion designer's, where she seduces him by modeling the latest undergarments. Her song, "Satin and Silk," expounds the power of such feminine clothing to make a woman feel alluring and attractive. Peggy's song and its effect on Boroff testify to the power of feminine wiles.

This scene is effectively juxtaposed with one in Ninotchka's room. Having called off a meeting with Boroff, she draws the curtains, turns Lenin's photograph face down, and exchanges her dark stockings for ones made from Parisian silk—garments she had sneered at upon her arrival in Paris. In a sensuous dance, she casts off her uniform for the Western accouterments she has secreted around her suite: delicate underwear, a bracelet, earrings, perfume, high-heeled slippers, and an evening gown. Her metamorphosis complete; she is ready for a night on the town with Canfield. She now represents the 1950's feminine concept, in contrast to her dowdy and severe appearance upon arriving in Paris. Returning at two o'clock in the morning after drinking much champagne, Ninotchka is even more starry-eyed. When she slips into a tipsy sleep, Canfield chastely lays her on a couch and leaves.

The next day at the movie studio where they have gone to watch the filming of Canfield's movie, Steve proposes marriage to Ninotchka, singing that they are "Fated to Be Mated." Although she yearns to accept, she fears the repressive Soviet government will prevent it. On the set itself the expected serious treatment of *War and Peace* turns out to be a travesty. Peggy, playing a sultry Josephine, performs Boroff's "Ode to a Tractor" in the style of American popular music. The Soviets, Ninotchka included, view this as an affront to their culture and return to Moscow.

In one of the film's few technical lapses, we find ourselves without transition in Russia about a year later. The Soviets meet for a reunion in Ninotchka's portion of a somber flat shared with several others. Soviet life is depicted as void of luxury, privacy, pleasure, and beauty. Ninotchka receives a letter from Canfield, completely censored except for the salutation and closing. Boroff reveals that he has adopted a new musical style and performs "The Red Blues." The other occupants of Ninotchka's flat join the singing and dancing to express their dissatisfaction with Soviet life.

When Brankov, Bibinski, and Ivanov are sent to Paris again, an anonymous letter informs the Minister of Culture that they have again been taken in by the city's decadence. Ninotchka must go once more to bring them home to Russia. When she arrives at the hotel in Paris, she is struck by the Soviet motif in the decor. Her three comrades, dressed in Western clothing, insist that she see the show at the cafe. The production features Steve Canfield dancing and singing "The Ritz Roll and Rock," a piece written especially for the film by Cole Porter to comment on a brash new musical genre. In their office afterwards, the three Russians tell Ninotchka that they have bought the cafe and do not intend to return to Moscow. She also learns that the anonymous letter was sent by Canfield, who had finally decided it was the only way that he could get her out of Russia. He announces his intention to marry her, and the film ends with "Too Bad," the same song with which it began.

Silk Stockings was the last show which Cole Porter wrote for the stage, the last film directed by Rouben Mamoulian, and the last musical film in which Fred Astaire appeared as leading man. Contemporary critical response varied from the opinion that the story line was too ponderous for musical comedy treatment to rhapsodies over the dancing of Astaire and Charisse. The dancing is, indeed, the film's strongest point. Whether it be an expression of the sexual chemistry between the two principals, a manifestation of the frivolity of gay Paris, or merely a showcase for the talented cast, the dancing in *Silk Stockings* makes the film a worthwhile experience even in an age when the values of the 1950's seem peculiarly foreign.

Frances M. Malpezzi and
William M. Clements

SING AS WE GO

Released: 1934
Production: Basil Dean for Associated Talking Pictures
Direction: Basil Dean
Screenplay: Gordon Wellesley; based on a screen story by J. B. Priestley
Cinematography: Robert Martin
Editing: Thorold Dickinson
Running time: 80 minutes

Principal characters:

Grace Platt	Gracie Fields
Hugh	John Loder
Phyllis	Dorothy Hyson
Policeman	Stanley Holloway
Uncle Murgatroyd	Frank Pettingell
Sir William Upton	Lawrence Grossmith
The Cowboy	Morris Harvey
The Great Maestro	Arthur Sinclair
Madame Osiris	Marie O'Neill

Gracie Fields was a British vaudeville and film star who held a unique place in the hearts of English people everywhere; she was known simply as "Our Gracie" and loved by two generations for her simple, working-class approach to life. The songs she made famous, "In My Little Bottom Drawer," "The Biggest Aspidistra in the World," "I Took My Harp to a Party," and "I Never Cried So Much in All My Life," typified this approach, which stemmed from a childhood spent in the grimy, industrial Lancashire town of Rochdale, where she was born in 1898. She came to fame during the 1920's at the British Music Hall and in revues, and by 1930 had even achieved the ultimate in American vaudeville by headlining at New York's Palace Theater. Her down-to-earth charm, her unpretentious singing voice with its working-class accent and manner, and above all her energy completely won over audiences everywhere. It was obvious that the next step was a career in films.

To guide her film career, Gracie Fields was fortunate in choosing—or having chosen for her by her husband—Basil Dean, an extraordinary figure in the history of British theater and cinema. As a stage director and producer, he was without equal in the 1920's, a stern disciplinarian responsible for such successes as *Rain*, *They Knew What They Wanted*, *The Constant Nymph*, and *Autumn Crocus*; authors who owe much of their fame to him include John Galsworthy, Clemence Dane, and J. M. Barrie. In 1930, he created Associated Talking Pictures and founded Ealing Studios, whose success too many historians have credited to its later head, Michael Balcon. At Associated Talking Pictures, Basil Dean must be given full credit for establishing two

British Music Hall stars, George Formby and Gracie Fields, as that country's biggest film performers of the 1930's.

Gracie Fields's first feature was *Sally in Our Alley* (1931), a minor production notable for giving its star what was to become her theme song, "Sally." Three further films followed—*Looking on the Bright Side* (1932), *This Week of Grace* (1933), and *Love, Life and Laughter* (1933)—before Gracie Fields and Basil Dean made *Sing as We Go*, which was to be the star's greatest British production, and which, more than any of her other films, symbolized the British people's courageous and light-hearted approach to the depression. To furnish the story, Basil Dean turned to novelist J. B. Priestley, whose North Country background was as well known as Gracie Fields's. Priestley saw in Fields all the attributes which assured the performer of a sympathetic popularity with the English working classes: "shrewdness, homely simplicity, irony, fierce independence, an impish delight in mocking whatever is thought to be affected and pretentious." He took a simple story and embroidered it with the use of British Music Hall humor and scenes and situations which typified life for the majority of North Country English people. They could empathize with the Gracie Fields character and with the persons and problems which she encountered, and therein lay the ultimate reason for the success of all of the Gracie Fields films.

Gracie Fields plays Grace Platt, whom the depression leaves unemployed through the closure of the cotton mill where she works. In search of a new life, she goes to Blackpool, a North England seaside resort, where she becomes involved with a policeman (Stanley Holloway). Eventually the cotton mills are reopened, and Gracie leads the workers back to the factory, all of them waving Union Jacks and singing the theme song, "Sing as We Go." It is a marvelous moment of patriotism, unsurpassed in its feeling of unrehearsed fervor and spontaneity. The song was to become the theme song of the depression in England, and Fields used it as the title for her 1960 autobiography.

Blackpool was famous for its amusement park; its tower where Reginald Dixon had become a national figure entertaining at the organ; its ballroom which was a rendezvous for a generation of courting couples; its illumination—a glittering display of fairy lights; and its musical comedies and farces performed in the theaters at the ends of its many piers. Producer and director Basil Dean uses an almost *cinema verité*-type approach to the film in order to capture the essence of this great seaside resort, and he shows Gracie cycling around town or enjoying the delights of the big dipper, as ferris wheels are called in England. The strength of *Sing as We Go* lies in the fact that it captures the endurance of the British people and celebrates their ability to overcome adversity. The cornerstone of *Sing as We Go*, and of its appeal, is Gracie Fields, a reminder that an individual can overcome any obstacle by sheer perseverance, courage, and something that has disappeared very much from the world—the will to survive and to "get up and go."

Sing as We Go, made for the trifling sum of one hundred thousand pounds, was one of the studio's biggest hits, and supposedly financed the construction of five new cutting rooms and two new sound stages. Although it is hard to believe that much, if not all, of the credit for *Sing as We Go* should go to Basil Dean, Thorold Dickinson has claimed credit for the pacing of the production because of his editing, particularly in the chase sequence through the Blackpool fun fair, and has stated that Basil Dean did not supervise the editing and indeed did not see the film, following its shooting, until the production's release. Because of the high regard in which Dickinson is held by today's film scholars, it has become fashionable to denigrate Dean's contribution to the film. There should be no doubt, however, that it was Dean, and Dean alone, who conceived of the production, handled the Blackpool locations, and was ultimately responsible not only for the success of the film but also for the lasting fame of its star.

Gracie Fields continued her successful film career and even starred in a number of Hollywood productions, the best of which are *Holy Matrimony* (1943), in which she appeared opposite Monty Woolley. She died on the Isle of Capri, where she had made her home since the 1930's, on September 27, 1979. She was one of a small group of British performers—others being George Formby, Flanagan and Allen, and Vera Lynn—whom generations of English people held in special esteem since each went far beyond being successful in one particular medium of show business, and became national symbols of Britain and the British way of life.

Anthony Slide

SINGIN' IN THE RAIN

Released: 1952
Production: Arthur Freed for Metro-Goldwyn-Mayer
Direction: Gene Kelly and Stanley Donen
Screenplay: Adolph Green and Betty Comden; suggested by the song of the same name by Arthur Freed and Nacio Herb Brown
Cinematography: Harold Rosson
Editing: Adrienne Fazan
Choreography: Gene Kelly and Stanley Donen
Music direction: Lennie Hayton
Music: Arthur Freed and Nacio Herb Brown
Running time: 102 minutes

Principal characters:
Don Lockwood .... Gene Kelly
Cosmo Brown .... Donald O'Connor
Kathy Selden .... Debbie Reynolds
Lina Lamont ....Jean Hagen
R. F. Simpson ....Millard Mitchell
Dancer ....Cyd Charisse

Often called Hollywood's most enjoyable musical, *Singin' in the Rain* is also one of the most optimistic and charming. Its appeal is due largely to its glossy, colorful look and its humorous view of a Hollywood in transition from silents to talkies. It was produced by the Freed Unit, which was responsible for M-G-M's best musicals of the 1940's and 1950's, such as *Meet Me in St. Louis* (1944), *An American in Paris* (1951), and *The Band Wagon* (1953), Arthur Freed, head of the unit, was a former lyricist who had written many songs with Nacio Herb Brown and had become a producer at M-G-M in the late 1930's. He asked scriptwriters Betty Comden and Adolph Green to write a script that would use songs he had written with Brown. Realizing that most of the songs had been composed during the early sound phase of films, 1927-1931, they were inspired to set their story during this period, a time they both knew and loved.

The film opens with an exciting 1927 premiere at Grauman's Chinese Theatre in Hollywood of the latest film of Don Lockwood (Gene Kelly) and Lina Lamont (Jean Hagen). When Don and Lina arrive at the premiere, a famous gossip columnist, supposedly modeled on Louella Parsons, asks Don to comment on his success. Wearing a white polo coat and a white felt hat, Don recounts with a toothy grin his version of his rise to stardom as we see on the screen what actually happened. He assures his fans that he was educated at the finest schools, but we see him tap dancing in pool halls; he claims he received his musical training at a Conservatory, but we see him performing in a burlesque house with his friend, Cosmo Brown (Donald O'Connor).

Lina has always encouraged him, he says, but we see her snubbing him until his stunt work attracts the attention of the director and he becomes her costar. Significantly, Don does all the talking for the pair, and later we learn why. Lina's speaking voice is shrill and her accent uncouth, a handicap that destroyed the careers of many stars when talkies arrived.

On his way to a party after the film's premiere, Don is attacked by autograph seekers and is forced to escape by jumping into a car driven by Kathy Selden (Debbie Reynolds), an aspiring actress. She discourages Don's advances by saying she has not seen his films and does not think silent film stars really act. At the party, which is given by R. F. Simpson (Millard Mitchell), the head of the studio, there are two surprises for Don. First, Simpson shows a short demonstration of a talking picture. The guests are surprised, but they refuse to take it seriously. Then a huge cake is rolled into the room and out of it pops Kathy Selden, who is soon joined by a group of chorus girls performing the song "All I Do Is Dream of You." Don teases Kathy until finally, stung by his gibes, she throws a cake at him, but misses and hits Lina instead. Flustered, Kathy runs away although Don tries to stop her.

Sound pictures become more than a joke for a party when Warner Bros. makes a full-length sound picture, *The Jazz Singer*, and it becomes a huge success. Simpson stops the production of Don and Lina's current film, *The Dueling Cavalier*, in order to convert it to a sound film. Worried about Kathy Selden, whom he has not seen since the party, and worried about the impact of sound on his career, Don goes to the studio with his friend Cosmo. As they walk by movie sets, we catch glimpses of films in various stages of production—Westerns, comedies, costume dramas—all existing side by side in the same building. This brief look at the world of silent films and how they were made adds much to the charm of *Singin' in the Rain*. To cheer Don up, Cosmo does a cheerful, wacky song "Make 'Em Laugh," in which, among other antics, he falls down, runs into a brick wall, and falls off a couch.

Next, a montage of excerpts from musicals currently in production at the studio leads into a musical fashion show. This number serves as an excuse for a colorful display of 1920's fashions, and closes with an overhead shot of the chorus girls surrounding the male commentator in a kaleidoscopic pattern in the manner of Busby Berkeley. When Cosmo points out to Don that one of the girls in the show is Kathy Selden, he is delighted. After getting her a minor film role, Don then wins her love by singing to her "You Were Meant for Me," using a wind machine and dramatic lighting to create a romantic atmosphere on an empty sound stage.

By now everyone at the studio is taking diction lessons, including Don and Lina. Lina is not coping well with sound, but Don and Cosmo prove how well they have mastered their lessons by doing a novelty number for their diction coach, "Moses Supposes."

The production of *The Dueling Cavalier* as a sound film provides some funny scenes, faithfully researched to give the proper look. The booth that houses the camera, the design and placement of the microphones, even the gate and sign "Monumental Pictures," are all based on photographs and designs of the period. The film tries, in fact, to duplicate M-G-M as it looked in 1927. These scenes contain some of the best comedy in the film. In order to pick up Lina's voice, the microphone is placed first in a bush, and finally in the bosom of Lina's low-cut gown. There, however, it also picks up Lina's heartbeat. Finally, the microphone is hidden in a corsage on her shoulder, but Simpson, visiting the set, trips over the cord and tips Lina head over heels. After many such problems, the film is finished; but at its preview the audience laughs at Lina's shrill, ungenteel voice, the uneven sound, and terrible synchronization. It looks as if Don and Lina's careers may be ended.

During an all-night talk session at Don's house, however, Don, Cosmo, and Kathy try to cheer one another up. Finally, Cosmo has the idea of turning the film into a musical, with Kathy, who has a lovely singing and speaking voice, dubbing Lina's voice. Their relief and joy is evident as they sing "Good Mornin'," dancing on the furniture and around the house. Don then takes Kathy home; and after he leaves her, he expresses his happiness in the song "Singin' in the Rain." As a musical, the film, now called *The Dancing Cavalier*, is a great success. At the premiere the audience, especially impressed by Lina's singing, begs her to perform a number on stage for them. Lina prepares to mouth the words while Kathy sings behind a curtain, but Don, Simpson, and Cosmo pull up the curtain hiding Kathy to reveal the deception to the audience. Lina is laughed off the stage, and Don and Kathy have their happy ending.

Two of the musical numbers must be singled out for special comment: the title song, "Singin' in the Rain," and the film's big production number, "Broadway Rhythm." Many believe Kelly's solo dance on a rainy street with an umbrella represents some of his best work; it is a spontaneous expression of happiness. After kissing Kathy Selden good night, he walks along the street in the rain, singing. He is so happy that he lets water from a drain pipe splash on his upturned face, kicks up water with his feet, and splashes in puddles like a child. When a policeman finally walks over to see what he is doing, he reacts guiltily, then walks off defiantly, waving good-bye to the policeman. It is one of Kelly's most successful pieces of choreography, largely because it is unpretentious and unaffected. Unfortunately, the number's impact is lessened because it is not built up to with enough care to support all the exhilaration it expresses. Don and Kathy have already fallen in love, and he has already told her so in song ("You Were Meant for Me").

"Broadway Rhythm" is led up to by the simple device of having Don Lockwood first explain his idea for a big musical number to Simpson, and then we see the number he describes, which has no direct relation to the plot. Lockwood is a naïve, eager young dancer who arrives on Broadway with glasses and a suitcase, looking for a break. He is rejected by several agents before being taken to a speakeasy where he lands a job. In an extraordinary scene Kelly and the audience suddenly see a woman's long shapely leg extended into the frame with Kelly's hat on the end of her foot. His eyes and the camera follow the shapely leg to the shapely figure of a dancer (Cyd Charisse). Leaving her silver-dollar-flipping gangster boyfriend, she flirts with Kelly, shaking her hips and blowing cigarette smoke into his face. Finally, she removes his steamy glasses, wipes them on her thigh, and kicks away both the hat and the glasses. When he tries to retrieve them, she puts her long cigarette holder in his mouth. They dance closely and sensuously, and she starts to kiss him but is lured away by the sight of a diamond bracelet in the hand of her gangster boyfriend. Later, the young dancer becomes a star, meets the beautiful girl again, and in his imagination sees himself dancing with her in a romantic setting, but in reality she spurns him again. After the number, Don asks Simpson what he thinks of the idea. "I can't quite visualize it," he responds. "I'll have to see it on film first." Like the rest of *Singin' in the Rain*, the ballet was inspired by the 1920's. The gangster boyfriend is a parody of the roles often played by George Raft, and Cyd Charisse is made up to look like Louise Brooks, a star of silent films.

Besides Gene Kelly's dance in the rain and Cyd Charisse's seductive dance in "Broadway Rhythm," another joy of the film is Jean Hagen's memorable comic performance as Lina Lamont. Comden and Green had Judy Holliday in mind when they created the character, and Hagen was instructed to act similar to Holliday portraying Billie Dawn in *Born Yesterday* (1950). Her characterization, from shrill voice to simpering mannerisms, is both funny and appealing.

Ideal in the leading role are Gene Kelly, Donald O'Connor, and Debbie Reynolds. All are exuberant, vivacious, and irrepressible, and work well together. As Don Lockwood, Kelly, who also collaborated in the direction and choreography, has several opportunities to show off his dancing style at its best—athletic and unpretentious. As Cosmo Brown, whose irreverent remarks and clever ideas provide not only a comic background but also solutions to the other characters' dilemmas, O'Connor demonstrates his abilities as a comedian and as a dancer, especially in the "Make 'Em Laugh" number; and Debbie Reynolds is a fresh and engaging Kathy Selden.

In *Singin' in the Rain* the dramatic and comic elements are as entertaining and as inventive as the musical ones, so there is no slackening of energy after a musical number. All the parts are expertly woven together under the direction of Stanley Donen and Gene Kelly. Certainly the clever, humorous script, the careful attention to detail and lavish production values, and the cheerful songs of Freed and Brown all contribute to the enduring popularity of this fine musical.

Julia Johnson

SITTING PRETTY

Released: 1948
Production: Samuel G. Engel for Twentieth Century-Fox
Direction: Walter Lang
Screenplay: F. Hugh Herbert; based on the novel *Belvedere* by Gwen Davenport
Cinematography: Norbert Brodine
Editing: Harmon Jones
Running time: 84 minutes

Principal characters:
Harry King .... Robert Young
Tacey King .... Maureen O'Hara
Lynn Belvedere .... Clifton Webb
Mr. Appleton .... Richard Haydn

An entertaining comedy, *Sitting Pretty* takes some surprising turns as it depicts the adventures of an eccentric self-proclaimed genius in a suburban town. The situations are intriguing, and Clifton Webb is superbly haughty as the egotistical genius. The audience is informed by a title that the film's location is Hummingbird Hill, "where everybody knows a little more than a little about everybody," and we meet Mr. Appleton (Richard Haydn), a fussy busybody. The story is then set in motion by the maid of a young couple, Harry (Robert Young) and Tacey King (Maureen O'Hara), who quits because she has completely lost patience with their unruly children. Tacey cannot possibly manage three children herself, so she advertises for and hires by mail a live-in baby sitter, who, quite to her surprise, turns out to be a man. She assumes that only a woman would apply for the position, and the name Lynn Belvedere does not tell her otherwise.

Tacey and Harry are taken aback by this situation and try to tell Belvedere (Clifton Webb) that it will not work out; however, he rationally states that he is fully qualified and sees no reason why he should not stay. Their doubts are dispelled when, in his first day on the job, he tames all three children, fixes the icebox, and makes a "divine combination salad." They become used to his eccentricities, such as practicing yoga and being a vegetarian, and his ego. When Harry tells him he has "got something," Belvedere responds, "You might even say I have everything." Indeed, later on when Tacey tells him that the only virtue he lacks is modesty, he simply says that he does not consider that a virtue. Even though he is very strict with them, the children are devoted to Belvedere, and everything goes smoothly, until Harry, who is a lawyer, has to take a business trip to Chicago. He decides that Tacey cannot spend the nights that he is away in the same house with Belvedere, and insists that she sleep at the house of their friends Bill and Edna Philby. However, one of the children gets sick in the middle of the night and Tacey goes to comfort him when Belvedere telephones her because the "child expressed a maudlin desire for his mother." The nosy neighbor, Mr. Appleton (Richard Haydn), sees the lights in the night and comes to see what is happening. The next day he spreads the rumor that Tacey and Belvedere were engaged in a drunken orgy, and the moment Harry returns, his boss confronts him with the story. Although he is willing to believe that nothing suspicious has happened, Harry thinks matters would be solved if Belvedere left. He has to relent, however, when the children protest.

All settles down once again until Appleton starts more gossip about Tacey and Belvedere. This time Tacey gets so upset with Harry that she goes home with one child to her parents, leaving Harry with Belvedere and the other two. This standoff contines until a new novel is published and immediately becomes a best seller, especially in Hummingbird Hill. The novel, called *Hummingbird Hill*, and written by Lynn Belvedere, is a very thinly disguised story of the activities of the citizens of the community. The book creates a great uproar and causes Harry's boss to fire him for harboring such a person. The end of the film finds Tacey and Harry back together and Belvedere hiring Harry to represent him in the libel suits people are filing against him. Despite his success and fame, however, Belvedere plans to continue as a baby sitter for the Kings, and when Tacey announces that they are going to have another child, he replies that he will be useful since he was once an obstetrician.

The strength of *Sitting Pretty* lies, of course, in the character of Belvedere. Hollywood has a habit of portraying an intellectual as a stuffy, inhibited person with a great deal of very specialized and useless knowledge but no idea of how to enjoy life. Belvedere, however, quickly surprises everyone, as he not only tames the previously ungovernable children but also reveals that he has been, among other things, a locksmith, a beekeeper, a medical doctor, and the dance instructor who taught Arthur Murray how to dance. In exasperation, Harry asks him if there is anything he has not been. "I've never been an idler or a parasite," he replies. He is also unlike the Hollywood stereotype of the genius in that, although he does not become romantically involved with any of the women in the film, he is attractive to and attracted by them.

Robert Young and Maureen O'Hara contribute excellent performances as the young couple, Tacey and Harry King, as they try to cope with the imperious Belvedere. Tacey is able to adjust rather quickly to the situation and finds Belvedere's wealth of knowledge and experience stimulating, but it is more difficult for Harry, who cannot help being jealous. Richard Haydn gives fine support as Appleton, the fussy busybody neighbor.

Sitting Pretty was one of the top-grossing films of its year, and Twentieth Century-Fox tried to capitalize on its great popular success with two sequels,

Mr. Belvedere Goes to College (1949) and *Mr. Belvedere Rings the Bell* (1951), but neither is nearly as engaging as the original.

Timothy W. Johnson

SLEUTH

Released: 1972
Production: Morton Gottlieb for Twentieth Century-Fox
Direction: Joseph L. Mankiewicz
Screenplay: Anthony Shaffer; based on his play of the same name
Cinematography: Oswald Morris
Editing: Richard Marden
Running time: 137 minutes

Principal characters:
Andrew Wyke .... Laurence Olivier
Milo Tindle .... Michael Caine

The theater lights dim and the screen reveals a miniature stage. The playful music suggests that this will be a light, theatrical game of detective work. But then the camera closes in on the tiny stage's depiction of a crime and hesitates for a moment. There is a break in the music, and the audience thinks that perhaps there is something more serious afoot after all. But then the music returns, the camera moves on to another tiny stage, and the mood is light again. What the audience does not know is that director Joseph Mankiewicz is playing tricks. The credits tell the audience that they will see a cast of seven; only at the end of the film will the audience know that Laurence Olivier and Michael Caine make up the entire cast.

The camera moves on to the last little scene of crime: a beautiful sixteenth century English country house. Here the detective story about a detective story writer and the theatrical game about a highly theatrical game player begins. Milo Tindle (Michael Caine) searches along a remarkable maze of hedges until he finally discovers the master game player and detective writer, Andrew Wyke (Laurence Olivier). Wyke is listening with pleasure to the playback of the new dictation on his latest thriller. But it will not be as good as the real event he is planning. The aristocratic writer abhors Milo's trade and his origins—Milo is a beauty shop owner and hairdresser of poor Italian ancestry—but most intolerable to Andrew is the knowledge that his wife Marguerite and Milo are lovers. Andrew will have his revenge on the younger man; and since he loves games, it will be a gamelike revenge.

Playing the proper host, Andrew invites Milo inside for a drink and shows him some of the remarkable mechanical toys that fill his house. Then, in the same light spirit, he persuades Milo to steal Marguerite's valuable jewelry so that Milo and Marguerite can live together in the style to which she has become accustomed. According to Andrew's plan, Milo can sell the jewelry and Andrew will collect the insurance. He also convinces Milo that a clown costume is the only appropriate attire for the theft. With a grand effort, and unintentional comedy on his part, Milo "steals" the jewels. But then Andrew tells Milo that the theft was just a setup. His real intention is to murder the hairdresser and make the police think he has killed a dangerous burglar. During a very dramatic scene the audience watches a tearful Milo beg for his life. Nevertheless, after alternating between amusement and anger, Andrew shoots him.

After what appears to be a few days, the audience sees Andrew festively preparing a snack of caviar and drinks for himself. But the light mood is broken by the sound of the doorbell. The police have arrived. Soon a simple but skilled Inspector Doppler creates a strong murder case against Andrew. At first, the writer proudly describes the trick he has played on Milo. He has not really murdered him, he insists, but has only given him a good scare and taught him a lesson by shooting him with a blank. But when the Inspector discovers bullet holes in the wall and dried blood on the stairs, it is Andrew who becomes scared. At the height of Andrew's fear, Doppler pins him down on the sofa and then slowly and dramatically removes his disguise. Both Andrew and the audience are amazed to see that the Inspector is none other than Milo. Milo proudly describes how he stole into the house a few days before and set up all of the evidence against Andrew.

It would seem now that Andrew and Milo are even. But the tricks are not finished. Milo says he still has one more game. He tells Andrew that he has made love to Teya, Andrew's present mistress, and then murdered her. The evidence, however, indicates that Andrew is the murderer. Milo challenges Andrew to discover and erase four pieces of incriminating evidence which Milo has planted in the house. Andrew must hurry, for the police will be arriving very soon. Following Milo's clever, gamelike hints, Andrew races frantically through the house to discover each clue. Finally finished, he sinks into a chair. Then Milo reveals that this has once again been a game, a game that Teya herself helped him play. He adds that she has also revealed that Andrew is impotent and that she is not really his mistress at all.

This confrontation is intolerable for the egotistical writer. When Milo goes upstairs to get Marguerite's fur coat, Andrew purposefully drops bullets into a revolver. By now, both Milo and the audience think this will be still another game; but when Milo ironically tells Andrew that "the game's over," Andrew pulls the trigger, and the camera reveals blood on Milo's mouth. Soon a police car's flashing lights shine through the windows of the big house. For a moment, Milo pulls himself up to warn: "Andrew, don't forget. Be sure and tell them it was just a bloody game." Then he falls back, and all the toys in the room simultaneously begin their grotesque antics. Their controls are locked in the death grip of Milo's hand.

Sleuth is a fine detective story. Anthony Shaffer, who wrote both the screenplay and the original successful stage play, is one of Britain's best writers of thrillers. Oswald Morris' camera work helps to increase the tension of Shaffer's script; close-up shots and occasional stills of Andrew's toys add a special gothic quality. When the camera goes outside the house to look in on Andrew, it suggests that an unidentified person is staring in at him. To further the tension and excitement of the script, the soundtrack uses music traditional to detective stories. A harpsichord begins to create a quick, playful mood, and then becomes slow and foreboding. When more instruments join in, they also alternate between a quick, teasing tempo and a slower, more ominous one.

Sleuth, however, is more than a detective story—it is also a highly theatrical comedy. As early as the credits, Mankiewicz sets up a comic tone. One of the supposed cast of seven is an actress named "Eve Harrington": a playful allusion to the main character of Mankiewicz's earlier film, *All About Eve* (1950). At one point in the film the audience sees a photograph of "Marguerite," which is, in fact, a picture of actress Joanne Woodward. Noted for his appreciation of fine dialogue, Mankiewicz remains true to the witty dialogue of the stage play and reinforces it with the camera work and music. Paralleling the alternating tempos of the music, the dialogue between the two actors suddenly shifts from light repartees to joltingly serious lines. In the midst of a light conversation about detective writing, Andrew casually hands Milo a drink and then says, "So, you want to marry my wife." Later, during the staged theft, he urges that Milo should ransack the house in a manner that is "convincing but not Carthaginian."

Olivier and Caine develop the dialogue to its fullest. Seeing these two outstanding actors work together is the best part of the film. They turn a pool game into an escalating cold war. Trying on costumes together, they stretch acting to its most theatrical, and Olivier especially seems to be having a wonderful time. Caine certainly keeps pace with Olivier, however, from his slapstick attempts to climb a ladder to his fine characterization of Inspector Doppler.

In addition to being a detective story and a sophisticated comedy, *Sleuth* has still another dimension. Mankiewicz has a reputation for imparting liberal messages. In *Sleuth*, he exposes the pomposity and amorality of the upper class. In contrast to the lightness of the detective story, a class struggle between the aristocratic writer and the proletarian hairdresser becomes increasingly serious as the film develops. At first, Andrew seems to be a refined and witty gentleman. His enthusiasm and his remarkable theatrics are great fun for the audience, and he often does make Milo appear crude and greedy. But then, ironically, Andrew begins to reveal his own crudeness and cruelty. During the pool game, he envisages Milo and Marguerite's lovemaking in especially ugly imagery. He winces at Milo's slang, but then with good, upper-class British slang, he immediately describes one of his stories as "an absolute corker." In the course of the film, he shows that it is only concern for reputation and not love that makes him want to keep his wife and his mistress. Most dramatically, he shows himself to be remarkably cruel. He not only convinces Milo that he is about to kill him, but at the same time, he totally humiliates him.

In contrast, throughout much of the film, Milo is the underdog whose openness and honesty quickly draw the audience to his side. Andrew is cunning and clever and tries to divulge little about his real feelings, but Milo readily answers the writer's unfair questions and gives a moving description of his immigrant father's difficulties in England. Andrew makes such a fool of Milo that the audience is later delighted to discover that the bright, practical Inspector Doppler is actually Milo in disguise and that the nice guy is finally getting the upper hand. Later in the film, however, the nice guy becomes a little less nice. Maybe he has been around the callous upper class too much, for Milo begins to act more and more like Andrew. When he sends Andrew on a frantic search for clues to Teya's "murder," for example, he leans back on the plush steps and enjoys his new power perhaps a little too much. Knowing how he can hurt Andrew most, he mocks his impotence after he already has humiliated him sufficiently.

In spite of these changes, Milo nevertheless continues to fare better than Andrew. Perhaps Mankiewicz gives Milo an unfair share of sympathy. As the film develops, Andrew's life seems increasingly foolish and hollow. A stereotyped member of the upper class, Andrew amuses himself with games in order to fill the emptiness of his life. He surrounds himself with expensive and intricate toys, and his only friend seems to be the mechanical Jack the Sailor. When Andrew tells Doppler that playing the game is his whole life, the Inspector comments that it "sounds a bit sad, like a child."

The real twist of the film is that the master game player is Mankiewicz himself, since he criticizes Andrew's aristocratic game playing, and then turns around and plays game after game on the audience. The acting, music, and camera work make the audience expect a comic scene; then the mood suddenly becomes serious and even ominous. Then, the moment when the audience expects the worst, everything becomes light and playful again. Sometimes Andrew wins a game and sometimes Milo wins, but the audience gets tricked every time.

The characterization of Milo places a still greater and less playful demand on the audience's credulity. Would a hairdresser from Soho have the acting ability to play Inspector Doppler and the verbal skills to create intellectual word games? Would Milo's pride allow him to follow Andrew's burglary scheme? And would Andrew's girl friend go along with Milo's trick? The answer to all these questions is that it doesn't matter—*Sleuth* is a paced, witty detective story, and getting tricked is, after all, inherent in the plot of detective stories. In *Sleuth*, the fine dialogue and acting are likely to capture even the most critical viewer.

There are some difficulties, however, that *Sleuth*'s wit and sophistication do not solve. After the second game, the film begins to seem long. In spite of the strong acting, Milo's word games become tiresome. By the end of the film, one is tempted to agree with Andrew when he tells Milo that three games are too many. Even the fine close-ups of Andrew's toys finally become a little too frequent and predictable. A second difficulty with *Sleuth* is its class theme. As a witty detective story, it is successful, but when Mankiewicz also tries to include a criticism of upper-class values, the film's direction becomes confused. It is the theatricality and playfulness of the film that make it work; the messages do not.

The music, the camera work, and the dialogue give *Sleuth* a delightful tempo and variety. Its greatest strength, however, lies in the acting. Both Olivier and Caine were nominated for Academy Awards for Best Actor, and, for his performance in *Sleuth*, the New York Film Critics voted Olivier the Best Actor of 1972. Ultimately, *Sleuth*'s impact comes not from any message it attempts to convey but from the fact that the two actors and the audience have such a good time together—and that the game is played so well.

Elaine McCreight

SMILE

Released: 1975
Production: Michael Ritchie for United Artists
Direction: Michael Ritchie
Screenplay: Jerry Belson
Cinematography: Conrad Hall
Editing: Richard Harris
Running time: 113 minutes

Principal characters:
"Big Bob" Freelander .... Bruce Dern
Brenda DiCarlo .... Barbara Feldon
Tommy French .... Michael Kidd
Wilson Shears .... Geoffrey Lewis
Andy DiCarlo .... Nicholas Pryor
Robin Gibson/Miss Antelope Valley ..... Joan Prather
Doria Houston/Miss Anaheim .... Annette O'Toole
"Little Bob" Freelander .... Eric Shea

Competition and its effect upon human principles is one of director Michael Ritchie's favorite themes. Ritchie surveyed this theme as it pertained to the world of sports in *Downhill Racer* (1969) and to politics in *The Candidate* (1972). Having discovered that competition pervades the adult world, *Smile* assures us that it is also present in the seemingly innocuous world of a teenage beauty pageant.

Smile is set in the town of Santa Rosa, California, during its major "cultural" event of the year, the annual "Young American Miss" beauty pageant. The director of the pageant is "Big Bob" Freelander (Bruce Dern), who owns the town's recreational vehicle dealership. His assistant is Brenda DiCarlo (Barbara Feldon), an efficient woman who was once a Young American Miss herself.

As in many of Ritchie's films, *Smile* is drawn from reality. According to the director, "Everything in *Smile* is true." Anyone who has seen a beauty pageant will agree that the mood, flavor, dialogue, and characters presented in the film are accurate. Certainly, the fact that Ritchie once served as a judge at an actual Santa Rosa beauty pageant gave him an inside knowledge of such events. Nevertheless, the film is not a documentary on beauty pageants, but a study of the men and women who organize, participate in, and attend them.

In order to provide the film with the proper spirit and feeling, the filmmakers staged what was in essence a real beauty contest. Most of the contestants are either nonprofessionals or young actresses with limited experience. Some are daughters of people in the motion picture industry, such as Maria O'Brien (Edmund O'Brien's daughter) and Melanie Griffith (Tippi Hedren's daughter). Thus, during the filming, the girls developed relationships and experienced tensions and excitement as they would in a real beauty contest. However, unlike the contestants in a real contest, these girls were allowed to hide behind fictional characters, allowing them to remain more natural and freeing them from the fear of the camera intruding on their daily lives. In all, thirty-three girls took part in the filmed pageant, with many chosen from open auditions held for that very purpose. However, the distinction between professionals and nonprofessionals is largely indeterminable and creates a highly energetic environment.

While much of the film is concerned with the thirty-three teenage contestants, those involved in other areas of the pageant are also of interest, in particular "Big Bob." He is the focal point of the pageant. As chief judge, he sets the standards by which these young girls will be judged; his values pervade the entire pageant. Although he is not the originator of these values, he has accepted them so enthusiastically that they pervade both his personal and professional life. His assistant Brenda represents the aftereffects of the beauty contest experience. She remains a true articulation of the "Young American Miss" attitude.

We follow the contest through several days of rehearsal and two nights of pageantry. In the process, we become acquainted with both the contestants and the organizers. We are shown how the contest affects the values of the girls and how some come to adopt the values which make a beauty contest winner. We are also taken on a series of adventures which shed light on the characters of the organizers.

Andy (Nicholas Pryor), Brenda's husband and Big Bob's best friend, is unlike almost everyone else in the film; he is neither enraptured by the beauty pageant nor by his life. He has begun to drink heavily and must soon go through the "Exhausted Rooster" ceremony at the Bears Club. The ceremony, which serves as a symbolic passage from youth to "old age," occurs at one's thirty-fifth birthday and includes kissing a chicken's ass. Andy finds this particularly revolting and humiliating. Bob finds Andy's reluctance to kiss a chicken's ass confusing, as does Brenda, who is alienated by what she calls his "sarcasm and self-pity." Andy, frustrated by his inability to communicate his dissatisfaction with life, threatens to shoot himself. However, Brenda reprimands him for potentially soiling her clean rug and reminds him that it would solve nothing; he should take care of the real problem. Andy sees the light and shoots her. Fortunately for him, he only hits her in the arm, and she is back at the pageant in no time sporting an impeccable sling.

Big Bob's euphoric state is threatened by the behavior of his son "Little Bob." In true capitalistic spirit, Little Bob has contracted with a number of schoolmates to provide them with Polaroid pictures of naked contestants. However, he is caught and sentenced to see a child psychiatrist. Big Bob, on the other hand, after being accused by Andy of being himself a "Young

American Miss," is forced for perhaps the first time in his life to examine his own and the pageant's values.

The film draws its humor largely from the contestants' individual and collective lack of talent. However, we never feel any animosity or hostility towards the girls. Ritchie does not exploit them; they are innocents being swept along by a society which measures a person's worth by physical appearance. In a series of vignettes, we are given samples of their talent, which include a striptease set to a dramatic reading, a combination song and saxaphone solo of "Delta Dawn," and an exhibition of the proper method of packing a suitcase.

The primary focus of interest among the contestants falls on Miss Antelope Valley (Joan Prather) and Miss Anaheim (Annette O'Toole). The former is an intelligent, mature, but innocent young woman with a real talent for playing the flute. The latter is a beauty contest veteran who knows all the tricks. In one revealing scene, the two are discussing the pageant. Miss Antelope Valley suggests that perhaps beauty pageants are a little demeaning. Miss Anaheim replies, "Boys get money for making touchdowns, why shouldn't girls get money for being cute?" The first girl considers this and then replies, "Yeah, but maybe boys shouldn't get money for playing football." Eventually, tasting the possibility of victory, Miss Antelope Valley develops the competitive spirit.

When the pageant climaxes, the girl who demonstrated the proper procedure for packing and displays a well-developed body proves to be the most talented. She is declared the winner, showing the shallowness of the pageant's lofty ideals and verbiage.

Unfortunately, *Smile* never achieved the success or recognition it deserved. Nevertheless, to anyone who has seen the film, the pageantry of real beauty contests will forever elicit a knowing laugh.

James J. Desmarais

SNOW WHITE AND THE SEVEN DWARFS

Released: 1937
Production: Walt Disney (AA Special Award)
Supervising director: David Hand
Screenplay: Ted Sears, Otto Englander, Earl Hurd, Dorothy Ann Blank, Richard Creedon, Dick Richard, Merrill de Moris, and Webb Smith; based on the fairy tale *Snow White* from *Grimm's Fairy Tales*
Character designers: Albert Hurter and Joe Grant
Music: Frank Churchill, Leigh Harline, Paul Smith, and Larry Morey
Running time: 83 minutes

Voices of principal characters:

Snow White	Adriana Caselotti
Prince Charming	Harry Stockwell
The Queen	Lucille LaVerne
Magic Mirror	Moroni Olsen
Sneezy	Billy Gilbert
Sleepy and Grumpy	Pinto Colvig
Happy	Otis Harlan
Bashful	Scotty Mattraw
Doc	Roy Atwell

Snow White and the Seven Dwarfs made film history in 1937 by establishing a new genre: the feature-length cartoon. Cartoons had previously screened only as one- or two-reel fillers lasting eight to ten minutes. But the introduction in the early 1930's of the double feature lessened the demand for the comedy shorts of the type Walt Disney had been producing since 1927. Out of economic necessity and the desire to expand upon his talents, Disney sought to create a competitive, full-length film of animated drawings. The seven-reel fruition of three years' labor was a great success and silenced all those who had hastily dubbed the endeavor "Disney's folly."

Seven hundred and fifty artists perfected 250,000 drawings out of an estimated one million to bring to life the Grimm Brothers' folk tale of the orphaned princess, Snow White. Those preferring to draw pretty girls were set to work characterizing the tale's heroine, with her rose-red lips, ebony hair, and skin as white as snow. The princess was imbued with the qualities of a dream girl, as idealized by Disney's staff of young men. She became sweet, a little shy, vivacious, and possessed of a distinct sense of humor. Marge Champion, then married to a studio artist, modeled Snow White for the cartoonists all of whom had previously animated only nonhuman subjects. The dwarfs, barely identified in the Grimm story, were lent individuality by assigning them names denoting personality traits—Happy, Sleepy, Grumpy, Dopey, Sneezy, Bashful, and Doc—making them readily distinguishable from one another on the screen. These dwarfs are the only cartooned and caricatured humans. The other characters simulate adult appearance and behavior.

Remaining otherwise faithful to the original, Disney's adaptation deemphasized suffering and cruelty. Early in the Grimm's *Snow White*, for example, the princess' mother dies at her infant's birth; the film version first comes upon the grown girl, dressed in rags, dreaming of the day a prince will come to release her from her life of toil at the hands of her mean and hateful stepmother, the queen.

Vain as well as cruel, the wretched woman has cast Snow White into the scullery as a drudge to conceal the girl's blossoming beauty. The queen wishes to remain the fairest in the land, and she consults her magic mirror daily for assurance. As the mirror never lies, it is soon compelled to admit to the queen that Snow White is the fairest. Enraged, the queen dispatches her huntsman to kill the threat to her reigning beauty. But once in the forest, his knife poised, the huntsman is moved by the innocent tenderness of his victim. Instead of killing her, he bids her to flee deeper into the woods to escape from her murderous stepmother. The dark of night and Snow White's fear-filled imagination render the trees of the forest into looming monsters which snag at her clothes and the creatures into huge-eyed specters about to devour her. This montage sequence is made unforgettably real by the multiplane camera, a Disney innovation which achieves the illusion of depth. The craggy trees and monstrous shapes pass both in front of and behind Snow White as she penetrates and then emerges from the thickets, running for her life.

At daybreak, with the help of the forest's four-footed inhabitants, she comes upon a tiny dwelling. The thatch-roofed Tudor cottage appears to her to be the home of children because of its size and messiness. But before collapsing in exhaustion upstairs, she puts her years of experience as a maid to use in tidying the cottage, assisted by the animals. Returning home from their day's labor in a diamond mine, its seven residents discover a new sense of domesticity in their orderly home and adopted housekeeper. All is well.

Meanwhile, the tactless mirror again reveals to the queen the true beauty in the realm. Realizing that Snow White is still alive, the jealous woman consumes a boiling potion which will conceal her identity long enough to administer a final poison to her bothersome stepdaughter. Disguised as a stooped and warty old woman, the queen finds her way to Snow White's new home through a mysterious underground waterway. Knowing what will happen, the ever-helpful animals race to the mine to warn the dwarfs, but they arrive too late. Snow White has bitten into the apple offered her by the fruit-peddling hag. The dwarfs pursue the evil woman up a mountaintop, where she is struck by lightning and falls over a precipice to her death.

Unable to part with the beautiful Snow White, the dwarfs build her a coffin of glass. As they stand around it grieving, a prince who had fancied the ragged maiden from a distance back at the castle scullery is relieved at finally finding her. His kiss upon her cold red lips rouses her from her deathlike slumber, a poison-induced state which only love's first kiss can alter. The forest rings with excitement for the happy Snow White whose prince has indeed come.

The song with which she had earlier wished for him, and which in the end celebrates his arrival, is one of eight tunes finally selected as suitable for the film. "Some Day My Prince Will Come," "Heigh Ho," and "Whistle While You Work" have become melodies known to everyone. Out of twenty-five songs originally composed, these eight set the rhythm for the film, which was entirely planned to a musical beat. Evident in some scenes more than others, all movements and dialogue are enacted in cadence.

Such artistic care and attention to detail is indicative of the high production quality of the film, which increased in cost from the budgeted $150,000 to 1.5 million dollars, an outrageous sum during the Depression. Though Disney was plunged deeply into debt to finish *Snow White and the Seven Dwarfs*, he recouped his fortune well before the first year's showing was over. Clearly a financial success, the film also won a Special Oscar in 1938, represented not by only the one familiar golden statuette but also by seven miniatures lined up alongside. On behalf of the children of the world, it was presented to Disney by Shirley Temple.

Nancy S. Kinney

SOME LIKE IT HOT

Released: 1959
Production: Billy Wilder for the Mirisch Company; released by United Artists
Direction: Billy Wilder
Screenplay: Billy Wilder and I.A.L. Diamond; suggested by a story by R. Thoeren and M. Logan
Cinematography: Charles Lang
Editing: Arthur Schmidt
Costume design: Orry-Kelly (AA)
Running time: 120 minutes

Principal characters:

Sugar	Marilyn Monroe
Joe/Josephine	Tony Curtis
Jerry/Daphne	Jack Lemmon
Spats Colombo	George Raft
Mulligan	Pat O'Brien
Osgood Fielding III	Joe E. Brown

Billy Wilder's *Some Like It Hot* is an outrageous, satirical spoof of the 1920's in which Wilder deftly spends two hours milking one joke, that of two musicians on the run from Chicago mobsters, who disguise themselves as women and join an all-girl band. With its broad humor and its period costumes, *Some Like It Hot* is reminiscent of the Marx Brothers, early Woody Allen films, and Mack Sennett comedies. It is a madcap lampoon of the 1920's, encompassing speakeasies, gangsters, gambling, bootlegging, and even murder by machine gun.

Musicians Joe (Tony Curtis) and Jerry (Jack Lemmon) accidentally witness the St. Valentine's Day massacre. With an angered Spats Colombo (George Raft) and his boys on their trails, they have to flee. First, however, they need disguises, and the presence of an all-girl band is the answer to their problems—but only after they shave their legs and become members. In a clever, breezy transition, the boys discuss the possibility of shaved legs in one scene; the next scene begins with a close-up of their legs wobbling on high heels.

Disguised as Josephine (Joe) and Daphne (Jerry), the two share a train car with other members of the band, including the luscious (and a bit of a "lush") Sugar (Marilyn Monroe). Both experience uneasy moments during the train ride, Joe's (Josephine's) taking place when the train makes an unexpected stop, throwing the lovely Sugar into his arms. Jerry's (Daphne's) dilemma occurs when Sugar climbs into his berth to thank him for saving her job; when she was going to get the ax because of her drinking, Daphne stepped in to take the blame. Lonely Sugar in a seductive black nightgown proves too much for Jerry to handle, and he asks Sugar to join him in a drink, at which time a surprise—his real identity—will be revealed. In no time at all, Sugar has passed the word about the drinking party, which Jerry had wanted to be private. Thus, Jerry winds up with an eight-girl slumber party in his berth.

Some Like It Hot is highlighted by a delicious tangle of identities. Once the all-girl group arrives in Florida, for example, Jerry is coaxed by Joe into encouraging the advances of the wolfish Osgood Fielding III (Joe E. Brown), who has admired Daphne's legs, in order that Joe can assume another identity. Josephine, who, like Daphne, has become one of Sugar's best "girl friends," has talked with her about the kind of man she is looking for. Joe is determined to be it. With Jerry as Daphne flirting with Osgood, Joe can assume the identity of "Junior" (of "Vanity Fair and Shell Oil fame"). In order to appear with the accouterments to be "Junior," Joe requires the use of the preoccupied Osgood's yacht.

As Junior, Joe dons glasses, a Cary Grant accent, and yachting jacket and cap. After luring Sugar to his yacht, he tries to evoke the indifference of the upper class. He keeps a copy of the *Wall Street Journal* at hand, discusses the art of water polo (on horses), and, in pointing out the difference between the fore and aft of a ship, explains that it depends "whether you're coming or going." Junior, who maintains he gets no thrill at all from women, utilizes psychiatric jargon so that Sugar will ask for the privilege of seducing him. Although he gets no "thrill" from women, however, his glasses begin steaming when Sugar tries to help him overcome his "problem."

While Joe carries on his Junior identity, Jerry as Daphne is also undergoing an identity crises. The absurdity of the tangled identities comes into focus when Daphne, after a night of dancing the tango with Osgood, decides to marry him. "It's my only chance to marry a millionaire," insists Jerry, explaining that "security" is what he is seeking; and improbably, he winds up becoming engaged to Fielding.

The romances, however, are all cut short when the mob makes its appearance at the hotel. Both Joe and Jerry think their numbers are up, but in typical Wilder fashion, the gangsters themselves come to an untimely and comical end with Spats being machine-gunned through the vehicle of a six-foot-tall birthday cake out of which pops the assassin. The remainder of the mob then kill one another off.

Joe is now ready to reveal the truth about "Junior" to the unsuspecting Sugar, who loves both his personalities, Josephine as well as Junior. Jerry, in the meantime, sadly realizes that he must break the news of his identity to Osgood, who is looking forward to marriage. In the film's classic closing scene, Jerry, who now wants to discourage Osgood's affection, rips off his wig, revealing his true identity. Unruffled by it all and with his love apparently still intact, Osgood merely replies, "Well, nobody's perfect."

Visually and verbally, *Some Like It Hot* is a frantic, nonstop barrage of one-liners and comic invention. Tony Curtis as Joe/Josephine/"Junior" and Jack Lemmon as Jerry/Daphne deliver their lines with expert timing; and Lemmon garnered an Oscar nomination for his work. Marilyn Monroe is the wistful Sugar, the ukelele-strumming singer who joins the all-girl group because when she works for male groups, she always falls for the saxophone player. This was Monroe's second film with Wilder (the first was *The Seven Year Itch*, filmed in 1955), and although he managed to elicit a fine comic performance from her, as well as several highly entertaining musical numbers (including "Running Wild," and "I Wanna Be Loved by You"), the battles the two had on the set have become part of Hollywood lore. One sequence in *Some Like It Hot* that involved Monroe required a legendary fifty-nine takes.

In its final form, *Some Like It Hot* was a box-office bonanza, grossing more than twenty million dollars. With its fast and furious premise, as well as its constant humor, *Some Like It Hot* was the funniest film of 1959. Its humor runs the gamut from broad slapstick to sly sexual innuendo. With Lemmon and Curtis delightfully appearing in women's clothes, the film suggests transvestite jokes but never plays on them seriously. Curtis, a frequently underrated actor, delivers an especially good Cary Grant take-off; and the supporting players, including Joe E. Brown as Osgood, are slickly in control all around.

Some Like It Hot was Wilder's fifteenth film, following dramatic successes such as *Double Indemnity* (1944) and *Sunset Boulevard* (1950), as well as comedies such as *Stalag 17* (1953) and the more fanciful *Sabrina* (1954). It ranks as Wilder's funniest film, and paired him for the first time with Lemmon; the two would go on to collaborate in films such as *The Apartment* (1960), *The Fortune Cookie* (1966), *Avanti* (1972), and *The Front Page* (1974).

With the exception of Lemmon's Best Actor nomination, *Some Like It Hot* did not get any major award nominations, although Orry-Kelly's costumes did take an award. The film nevertheless remains a classic comedy whose genuinely affectionate nostalgia merges with an irreverent story line that tampers with social taboos and sensibilities. With their portrayals of Joe/Josephine and Jerry/Daphne, Tony Curtis and Jack Lemmon made their marks as a great and decidedly unsung cinema team.

Pat H. Broeske

THE SONG OF BERNADETTE

Released: 1943
Production: William Perlberg for Twentieth Century-Fox
Direction: Henry King
Screenplay: George Seaton; based on the novel of the same name by Franz Werfel
Cinematography: Arthur Miller (AA)
Editing: Barbara McLean
Art direction: James Basevi and William Darling (AA)
Interior decoration: Thomas Little (AA)
Costume design: Réne Hubert
Music: Alfred Newman (AA)
Running time: 158 minutes

Principal characters:

Bernadette Soubirous	Jennifer Jones (AA)
Antoine Nicolau	William Eythe
Peyramale, Dean of Lourdes	Charles Bickford
Dutour, the Imperial Prosecutor	Vincent Price
Dr. Dozous	Lee J. Cobb
Sister Marie Theresa Vauzous	Gladys Cooper
Louise Soubirous	Anne Revere
Francois Soubirous	Roman Bohnen

Bernadette Soubirous was a young French maiden who lived in the provincial village of Lourdes in the nineteenth century, and who, as a result of a religious vision, became a saint. *The Song of Bernadette* recounts her story, concentrating explicitly upon the effect of her vision on her life and the lives of the people who were involved with her. Although the vision is presented, it is rendered visually as Bernadette's subjective experience: the audience sees the beautiful lady whom Bernadette describes only through her eyes, and even in these scenes, the emphasis is on the bliss reflected in Bernadette's gaze. The purpose of the film is not to convince the audience that what Bernadette sees is the result of a divine gift; it seeks rather to describe a spiritual process which ultimately creates meaning for her existence. Her life was marked by the scorn and hostility of her tormentors and by the denial of earthly pleasures. She suffered without complaint the physical anguish of an incurable affliction and the emotional isolation which became inevitable when she was no longer perceived as an ordinary young woman. Her life, however, is never portrayed as a tragic one, and without requiring the literal religious faith of its audience, the film lucidly and methodically affirms that Bernadette achieved a state of grace which was to be envied.

The opening sequences of the film, in which Bernadette (Jennifer Jones) herself is a marginal figure, beautifully illuminates the significance of the film as a whole, providing the key to Bernadette's struggle to reconcile material existence and the transcendent way of life. Bernadette's father Francois (Roman Bohnen) awakens early in the morning to look for work. As the children sleep, he and his wife Louise (Anne Revere) exchange a few words to enable the audience to learn that he had been a miller and has fallen on hard times. Desperate, he takes a job burning the infected linen from the hospital, and we follow him as he goes to the edge of a precipice with his cart and dumps the linen. This prelude to Bernadette's story is presented at some length, with director King daringly establishing the slow pace at which the story will unfold, lingering first on the scene in the Soubirous home, and then on the father's search for work and performance of his task. The story does not seemingly call for this kind of treatment, nor for the impassioned music with which Alfred Newman scores the conclusion of the sequence. Thus, with a minimum of dialogue and a series of forceful images enhanced by music, the film creates a world, but allows the meaning of this world to remain mysterious. It seems initially that the only way to interpret the treatment given to this sequence is to anticipate that the father will become infected and die as a result of his labors. This, however, does not occur; instead, Bernadette beholds her vision for the first time later that same day.

Although Bernadette herself does not identify the lady whom she sees as the Virgin Mary, it is evident to everyone in the village from her description that it is indeed the Blessed Virgin who has appeared to her. Has the miserable task performed earlier by the father reverberated into eternity, prompting this gesture of solace to the daughter? Bernadette herself is presented as unhappy and lonely, unable to grasp the simple teachings which the other girls learn easily. In one scene, Sister Vauzous (Gladys Cooper), her teacher, denies her the reward of a holy picture which she glimpses only briefly, but which perhaps creates in her the need for a relationship with the understanding mother of Christ. Without explicitly proclaiming that there are complex and interrelated reasons why Bernadette is chosen by God, the film persuades us that she is deserving, and that through her, others may find a liberation of the spirit, if they choose.

Bernadette's characterization is always the center of the film, and the other characters are defined, sometimes surprisingly but always effectively, in relation to her. The father, initially bitter over his fall from fortune, is irritable and treats his family without warmth. However, he is one of the first to stand beside his daughter, and he unfailingly defends her in the face of adversity. As the story progresses, he is revealed to be a warm and sensitive man who cares deeply for those he loves. Similarly, Bernadette's mother is loving and compassionate beneath her reserved exterior. The spiritual path taken by Bernadette seems to bring a serenity to her parents, altering their own attitudes toward their lives. Antoine (William Eythe), the young man who is drawn to Bernadette, is so touched by her that when she finally makes the decision to become a nun and live in a convent, he renounces his own desire ever to marry. Most importantly, Bernadette profoundly influences the lives of four people, who are cleverly paired and opposed according to their secular and ecclesiastical vocations.

On the secular side, there is Dr. Dozous (Lee J. Cobb), who, although a man of medicine, finds no psychological disturbance in Bernadette which would contradict the truth of her vision and who becomes her ally in the face of political pressure. His counterpart is Dutour (Vincent Price), the Imperial Prosecutor, a man convinced of his superiority to the superstitions and ignorance of the people; for him, the destruction of Bernadette is a personal obsession. As multitudes of people are cured at the spring which flows from the site of the visitation, Dutous remains steadfast in his resistance to divine mysteries which he cannot comprehend, and in doing so, this arrogant man becomes pathetic. On the religious side, Sister Vauzous is contrasted to the Dean of Lourdes (Charles Bickford). The Dean becomes Bernadette's truest friend, somewhat surprisingly, as he appears to be an aloof and practical man, at first taking the attitude that the Church should not acknowledge Bernadette at all. Through a series of meetings in which his response to her is at first ambiguous, he unexpectedly becomes her adviser and then her most ardent defender. More than anyone else, he is moved by her, perhaps because she arouses in him a compassion which his position as a spiritual leader paradoxically does not require.

Equally fascinating is the portrayal of Sister Vauzous, a severe and tormented woman who has gained no measure of tranquility from the religious life. Almost to the end, she believes that Bernadette is a fraud, convinced that the girl could not have been chosen because she has never suffered and is therefore undeserving. Her hatred of the young woman is the result of selfish resentment which she finally cannot resist expressing, and as a result, Bernadette reveals the tumor which is the symptom of a bone cancer which is killing her. Her enemy is then chastened by Bernadette's goodness of heart and strength of will in having never cried out against her misfortune.

The film portrays Dutour and Sister Vauzous, Bernadette's antagonists, as people who deserve the audience's sympathetic understanding as much as Dozous and the Dean of Lourdes, who have revealed their nobility. In a sense, the two antagonists who have lived their lives without being blessed by their relationship to the girl are the most compelling figures in the film because they are seen to be most in need of an elusive faith. Both of these characters ultimately acknowledge this and are perhaps redeemed. We may therefore perceive that the film, though centrally about Bernadette, describes a spiritual need which exists in everyone. Although hers is the direct path to heaven and the most difficult to tread, there is for each man and woman a search for enlightenment, for a sign that some eternal truth exists which gives meaning to the burdens of life.

Although it has been suggested that expensively produced films such as this one are devoid of true artistry and spirituality, *The Song of Bernadette* is never guilty of superficiality. Its visual tone has more in common with the work of Carl Dreyer and Robert Bresson than with most Hollywood films concentrating on religious subjects, always excepting other films by Henry King. A visual concept is in evidence throughout the film, attesting to a unity in the work of the art directors and interior decorators, the costume designer, and the cinematographer. Black-and-white lighting, of which Arthur Miller was a major master, is at its most expressive in the film. Miller's work is that of a painter on film, and his ideas are always in harmony with those present in the sets, decor, and costumes. When one looks at any scene in the film, exterior or interior, there is always a plasticity of visual expression since the characters exist in relation to the varying black-and-white images which define them at once both artificially and realistically. The beauty of the film's visual tone is matched by that of its sound track, in which the most dramatic element is not the voices of the actors but the outstanding music of composer Alfred Newman.

On the whole, the actors provide very thoughtful and modulated performances. Charles Bickford is especially notable for expressing the depth and sensitivity of the Dean without the benefit of even one obviously dramatic personal scene. Jennifer Jones always possesses an intensity whose many facets allow her to be a different woman from film to film, invariably adapting to the director's concept of her character. Thus, she is well-cast in any role, from Bernadette in her first film to Pearl Chavez in *Duel in the Sun* (1946), directed by King Vidor.

The Song of Bernadette owes its artistry most of all to Henry King. The handsomeness of the production and the moving interpretations of the actors reflect directly on the individual contributors, but because King's patience with visual detail and performances are characteristic of his work, he also directly shares credit for the film's strong qualities. More crucially, it is his interpretation and deep conviction which make the film one of the most profound expressions in cinema of an explicitly spiritual theme. With unfailing seriousness and a moving sincerity, King instills, through his patience with visual details and performances, a belief in the truth of the story. He fills intimate scenes with silences and hesitations, places the actors in such a way that the space between and around them becomes beautifully expressive, and never allows a scene to end before it is fully realized. He, as other classical directors, has the ability to save the use of close-ups for those moments in which they will be most expressive, and his camera's eye never becomes empty because he never loses touch with the emotional heart of his subject. *The Song of Bernadette* has in common with many other of his films a certain ponderousness; far from being a negative quality, however, this very slow pacing is effective, manifesting a density of feeling and an absence of superficiality in his films.

Once highly regarded, King has become unfashionable, and the popularity and critical appreciation enjoyed by many older films is denied to his many outstanding works. His preference for religious subjects such as *The White Sister* (1933), *David and Bathsheba* (1952), and *Captain from Castile* (1947), and for old-fashioned Americana as represented by *State Fair* (1945), *Margie* (1946), and *Wait Till the Sun Shines Nellie* (1952), have made him a remote figure in cinema. Similarly, *The Song of Bernadette*, acclaimed as a great film at the time of its release, is now rarely revived or spoken of favorably. Just as King is a neglected master whose work as a whole deserves reconsideration, this film is an unusual and rewarding one which is undeserving of its present lack of reputation. It demonstrates King's gift for expressing spiritual rapture with a beautiful simplicity.

Blake Lucas

THE SOUND OF MUSIC

Released: 1965
Production: Robert Wise for Twentieth Century-Fox (AA)
Direction: Robert Wise (AA)
Screenplay: Ernest Lehman; based on the musical play by Richard Rodgers and Oscar Hammerstein II, adapted from the novel of the same name by Howard Lindsay and Russell Crouse
Cinematography: Ted McCord
Editing: William Reynolds (AA)
Sound: James P. Corcoran for Twentieth Century-Fox Studio Sound Department and Fred Hynes for Todd-AO Sound Department (AA)
Music: Irwin Kostal (AA)
Song: Richard Rodgers and Oscar Hammerstein II
Running time: 174 minutes

Principal characters:

Maria	Julie Andrews
Baron Von Trapp	Christopher Plummer
The Baroness	Eleanor Parker
Mother Abbess	Peggy Wood
Max Detweiler	Richard Haydn
Liesl	Charmain Carr
Sister Margaretta	Anna Lee
Sister Sophia	Marni Nixon

The film musical had gone through many changes and problems by 1960 and had become generally unsuccessful at the box office because it lacked sufficient realism or sophistication for the new audiences of the 1950's and 1960's. The "black and white message films" of this period expressed certain realistic social ideals while the musical depicted a dream world. As a result of this change, and the increasing cost of producing musicals, only presold vehicles, such as Broadway shows, were considered by the studios.

The Sound of Music, which had been very successful on Broadway, certainly did not portray realistic ideals; it was in the style of the traditional musical—pure entertainment and fun. It proved a successful cinematic achievement, however, garnering five Academy Awards, including one for Best Picture of 1965. The producer, Twentieth Century-Fox, had gambled in filming this "unsophisticated" motion picture for a 1960's audience, but nevertheless succeeded in producing a box-office smash. *The Sound of Music* became the highest grossing film of all time, topping the longtime leader, *Gone with the Wind* (1939), and continued to be number one until the early 1970's. It remained the most successful musical film until 1978 when it was surpassed by *Grease*.

This musical film about the famous singing Von Trapp family who fled

Austria from the Nazis was not as warmly received by the critics. Some found it too sentimental, silly, and unrealistic. However, it remained popular at the box office for exactly these reasons. The film entertained audiences and allowed them to forget their concerns over the Vietnam War and other issues occurring during the "Radical Sixties." The critics were perhaps most disappointed in the film because it did not depict the harsher effects of the Nazi takeover of Austria. The annexation to Germany was treated almost as any other daily event in the lives of the Von Trapp family, although it was to change their lives forever.

Julie Andrews portrays Maria, the governess who becomes Baroness Von Trapp and stepmother to the Von Trapp children. She is sent to their home by the convent in which she lives as an unsuccessful postulant, in hopes that the vocation of governess will better suit the adventurous girl. She is confronted by the militaristic home of the Baron Von Trapp (Christopher Plummer) and his mischievous children, who are noted for playing tricks on their governess behind their father's back. She soon wins the children to her side but continues to have problems with the Baron through her refusal to obey his strict orders. She also falls in love with him. When he announces his engagement to a wealthy Austrian Baroness (Eleanor Parker), Maria runs back to the convent; but she is persuaded by the Mother Superior (Peggy Wood) to return to the Von Trapp home. The Baron soon realizes that he loves Maria. He leaves his fiancée, and after a brief courtship he and Maria are married.

When Austria is annexed by Germany, the Baron refuses to serve under the Nazis as a military specialist. The family attempts to flee the country one night but is detained. The Baron and Baroness easily convince the Nazis that they are actually on their way to a musical festival in which they are to perform, thus explaining their traveling clothes. The Von Trapps perform at the festival and flee at the completion of the program to the convent. They soon take the convent car and are last seen climbing the beautiful mountains of Austria to freedom in Switzerland.

The tunes of Richard Rodgers and Oscar Hammerstein are the film's most appealing feature and the primary reason for its success. They delighted audiences then and are still popular. The title song, "Do, Re, Mi," "My Favorite Things," and "You Are Sixteen, Going on Seventeen" are only a few of the hit songs from this musical. The tunes were already so well known from the Broadway success that their performance and presentation provided a challenge in the film. The choice of Julie Andrews in the starring role of Maria was a wise one because of the combination of her magnificent soprano voice and outstanding acting ability. The selection of Christopher Plummer as Baron Von Trapp was also appropriate. Plummer does not have a great singing voice like his costar, but his sophistication and air of arrogance is sufficient to carry off the part of the noble Baron. Ted McCord's cinematography, particularly that of the Austrian Alps, is as much a star of the film as was Andrews or Plummer. Under the direction of Robert Wise, the beautiful mountains of Austria are majestically portrayed and hold audiences in awe, including the critics. In the opening scene of the picture, for example, the camera scans the Alps and Andrews suddenly appears singing "the hills are alive with the sound of music," a film device which truly enhances the title tune.

Robert Wise had won the Best Director and Best Picture Academy Awards for an earlier picture that he produced and co-directed with Jerome Robbins: *West Side Story* (1961). *The Sound of Music* earned him additional Oscars and established him as an excellent musical director and producer in the tradition of the great film musical pioneers: Vincente Minnelli, Arthur Freed, and Busby Berkeley. His direction throughout the musical scenes is excellent, in spite of the lack of dramatic appeal on the part of the actors. *The Sound of Music* did, however, bring the face of Marni Nixon to the screen for the first time in a minor role as Sister Sophia. She had previously only "voiced-over" the songs of other famous actresses who had poor voices, such as Natalie Wood in *West Side Story* and Audrey Hepburn in *My Fair Lady* (1964).

The uncertainty surrounding the future of the motion picture musical added to the interest of *The Sound of Music*. The personal magnetism of its star, 1964 Academy Award-winner Julie Andrews (for *Mary Poppins*), undoubtedly had much to do with its success, as did the tunes of Rodgers and Hammerstein. Some critics may continue to argue that this picture has no cinematic value, that the dramatic performances are poor, and that the story line could not hold up without the musical score and cinematography. But in spite of these debatable flaws, *The Sound of Music* provides entertainment, and it will continue to enliven audiences both old and new for years to come.

Carl J. Mir

SOUTH PACIFIC

Released: 1958
Production: Buddy Adler for Magna Theatre Corporation; released by Twentieth Century-Fox
Direction: Joshua Logan
Screenplay: Paul Osborn; based on the musical play of the same name by Richard Rodgers, Oscar Hammerstein II, and Joshua Logan, adapted from *Tales of the South Pacific* by James A. Michener
Cinematography: Leon Shamroy
Editing: Robert Simpson
Sound: Fred Hynes and Todd-AO Sound Department (AA)
Song: Richard Rodgers and Oscar Hammerstein II
Running time: 165 minutes

Principal characters:

Emile de Becque	Rossano Brazzi
Nellie Forbush	Mitzi Gaynor
Lieutenant Joe Cable	John Kerr
Bloody Mary	Juanita Hall
Luther Billis	Ray Walston
Liat	France Nuyen
Captain George Brackett	Russ Brown
Bill Harbison	Floyd Simmons
Ngana	Candace Lee
Jerome	Warren Hsieh

South Pacific is the fourth of Rodgers and Hammerstein's five spectacular Broadway successes (after *Oklahoma!*, *Carousel*, and *The King and I*, and preceding *The Sound of Music*) to be made into a film which then became a classic in its own right. Like the Pulitzer Prize-winning play, the film combines romance, drama, and comedy, set to one of Rodgers' and Hammerstein's loveliest and most versatile scores.

The story takes place, as the title indicates, on an island in the South Pacific; the time is World War II and the United States Navy is battling the Japanese and losing badly. Against this background the film's two love stories unfold: one between young Navy nurse Nellie Forbush (Mitzi Gaynor) and wealthy French planter Emile de Becque (Rossano Brazzi), and the other between Marine Lieutenant Joe Cable (John Kerr) and a native Tonkinese beauty named Liat (France Nuyen).

The drama of the romances is lightened by the comic relief provided by the American sailors, which—after a brief opening scene of Cable's flight to the island—gets under way with the men's humorous serenade, "Bloody Mary Is the Girl I Love." Mary (Juanita Hall) is an earthy Tonkinese souvenir-seller who shrewdly gets the better of her chief business rival, blustery Luther

Billis (Ray Walston), by selling him a boar's tooth bracelet for an exorbitant fee. The bracelet is from the mysterious island of Bali Hai, where one can find valuable souvenirs and the most precious commodity of all—women. Unfortunately, though, only officers can requisition boats to go there. In one of the film's most memorable highlights, "There Is Nothing Like a Dame," the frustrated sailors lament the absence of women in their lives.

Having landed, Cable joins the men and Mary on the beach. Mary is immediately taken with his good looks; she tells him that Bali Hai ("Your special island") is beckoning him, and sings the hauntingly beautiful "Bali Hai." Cable is spellbound, but rejects Billis' eager offer to requisition a boat in order to report to Captain George Brackett (Russ Brown), the island commander, and his assistant, Bill Harbison (Floyd Simmons). He tells the men of his top-secret assignment: to set up a coast watch on nearby enemy-held Marie Louise Island to acquire firsthand intelligence on Japanese warship movements, which could then be radioed to Brackett. It is a dangerous mission, but with the help of Emile de Becque—a former Marie Louise Island resident who knows the island and whom Cable has been instructed to contact—he feels it can be successful.

Meanwhile, Becque and Nellie Forbush are at Becque's plantation home. They had met two weeks earlier at an Officers' Club dinner, and have fallen in love, but they are from vastly dissimilar backgrounds. Nellie herself admits that she is a naïve hick from Little Rock, Arkansas, far younger and less worldly than the cultured Becque. Each expresses doubts about the relationship in song. Becque declares his love for Nellie in the moving ballad, "Some Enchanted Evening," then confesses that he came here from France because he had killed a man. Nellie accepts his explanation that the man was a wicked bully and agrees to think about his marriage proposal.

Later, Brackett asks Nellie what she knows about Becque and requests that she try to learn more. Realizing that she really does know little about him, she decides to break off the romance in the lively "I'm Gonna Wash That Man Right Outa My Hair." However, she changes her mind when Becque invites her to a party in her honor and proposes again, and she expresses her feelings by singing "I'm in Love with a Wonderful Guy"—a buoyant song and dance which her friends also perform.

Brackett asks Becque to go along on Cable's mission but he refuses, not wanting to jeopardize his future with Nellie. Meanwhile, Cable, who has some free time before he leaves on his mission, decides to go to Bali Hai. There, Mary takes him to her hut, where he meets her daughter, an exquisite young Tonkinese girl, Liat (France Nuyen). It is love at first sight for both, and after consummating their love, Cable expresses his feelings to her in the tender ballad, "Younger Than Springtime."

After Becque's party, Becque and Nellie draw closer together, for, as she says, despite their different backgrounds they are alike "fundamentally."

Becque introduces her to two native children, Ngana (Candace Lee) and Jerome (Warren Hsieh). Though enchanted by them, Nellie is shocked when he tells her that he is their father and that their dead mother was a Polynesian. Stunned, she flees, later requesting a transfer to another island, but Brackett convinces her to remain for the Thanksgiving Day variety show she has been preparing for the sailors.

Meanwhile, Cable and Liat have been having a passionate affair, much to Mary's great delight. She tells Cable that a French planter wants to marry Liat, and, in "Happy Talk," she sings of the carefree life he and Liat could have together. Deeply disturbed, Cable tells Mary that he cannot marry her daughter. Furious, Mary says that Liat will now marry the planter, and drags her away.

The two love stories intersect after the Thanksgiving show when the disconsolate Nellie and Cable reflect together on their similar romantic problems, and the contrast between America and the Pacific, in "My Girl Back Home." Becque joins them, and Nellie tearfully tells him she cannot marry him because of his Polynesian first wife. She cannot give him a good reason; her feeling, she says, is purely emotional, "something that is born in me." Becque angrily protests, but she runs off. "It's *not* born in you!" Cable exclaims, "It happens after you're born!" He sings of the intolerance of prejudice in the stinging "You've Got to be Taught." Finally realizing that all he cares about is Liat, Cable resolves to remain with her if he survives the war.

Becque sings of his lost chance for happiness in the aching "This Nearly Was Mine." Seizing the opportunity, Cable asks him to reconsider participating in the mission, and this time Becque consents. Successfully landing on Marie Louise Island, the men transmit reports to Brackett. Nellie learns that Becque is behind enemy lines, and soon thereafter, hears his sad report that Cable has been killed. Grief-stricken, Nellie realizes how foolish she has been about Becque's first wife, and realizes that all that matters is their being together. "Live, Emile," she pleads over and over. When Mary suddenly appears with Liat, saying that Liat will marry no one but Cable, Nellie, having information about Cable's death, clutches the girl to her.

Thanks to the efforts of Cable and Becque, the tide of the war turns. Landings are made on Japanese-held islands and the Americans begin to move out, although Becque's fate at this point is unknown. On Becque's terrace, Nellie, Ngana, and Jerome eat dinner. Unseen by them, Becque approaches, then joins them at the table. He and Nellie clasp hands, and as they gaze enraptured at each other, the film ends.

The names of Rodgers and Hammerstein have long been associated with musicals of superior quality—rich in emotion, imaginatively conceived, and skillfully written and performed—and *South Pacific* more than lives up to this tradition. The film's strongest asset is, of course, its wonderful score. All of the songs from the play have been retained, with one addition, "My Girl Back Home." The score once again demonstrates Rodgers' and Hammerstein's genius for creating songs that not only capture, but also enhance, the emotions of the story. This is accomplished through fresh, literate lyrics and melodic music that corresponds appropriately to the particular mood. Since *South Pacific* is a film of many moods—love, despair, hope, exhilaration, anger—the team's skill and versatility are never more in evidence.

The reprising of several songs at crucial points of the story is most effective. For example, Becque repeats "Some Enchanted Evening" when proposing again to Nellie, and when Mary drags Liat out of Cable's life, he sings "Younger Than Springtime," but in the past tense. Indeed, so much is told through song that *South Pacific* at times verges on the operatic.

Less successful is cinematographer Leon Shamroy's technique of putting colored filters over the camera lens during some songs—bathing people and setting in purples, greens, and yellows—to differentiate between reality and the romance of the songs. This works well for "Bali Hai," for the island is supposed to be mystical and otherworldly, but is too disconcerting and theatrical for the other numbers. The songs are strong enough on their own to create a romantic mood without depending on artificial devices. Use of the filters detracts particularly from "Some Enchanted Evening," whose natural plantation setting is lush and lovely just as it is.

The acting is uniformly excellent. Mitzi Gaynor is appealingly fresh and wholesome as the unsophisticated Nellie, and Rossano Brazzi's deeply felt Becque is strong but sensitive. There is less chemistry between them, though, than one might have hoped. On the other hand, John Kerr, perfect as the virile, attractive Cable, and France Nuyen, whose role as Liat calls primarily for eloquent facial expressions rather than dialogue, are electric together. The liveliest performances come from Ray Walston as the conniving Billis and Juanita Hall, re-creating her Broadway role as Mary. Russ Brown is authoritative yet caring as Brackett, and the sailors are rowdy and comical.

Except for Gaynor's strong, lilting soprano, the singing voices of the major characters are dubbed, each carefully matched to the actors' personalities and vocal qualities. Opera star Giorgio Tozzi receives screen credit for the vocal role of Becque.

The screen version of *South Pacific* is of a greater visual scope than was possible on the stage; most of the filming was done on the lush island of Kauai, and the Bali Hai sequence features a montage of shots of Fiji and other tropical locales. Thus, the scenic beauty of the beaches, valleys, and Becque's plantation, which could only be suggested by theatrical sets, is fully captured on film.

The play has been expanded upon in other ways as well. For example, actual Navy ship maneuvers are seen, and Billis' escapade of stowing away on the plane to Marie Louise Island and then falling out in midair, only mentioned in the play, is shown here in a very funny sequence. Also included is the Boar's Head Ceremonial Dance, which is extraneous to the plot but adds to the feeling of tropical authenticity.

In addition to expanding the play, Paul Osborn's script strikes an effective balance between drama and comedy, romance and realism. Osborn knows when to inject humor in order to lighten a mood, but also when to let the full drama emerge for the greatest impact on the audience. Although much dialogue and action are taken directly from the play, certain scenes have been tightened or their order shifted for a more cohesive, compelling story line.

With so many elements involved in the making of the picture, Joshua Logan, who coauthored, staged, and directed the play, was the suitable choice for its director. Under his caring, capable control everything fits together neatly, and the film moves along fluidly and briskly—seeming far shorter than its nearly three-hour running time.

The movie received almost unanimous glowing reviews and became one of 1958's box-office smashes. Surprisingly, though, it was nominated for only three Academy Awards: musical scoring, color cinematography, and sound, winning only in the latter category.

War and racial prejudice seem unlikely subjects for an entertaining musical, but thanks to its creators' considerable talents, *South Pacific* is just that—warm, moving, and uplifting. Without preaching, it delivers its message of racial tolerance in an opulent, tuneful production filled with charm and humor.

Libby Slate

THE SOUTHERNER

Released: 1945
Production: David Loew and Robert Hakim for United Artists
Direction: Jean Renoir
Screenplay: Jean Renoir and Hugo Butler; based on the novel *Hold Autumn in Your Hand* by George Sessions Perry
Cinematography: Lucien Andriot
Editing: Gregg Tallas
Music: Werner Janssen
Running time: 91 minutes

Principal characters:

Sam Tucker	Zachary Scott
Nona Tucker	Betty Field
Granny Tucker	Beulah Bondi
Daisy Tucker	Bunny Sunshine
Jot Tucker	Jay Gilpin
Harmie	Percy Kilbride
Ma Tucker	Blanche Yurka
Tim	Charles Kemper
Devers	J. Carrol Naish
Finlay	Norman Lloyd
Bartender	Nestor Paiva
Ruston	Paul Harvey

The Southerner is Jean Renoir's film hymn to the earth, in the same manner that *The Grapes of Wrath* had been John Ford's five years earlier. It is about sharing experiences and needed goods with one's family and neighbors as well as understanding one's place in both the universal community of man and the smaller personal community of friends and family. It documents the strength that family provides and defines what is owed it in return.

Sam Tucker (Zachary Scott), a Texas field hand, learns of a vacant farm near where he and his wife, Nona (Betty Field), are picking cotton. He arranges to rent the land in return for a share of his crop and transports his family there, including Granny (Beulah Bondi), Daisy (Bunny Sunshine), and Jot (Jay Gilpin). Although the house on the land is in shambles, Nona makes it livable, and they all begin to work the fields. In this experience, they are dependent on their neighbor, Devers (J. Carrol Naish), a selfish but successful farmer, for well water. The first winter leaves the Tuckers cold and hungry, and spring brings a case of pellagra to Jot, who needs milk and fresh vegetables which the Tuckers can ill afford. Devers has been trying to catch a huge fish, nicknamed Lead Pencil because of the thickness of his whiskers, in the nearby river; when Sam succeeds, Devers bargains with him, exchanging vegetables from his garden and the use of his well rope for the credit of catching Lead Pencil.

Sam's mother, Ma Tucker (Blanche Yurka), and Harmie (Percy Kilbride), the proprietor of the local store, decide to marry. After a riotous, drunken wedding party, there is a tremendous downpour which ruins the Tuckers' cotton crop. Because of this defeat, Sam nearly gives up; however, when he finds Nona repairing the house again and Granny cheerfully hanging clothes on the line, he gains strength to continue. The next season finds Sam and Nona still poor and struggling, but confident and happy.

From the initial scene of the film, when Sam's Uncle Pete dies in the fields, admonishing him in his last words to work for himself and grow his own crops, Sam is instilled with the concept of being independent, of being able to provide for his family from his own land. Yet Renoir's script, adapted by Hugo Butler with uncredited assistance from William Faulkner, consistently emphasizes how contingent the Tuckers' existence is on other people: Sam strikes a bargain with Devers for good well water; Granny has to give up her best blanket in order to make a coat for Daisy so that she can attend school in the winter; Sam's mother comes to help out; a friend, Tim (Charles Kemper), brings a cow so that Jot can have milk; and Devers must rely on Sam's discretion about telling who really caught Lead Pencil to retain his own feeling of self-importance.

Everyone depends on nature: the earth provides, but the rain can also take away. At the end of the film while discussing the interchange between farmer and factory worker, Sam and Tim outline what each supplies the other: the farmer grows crops and meat to feed the worker, who in turn manufactures plows, guns, and clothes for the farmer. The film clearly demonstrates that there is no existence without coexistence, and that reciprocity means a better life for all. But the film is not a socialist tract; it is a simple story about nurture and labor, about the dignity of honest work and the solidarity one feels with one's fellow human beings.

The one person who does not feel this sense of kinship is Devers, whose struggle and losses have soured him and poisoned his relationships. He does not like people to appear better than they are, and he warns Sam not to be so ambitious; but even Devers softens in his attitude when the opportunity arises to feed his ego.

Renoir's direction is unaffected and straightforward. Many of the scenes are filmed in medium or long shots such as Scott and Field striding along the fields, the family gathered around the table, or Scott and Naish hauling in Lead Pencil. There are no fancy angle shots calling attention to the presence of the director behind the camera. Scenes are simple and unpretentious, such as the one in which Nona and Sam are in bed on the porch, illustrating simply a line spoken earlier about summer being an opportunity for them to have a room of their own; or that in which Ma and Harmie lie on the ground smiling contentedly as they announce their engagement. At the party for the couple, Ma counts her blessings before the celebration erupts into humorous chaos; this sequence is one of the few which admits humor into the proceedings. The men share a jug of whiskey; there is a rambunctious square dance; and Tim and Sam, scuffling over a three-dollar whiskey bottle that has been dropped, eventually fall in a drunken stupor onto a bed which collapses under them.

Through his direction, Renoir reveals his great fondness for these characters, for their goodness and honesty, as well as for their human failings. Certainly, the characters cherish warm feelings for one another within the family unit and beyond it as well. Even cantankerous old Beulah Bondi, pigheaded and whining though she may be, bestows and receives affection and kindness. The film abounds with tenderness and love—love of people for one another (with Renoir using Naish as a contrast to show how truly warped man can become when denied affection) and the love man has for the earth because of his certainty that it will yield. There is also the certainty that man can find self-esteem by working the soil.

Renoir is not always as well-served by his cast as he is by his own ability to evoke his themes. Betty Field is sweet, plain-faced, and simple as Nona, but she is not natural enough, despite her efforts to develop a regional Southern accent and to seem like a real farmer's wife. Beulah Bondi's portrayal as Granny is all caricature, from her peculiar, pinch-mouthed delivery to her down-home spitting and her obvious old-age makeup. Percy Kilbride made a career out of playing Pa Kettle types, but his Harmie is not particularly Southern and his acting seems a collection of mannerisms looking for a real person to inhabit. J. Carrol Naish, more successful as the narrow-minded Devers, provides a disciplined performance, attentive to nuances of character. Charles Kemper is excellent as the kindhearted Tim and uses his bulk to add substance to his role as the compassionate friend. Best, however, is Zachary Scott, a Texan of thin frame and narrow face whose natural drawl correctly fits the dialect of the film's Texas setting. Scott's features are not those of a leading man; he looks more like a character actor than a conventional hero, and his manner is also convincing. He can be humble when thanking the Lord and spirited when declaring his need to control his life.

The Southerner is Renoir's most successful American film and is imbued with man's love of the soil and respect for his labor. It showcases the theme of the interdependence of men upon one another, and the satisfaction they receive from that bond.

Judith M. Kass

SPELLBOUND

Released: 1945
Production: David O. Selznick for Selznick International; released by United Artists
Direction: Alfred Hitchcock
Screenplay: Ben Hecht; based on Angus MacPhail's adaptation of the novel *The House of Dr. Edwardes* by Francis Beeding (Hilary St. George Saunders and John Palmer)
Cinematography: George Barnes
Editing: William Ziegler and Hal C. Kern
Music: Miklos Rozsa (AA)
Running time: 111 minutes

Principal characters:

Dr. Constance Peterson	Ingrid Bergman
John Ballantine (J. B.)	Gregory Peck
Dr. Murchison	Leo G. Carroll
Dr. Edwardes	Edward Fielding
Garmes	Norman Lloyd
Mary Carmichael	Rhonda Fleming
Dr. Alex Brulor	Michael Chekhov

Alfred Hitchcock is one of the best-loved and most widely respected directors in American and British cinema. His films are financial, critical, and popular successes that continue to be named among the "ten best films of all time." The enormous satisfaction people find in his greatest works is a function of his admirable union of visual and narrative expression, and of the metaphors he uses for the emotional malaise with which twentieth century audiences can readily identify.

Hitchcock's characters suffer from dislocation and isolation which is expressed in terms of identity confusion (*North by Northwest*, 1959; *Psycho*, 1960; *Marnie*, 1964; *The Birds*, 1963; *Spellbound*); dislocation in which a character finds himself or herself on the wrong side of the law (*Young and Innocent*, 1937; *Spellbound*, *Strangers on a Train*, 1951; *The Man Who Knew Too Much*, 1955; *The Wrong Man*, 1957); isolation from land itself (*Lifeboat*, 1944); political dislocation (*Torn Curtain*, 1966; *Topaz*, 1969; *Sabateur*, 1952; *Sabotage*, 1936); or dislocation from their own sexuality and their very souls (*Marnie*, *Vertigo*, 1958). The unity of all forms of isolation is the genius of Hitchcock's vision: the inner, psychological forms lead to the external, legal, or physical forms and are accurate maps of the characters' souls. For Hitchcock, the rectifying of any of these states of isolation is part of and a metaphor for emotional integration. Even in his thrillers and whodunits, the crime or mystery in which the hero is embroiled is an indication of his or her emotional integration, and only through reaching out emotionally (usually in the form of sexual love) do these characters break through their isolation. Or, if they are unable to break through they are lost (*Psycho*, *Vertigo*).

In Hitchcock's early films, the external dislocation (usually legal) was the focus of the narrative, and the accompanying emotional health achieved by the characters was almost a side benefit. In his later films, however, and in all of his great 1950's and 1960's masterpieces, the emotional (usually sexual) integration of the characters is the real subject (*Marnie*, *The Birds*, *Vertigo*, *Rear Window*, 1954; *Notorious*, 1946; *Psycho*, *North by Northwest*).

With *Spellbound*, Hitchcock wanted to "turn out the first picture on psychoanalysis." It is not, of course, the first, but it remains one of the best of the "madmen take over the asylum" genre films. An amnesia victim, John Ballantine (Gregory Peck), thinks he has murdered his friend, Dr. Edwardes (Edward Fielding), a psychiatrist due to take over the head position at a mental hospital. Ballantine masquerades as the murdered man, joins the hospital staff as their leader, and falls in love with Dr. Constance Peterson (Ingrid Bergman). Ballantine behaves strangely when he sees parallel lines, and Constance discovers he has amnesia and believes himself to be a murderer. She takes him to her old teacher and psychoanalyst, and together they analyze his dreams (surreal sequences created by Salvador Dali) to find the source of his trauma. The dream imagery reveals the source of his problem to be his guilt over his role in the accidental death of his younger brother. This was transferred when he saw the murder of Dr. Edwardes by the man Edwardes was to replace at the hospital, Dr. Murchison (Leo G. Carroll). Murchison kills himself in a spectacular burst of red (a subjective shot, with the audience in Murchison's place as he pulls the trigger), and the lovers are free to begin their life together.

The joining of the crime (or at least its essential clue) to a psychological neurosis is the essence of Hitchcock's vision. Ballantine's legal dislocation is bound up in his mental loss of identity, and the solution to both is primarily love and secondarily analysis. The dream interpretation of Ballantine's symptoms (aversion to parallel lines) are too simplistic, but the essential unity of all forms of isolation is as clear here as it was to be in Hitchcock's later, greatest films.

John Ballantine is not the only dislocated character in the film. Hitchcock's films are insistent that the seemingly "normal" characters are implicated as well, and Dr. Peterson is characterized as a psychiatrist who is unfeminine, cold, and emotionally crippled, and who is perhaps unable to give her patients the understanding they require because she is so shut off from the world and the range of human emotion. In the first scene she is accused by a fellow doctor (who would like to initiate her into the world of romance) and then by a woman patient (who appears to be a nymphomanic, making the contrast clear) of having only a textbook knowledge of life. Her pulled-back hair and glasses further lock her into a stereotyped image of a frigid woman.

This aspect of the film is rather grating; it is never implied that the male doctors are hiding from their real selves in their work. Constance's professor (Michael Chekhov) is the perfect father and the perfect psychiatrist, complete with Austrian accent. Constance's oppressively narrow character development is a flaw of the kind which does not occur in Hitchcock's later films (such as *Marnie* and *The Birds*), where women's sexual neuroses are fully as complex as men's and proceed from more than their choice of a traditionally male profession.

In *Spellbound*, it is John who will awaken Constance from her frigidity. Their meeting, in a scene that is rather irritating because of its conventional romance cues, is accompanied by an upsurge of music. The climactic opening of doors, while questionable as a cinematic device, certainly makes clear Hitchcock's feelings of what is wrong with Constance: she has been isolated from the world of feeling, and in a graphic depiction of her reaction to Ballantine, superimposed doors actually open in her psyche. The job of the film is for both characters to rediscover themselves, to break through their own isolated situations into emotional commitment, and they do this through each other's love. This is not easily accomplished, and the fact that surrealism is used in the film is perhaps a key to understanding a cinematic device of Hitchcock's which is widely misunderstood. The effect of his artificial backgrounds and rear-screen projection is to cut his characters off from their physical surroundings and thus to put them into closer contact with their inner environment.

This cutting off seems the point of the surrealism in *Spellbound*: through a total warping of the objects of reality and their environment, the inner conflicts of the character whose surrealism we are seeing are better brought into focus. The effect is the same in the skiing sequence: the obviousness of the rear-screen projection may annoy people seeking unobtrusive, technical realism, but it seems that what Hitchcock is forcing us to do is to see that artificial background as a metaphor for the character's inner state. By isolating him from his environment totally, he has achieved a condition of unreality that is responsive to the demands of the characters' emotional torments and release: we see what they are feeling, not what they are seeing, and their emotions which are reflected in their surroundings are the impressions to which we respond.

Hitchcock carries out his theme of isolation in visual nuances as well. When John and Constance are at her old teacher's house, joined in two-shot and talking intimately, the wall behind her is a totally different tone from the one behind him, thus separating them emotionally even though they are together in the shot. Sometimes John's head is perfectly framed by the frame of a picture behind him, cutting him off from the rest of the composition and presenting him in a metaphoric cage. This meticulous attention to technical detail as well as to narrative is characteristic of Hitchcock, and makes his films textbooks for the creation of an idea through both formal and narrative means.

Spellbound was both a commercial success and a critical success, and it earned a place on the *New York Times* "Ten Best Films of 1945" list. Ingrid Bergman was the New York Film Critics Circle Award's choice for Best Actress of 1945. Although the 1945 film does not achieve the total artistic success of Hitchcock's later films, it points to them in its themes and formal expression, and is one of his finest pre-1950 productions. *Spellbound* was parodied, along with other Hitchcock films (notably *Vertigo*), in Mel Brooks's 1978 tribute to the master, *High Anxiety*.

Janey Place

THE SPIRAL STAIRCASE

Released: 1946
Production: Dore Schary for RKO/Radio
Direction: Robert Siodmak
Screenplay: Mel Dinelli; based on the novel *Some Must Watch* by Ethel Lina White
Cinematography: Nicholas Musuraca
Editing: Harry Marker and Harry Gerstad
Music: Roy Webb
Running time: 83 minutes

Principal characters:

Helen Capel .... Dorothy McGuire
Professor Warren .... George Brent
Mrs. Warren .... Ethel Barrymore
Dr. Parry .... Kent Smith
Blanche .... Rhonda Fleming
Steve Warren .... Gordon Olivier
Mrs. Oates .... Elsa Lanchester
Nurse Barker .... Sara Allgood
Mr. Oates .... Rhys Williams

The Spiral Staircase is an old-fashioned, spine-tingling murder mystery that depends as much on psychological shocks as visual ones. Directed by Robert Siodmak and adapted by Mel Dinelli from a novel by Ethel Lina White, the film is full of eerie atmosphere and dark shadows. Its heroine is a young mute servant girl who witnesses horrifying events but cannot comment on them. The action occurs in a heavily decorated mansion full of secret doors and heavy draperies with a winding staircase that is central to the plot. The inhabitants of this strange house are no less baroque: an afflicted old woman with amazing powers of perception, her antisocial biologist son, another son who is irresponsible, various servants, and a secretary.

A sense of chill comes over the proceedings when it is revealed early in the film that a series of murders has taken place in the neighborhood of the old house, and that all the victims are young women with physical defects. The camerawork contributes to the viewers' sense of unease by lingering on closeups of the killer's glaring eyeball, or on feet lurking behind curtains. The film builds to its climax of horror by establishing in the opening scenes the tension which exists both in the mansion and in the town, where the residents are frightened by the maniac in their midst. Most of the film takes place during a gothic New England thunderstorm, which certainly adds to the atmosphere of terror. In short, *The Spiral Staircase* has all the trappings of the horror genre, and the skillful way in which its story is presented makes it entirely convincing. If the filmmakers' purpose was to frighten the audience out of their wits, then they succeeded.

With less than ten words to speak throughout the film, Dorothy McGuire gives a sensitive performance as Helen, the servant girl. Without uttering a word, she conveys the girl's quick intuition and basic intelligence, as well as her sense of panic when she finds herself trapped with a killer. Ethel Barrymore plays the bedridden head of this bizarre household, while George Brent and Gordon Olivier are both rather wooden as her two sons. The rest of the roles are effectively performed by Kent Smith, Rhonda Fleming, and a group of servants that includes Elsa Lanchester, Rhys Williams, and Sara Allgood.

Particularly effective is the music by Roy Webb, whose themes orchestrate and coordinate with the recurrent thunderstorm. Music and background noises are doubly urgent in the film since the principal character cannot speak, but must merely react to what is going on around her. Some of the most chilling scenes take place in absolute silence, with the incessant score contributing to the mounting horror that the young girl is experiencing.

The film is set in a small New England town at the turn of the century. Three girls from the village are murdered mysteriously. They all had in common a physical handicap of one sort or another. Helen (Dorothy McGuire), a young servant employed by the bedridden Mrs. Warren (Ethel Barrymore), seems likely to be the next victim because she is a mute, having lost her power of speech as a result of the childhood shock of seeing her parents die in a fire. At the beginning of the film, Helen is at a movie theater, and through her response to the picture it can be seen that she is a quite impressionable young girl. As she walks home, her fear mounts and she gratefully accepts a ride home in his carriage from Dr. Parry (Kent Smith), physician to her employer.

The inhabitants of the household where Helen works are a depressing group. Besides Mrs. Warren, there are her Professor stepson (George Brent) and her rather callous younger son Steve (Gordon Olivier), both of whom are ill-tempered and moody. Blanche (Rhonda Fleming), the bespectacled secretary to the Warren family, is the next victim of the unknown killer, and Helen begins to suspect that Steve is the murderer because of his odd behavior. Helen's terror quickens, while the audience witnesses the eye of the killer as he views Helen. Through his eyes she has no mouth. Dr. Parry warns Helen that she should leave the house. He is the girl's only friend, and there is more than a hint of a possible romance between the two. On a stormy night when all of the servants have left on various errands, Helen locks Steve up, only to play into the hands of the real killer, who turns out to be the Professor. He very nearly succeeds in killing Helen, but Mrs. Warren spectacularly saves the girl's life by staggering out of bed and shooting her stepson. The old woman falls back in a faint after the shot, and Helen is left to communicate somehow with the outside world. As she struggles to use the telephone, she finds that the terrifying experience has restored her powers of speech. She dials Dr. Parry's number and after much struggle and hesitation, utters her first words in years.

The ends are neatly wrapped up in the film as it reaches its terrifying climax. Helen's futile efforts to use the telephone before her speech is restored foreshadow what is later to come, and the Professor's proclivity for young, defective girls is satisfactorily explained as caused by a psychotic attempt to rid the world of imperfection and weakness. The pace speeds up as events crowd in upon Helen, and the slow, artful build-up of the first half of the film makes the last part all the more effective.

Robert Siodmak was one of a group of distinguished German *émigré* directors who came to Hollywood to flee the Nazis before World War II. Like most of his compatriots, he employed many of the techniques in his films that were used in the great period of German filmmaking prior to World War II. Large sets and overstuffed furnishings, expressionistic lighting and weird camera angles all contribute to the European look of the film. Indeed, some critics compared the ambience of *The Spiral Staircase* to that of Fritz Lang's *M* (1930).

General critical response to *The Spiral Staircase* was favorable, with most reviewers admitting to being so frightened that they were relieved when the lights went on. The film was remade in 1975 with Jacqueline Bisset as the mute girl, Christopher Plummer as the Professor, and Mildred Dunnock as Mrs. Warren. Like so many remakes, however, there were too many people who remembered the original, and the new version did not fare well at the hands of the critics. Directed by Peter Collinson, it lacked the tension and excitement of the first version and had the feel of a film made for television. It does not come close to Siodmak's rendition of *The Spiral Staircase*, a film fondly remembered by those who experienced it as children as one of the most frightening films to come out of Hollywood.

Joan Cohen

THE SPY WHO CAME IN FROM THE COLD

Released: 1965
Production: Martin Ritt for Salem Films; released by Paramount
Direction: Martin Ritt
Screenplay: Paul Dehn and Guy Trosper; based on the novel of the same name by John LeCarré
Cinematography: Oswald Morris
Editing: Anthony Harvey
Running time: 112 minutes

Principal characters:

Alec Leamas	Richard Burton
Nan Perry	Claire Bloom
Fiedler	Oskar Werner
Hans-Dieter Mundt	Peter Van Eyck
George Smiley	Rupert Davies
Control	Cyril Cusack

By 1965, America was spy-happy. Terence Young's marvelous *Doctor No* (1963), *From Russia with Love* (1964), and *Goldfinger* (1964), the first and best of the James Bond films, started the superspy craze, and others—including television's *The Man from UNCLE* (which begat *The Girl from UNCLE*) and *Get Smart*—quickly jumped on the bandwagon. All featured, or spoofed, a suave hero adept at foiling exotic villains with even more exotic weapons, all the while surrounded by hordes of beautiful and willing women. Martin Ritt's film adaptation of John LeCarré's *The Spy Who Came in from the Cold*, however, entered this milieu like Coleridge's Ancient Mariner accosting an unsuspecting reveler. *The Spy Who Came in from the Cold* is the precise antithesis of the James Bond films. Alec Leamas (Richard Burton), the film's protagonist—"hero" is an utterly inappropriate term—lives in an ugly, sordid world in which the good guys and the bad guys are hard to tell apart. Gone are the black and white moral choices that await the Bondlike superspy. Alec Leamas' world is a study in gray.

The film opens with Leamas, the head of Britain's German espionage network, at that bleak symbol of the Cold War, the Berlin Wall. He is waiting near Checkpoint Charlie for one of his agents to attempt an escape from the Communist sector, and he has been waiting a long time. Finally, hours past the scheduled time, his man makes a break for safety, only to be gunned down by the East German police. This scene tells us a great deal about Leamas, about his character and about his fate. He is not heroic; his strength as a spy is a dogged, almost fatalistic patience, a willingness to let things develop. His fate is disappointment and death.

Leamas' opposite is an East German named Hans-Dieter Mundt (Peter

Van Eyck). It is Mundt who is responsible for killing Leamas' agent; in fact, Mundt has reduced Leamas' Berlin operation to a shambles. Thus, when Leamas is summoned to London, he fully expects to be fired. Instead, he finds himself involved in a complicated plot to subvert the entire East German spy network. Once again, Ritt, following LeCarré's lead, very quietly foreshadows the stunning plot twist that gives the film its force. We are warned, early and very subtly, that, although the film's narrative proceeds from Leamas' point of view, his perceptions are not always accurate, and that he is a cog in an incredibly complex set of wheels.

Leamas' initial orders are to act precisely as though he had been fired. His job is to play the disillusioned, disgraced ex-spy who has turned to alcohol in an effort to forget his failures. Leamas proves unnaturally adept at such a role, and he deteriorates quickly. He begins drinking heavily and conspicuously, leading a solitary life and barely supporting himself by doing clerical work in a strange library devoted to occult phenomena. His only friend is Nan Perry (Claire Bloom), one of his coworkers.

Leamas' friendship with Nan is curious, yet oddly affecting. Although she is younger than he by some fifteen years, it is she who initiates their relationship. They appear to have little in common; Nan, it turns out, is a devout Communist, a fact which Leamas finds grimly amusing. He has seen a workers' paradise close up, a fact which his present mission prevents him from explaining to Nan. The two share a common loneliness, however, and against all odds, they become lovers. Leamas denigrates the relationship, but it is clear that, against his will, he has come to care for the girl.

Their affair is complicated by Leamas' pretended degeneration. He hits bottom when he is imprisoned for a short time for assaulting a grocer who has refused him credit. When he is released, two people are waiting for him—Nan and a man who represents the East German secret service. Leamas' act has been successful. The East Germans are convinced that he is an embittered, disgraced ex-spy, ready to defect if approached properly.

Before his rendezvous with the East Germans, Leamas visits his superiors, George Smiley (Rupert Davies) and a man known only as Control (Cyril Cusack), who reveal a bit more of the game plan to him. Mundt, it seems, has an ambitious young second in command named Fiedler (Oskar Werner), and there is no love lost between the two; their rivalry is exacerbated by the fact that Mundt is a former Nazi while Fiedler is a Jew. The British, Control explains, have spent months laying the intricate groundwork for a plan to use Fiedler to get at Mundt. Leamas is to pretend to defect and to reveal a few seemingly insignificant details about a series of obscure financial transactions in Sweden. When examined closely by Fiedler, they will make it appear that Mundt has sold out to the British.

Leamas agrees to do his part, asking only that Nan Perry be left alone. Control promises that she will not become involved. Here Ritt uses Leamas' seemingly gratuitous insistence on leaving Nan out of the plan (there was no suggestion by Control that she would figure in the plot) in two ways. First, the vehemence of Leamas' request is an indication of the depth of his feeling for Nan; and second, the incident warns the perceptive viewer that Nan will inevitably become enmeshed in the scheme sooner or later.

The scene thus set, the film picks up momentum as it builds towards its climax. In return for the promise of a substantial sum of money, Leamas agrees to accompany an East German agent to Holland, where he answers their questions just grudgingly enough to keep them believing that he is bona fide. Complications arise, however, and Leamas is taken to East Berlin where Fiedler takes over the interrogation. Fiedler's excitement mounts as he pieces together the information that appears to implicate Mundt. Finally he acts. Mundt is arrested and brought to trail; Leamas is to be the prosecution's chief witness.

Fiedler puts together a damning case. Leamas' information, coupled with a record of Mundt's movements around Europe, seem to indicate clearly that Mundt has been receiving payoffs from the British. Given the opportunity to cross-examine Leamas, Mundt angrily asserts that Leamas is still a British spy and that the whole thing is a set-up. His attorney repeatedly questions Leamas about his connection with George Smiley, and Leamas doggedly denies ever having met the man. Mundt's attorney exhibits an alarming insight into the British scheme, however, and he has yet to play his trump card. As Leamas looks on in dismay, Nan Perry is brought into the room. She has been brought to East Germany by the Communists under the pretense of attending a Party Congress and is to undergo interrogation by Mundt's attorney. Although she is mystified by the question, she admits to having been visited by a man named George Smiley, who described himself as a close friend of Alec Leamas.

Thus, both Leamas and Fiedler are thoroughly discredited. The stunned Leamas gradually comes to realize that this has been Control's plan all along. Mundt really is a double agent in the pay of the British, and the whole operation has been designed to eliminate Fiedler. Control has used Leamas just as surely, and just as coldly as he has used everyone else. Although Leamas had fancied himself a cynic, he now knows that there are depths of cynicism which he has never imagined.

The film ends where it began, at the Berlin Wall. Mundt arranges for Leamas and Nan to escape. As they drive towards the Wall, Leamas bitterly summarizes the situation for Nan; and his remark that "There's only one rule—expedience" proves to be their epitaph. Control has arranged for Leamas to escape alone. Nan now knows too much to be permitted to live, and she is shot by an East German border guard as the two clamber over the wall. This final betrayal is too much for Leamas. Ignoring the pleas of his "friend" George Smiley on the west side of the Wall, he turns around and climbs back down into the Eastern sector where he awaits the bullet that ends his life. Alec Leamas has come in from the cold.

The Spy Who Came in from the Cold stands the imaginary spy world of James Bond on its head. Gone are the invincible heroes, the exotic locations, the nobility of purpose—all of the certainties on which the world of the heroic superspy is based. In their place is confusion, grimness, and an inability to tell right from wrong. In bringing John LeCarré's novel to the screen, Martin Ritt and writers Paul Dehn and Guy Trosper are uncompromising. In addition to following the novel's story line closely, Ritt steadfastly refuses to enliven the film artificially in any way. It is shot in stark black-and-white cinematography which emphasizes the bleakness of Leamas' world, and the pacing of the film is deliberately slow.

Despite its slow pace, however, the film never becomes boring, and much of the credit for this must go to the fine cast. Claire Bloom and Oskar Werner are more than adequate as Nan Perry and Fiedler, the major supporting roles; and Cyril Cusack as Control and Peter Van Eyck as Mundt are particularly effective in smaller roles. Richard Burton's portrayal of Alec Leamas, though, is the film's centerpiece. The mid-1960's found Burton at the height of his powers as a screen actor, and his performance as the disillusioned British spy is arguably one of his best. Burton excels at playing broken men who refuse to relinquish their dignity even in despair, using his face, and particularly his eyes, to reveal first the shock and then the numbness that Leamas feels as his world disintegrates. It is an outstanding performance.

The Spy Who Came in from the Cold was a very salutary film. Coming as it did in the midst of the James Bond craze, it served to remind audiences that the Bond films were, after all, mere escapism (albeit high-class escapism), and that the real world of espionage was a good deal colder and more morally ambiguous than the imaginary one inhabited by 007. More importantly, however, the film stands the test of time. With its well-crafted plot, its deliberate, somber direction, and Richard Burton's classic character study of a burnt-out spy, *The Spy Who Came in from the Cold* stands in the first rank of cinema thrillers. It is a classic of its genre.

Robert Mitchell

THE SPY WHO LOVED ME

Released: 1977
Production: Albert R. Broccoli for Eon Productions; released by United Artists
Direction: Lewis Gilbert
Screenplay: Christopher Wood and Richard Maibaum; based on the characters created by Ian Fleming
Cinematography: Claude Renoir
Editing: John Glen
Production design: Ken Adam
Running time: 125 minutes

Principal characters:

James Bond	Roger Moore
Major Anya Amasova	Barbara Bach
Stromberg	Curt Jurgens
Jaws	Richard Kiel
General Gogol	Walter Gotell
"M"	Bernard Lee

When the tenth James Bond film, *The Spy Who Loved Me*, opened during the summer of 1977, it was advertised as "The Biggest of the Bonds" and "It's Bond and Beyond." For many aficionados of the James Bond films, these two statements were somewhat contentious. Many proponents of the earlier and more-faithful-to-the-book Bond sagas felt that being "Bond and beyond," was a betrayal of Ian Fleming's original creations, while others felt that the film was indeed the best as well as the "biggest" of the filmed Bond stories. Perhaps more than any other of the previously filmed titles, *The Spy Who Loved Me* reflects the passage of time from the first venture, *Dr. No* (1963), to the present.

There are many reasons why the first and the tenth of the Bond films are so different. Most importantly, the character of James Bond is played by a different actor. Sean Connery, the original Bond, typified the rugged, almost cruel appearance and behavior of Fleming's Bond. Roger Moore, who has portrayed Bond four times, brings a less cruel, more sophisticated aspect to the role. While in the early Connery films, animal magnetism and cunning seemed to be Bond/007's most valuable assets, in the later Moore films, tongue-in-check charm works more effectively. Many critics and fans alike yearn for the days of the "real" James Bond—that is, Sean Connery—although others find the more subtle, more vulnerable Roger Moore Bond very appealing. George Lazenby, who played Bond in *On Her Majesty's Secret Service* (1969), financially the least successful of all Bond films, was more of a "road company" Sean Connery than a different character, and his interpretation of the role is all but overlooked by Bond critics. Another overlooked string of James Bonds appeared in the film *Casino Royale* in 1967, the only Bond story not to be filmed either by the production team of Harry Saltzman and Albert R. Broccoli, or by Broccoli alone. This unsatisfying parody boasted several James Bonds, including David Niven and Woody Allen. Although the film was relatively successful, it is so far removed from the mainstream of James Bond films that it hardly seems to be dealing with the same characters.

Another reason for the differences between various Bond films is changing public tastes. *Dr. No* and *From Russia with Love* (1964) attempted to be faithful to the original Fleming novels and relied more on story than gadgetry. Recently, however, with the increased popular enthusiasm for glamorous locales and impossible stunts, James Bond cannot simply rely on his wits and his Biretta. Now he is surrounded by cars that fly and turn into submarines, beautiful women by the score, and magnificent locations.

As with several of the other Bond films, *The Spy Who Loved Me* begins with a mysterious catastrophic occurrence. A British nuclear submarine inexplicably starts to shake, and the captain looks through his periscope and utters "My God!" The audience is then cinematically whisked away to British Intelligence Headquarters where an official reports that a nuclear submarine is missing without a clue. Next, against the mellow strains of a Russian balalaika, we see the head of Soviet intelligence as he discovers that the Soviets have also mysteriously lost one of their nuclear submarines. In order to solve the mystery, General Gogol (Walter Gotell) decides to put his best agent, "Triple X," on the case.

As it turns out, Triple X, Major Anya Amasova (Barbara Bach), is a beautiful woman who is carrying on an affair with another Russian spy who leaves their tryst at a "people's rest and recuperation center" for a special assignment in Austria. The assignment involves an attempt to kill James Bond (Roger Moore), who is also there on a mission. In the next sequence, in perhaps the most breathtaking and daring stunt ever filmed, Bond, in this instance played by a professional skier and stuntman, kills the Russian agent, is chased down a mountain on skis to a precipice where he jumps, free falls for a seemingly endless period of time, and is saved by a parachute opening up to reveal the Union Jack. Immediately after this stunt, Maurice Binder's credits come across the screen, beautifully orchestrated by Marvin Hamlish's and Carole Bayer Sager's background theme, "Nobody Does It Better," and placed against a shadowed background of gymnasts performing acrobatics symbolic of both the action and sexual innuendoes of the title song, performed by Carly Simon. Though the phallic symbols of this sequence may be overdone, the staging is so beautiful that the heavy-handedness can be overlooked.

After this spectacular beginning, the plot settles down to reveal the usual Bond type of action, as Bond and Anya must cooperate on a joint Soviet-

British operation to find the missing submarines. It is discovered that there may be a connection between the multimillionaire shipping magnate Stromberg (Curt Jurgens) and his supertankers, and the disappearance. During the mission, Bond and Anya hurry across Egypt and Sardinia to catch their villain.

Amid the usual fights and loves scenes, Bond encounters a giant steel-toothed killer named Jaws. Although similar to Odd Job of *Goldfinger* (1964), Jaws, with his almost boyish smile and tenacious ability to defy death, appeals to the audience. Played by a seven-foot-three giant of an actor named Richard Kiel, Jaws was so popular as a villain that he was brought back for the next Bond caper, *Moonraker* (1979). Defying electrocution, falling pillars, car crashes, and explosions, Jaws's brawn is clearly a match for Bond's brain.

The part of Stromberg is typical of Bond films. He is an enormously wealthy man bent on revenge against humanity for its destruction of the seas by pollution. He has a beautiful submarinelike headquarters which can submerge or fly above the water at will. He seems to prefer fish to people and even displays hands that are partially webbed—a physical abberation which also has parallels in earlier Bond films. The prime villain is never simply evil, he is also deformed in some way, and despite his wealth or power, he is obsessed with his goal, be it money, world domination, or the death of James Bond.

Barbara Bach as Anya is certainly one of the most beautiful of all Bond heroines, but her acting abilities leave something to be desired. She is unable to match the screen charisma or talents of such actresses as Diana Rigg or Ursula Andress of earlier Bond films. Her position as a Russian agent may make her appear to be a match for Bond, but in many of her scenes she appears rather helpless. Also unfortunate is the fact that Bach, an American, falters occasionally in her Russian accent. In spite of such weaknesses, however, a certain chemistry between Bach and Moore works well and pleased audiences. As in all of the other Bond pictures, James Bond and his female accomplice are able to save the world from destruction and the villain is killed. The final portions of the film move very quickly with explosions and daring escapes from Stromberg's underwater refuge. The set used for Stromberg's headquarters is the largest indoor set ever built. Because of the necessity for huge water tanks to house studio-made submarines, a new sound stage had to be specially made at Pinewood studios, England, for the filming.

The film is successful overall. The story may be a scissors-and-paste edition of several earlier stories, but the music, cinematography, location shooting, and stunts distinguish *The Spy Who Loved Me* from previous efforts. The set designs of longtime Bond collaborator Ken Adam and the camerawork of Claude Renoir are particularly noteworthy. What makes the film such a success (it grossed more than $85,000,000) is its unabashed refusal to take itself seriously. Being the first of the Bond films to be solely produced by Albert R. Broccoli without the collaboration of Harry Saltzman, this film surrenders completely to self-mockery and "inside" humor. There is not the slightest attempt to make the audience believe the story and the shenanigans. The story, which was the first to be written for the screen rather than being based on a Fleming novel, is subservient to the escapist fun of the gadgetry, the magnificent cinematography, and Moore's wry, tongue-in-check performance. Whereas the previous two Roger Moore efforts were weakened by attempts to make him fit into the Connery mold, *The Spy Who Loved Me* takes advantage of Moore's own screen *persona* rather than relying on the audience's preconceived notions of what James Bond should be like.

There are many scenes in which the film's self-parody is evident. In the scene at the Pyramids during the Sound and Light show, after Bond has successfully fought off several Russian attackers, he walks off into the distance illuminated by spotlights, amid a fanfare, slightly bowing his head in open acknowledgment of his "performance" of a few moments before. Another example of humorous self-mockery occurs when Moore introduces himself to the owner of a Cairo night club who is involved in the submarine disappearance. When Moore announces, deadpan, "I'm James Bond," the man responds, equally deadpan, "What of it?" This is perhaps the key to the change in the most recent Bond films. The emphasis has shifted from a story with some sex and satire, to sex and satire with some story. Those who are willing to accept the good points of the later films without making disparaging comparisons to the earlier ones can also say "What of it?" and sit back and enjoy unabashed escapism at its best.

Patricia King Hanson

STAGECOACH

Released: 1939
Production: John Ford and Walter Wanger for United Artists
Direction: John Ford
Screenplay: Dudley Nichols; based on the short story "Stage to Lordsburg" by Ernest Haycox
Cinematography: Bert Glennon
Editing: Dorothy Spencer and Walter Reynolds
Art direction: Alexander Toluboff
Costume design: Walter Plunkett
Music: Richard Hageman, Franke Harling, John Leipold, Leo Shuken (AA)
Running time: 96 minutes

Principal characters:

Ringo Kid	John Wayne
Dallas	Claire Trevor
Doc Boone	Thomas Mitchell (AA)
Buck	Andy Devine
Curly Wilcox	George Bancroft
Mr. Peacock	Donald Meek
Lucy Mallory	Louise Platt
Hatfield	John Carradine
Mr. Gatewood	Berton Churchill
Lieutenant Blanchard	Tim Holt
Luke Plummer	Tom Tyler
Ike Plummer	Joe Rickson

Stagecoach is a landmark in the evolution of the Western genre and in the career of its director, John Ford. After the introduction of synchronized sound during the 1930's, Westerns were mostly "B" type films. There were singing cowboys, (Gene Autry and Roy Rogers), action heroes (Hopalong Cassidy and George O'Brien), serials (the Long Ranger and Johnny Mack Brown), and a stampede of cheaply made quickies from the backlots of independent studios such as Republic, Monogram, and Resolute. However, when an upbeat spirit of national optimism emerged in the late 1930's, as exemplified in *Stagecoach* and Cecil B. DeMille's *Union Pacific*, the Western became a means of transmitting themes of national progress and consequently a genre to be seriously considered. *Stagecoach* also helped reestablish the epic Western as a solid box-office commodity.

For Ford, regarded as one of the genre's seminal auteurs, *Stagecoach* marked a return to the Western after a thirteen-year hiatus. (His last Western had been *Three Bad Men*, a silent film made in 1926.) The overwhelming success of *Stagecoach* with both critics and the public brought Ford the prestige and recognition that enabled him to take a fairly independent course, at least by Hollywood standards. It also paved the way for other memorable Ford Westerns such as *My Darling Clementine* (1946), *Fort Apache* (1948), *She Wore a Yellow Ribbon* (1949), *Wagon Master* (1950), and *The Man Who Shot Liberty Valance* (1962).

Though Dudley Nichols' screenplay is based on Ernest Haycox's "Stage to Lordsburg," which first appeared in *Collier's* magazine in April of 1937, Ford has stated that Haycox's inspiration probably came from Guy de Maupassant's *Boule de Suif*, a tale of a prostitute traveling by carriage through war-torn France with important members of the bourgeoisie. The dramatic structure of *Stagecoach* is based on a time-tested convention: a group of widely varied characters is placed in a dangerous situation which, like a litmus test, reveals each individual's true character. Specifically, eight passengers are brought together from an overland stagecoach journey from Tonto to Lordsburg through the perilous American Southwest, which was terrorized by Geronimo's Apache warriors during the 1870's.

The band of travelers includes Doc Boone (Thomas Mitchell), an intoxicated man of medicine; Hatfield (John Carradine), a Southern officer-turned-cardsharp; Dallas (Claire Trevor), a prostitute driven out of Tonto by the self-righteous Ladies' Law and Order League; Mrs. Lucy Mallory (Louise Platt), the pregnant wife of a Cavalry lieutenant; Mr. Gatewood (Berton Churchill), a pompous banker in flight with embezzled band funds; Mr. Peacock (Donald Meek), a timid whisky drummer who is consistently mistaken for a clergyman; Buck (Andy Devine), the skittish driver of the stage; Marshal Curly Wilcox (George Bancroft); and his prisoner, the Ringo Kid (John Wayne). In the course of their trying adventures, these characters are manipulated by Ford and Nichols so that conventional social levels are turned upside down. As a result, it is the social outcasts—the outlaw and prostitute—who emerge as most noble, while the outwardly most "respectable" member, the banker, turns out the most despicable, a man consumed by greed and self-importance.

During the journey, two major events serve as primary catalysts for revealing character. The first occurs at the Apache Wells station where Lucy Mallory goes into labor. Doc, drunk with "samples" provided by the reluctant Mr. Peacock, realizing his professional responsibility, calls for coffee. While Ringo, Dallas, and Curly help Doc sober up, Hatfield looks on with suppressed fury: "A fine member of the medical profession! Drunken beast!" Hatfield's angry disgust is based on his concern for Lucy, a concern based on a shared Southern heritage and his chivalrous stance as her protector.

Gatewood, on the other hand, complains not about Doc, but about their situation. "A sick woman on our hands! That's all we needed!" Gatewood's outburst is totally selfish; his sole concern is getting to Lordsburg as quickly as possible. Dallas, however, proves her true worth during the childbirth by assisting Doc and then sitting up all night tending to Lucy and her baby girl.

During the evening, Dallas takes a break and strolls outside the station to get some fresh air. She meets Ringo, who explains that he must get to Lordsburg to avenge the murder of his father and brother. He then tries to tell Dallas how impressed he was with her way of handling the baby. Though his words are awkward, he proposes by stating "You're . . . the kind of girl a man wants to marry." Dallas appears nonplused and tells him not to talk like that. Rushing off, however, her tears betray her deep feelings for Ringo, her concern for his impending shoot-out with the Plummer gang, and the shame she feels over being a prostitute. The next morning, Doc suggests the stage's departure be postponed for a day to allow Lucy to regain some of her strength. In spite of the threat of Geronimo, all endorse Doc's advice except Gatewood, who vehemently protests the delay.

Back on the trail, the ongoing bickering suddenly ceases as an arrow hits Peacock in the shoulder. The group's ultimate test is about to begin. Apaches swarm down from the hills in pursuit of the stage hurtling across the broad, flat plain. Gatewood, in a mad panic, cries "Stop the stage! Let me out of here!" Doc Boone bandages Peacock's shoulder. Buck drives his frenzied team of six horses with wild yells. Curly, Ringo, and Hatfield attempt to fight off the Apaches. As their end seems near, Hatfield, with one bullet left in his chamber, points his gun toward the huddled figure of Lucy muttering prayers: he obviously intends to save her from a fate worse than death. Hatfield pauses, a gunshot is heard, his gun drops and falls to the ground. Hatfield has been hit.

Suddenly, a bugle is heard in the distance blowing the charge. The cavalry has arrived. The Apaches halt and turn in flight as the troopers charge. As the coach comes to a stop, Hatfield turns to Lucy and utters his last words: "If you ever see Judge Ringfield . . . tell him his son. . . ." The others, however, are safe and proceed without further incident to Lordsburg escorted by the cavalrymen.

The stage is met by Lordsburg's sheriff, who surprises the blustering Gatewood: "You didn't think they'd have the telegraph wires fixed, did you?" Gatewood struggles to no avail, is handcuffed and marched away to the local jail. Peacock is carried off on a stretcher for more medical attention, and Lucy is assured by a Captain sent to meet her that her husband is safe. Before departing, Lucy, whose initial scorn of Dallas has mellowed because of Dallas' unselfish help, attempts to reach out by saying, "If there's anything I can ever do for. . . ."

The film concludes with Ringo's showdown with the Plummers. Having gained the marshal's respect, Ringo is given ten minutes by Curly to take care of business. In another part of town, Dallas hears a volley of shots. Fearing the worse, she cries out Ringo's name; then a figure looms in the darkness—it is Ringo. Dallas rushes forward to embrace him; the Plummers have been vanquished. Curly directs Dallas and Ringo to a buckboard. Once seated,

Curly and Doc shoo the team of horses and shout best wishes to the pair as they head out to establish new lives on Ringo's ranch in Mexico. As the buckboard rumbles into the night, Doc comments: "Well, they're saved from the blessings of civilization." The marshal then offers Doc a drink. After a majestically grand pause, Doc replies, "Just one." It is the perfect note of irony for a film whose portrait of society is itself ironic.

Stagecoach, aside from its value as a well-told tale of the West, is an incisive comment on the virtues and limitations of society. Doc, the poet of the group and Ford's voice within the film, is a man whose training was made possible by the institutions of civilization; at the same time, because of his passion for drink, he is regarded by society's mainstream as an outcast. When the chips are down, however, Doc is equal to the tasks of delivering a baby or patching a wound. Curly also straddles the line between society and the wilderness. Though his oath as a lawman requires him to return Ringo to the prison from which he escaped, Curly responds to a higher law, the code of honor of the old West. In Curly's eyes, Ringo has proved himself and repaid his debt to society; that allows Curly to give him an opportunity to face the Plummers and, later, a fresh chance at a new life in Mexico. In these and other incidents, the values of society are shown as cold, unfeeling, and even corrupt. It is clear that Ford's values are aligned with the primitive and natural society of an old West unfettered by the stultifying pressures of civilization. The beauty and freedom of the wilderness represent the ultimate in values.

Underscoring Ford's broad theme is the magnificent landscape of Monument Valley. With his broad panoramas of weathered plains, mesas, and majestic clouds, Ford creates a universe of natural order which dwarfs the actions of the men who travel through it. There is, however, the implication that those who live by the spirit of the land instead of by society's dictates will live most nobly.

Mood and atmosphere are effectively established by an outstanding score by Hageman, Harling, Leipold, and Shuken, which incorporates seventeen American folk songs from the period. The score won an Academy Award. The performances by John Wayne, Claire Trevor, Andy Devine, George Bancroft, Donald Meek, Louise Platt, John Carradine, and Berton Churchill are all outstanding as is that of Thomas Mitchell who won an Academy Award as Best Supporting Actor for his portrayal of Doc Boone.

Today, *Stagecoach* stands as one of the brightest examples of the American Western and as one of the most mature of John Ford's films. Ford was honored as the Best Director of 1939 by the New York Film Critics for his direction of *Stagecoach*.

Charles M. Berg

A STAR IS BORN

Released: 1937
Production: David O. Selznick for Selznick International; released by United Artists
Direction: William A. Wellman
Screenplay: Dorothy Parker, Alan Campbell, and Robert Carson; based on William A. Wellman's and Robert Carson's screen story (AA), adapted from the 1932 film *What Price Hollywood?*
Cinematography: W. Howard Greene (AA Special Award)
Editing: Hal C. Kern and Anson Stevenson
Running time: 111 minutes

Principal characters:

Esther Blodgett/ Vicki Lester	Janet Gaynor
Norman Maine	Fredric March
Danny McGuire	Andy Devine
Oliver Niles	Adolphe Menjou
Matt Libby	Lionel Stander

The continuing public fascination with Hollywood and its fantasy world has created a ready audience for films which purport to show the real Hollywood, and the industry, capitalizing on this interest, has produced many films about itself. One of the first films to expose the inner workings of the star game was the 1937 version of *A Star Is Born*, which is loosely based on a 1932 production entitled *What Price Hollywood?* and whose same story line was used for remakes in 1954 and 1976. For many, the William Wellman version of 1937 remains the most outstanding to date; it is a compelling and well-directed character study as well as an extensive examination of the creation and destruction of stars.

Leaving her Colorado home to find fame and fortune in Hollywood, Esther Blodgett (Jaynet Gaynor) is pursuing a lifelong dream of becoming a star. She is told her chances are "100,000 to 1," but clinging to the belief that she is the one destined to stardom, she persists. Befriended by kindhearted Danny McGuire (Andy Devine), she is able to find work as a waitress at a party, where she meets Norman Maine, a suave star with a reputation for drinking too much. A screen test is arranged by Maine, and thus begin the intricacies of transforming unknown Esther Blodgett into the movie star, Vicki Lester.

Janet Gaynor's portrayal of the innocent and excited Esther is very well done; she watches wide-eyed as every aspect of her life is re-created to fit the studio's needs. A new biography is written to go with her new name and to overshadow the mundane facts of her real life. She is remolded by the makeup artists, and, after going through numerous styles, Vicki Lester is created;

even her walking and talking are reprogrammed into something new. This was one of the first real treatments of star-building depicted on the screen, and although the machinations of identity building are well known today, in 1937, such information was new and was eagerly devoured by the public.

In Vicki's first film she plays opposite Norman Maine as leading man; the critics adore both her and the movie. The only negative remarks are regarding Norman, whose appearance is far overshadowed by Vicki. By this time, however, Vicki and Norman are in love and announce their intention to marry. Once again the audience is privy to the inner workings of Hollywood as the wedding is turned over to the publicity department and its obnoxious head, Matt Libby (Lionel Stander); but to escape the fantasy wedding designed by Libby, the two elope and are married under their real names.

With future films, it becomes obvious that Vicki's popularity has risen as quickly as Maine's has fallen. The film deftly outlines the pair's fickle change of fortunes, as the cruelty and spite suffered by Norman are contrasted beautifully with the adulation and goodwill received by Vicki. The personal destruction of Norman Maine is finely interpreted by Fredric March. Unable to cope with being seen as Mr. Lester, Norman finds increasing escape and solace in alcohol. In one particularly moving scene, Maine's long-time friend and producer, Oliver Niles (Adolphe Menjou), tells Norman that the actor's career is finished and offers to buy out his contract. The emotions felt by both characters are apparent and well acted.

Vicki's love for Norman has not dwindled, but is, rather, strengthened by his troubles. One evening, after bailing her husband out of jail for drunkenness, Vicki confides to Niles that she is going to sacrifice her career to take care of Norman. Unfortunately, Norman overhears this, and through a combination of self-pity and love for Vicki, takes his life by walking out to sea. One criticism of the film is that it could have ended here; indeed, any further action is anticlimactic after Norman's suicide. However, the film continues and, after a harrowing funeral encounter with her "fans," Vicki returns to the screen. At the debut of her new film, she triumphantly steps to the microphone and says "Hello everybody, this is Mrs. Norman Maine."

A Star Is Born is truly an outstanding motion picture that holds the audience's attention from the start until the final scene. This is surely due in part to William Wellman's direction and writing, for which he, with Robert Carson, won the Academy Award for Best Original Story. Despite the many outstanding aspects of the film, this was the only Oscar *A Star Is Born* received, although it was also nominated for Best Picture, Best Actor, Best Actress, Best Direction, and Best Assistant Director (Eric Stacey), an award category which was later discontinued by the Academy.

Another reason why this film's reputation has endured through the years is its use of color, with well thought-out set decorations such as the dull boarding house contrasting to the colorful but tasteful star's home. The color cinematography work of W. Howard Greene received a special award from the Motion Picture Academy. All of the ingredients in *A Star Is Born* blend together well to form an excellent movie, and although remade several times later, many critics feel that this production has not been equaled.

Elaine Raines

A STAR IS BORN

Released: 1954
Production: Sidney Luft for Transcona Enterprises; released by Warner Bros.
Direction: George Cukor
Screenplay: Moss Hart; based on the screenplay for the 1937 film of the same name
Cinematography: Sam Leavitt
Editing: Folmar Blangsted
Running time: 154 minutes

Principal characters:

Esther Blodgett/
Vicki Lester .... Judy Garland
Norman Maine .... James Mason
Matt Libby .... Jack Carson
Oliver Niles .... Charles Bickford
Danny McGuire .... Tommy Noonan

"Inside Hollywood" stories have provided the material for many filmmakers' products over the years, and few variations on this theme have been repeated more often or more successfully than that of *A Star Is Born*. No than three films with this title have been made, the first by William Wellman in 1937, and the latest by Frank Pierson, who in 1976 made his protagonists rock stars instead of actors. The best of these films, however, is arguably the 1954 version, directed by George Cukor and starring Judy Garland and James Mason.

Like its predecessor, Cukor's *A Star Is Born* is the story of Norman Maine (James Mason), a talented but alcoholic movie star who discovers young Esther Blodgett (Judy Garland), propels her to stardom under the stage name of Vicki Lester, marries her, and finally commits suicide when he realizes that his alcoholism is ruining her career. Into the midst of this drama, however, Cukor inserts musical comedy of the highest order. It is a tribute to the talent of the director, and his two stars, Garland and Mason, that the two apparently conflicting genres mesh and complement rather than detract from each other.

A Star Is Born is at least nominally about Hollywood, and Cukor uses three official Hollywood ceremonies, strategically placed at the beginning, middle, and end of the film, to comment on the Hollywood scene as well as to advance the plot. The first of these ceremonies is a concert for a benefit known as "The Motion Picture Relief Fund," the proceeds of which go to out-of-work actors. "Hollywood never forgets its own," boasts the Master of Ceremonies, but Cukor underscores the irony of this statement throughout the picture as he chronicles the downfall of Norman Maine. Although Norman is sufficiently self-destructive to ruin his own career, the way is made easier for him by his studio, most notably by Matt Libby (Jack Carson), the mean-spirited publicity man.

As the film opens, however, Norman has just begun his descent from the top. He arrives at the benefit late and obviously drunk. After disrupting things backstage and insulting Libby, he lurches onstage into a performance by the Glenn Williams Orchestra. Esther Blodgett, the orchestra's singer, cleverly incorporates Norman into their song and dance routine, saving everyone from major embarrassment. Even in his inebriated condition, Norman is aware of what an extraordinary gesture Esther has made; for her part, Esther is more amused than offended. "Mr. Maine is feeling no pain," she quips, but later adds "drunk or not, he's nice." A sullen Libby sees to it that Maine gets home safely. By showing the evident hostility between the two men, Cukor lays the groundwork for a time when the worm will turn.

Later that same night, Norman awakens and, haunted by the memory of the girl in the Glenn Williams Orchestra, tracks Esther down at an afterhours club where she and her fellow musicians hang out. In this scene, Cukor makes effective use of the soundtrack by playing a very quiet orchestral reprise of one of Esther's songs to suggest that she is in Norman's thoughts. As Norman enters the club, he is transfixed by Esther's rendition of "The Man That Got Away." After witnessing this performance, both Norman and the audience realize that Esther Blodgett is not simply a cute and talented singer; there is a spark of genius in her, a rare star quality just waiting to be discovered. "The Man That Got Away" scene is one of the keys to the believability of the film. Garland's performance of the Harold Arlen-Ira Gershwin song has been justifiably praised as one of the classics of the Hollywood musical film. We do not have to take Esther's potential on faith—Garland makes it abundantly obvious.

Norman is happy to sponsor Esther's entry into show business, and he cajoles the reluctant head of the Oliver Niles Studios (Charles Bickford) into giving her a screen test. She passes the test and becomes a part of the studio. Cukor emphasizes, however, what a minor part she is in a hilarious sequence in which Esther, now renamed Vicki Lester, is shuttled from person to person, each of whom, from the wardrobe lady to the head of the studio, greets her with a cordial "Glad to have you with us," and then promptly proceeds to ignore her. Finally, again through the good offices of Norman, she gets a chance at a starring role in a musical comedy. Cukor shows us a long sequence from this film at a special screening at which Norman's new film is also being previewed. The sequence is an exquisitely staged musical "biography" of Vicki Lester's character. She opens and closes with "Born in a Trunk." In between, interspersed with her ironic commentary on being a "ten-year-overnight sensation," come such classics as "I'll Get By," "You Took Advantage of Me," "Melancholy Baby," and "Sewanee." The screening is a sensation; the title of the film has become a reality. Vicki Lester has become a star.

Norman has mixed feelings about his protégé. His own film has been ignored in the fanfare that greeted Esther's smash debut. He knows himself well enough to be aware that he destroys everything to which he gets close; nevertheless, he loves Esther, and she persuades him to give marriage a try. After losing the frustrated Libby, who has hoped to get some publicity mileage out of their elopement, Norman and Esther are married by a sleepy country justice of the peace under Norman's real name, and become Mr. and Mrs. Ernest Sidney Gubbins.

Despite an idyllic honeymoon, both Norman and his marriage soon begin to unravel, and Cukor uses another Hollywood ceremony to demonstrate this fact. It is Oscar night, and Vicki Lester has won an Academy Award. She is about to make her acceptance speech when Norman once again lurches drunkenly onstage. He makes a rambling, self-pitying speech about his inability to get work; and, gesturing wildly, accidentally slaps Vicki. As the audience gasps in shock, Vicki somehow manages to get offstage. However, the damage is done: Norman Maine's career is finished.

Norman makes an effort to adjust to his new circumstances, and even has himself committed to a sanitarium in an effort to dry out; but the lure of alcohol proves to be too strong. When his old adversary, Matt Libby, provides him with an excuse to go off the wagon by picking a fight with Norman at a racetrack and beating him, the humiliated Norman responds by going on a monumental drunk, ultimately turning up in a local drunk tank and bringing more scandal down upon himself and his wife. Esther, for her part, feels helpless. She loves Norman, but admits that she hates him as well. Torn between her husband and her career, she tells Oliver Niles that she is quitting her career to stay with Norman at their Malibu home. Norman, who has been in a drunken sleep in the next room, overhears the conversation; a look of agonizing self-loathing crosses his face, followed by a look of grim determination. After Niles leaves, Norman, with a huge smile, comes to Esther, wearing swimming trunks. He is turning over a new leaf, he vows, and will begin his healthy new life at once by getting in some swimming. He stops short, however, and looks wistfully at his wife for a long moment. As Esther goes inside to prepare dinner, Norman runs into the ocean and drowns. Although his death is officially ruled an accident, it is obvious that he has sacrificed his own life for the sake of Esther and her career.

Cukor closes the film with a third Hollywood ceremony; it is another benefit and a grief-stricken Esther is persuaded to come out of mourning in order to perform. When an excited announcer introduces her as Vicki Lester, she corrects him emphatically: "Hello everybody. This is *Mrs.* Norman Maine!" As the audience applauds ecstatically, the camera pulls back slowly, and the film ends with a long shot of Esther, smiling through her tears.

In 1932, George Cukor directed his sixth film, *What Price Hollywood?*, which traced the rise and fall of a young actress whose film career was masterminded by an alcoholic director. This film provided the inspiration for William Wellman's original *A Star Is Born* in 1937, which Cukor, in turn, remade seventeen years later. It was through this circuitous path that George Cukor produced the film that has been acclaimed by some as Hollywood's greatest musical. Among a host of first-rate actors, three performances stand out. James Mason's thoughtful, unmannered portrayal of Norman Maine won him an Academy Award nomination. Because Mason has no illusions about Norman, neither does the audience, but Mason is a good enough actor to show us the talent and the warmth beneath Norman's dissipation. We can understand why Esther loves him, and his demise, though inevitable, is thus genuinely tragic. In a supporting role, Jack Carson is similarly effective as Matt Libby, Norman's chief antagonist. Libby is the film's only real villain, and Carson's performance is appropriately mean-spirited. His Libby is a classic today, a man who despises those whom he serves. As good as Mason and Carson are, however, *A Star Is Born* belongs to Judy Garland; she does not so much overshadow her colleagues, however, as illuminate them. She performs with such an intensity that at times she almost seems to glow. It is not inconceivable that actors other than Mason and Carson could have handled the roles of Norman Maine and Matt Libby; it is almost impossible to imagine anyone other than Judy Garland as Esther Blodgett. Her performance lifts *A Star Is Born* into the first rank among Hollywood musicals.

Robert Mitchell

STAR WARS

Released: 1977
Production: Gary Kurtz for Lucasfilm Productions; released by Twentieth Century-Fox
Direction: George Lucas
Screenplay: George Lucas
Cinematography: Gilbert Taylor
Editing: Paul Hirsch, Marcia Lucas, and Richard Chew (AA)
Art direction: John Barry, Norman Reynolds, and Leslie Dilley (AA); set decoration, Roger Christian (AA)
Special effects: John Dykstra, John Stears, Richard Edlund, Grant McCune, and Robert Blalack (AA)
Sound effects editing: Benjamin Burtt, Jr. (AA Special Award)
Costume design: John Mollo (AA)
Sound: Derek Ball, Don MacDougall, Bob Minkler, and Ray West (AA)
Music: John Williams (AA)
Running time: 119 minutes

Principal characters:

Luke Skywalker .... Mark Hamill
Han Solo .... Harrison Ford
Princess Leia Organa .... Carrie Fisher
Ben (Obi-Wan) Kenobi .... Alec Guinness
Grand Moff Tarkin .... Peter Cushing
Lord Darth Vader .... David Prowse
(voice, James Earl Jones)
R2D2 (Artoo Detoo) .... Kenny Baker
C3PO (See Threepio) .... Anthony Daniels
Chewbacca .... Peter Mayhew

The highlight of *Star Wars* is the multitude of well-executed special effects, the most ambitious level of technical wizardry in science fiction film since Stanley Kubrick's *2001: A Space Odyssey* (1968). Writer-director George Lucas expanded the technical side of film further than any other director of his day, not only creating a special effects shop to handle the film's many optical and mechanical needs, but also encouraging the supervisor of special photographic effects, John Dykstra, to invent a new camera called the Dykstraflex, which was needed to film the kinds of shots Lucas wanted. Although Lucas did use Kubrick's technique of superimposing images on each frame, he attached a computer to the camera which enabled him to record each shot and play it back exactly as filmed, producing more elaborate scenes in less time than Kubrick had spent on his film. The result is that *Star Wars* has three hundred sixty-three different special effects in contrast to *2001: A Space Odyssey*, which has only thirty-five.

Unlike the realistic yet disheartening films of the 1960's, *Star Wars* is a return to the adventure and fantasy films of early Hollywood; the plot is influenced by Westerns, comic-book characters such as Buck Rogers and Flash Gordon, medieval knights and sorcerers, and other science fiction films. Lucas wanted to re-create for contemporary young people the fantasy and excitement of old movies which he had seen as a child. Audiences wholeheartedly welcomed this "old-fashioned" swashbuckling tale complete with the happy ending, and within a year of its release, *Star Wars* had become the most profitable film ever made, surpassing the former first-place film, *Jaws* (1975), the leader of disaster films.

The saga begins with an introductory crawl describing the war between the Imperial forces and the Rebel Alliance, an eye-catching device which moves into the background rather than disappearing at the top of the frame as is the usual custom. It is a device which initiates in the audience the anticipation of new sights, and the action begins.

An Imperial spacecraft rumbles across the screen chasing a rebel ship belonging to the Princess Leia Organa (Carrie Fisher), one of the leaders of the Rebel Alliance. The Imperial cruiser shoots lasers at the smaller ship, causing much damage and buffeting the passengers, including two robots, C3PO (Anthony Daniels) and R2D2 (Kenny Baker), who, reminiscent of Laurel and Hardy, provide the comic relief of the film. As C3PO hides from the invading Imperial troopers, he notices the Princess feeding information into R2D2, but has no time to puzzle over this incident because the Princess is subsequently captured and most of the other humans onboard killed. R2D2 searches for C3PO and insists that they jettison away from the ship in an escape pod. The Imperial navigators spot the pod as they launch, but allow it to leave since they do not scan any life forms aboard. However, Darth Vader (David Prowse), Dark Lord of the Sith, later deduces that the plans stolen by the rebels are aboard the pod and sends Imperial troopers to retrieve the pod's contents.

R2D2 and C3PO crash on a desert planet called Tatooine and are captured by Jawas, scavengers of the planet, who deactivate them and load them onto a tank-sized vehicle called a sandcrawler. The Jawas sell the two robots to a local moisture farmer and his nephew Luke Skywalker (Mark Hamill). As Luke cleans R2D2, he accidentally sets off part of the Princess' message which appeals for help to an unknown Obi-Wan Kenobi (Alec Guinness) in a three-dimensional hologram message.

R2D2 runs away to find Obi–Wan Kenobi, with Luke and C3PO giving chase in Luke's jet-propelled landspeeder, a vehicle which skims along about a foot above the ground. They find R2D2, but the dangerous Tusken Raiders, better known as the Sand People, attack the three and almost kill Luke, who is rescued in time by an old hermit named Ben Kenobi. After bringing the group back to his cave, Ben Kenobi, *alias* Obi-Wan Kenobi, last of the Jedi knights, listens to Princess Leia's message, which tells him about the stored secret Death Star plans inside R2D2, and begs Ben Kenobi to deliver the plans to her father on Alderaan. Although Ben Kenobi asks Luke to join them on the mission, Luke refuses, saying that his uncle needs him during harvest. However, when Luke returns home and finds that Darth Vader's Imperial troops have murdered his uncle and aunt and burned the farm while searching for the plans, he vows vengeance and travels with Ben Kenobi and the robots to Mos Eisely, Tatooine's spaceport, in order to locate and hire a space pilot to take them to Alderaan.

Ben Kenobi heads for the local cantina and finds a Corellian smuggler named Han Solo (Harrison Ford) to ship them to Alderaan. Solo's first mate is a Wookiee called Chewbacca (Peter Mayhew), a seven-foot apelike being who is similar in personality to the Cowardly Lion in *The Wizard of Oz* (1939). As Solo's ship, the Millenium Falcon, takes off, it is pursued by Imperial ships but Solo calculates an accurate jump to hyperspace speed (faster-than-light speed), and the ship escapes capture. This hyperspace jump is one of the more spectacular effects, combining the sight of blurring stars as the jump is made with the roar of ship acceleration to create an exciting moment.

When the ship nears Alderaan and Solo returns to normal speed, the Death Star, an Imperial ship the size of a small planet, is in the area and traps the Falcon in its tracking beam. The Death Star's commander, Grand Moff Tarkin (Peter Cushing), Governor of the Imperial Outland Regions, has destroyed Alderaan because the Princess has refused to reveal any information about the stolen plans or the secret Rebel base. Imperial troopers board the Falcon but the occupants hide in Solo's smuggling holds and ambush them. Disguised in trooper uniforms, Luke and Solo rescue the Princess by pretending to take Chewbacca as prisoner to the incarceration levels, while Ben Kenobi shuts off the tracking beam and stalks his former protégé, Darth Vader. Ben Kenobi and Darth Vader duel with laser swords until, in order to divert attention from the rest of the Falcon party, Ben Kenobi allows himself to be killed. Moments later, Luke hears Ben Kenobi's voice, reminding him to use the Force, a mystical power Ben Kenobi and other Jedi knights used and lived by. The Falcon escapes from the Death Star and flies to the planet Yavin, the location of the secret Rebel base where the Alliance leaders peruse the plans and discover the only way to destroy the Death Star. A fighter craft must fire a laser into the center of the gigantic ship setting off a chain reaction which will detonate and destroy the Death Star. Luke tries to persuade Solo to join the mission but Solo refuses, considering the whole idea foolish and suicidal.

Darth Vader launches a group of fighters against the Rebel pilots, eventually destroying all Rebel fighters except Luke in an impressively choreographed space battle. Darth Vader himself is about to kill Luke when Solo appears in the nick of time and sends Darth Vader's fighter craft hurtling out into deep space. When Luke hears Ben Kenobi advising him to use the Force, Luke succeeds in destroying the Death Star and saving the Rebel Alliance.

Lucas originally wanted to make a new "Flash Gordon" picture laden with the special effects he thought the story deserved; but he could not get the rights to the characters and therefore decided to write *Star Wars*. Despite numerous obstacles in portraying another galaxy on film, Lucas persevered in expressing his imaginative visual ideas. He filmed Kenny Baker as R2D2 in standing shots only, using radio-controlled models for walking, plugging into outlets, and other moving scenes; these radio models behaved only on the first day of filming, after which they scurried everywhere in response to any stray radio signal. The hologram messages and the three dimensional chess game were created by transferring the pictures from film to videotape and then back to film, giving the images their wavering eerie quality. The laser swords were wrapped with material which reflected black light at two hundred times its original intensity, providing the swords with their glow. One very effective scene took place at a typical cantina, or bar, on Tatooine in which are assembled a motley mass of aliens, complete with a jazz combo playing a snappy tune on odd musical instruments. A humorous touch in this scene is provided by furnishing the audience with subtitles since all the aliens speak their own languages. For the space battles, Lucas scrutinized old World War II movie clips of air battles for plane positioning and sound mixing, imitating the sights and sounds but substituting laser beams for bullets. Lucas' idea was to film this galaxy as if he had packed up his film crew and shot everything on location, creating a "lived-in" look and conveying a believability.

In contrast to these strange sights, Lucas insisted that the music reflect the adventure and heroism rather than the alien galactic locations, and felt that the dramatic sounds of the Romantic era would be more appropriate than contemporary electronic music. John Williams wrote the Academy Award-winning score, which marked the current trend back to sweeping orchestral sounds and stirring fanfares in film music.

However, Lucas' talents lie more in the realm of film technique than film writing. The plot is a simplistic "shoot-em-up" war story of good *versus* evil, with stock characters such as the innocent hero, the beautiful damsel in distress, and the rogue with the heart of gold. The characters are shallow and always overshadowed by the technical aspects of the film and their dialogue is cartoonish and awkward. Although the sparse story line, weak characters, and lack of strong dialogue are obvious flaws, the visual effects are well done and so overwhelming that the impact of the film as a whole is not marred. *Star Wars* is very much like the youngsters for whom it was created: precocious yet naïve, charming and full of fun.

Ruth L. Hirayama

STATE OF THE UNION

Released: 1948
Production: Frank Capra for Metro-Goldwyn-Mayer
Direction: Frank Capra
Screenplay: Anthony Veiller and Myles Connolly; based on the play of the same name by Howard Lindsay and Russell Crouse
Cinematography: George J. Fosley
Editing: William Hornbeck
Running time: 124 minutes

Principal characters:

Grant Matthews .... Spencer Tracy
Mary Matthews .... Katharine Hepburn
Spike McManus .... Van Johnson
Kay Thorndyke .... Angela Lansbury
Jim Conover .... Adolphe Menjou
Sam Thorndyke .... Lewis Stone

The body of film work by Italian immigrant Frank Capra centers on the belief in "Life, Liberty and the Pursuit of Happiness" as set forth in the American Declaration of Independence. Often described as the principal Hollywood exponent of populism, Capra's ideologies support the individuality of the common man against the cynical world of political corruption and materialism. His films always show the triumphs of the honest man. While they have been criticized for the simplicity and naïveté of their politics and their inevitable happy endings, Capra at his best presents a heartwarming idealism which made him one of the most popular directors of the 1930's and early 1940's, with such films as *It Happened One Night* (1934), *Mr. Deeds Goes to Town* (1937), *You Can't Take It With You* (1939), *Mr. Smith Goes to Washington* (1939), *Meet John Doe* (1941), *Arsenic and Old Lace* (1944), and *It's A Wonderful Life* (1946).

It's a Wonderful Life was the first production of Capra's own company, Liberty Films, which he had formed with Samuel Briskin and directors George Stevens and William Wyler following World War II. The trademark for the company was appropriately the cracked Liberty Bell, and the first film was released through RKO/Radio, with whom Capra had arranged a deal to present nine films under the Liberty banner at a total cost of $15,000,000. However, when *It's a Wonderful Life* failed to return the profit RKO/Radio had expected, they refused to finance Liberty's next project, Capra's production of the popular Howard Lindsay and Russell Crouse play, *State of the Union*, which was budgeted at $2,800,000 and for which Gary Cooper had been discussed for the starring role.

When RKO/Radio vetoed the project, Capra became aware that M-G-M's

Spencer Tracy was interested in the role of Grant Matthews, and Capra took the project to Louis B. Mayer. He struck up a deal not unlike the one he entered into with David O. Selznick for *Gone with the Wind* in 1939. M-G-M would finance and release the production, Tracy would be the star, and M-G-M contractees Van Johnson and Angela Lansbury would join the cast. The part of the candidate's wife was to be played by Claudette Colbert.

Just three days before shooting was to begin, Colbert walked into Capra's office and informed him that a very important clause had been left out of her contract. In his autobiography, *The Name Above the Title*, Capra goes into great detail describing the scene. It seems that Colbert inserted into each of her contracts that she was not to work past 5 P.M. According to Capra, she told him her agent, who was her brother, always included this item in all her contracts because her doctor, who was her husband, said she got too tired if she worked any longer. Capra refused to acquiesce and Colbert walked out, an unwise career move for her as this film could have bolstered her greatly diminishing box-office appeal.

Capra first called Mayer, who told him to call Tracy before he heard the news from someone else. Tracy, who had been rehearsing his role with his friend Katharine Hepburn, suggested her for the part. Capra responded by asking, "You think she'd do it?" Tracy replied, "I dunno. But the bag of bones has been helping me rehearse. Kinda stops you, Frank, the way she reads the woman's part. She's a real theater nut, you know. She might do it for the hell of it." Hepburn agreed and the picture was on.

The Tracy-Hepburn relationship goes back to 1942 when they made *Woman of the Year*, the first of their nine films together. Hepburn had sold the idea for that film to M-G-M and felt that Tracy would be perfect as her costar in the picture which cast them as sparring newspaper columnists who marry. It was the beginning of one of the longest and most popular screen teams in motion picture history as they went on to make *Keeper of the Flame* (1942), *Without Love* (1945), *The Sea of Grass* (1947), *State of the Union*, *Adam's Rib* (1949), *Pat and Mike* (1952), *Desk Set* (1957), and *Guess Who's Coming to Dinner* (1967).

Lindsay and Crouse had written *State of the Union* as a vehicle for Helen Hayes. When Hayes turned down the role it was offered to both Margaret Sullavan and Katharine Hepburn, who both refused the role. When the play opened at the Hudson Theatre in New York City on November 14, 1945, its star was Ruth Hussey. The play ran for 765 performances. Sullavan later did the television version with Joseph Cotten on November 16, 1954.

Anthony Veiller and Myles Connolly fashioned the screenplay of the film. Wealthy aircraft manufacturer Grant Matthews (Spencer Tracy), an honest, liberal American hero-tycoon, is proposed as the dark horse Republican candidate for President of the United States. He and his wife Mary (Katharine Hepburn) are estranged, but she is talked into pretending that theirs is a solid marriage in order to help his campaign. She joins him in a cross-country campaign tour to alleviate any rumors of his romantic relationship with the seductive Kay Thorndyke (Angela Lansbury). Thorndyke is Matthews' most powerful supporter. She has inherited a chain of newspapers from her father who had once lost a presidential bid. She has her sights set on backing a candidate for president and being a powerful Washington influence, hostess, and, if she can pull it off, First Lady. Matthews' campaign manager is Jim Conover (Adolphe Menjou), an astute manipulator. Another strong supporter is Spike McManus (Van Johnson), a Drew Pearson-style newspaper columnist.

As his campaign progresses, Matthews gets caught up in the corruption of the political machinery and the variety of vested interests which must be pleased; he begins to sacrifice his ideals in order to win. The title of the play and film refers to not only the country, but also to the Matthews marriage. The Tracy-Hepburn chemistry works wonders with this aspect of the plot. On the cross-country tour they have a wonderful bedroom scene together. Mary has agreed to keep up the pretense of their marriage for his career but she is very much aware of his adulterous relationship with Kay Thorndyke, an element very much played down in the film. In their hotel room she takes over the bed and fixes a pallet for him on the floor. He presumes that the bed is to be his and in a typical Tracy-Hepburn battle of the sexes, he tries to convince her that they should share a bed. But she remains adamant.

Finally, Mary can no longer overlook the corruption of the campaign, and at an important dinner party she speaks out against the deceit and corruption. This spurs Matthews on to make a radio appeal in which he admits his dishonesty with the American people, withdraws from the race, and saves his marriage.

The play had relied upon sparkling Lindsay-Crouse topical political satire and jokes. Capra used the best of the play, adding and updating the political jibes to include many against Harry S Truman (the cross-country trip was not unlike the one Truman made) and Communism. The plot, in typical Capra style, takes on many facets of American political life—big business, agriculture, labor, the judiciary—all shown to wield considerable power over political aspirants. Some critics felt Capra's updating of the political satire weakened the script. For the most part it is a criticism which does not hold up when the film is viewed today with the retrospective knowledge of political corruption of the 1970's. While the politics may be oversimplified, as is the happy ending, the film packs a solid satirical punch at the business of politics, which is as valid today as ever.

The acting throughout is excellent. Tracy and Hepburn are ideal in their parts and a perfect screen team. Adolphe Menjou is properly cynical and unctuous as the unscrupulous campaign manager, and even Van Johnson gives an acceptable performance as the newspaper columnist. But the acting honors go to Angela Lansbury, whose icy bitchiness as Kay Thorndyke is a joy to watch. It is even more impressive when one realizes that at the time Lansbury was only twenty-two years old, depicting a woman in her mid-forties.

While the script makes numerous digs at Harry S Truman, he happily attended the Washington premiere of the film and found it so much to his liking that he ordered a print for the presidential yacht and showed the film repeatedly.

One additional note regarding *State of the Union* is the volatile political mood in Hollywood at the time the film was made, at the height of the House UnAmerican Activities Committee's investigation which led to hundreds being blacklisted and thus prevented from working in Hollywood. Adolphe Menjou was a rabid Communist hater and Hepburn was a known liberal. Capra says in his autobiography, however, that, while the two hated each other, there was never any hint of that animosity during the making of the picture.

Ronald Bowers

STELLA DALLAS

Released: 1937
Production: Samuel Goldwyn for United Artists
Direction: King Vidor
Screenplay: Victor Heerman and Sarah Y. Mason; based on the novel of the same name by Olive Higgins Prouty
Cinematography: Rudolph Maté
Editing: Sherman Todd
Running time: 108 minutes

Principal characters:

Stella Dallas	Barbara Stanwyck
Stephen Dallas	John Boles
Laurel Dallas	Anne Shirley
Helen Morrison	Barbara O'Neil
Ed Munn	Alan Hale
Mrs. Martin	Marjorie Main
Mr. Martin	Edmund Elton
Richard Grosvenor III	Tim Holt

Stella Dallas, adapted from the best-selling novel by Olive Higgins Prouty, is a story of frustrated mother love. It has had many lives, both in film and in radio. In 1925, Henry King directed a silent version of *Stella Dallas* starring Belle Bennett and Ronald Colman, and in 1937 King Vidor directed the best-known film adaptation with Barbara Stanwyck as the long-suffering Stella. So popular were the films and the novel that for years Stella Dallas, her daughter Laurel, and her various friends and neighbors were a staple on daytime radio. In short, *Stella Dallas* has been a part of American culture for a very long time.

The Vidor film is by far the most satisfying rendition of the story. Less sentimental than the book, and certainly less drawn out than the radio drama, it has the advantage of Barbara Stanwyck's performance as Stella. Stanwyck had shown early in her career that she had no peer when it came to playing women who were tough but goodhearted. A skilled comedienne (*The Lady Eve*, 1941) as well as a gifted dramatic actress, Stanwyck brought glamour, intelligence, and believability to all of her roles. In *Stella Dallas* she was called upon to enact some very emotional moments, and she handled such scenes with skill and delicacy, making them both poignant and touching. Indeed, she invested this old-fashioned melodrama with a quality that set it far above run-of-the-mill "tear jerkers."

The theme of the film is mother love and sacrifice. It deals with what happens when two basically decent people from different social classes marry, and how such a marriage affects the life of their child. It is, in a sense, reactionary, for in *Stella Dallas*, love across class lines does not work, although the film has no villains. Stella cannot blame anyone for her unhappiness or her lack of communication with her daughter: it is her background and circumstances that force her to make unhappy choices.

The film opens with the suicide of a well-known financier. His son, Stephen Dallas (John Boles), is ashamed and disgraced by his father's action and decides to move to another town to start life anew. Even Helen Dale (Barbara O'Neil), the woman he loves, cannot persuade him to stay. He goes to a mill town in New England and finds employment in a textile mill, eventually becoming assistant manager. When Dallas reads one day of Helen Dale's marriage to the wealthy Cornelius Morrison, he plunges himself into his work for consolation. He then meets the young and beautiful Stella Martin, daughter of a mill hand, when she brings her father's lunch to the office. Although clearly not a woman of much education, Stella is vivacious, kind, and lively. Stephen starts taking her out, much to the unease of her family, and within a few months, he marries her. It is apparent even before their marriage that trouble looms, for Stella and Stephen are not comfortable associating with the same kinds of people. Within a year, Stella gives birth to a baby girl, Laurel, whom she worships, but by this time, Stephen is already estranged from her. He is constantly aware of her essential vulgarity, which comes out at country club dances and at office functions. Stella, on her part, is bored by Stephen's colleagues, and finds a good friend of her own in Ed Munn (Alan Hale), a racetrack tout who begins dropping in to bring gifts for little Laurel. Stephen progresses in his business, and grabs the opportunity to be transferred to the company's branch office in New York. He insists that Stella stay behind, but comes home occasionally to see Laurel. It is now clear to Stella that their marriage, for all intents and purposes, is over.

Years pass, and Stella and Stephen become permanently separated. Laurel (Anne Shirley) goes to a select boarding school near Boston and meets her father from time to time in New York. Meanwhile, Stephen again meets Helen, now widowed, and they once more fall in love. Laurel gradually begins to turn against Stella; her boisterous conduct with Ed Munn makes Laurel stop inviting her friends home. Then she visits Helen Morrison in her fine home during summer vacation; her father is there too, and Laurel has a glimpse of a very different kind of life.

Stella finally becomes frightened that Helen and Stephen will take Laurel away from her, and she refuses to grant Stephen a divorce. She attempts to provide Laurel with better surroundings by taking her to an elegant resort, where Laurel meets Richard Grosvenor III (Tim Holt), a young man from a wealthy family. The two are immediately attracted to each other, but when Laurel overhears Richard's friends talking about her mother, she realizes that Stella has become a laughingstock because of her outlandish clothes and loud ways. Humiliated, Laurel insists that they return home. On the train, Stella hears a conversation between two of Laurel's friends from the resort that makes it perfectly clear why Laurel wanted to leave so quickly. When they arrive home, Stella takes the train to Boston to see Helen; she offers to divorce Stephen so that Helen and Stephen can make a proper home for Laurel. When Laurel hears from her father that she is to live with them, out of loyalty she tells him that she will not leave her mother. When she learns that it was her mother's idea and realizes that Stella is deliberately sacrificing herself, Laurel is more determined than ever to stay with Stella. But Stella is determined to do what is best for her daughter. When Laurel comes back to the house, Stella, in her most flamboyant outfit, greets her daughter feigning drunkenness. Ed Munn in tow, she pretends that Laurel is cramping her style. In the morning, Laurel is gone.

Several months later, in a kind of epilogue, we see Laurel's wedding day. Laurel is happy and excited, but feels badly that she has not heard from her mother. The house is beautifully decorated, and well-dressed guests are gathered to congratulate Laurel and Richard. Outside in the rain, a drab figure is able to peer into the brilliantly lit room because Laurel and Helen have deliberately left the curtains open. It is Stella Dallas.

Since the story is the stuff of which soap operas are made, it is a tribute to director King Vidor and to Barbara Stanwyck that *Stella Dallas* does not overflow into mawkish sentiment any more than it does. There are a few moments when the situations seem overdramatic, but the film is, for the most part, strong and effective melodrama. Alan Hale supplies much-needed comic relief as Ed Munn. John Boles is skillful in his role of the priggish Stephen, and Anne Shirley does well with a difficult part which requires that she show embarrassment tempered with love. Barbara Stanwyck's performance merited her an Oscar nomination, but she lost to Luise Rainer for *The Good Earth*.

Joan Cohen

THE STING

Released: 1973
Production: Tony Bill, Michael Phillips, and Julia Phillips for Universal (AA)
Direction: George Roy Hill (AA)
Screenplay: David S. Ward (AA)
Cinematography: Robert Surtees
Editing: William Reynolds (AA)
Art direction: Henry Bumstead (AA); set decoration, James Payne (AA)
Costume design: Edith Head (AA)
Music: Marvin Hamlisch (AA)
Running time: 129 minutes

Principal characters:

Johnny Hooker .... Robert Redford
Henry Gondorff .... Paul Newman
Doyle Lonnegan .... Robert Shaw
Luther Coleman .... Robert Earl Jones
Lieutenant William Snyder .... Charles Durning
FBI Agent Polk .... Dana Elcar
Billie .... Eileen Brennan
Loretta .... Dimitra Arliss

The Sting is an entertaining film about swindlers and hucksters which cons the audience just as cleverly as the protagonists trick their victim. What assured its popularity when it was released was the reunion of actors Paul Newman and Robert Redford with director George Roy Hill. The three had had tremendous success four years earlier with the release of *Butch Cassidy and the Sundance Kid* (1969), and *The Sting* was an attempt to repeat the formula. There are, however, some basic differences between the two: whereas *Butch Cassidy and the Sundance Kid* spun a more or less picaresque yarn—its two heroes traveling and bantering through a serial landscape of changing adventures—*The Sting*, after a short lead-in, pits the two against one villain and follows their single-minded quest to bring about his downfall.

Johnny Hooker (Robert Redford) is a small-time "grifter," or con-artist, working in Joliet, Illinois, during the worst days of the Great Depression. As the story begins, he and his partner Luther (Robert Earl Jones) inadvertently fleece a messenger for the mob. Although they become rich men for a day, the ultimate result is that Luther is murdered in retribution for the theft, and Hooker is forced to flee to Chicago, only steps ahead of the hit-men. The mobster who has Luther killed, Doyle Lonnegan (Robert Shaw), does not really need the money, the amount of which is inconsequential compared to his total wealth, but his pride is hurt. He also believes that he will lose control over the mob and respect for his authority if he allows even one such insult to his business and character to go unpunished.

Hooker arrives in Chicago and presents himself to Henry Gondorff (Paul Newman), a man of the "big con" whom Luther revered. Although Gondorff obviously has fallen upon hard times, he is, in fact, the great con-man that his legend purports him to be and desires just as much as Hooker to see Luther's death avenged. In addition, he could use a big sting, if only to boost his morale, and Lonnegan is too tempting an opportunity to pass up.

Hooker and Gondorff form an alliance for this purpose, and enlist the aid of a small army of con-men—most of whom also knew and respected Luther—to accomplish their goal. Setting out under assumed names, the two develop a detailed master plan which will cause Lonnegan to be "stung" gradually and step-by-step. Gondorff lays the bait by first humiliating Lonnegan at poker, and Hooker sets the trap by approaching him in the aftermath of this humiliation to offer him a share in the scheme he has developed for getting revenge against Gondorff. Lonnegan's greed and exaggerated lust for revenge are used against him by the con-men; and shown the lavish betting operation run by Gondorff, which Hooker claims can be bankrupted by the right bet placed at the right time, he is both impressed and persuaded to take a paternal interest in Hooker's future.

The plan is proceeding on schedule, but trouble arises in Hooker's private life: the hit-men that were on his trail in Joliet still pursue him; a corrupt detective (Charles Durning), also from Joliet, is snooping around; and the FBI also seems to be investigating him. Although the film at this point portrays a deep bond of affection between Hooker and Gondorff, it appears that Hooker may be forced to betray his friend and the whole operation. This, and many other allusions for both the audience and the film, reach their denouement in the climactic "sting." At a staged gambling casino, Lonnegan is lured into betting half a million dollars on what he thinks is both a sure thing and a way to bankrupt Gondorff; but he flies into a panicked rage when Hooker informs him that he has gotten his betting signals crossed and that the money cannot be retrieved. Lonnegan does not even have the comfort of knowing he was cheated. Just as the half-million-dollar loss begins to sink in, the FBI bursts into the fake casino, trailed by the Joliet detective. Gondorff is outraged by what he sees as this betrayal and shoots Hooker; then an FBI agent shoots Gondorff. Amid the confusion and apparent shootings, the detective persuades the confused and frightened Lonnegan to abandon his money and flee, not desiring his name to be associated with this mess; and the two escape together on the street.

The film, however, is not quite over: Hooker and Gondorff are not dead; they are not even wounded. The FBI, the betrayal, and the shooting were all part of the sting—steps taken to fleece money from Lonnegan, prevent his return, and get rid of the detective. Hooker and Gondorff get up, smiling, and to appreciative applause from the characters onscreen and, presumably, from the audience which has been stung by the hoax just as surely as Lonnegan was.

Time magazine panned *The Sting*, explicity commenting on its expensive sets and, in reference to Redford and Newman, its "screenful of blue eyes"; on the whole, however, the critical reaction to the film was positive, and it went on to become a big box-office hit in addition to sweeping the Academy Awards of 1973. Its first showing on network television netted a record share (61) of the viewing audience, and a survey taken five years after its first release listed it as number eight among the ten top moneymaking films to that time.

The credit for this success belongs equally to the actors, screenwriter, and director. Even apart from Paul Newman, Robert Redford, and George Roy Hill, whose contributions together would almost certainly have made the film a hit, it is the particular contributions of Robert Shaw as Lonnegan and of David Ward's script that make the film such good entertainment. Redford and Newman play their roles with a presence which is both dramatically effective and yet slyly self-aware. Redford's magnetic energy is perfectly offset by Newman's profounder, more serpentine quality; and both are complemented by Robert Shaw whose Lonnegan characterization is a model of style and subtlety. The incongruity of a dark, brooding gangster with an Irish brogue fits so well with the surrealist texture of the film that it virtually slips by unnoticed; Shaw calls no attention to himself except to provide the film with its one element of real menace.

David Ward's script is responsible for the major structural strategies—such as the use of titles for various segments of the film and the trick ending—as well as the minor ones. The story is believable in the manner of fantasy rather than probability, and the film's dialogue presents its own idiom, reflected in all the characters' speech, that seems extracted more from books than from experience. Since the parody also seems conscious, it has a unifying effect that supports the surrealist or dreamlike quality of the tale's geometry in outfoxing its audience as neatly as its protagonists do the villain. It thus becomes a metaphor for its own process. These subtleties would have been botched in the wrong hands. The film needed and received Redford, Newman, and Shaw to give some sense of a human life beyond its mere structure. It also needed George Roy Hill to give the film its visual texture and handle the actors sensitively so that an audience would care about the outcome.

Entertainment is the fundamental word that applies to any George Roy Hill film. Whatever their other virtues, his films—*The Sting*, *Butch Cassidy and the Sundance Kid*, *Slaughterhouse-Five* (1972), and *A Little Romance* (1979)—have entertainment as their prime motivation, and in *The Sting* this priority is raised to the level of a major preoccupation. "The Entertainer" by Scott Joplin is its musical theme; the illustrated title-cards that serve as chapter heads for the plot's developments also serve, not only as a lesson in con-artistry, but in the storyteller's creative artistry as well: "The Hook," "The Tale," "The Wire," "The Sting." Seldom has a popular film been so freely able to comment on itself without impeding the forward movement of the plot.

If *The Sting* has any weakness, it is that women are withheld from the mainstream of the plot. Eileen Brennan as Gondorff's whore-girl friend and Dimitra Arliss as a hit-woman sent after Hooker add nothing essential to the overall picture. *The Sting*'s contribution to film history seems minor if one overlooks its box-office record, yet the film is a 1970's archetype; escapist, romantic, and stylishly entertaining, it manages to seem timeless. Yet it would not have been possible in its final form except as a reaction to the more downbeat, antiheroic, conscience-haunted films that came out of Hollywood in the late 1960's.

F. X. Feeney

THE STORY OF G.I. JOE

Released: 1945
Production: Lester Cowan for United Artists
Direction: William A. Wellman
Screenplay: Leopold Atlas, Guy Endore, and Philip Stevenson; based on the books *Here Is Your War* and *Brave Men* by Ernie Pyle
Cinematography: Russell Metty
Editing: Albrecht Joseph and Otho Lovering
Music: Ann Ronell and Louise Applebaum
Running time: 108 minutes

Principal characters:

Ernie Pyle	Burgess Meredith
Lieutenant Walker	Robert Mitchum
Sergeant Warnicki	Freddie Steele
Private Dondaro	Wally Cassell
Private Spencer	Jimmy Lloyd
Private Murphy	Jack Reilly
Private Mew	Bill Murphy

"The greatest war picture I've ever seen," said General Eisenhower of *The Story of G.I. Joe*. Directed by veteran filmmaker William A. Wellman (*Wings*, 1927; *The Public Enemy*, 1931; *A Star Is Born*, 1937; *Nothing Sacred*, 1937; *Beau Geste*, 1939; *The Ox-Bow Incident*, 1942; and *Battleground*, 1949), the tense, dramatic, near-documentary film is based on the actual battle experiences of the famous war correspondent, Ernie Pyle, played by Burgess Meredith.

A native of Indiana, the eloquent Ernie Pyle studied journalism at Indiana University, and started his career by writing for the *Washington News* and the *New York World Telegram and Post*. After that, he became aviation editor for the Scripps-Howard newspapers; by 1940, he was in London, where he witnessed the severe bomb attacks on that city. In 1944, Pyle won the Pulitzer Prize for his distinguished reporting. He also won the Purple Heart for wounds he suffered during the invasion of Anzio, Italy.

A simple man who wrote simply of the common, unglorified, hard-fighting foot soldiers, Pyle wrote the books *Here Is Your War* and *Brave Men*, which served as the basis for the screenplay of *The Story of G.I. Joe*. Physically resembling the journalist, in terms of his thin face and slight build, Burgess Meredith successfully captures the character of the restrained, humble, and understanding observer.

Unlike the conventional Hollywood war films or action sagas, Wellman's well-crafted picture, enhanced by Russell Metty's subtle lighting, conspicuously lacks spectacular battle sequences. There are no phony heroics, no theatrics, and no major climax. Instead, the film deals with the human-interest side of combat as it captures the emotions of ordinary men. The sober, low-key, level-headed study focuses on the day-to-day, unglamorous struggles of the infantrymen as they try to survive. We witness the men's fears, foibles, weaknesses, and loneliness, their weariness, hunger, and boredom. We witness their longings to go home; and we see how they live and die.

The Story of G.I. Joe is not a story in the traditional sense; it has many scenes which end quite abruptly. The story is an authentic, unaffected narrative made up of small but significant incidents. Beginning in Africa, the movie shows us the idle nighttime conversation of the members of Company C (Charlie) of the 18th Infantry. New to his work as a war correspondent, Ernie Pyle (Burgess Meredith) wanders in. At dawn, the squad leaves for the front, and Pyle, at the suggestion of Lieutenant Walker (Robert Mitchum), joins them as they pass through Sicily into Italy and on into Rome. The men experience the effects of the Battle of San Vittorio. The streets are reduced to rubble; the cafés with their frightened barmaids are completely wrecked.

When the squadron receives orders from Eisenhower to bomb the monastery at Monte Cassino, there follows a bitter struggle with defending German forces which delays the Allied victory. With affection, camaraderie, and compassion, Ernie Pyle notes how Sergeant Warnicki (Freddie Steele) undergoes a mental breakdown from stress. He observes the many casualties, including the humane platoon leader, Walker who befriends him, and who dies before the company reaches Rome.

An uncompromisingly grim picture of war, *The Story of G.I. Joe* is totally realistic. Not only did the film receive technical guidance from The Army Ground Forces and War Correspondents, there is Signal Corps footage of the North African and Italian campaigns. A corps of extras were made up of more than one hundred and fifty combat veterans of the Fifth Army, some of whom had speaking roles. With an honesty and straightforward realism, the dirty, exhausted, drenched soldiers and their blood-and-sweat exploits are depicted with humor, poignance, and drama. While stark and factual, the film also has poetic and moving touches, including the sergeant who repeatedly plays the record of his baby son's voice; the German soldier who tolls his own death knell; the fighting of unseen enemies in the demolished church; and the farewell to the beloved Walker as his body is carried on the back of a mule through a mountain valley.

Although cast largely with unknowns, *The Story of G.I. Joe* enjoys the dignified portrayal of Pyle by Burgess Meredith; the drama is further enhanced by the fine performance of the stubby-bearded, lean-faced Robert Mitchum in the role of the stony, exhausted Lieutenant Walker. Bitter, hardened, steadfast, and stoic, the platoon leader, who says very little in the film, writes to his soldiers' families after they die, breaks in new men as their replacements, helplessly watches Warnicki go mad, speaks of his wife who walked out on him, and wonders about the war's misuse of human energy. In the end, the officer himself dies during the bloody Italian campaign. For his efforts, Mitchum was nominated for an Academy Award as Best Supporting Actor.

A heartrending, sincere tribute to the suffering and sacrifice endured by infantrymen, this nonhistrionic, classic World War II film makes very clear, in its subdued, unobtrusive manner, that war is hell. Without accusing any one faction, and without presenting any one remedy, *The Story of G.I. Joe* is as severe an indictment of war as any film ever made. Slow at times and sentimental in parts, the film resembles two other war films which were adapted from novels or news articles, which combined fiction and documentary, and which were done under experienced directors: John Ford's *They Were Expendable* (1945) and Lewis Milestone's *A Walk in the Sun* (1945).

Leslie Taubman

A STREETCAR NAMED DESIRE

Released: 1951
Production: Charles K. Feldman for Warner Bros.
Direction: Elia Kazan
Screenplay: Tennessee Williams; based on Oscar Saul's adaptation of the play of the same name by Tennessee Williams
Cinematography: Harry Stradling
Editing: David Weisbart
Art direction: Richard Day (AA)
Set decoration: George James Hopkins (AA)
Running time: 125 minutes

Principal characters:
Blanche .... Vivien Leigh (AA)
Stanley Kowalski ....Marlon Brando
Stella Kowalski .... Kim Hunter (AA)
Mitch .... Karl Malden (AA)

Elia Kazan's *A Streetcar Named Desire*, the 1951 film version of Tennessee Williams' Pulitzer Prize-winning play, draws heavily on the original. In it, Kazan, who also directed the Broadway version, created a film which challenged the censors at a time when adult drama was unacceptable on the screen. The number of changes required to please the censors was remarkably small, however, and does not diminish the impact of this story of a woman's demise. Many critics in 1951 applauded the adaptation, assuming that Hollywood censor Joseph Breen was allowing a more open treatment of sexual subjects in order for cinema to compete with the growing popularity of television. However, others viewed the film as going beyond the boundaries of good taste and faulted it for appearing too stagey. In retrospect, these latter criticisms seem linked more to the attitudes of the day than to aesthetic commentary.

The story concerns the mental destruction of Blanche (Vivien Leigh), a woman who has found her superficial genteel Southern propriety no match for the assaults of society. When she arrives in New Orleans to visit her sister and brother-in-law, Stella (Kim Hunter) and Stanley Kowalski (Marlon Brando), Blanche reveals her fragile emotional state through her demeanor. She has come to visit only because she has nowhere else to go. Vivien Leigh, in her first Hollywood film since *That Hamilton Woman* (1942), re-creates her role in the London production of the play and uses physical gesture and facial expression to portray Blanche sensitively. Her movements subtly betray her tenuous hold on reality and the struggle she is going through to maintain that hold. Should she abandon her role as a lady in a world of her own creation, she will abandon her reality. Her confrontation with the brutish Stanley Kowalski proves to be her downfall.

Stella, Blanche's younger sister, has turned her back on her decaying aristocratic background and found happiness with working-class, animalistic Stanley. She is pregnant, a condition she tries to hide from Blanche. Kim Hunter, who originally played Stella on Broadway, lends her role sympathy and warmth. Stella responds to her sister with loving memories of a shared childhood, willing to shelter her from the harsh realities of the present. Yet she has found love in a different milieu and is not willing to sacrifice this newly found stability in her life.

Blanche, left to care for the family holdings, has lost the home, her job, and her respect, yet she is unable to admit the truth to either herself or Stella. Stanley's insensitivity to Blanche's fragile emotional condition coupled with the feeling that Stella has been cheated out of her inheritance lead him to refuse to pamper Blanche, as Stella would have him do.

When Blanche meets Stanley's friend Mitch (Karl Malden), she finds a naïve admirer of her genteel ways. Mitch behaves as a gentleman, reponds to Blanche's coquettish behavior, and provides her with one final chance to realize her self-preserving fantasy. However, Stanley cannot allow what he perceives as dishonesty to exist. He learns of Blanche's tawdry past: losing her teaching position as a result of an affair with one of her students, turning to prostitution, and eventually being run out of town. He informs Mitch and Stella of Blanche's past, thereby destroying her last hope of maintaining her sanity.

Blanche learns of Stanley's actions at her birthday party. Mitch has been invited, but he does not appear. When Stella suddenly goes into labor, Blanche, left alone, drifts into her fantasy world. Mitch arrives, angry that Blanche has betrayed him. However, she gathers together what little emotional strength she has and confronts her past, telling Mitch even more than he wants to know. Again left alone, Blanche turns to the remnants of her world and dresses herself in faded finery to fabricate her nonexistent life.

When Stanley returns home, swollen with pride over being a father, he finds a drunken Blanche. His own small reserve weakened by liquor, Stanley rapes her, causing Blanche's final break with reality. As the film closes, Blanche is being taken to an institution. Her fantasy still intact, only "the kindness of strangers" convinces her to accompany the elderly gentleman to a place where fantasy becomes reality.

Only a certain degree of the play's frank treatment of sex has been retained, and that through suggestion rather than explicit statement. In the stage version, Blanche's demise begins when her youthful husband commits suicide because he has been caught in a homosexual encounter. Blanche relates this episode in the film, avoiding mention of homosexuality. In a similar manner, the rape scene, which was considered explicit at the time of the stage presentation, has been toned down in the film. A further bow to the censors occurs at the end of the film: Stella, instead of standing by Stanley, pushes the baby carriage off down the street in disgust and censure of Stanley's insensitivity.

In spite of the minor departures from the original, however, the film exemplifies a play successfully adapted to the screen. Tennessee Williams assisted in preparation of the screenplay and is said to have preferred the film to the stage version. The characters of Blanche and Stanley are more polarized in the film, Blanche eliciting sympathy and Stanley becoming totally unsympathetic. The restricted movement of the story proves an arresting quality in the film. In like manner, the monologues are effective in comparison with the undistinguished dialogue so often employed in screenplays.

The acting is exceptional throughout. Vivien Leigh portrays Blanche with the vulnerability of a trapped animal when confronted by Stanley, yet she is hard and cold when forced by Mitch to accept the truth about her past. She is coquettish when trying to win Mitch's attention, and effective as a lonely woman desperate for sexual attention when she flirts with a young delivery boy. In view of the task of portraying conflicting emotions often requiring sudden change, Leigh performs admirably. Her efforts were recognized with the Academy Award for Best Actress of the Year.

Marlon Brando, in his second screen appearance, re-creates his Broadway role as Stanley. His strong performance verges on overpowering the other excellent portrayals in the film. As a result of this role, one of the most memorable of his noteworthy career, the public often stereotypes him as the animalistic, physical man in the tee shirt that he portrays in this film. Nominated for an Academy Award for his performance, Brando lost to Humphrey Bogart for his role in *The African Queen*.

Both Karl Malden and Kim Hunter received Academy Awards for their supporting roles in the film, roles which they had also played on Broadway. Malden offers one of his most credible performances as the man who seeks propriety in the middle of his coarse environment. He effectively plays to Blanche and evidences his appreciation for what she represents in both his anger at her betrayal and his anger at Stanley's actions, which destroy what might have been. Despite the understandable flaws of Mitch's character, Malden gives him sympathy and a convincing quality of goodness. Likewise, Kim Hunter creates a sympathetic character in Stella. Her role, clearly one of support, points out the fragile balance in which Blanche lives. She shows both love and loyalty to her sister and to her husband, in spite of the internal conflict this creates.

The technical qualities of the film reinforce the stage heritage of the story. Filmed in black-and-white, the cinematography never detracts from the subjective views of the characters. Indirect light sources never illuminate the full set, in keeping with the shadowed secrets Blanche has to hide. Not only would direct light divulge her true age, but it would also render her vulnerable to the truth. The action is wisely confined to the apartment, the courtyard, and the dock where Mitch and Blanche talk under a lamppost. Art director Richard Day and set decorator George James Hopkins effectively lend the film the necessary seaminess and the atmosphere of New Orleans, which earned them the recognition of the Motion Picture Academy for their work.

All of these elements combine to produce a powerful piece of filmmaking. Yet credit must also go to Elia Kazan for bringing together technical specialists and performers who could blend their talents to create this film. Often derisively labeled a director of dreary films, Kazan demonstrates that such ventures can be artistic and successful in *A Streetcar Named Desire*. The demise of an individual is certainly not light fare; however, that such a film has remained engaging for years destroys the prejudice that "dreary" films cannot distinguish the work of a director.

Removed from the restrictive attitudes of its day, the film stands on its own merits. *A Streetcar Named Desire* combines excellent acting, sensitive use of technique, an impressive screenplay, and a faithful adaptation from another medium to prove that film can be art. It can be appreciated more objectively today, and, to its credit, the film's timeless look has earned it praise as a masterpiece of cinema.

Kenneth T. Burles

THE STRUGGLE

Released: 1931
Production: D. W. Griffith for D. W. Griffith, Inc./United Artists
Direction: D. W. Griffith
Screenplay: Anita Loos, John Emerson, and D. W. Griffith
Cinematography: Joseph Ruttenberg
Editing: Barney Rogan
Running time: 87 minutes

Principal characters:

Jimmie Wilson	Hal Skelly
Florrie	Zita Johann
Nina	Charlotte Wynters
Nan Wilson	Evelyn Baldwin
Johnnie Marshall	Jackson Halliday
Mary	Edna Hagan

The end of any great man's career is a sad occasion. In D. W. Griffith's case it was doubly so, for his last film, *The Struggle*, was greeted with universal contempt when it was first shown in 1931. It was not until after the director's death that critics and scholars alike came to recognize the film as a pioneering early talkie of considerable dramatic and emotional power. It is certainly far superior to Griffith's only other sound production, *Abraham Lincoln* (1930). In many respects, watching *The Struggle* is a reminder that tastes may change. A film considered extraordinary ten years ago may be dismissed as unimportant today; as with *The Struggle*, what contemporary critics might have described as poor cinematography can now be recognized as a realistic documentary style; or what was once old-fashioned can suddenly seem very modern. Tastes often change for the worse, but in this case they have changed for the better.

D. W. Griffith intended *The Struggle* as a protest against reformers in general and prohibition in particular. As far back as *Intolerance* (1916), he had preached against do-gooders and the harm they can create with their puritanical, unfeeling use of reform. Griffith had once angrily remarked that should Christ reappear in prohibition America, he would be jailed as a bootlegger. In *The Struggle*, the director used prohibition as a backdrop for his highly personal human drama. He described the film's title as symbolizing both the struggle of man against his own infirmities and the struggle of a nation against an adverse social condition.

The film begins on a beautiful and serene day in 1911; happy people sit in a beer garden, quietly relaxing and talking about "The Biograph Girl," a reminder of Griffith's beginnings in the cinema. From this idyllic scene, the director cuts to the present, to an America living under prohibition. To further emphasize his point, the director shows not a peaceful, outdoor restaurant-bar, but a typical shabby, working-class neighborhood in New York. Even the drab sets, which caused contemporary critics to complain, add to the feeling of a harsh life-style.

The central male character in the film is Jimmie, played by a stage and vaudeville performer named Hal Skelly. At the urging of his fiancée Florrie, played by the beautiful and vaguely exotic Zita Johann, Jimmie abandons his hip flask and settles down to what should be a happy marriage, a marriage which brings forth a daughter named Mary. However, events overtake the family and Jimmie returns to drinking, urged on by what appear to be trivial matters: his friends call him a "pansy" when he will not join them in a saloon. Because his wife wants him to wear a particular tie which he considers effeminate, Jimmie leaves his sister's engagement party, and again begins to drink heavily. Liquor is shown not only as a solace for the working classes, but also as its greatest danger, particularly in prohibition days when "bad liquor" had to be consumed quickly and furtively, rather than enjoyed as a relaxation. The engagement party offers the first major hint of what a serious problem alcohol will be for Jimmie. He is obnoxious to the party guests and insults the boss of his sister's boyfriend, forcing her to break off the engagement. (The sister is played by Evelyn Baldwin, who was later to become the second Mrs. D. W. Griffith.)

Life disintegrates for Jimmie and his wife. Urged on by a dance-hall tart, he cashes in an insurance policy in order to participate in a scheme to import liquor from Canada. Of course, he is swindled out of the money. His wife and sister are evicted from their apartment, and when Jimmie returns, he finds the place empty. As he wanders from room to room, the sound of a religious broadcast can be heard on the radio. "I am the Way and the Truth and the Light. No one cometh unto the Father but by me," says the voice, followed by an organ playing "Abide with Me." The scene could have become as maudlin as Jimmie himself becomes at that moment, but Griffith's careful direction keeps it both moving and impressive through the solo acting of Skelly and the use of sound.

Jimmie has now become a drink-sodden bum, wandering the streets of the Bronx around 175th Street—the location of the new Biograph studios, at which *The Struggle* was shot. Griffith's innovative documentary style is at its best in these scenes. The camera follows Skelly until some children spy him and run off to tell his daughter that her father has become a "beggin' bum." The girl tearfully runs after her wayward father and locates him on an abandoned floor of a tenement building. She runs back to find her mother, but she is not home. The girl leaves a note and returns to her father to plead with him to accompany her back home. By this time, Jimmie has gone into delirium tremens and attacks his daughter, whom he no longer recognizes

Just as all seems lost, the mother arrives, the door is broken down, and both Jimmie and the girl are saved.

Despite the slightly melodramatic nature of the editing, as well as the lightning flashes and the sound of thunder on the track, Griffith here demonstrates his favorite style of direction: the last-minute rescue that made him famous. His old flair for crosscutting to underline the urgency of the situation had not deserted him. There are elements of the rescue sequences in *The Birth of A Nation* (1914), *Way Down East* (1920) and *Orphans of the Storm* (1922) here, not to mention the famous closet sequence from *Broken Blossoms* (1919). Griffith had almost a fixation for scenes in which young, pure, innocent girls were under attack. He should have realized that by 1931 audiences were unwilling to accept such plot contrivances. No matter how good the acting was—and it is exceedingly good—audience sympathy could not be aroused, and most viewers would have agreed with one New York newspaper critic who contended that the film looked as if it had been made in New Rochelle in 1908.

In a brief ending, Jimmie is nursed back to sober health by his wife. The family moves into a new apartment, the sister and her boyfriend are reunited, and Jimmie proudly tells his wife that his new invention is to be installed in the factory where he works. As the family's happiness floods over the film frame, Florrie murmurs lovingly, "Jimmie, your eyes are all shiny." The ending mattered little at the film's premiere, for by this time most of the audience had walked out in disgust. Griffith, like his hero, found solace in liquor, and the career of the greatest film director the world has known came to a sorrowful end.

Considering Griffith's complete *ouvre* of films, from his Biograph shorts of the 1910's and pre-1910's through the masterpieces of the mid-1910's and the program pictures of the mid-to-late 1920's, *The Struggle* deserves a place. It is obviously not on a plateau with *The Birth of a Nation* or *Intolerance*, but it can stand proudly alongside *Hearts of the World* (1918) and *Isn't Life Wonderful* (1924) as one of the director's finer works.

Anthony Slide

SULLIVAN'S TRAVELS

Released: 1941
Production: Paul Jones for Paramount
Direction: Preston Sturges
Screenplay: Preston Sturges
Cinematography: John F. Seitz
Editing: Stuart Gilmore
Running time: 90 minutes

Principal characters:

John L. Sullivan	Joel McCrea
The Girl	Veronica Lake
Mr. Lebrand	Robert Warwick
Mr. Jones	William Demarest
Mr. Casalsis	Franklin Pangborn
Mr. Hadrian	Porter Hall
The Warden	Alan Bridge
Sullivan's Butler	Robert Greig
Sullivan's Valet	Eric Blore
The Preacher	Arthur Hoyt

Sullivan's Travels is Preston Sturges' version of Fellini's *8½* (1963) and Swift's *Gulliver's Travels* wrapped up into one. The titles begin on a book cover depicting Sullivan and his female companion dressed as hoboes. Slowly the book opens, and as it does, the viewer is taken inside, to be conducted on a Sturges tour of this "cockeyed caravan" called "life." Although the film concentrates, like Fellini's *8½*, on the art form from which it was produced, it also wanders periodically into the world of Lilliputians, Houyhnhnms, Laputans, and the like. The lives of railroad bums, frustrated widows, and mistreated prisoners are explored as far as Sturges' knowledge of these people and their situations could carry him, which admittedly, with his middle-class background, is not far. The film is Sturges' journey through this sometimes incomprehensible universe and into himself, to seek justification for his own existence. Because of its introspective probing, many consider *Sullivan's Travels* the director's most significant work; in any case, it is surely one of his most deeply felt.

The film opens with a fight between two men, a bum and a yard boss, atop a moving train. As their violent struggle continues, a series of gunshots resound on the sound track, and the two adversaries tumble into the water below. Superimposed over the gurgling river appears The End title. As it fades, the lights in the screening room come up and through an elaborate and rapidfire dialogue scene the viewer is informed that this was the finale of a "socially conscious" epic which director John L. Sullivan (Joel McCrea) has recently completed. Sullivan, through most of his career, has churned out comedies such as *Ants in Your Pants of 1939*; but now, to the consternation of the studio, he wants to direct more "meaningful" movies. A thick, ponderous book called *O Brother, Where Art Thou?* is his newest project. Before he can begin, however, he feels that he must learn about poverty and misery at firsthand; he must sample "the bitter dregs of vicissitude" and then use the material he uncovers for his film. So, contrary to the advice of friends and associates, Sullivan, dressed as a hobo, begins his "travels."

The worlds Sullivan encounters, like those upon which Gulliver stumbles, are somewhat misshapen by comic parody and, in Sturges' case, by a degree of sentimentality. On his first trek Sullivan is captured by a pair of lonely sisters, one of whom, a sexually voracious widow, locks Sullivan in a bedroom and watches him like a "bug in a jar." Before he becomes a permanent fixture on this isolated farm, however, he escapes. While buying a cup of coffee in a roadside diner, Sullivan meets a starlet (Veronica Lake) dressed in evening clothes and disappointedly heading for home. After buying Sullivan breakfast ("You know the nice thing about buying food for a man is that you don't have to laugh at his jokes"), he gives her a ride in a car which she suspects he must have stolen.

After Sullivan clears up a charge of stealing his own car, he returns to the studio environs with very little new experience to his credit. Still determined to break out of his environment, he sets out on another "voyage," this time accompanied by his new female companion. Hopping trains (after incongruously having been chauffered to the train yard in a limousine), sleeping in flophouses, attending mission revival meetings, and scraping garbage pails are a few of the items on the itinerary. After indulging themselves fully, and finally realizing that they are sick of this sample of poverty, the two travelers flee to the safety and comfort of Hollywood.

Sullivan's final expedition, however, proves to be his most educational, probably because it is completely unplanned. In a "generous" gesture Sullivan goes back to the flophouses and railroad yards to hand out five-dollar bills to those less fortunate than he. While performing this act of condescension he is knocked out and robbed by one of his beneficiaries. After a series of complications including an erroneous report of his death, Sullivan is arrested for striking a yard boss and sent to a work farm in the swamps. There he is beaten by a sadistic warden (Alan Bridge), punished in a sweat box, and forced to labor on a chain gang. Pain and misery permeate this hell-hole, yet in this most despicable of places Sullivan learns his most important lesson about himself, his art, and people in general.

One Sunday night the prisoners are invited by the black parishioners of a local church to share a "picture show" with them. The sequence opens with a dimly lit long shot of a slightly decrepit rural church surrounded by a light mist. Inside, the parishioners are singing an old spiritual, "Let My People

Go," as the weary prisoners—chained to one another—approach the building. As they enter, the camera cuts to a low angle, enabling the viewer to see the men's chained legs as they march up the center aisle with a funerallike cadence.

When they are finally seated, the Reverend (Arthur Hoyt) starts the ancient projector. It groans with age as it picks up speed. A Mickey Mouse cartoon flashes onto the improvised screen. As Pluto dashes across a room and falls, predictably, on his face, laughter rocks the old building. Sullivan looks about him in amazement. Gone is the pain from the faces of his cellmates; gone is the enmity between races; gone is the brutality of the warden as faces light up with laughter. Soon Sullivan finds that he, too, has been infected. In this admittedly sentimental sequence Sturges defends the act of moviegoing not only as an escape from the grim realities of life but also more significantly, as an almost religious experience where the ideal of brotherhood, rarely realized elsewhere, becomes a reality. It is ultimately a depressing statement in its implications, for it rejects the cinema as a tool for social change; yet it remains basically idealistic in its sentimental attachment to comedy as a therapeutic and enriching experience. It remains the vision of a man who pessimistically denies the revolutionary potential of the cinema but who dotes on the few hours we spend communally in movie theaters.

At the end of the film, Sullivan is returned to Hollywood by means of his false confession to a murder which places his picture on the front page of major newspapers, thereby enabling his friends to see that he is still alive. The director resolves to make only comedies in the future. This confirms the "message" of the earlier scene, while at the same time contrasting the finale with the opening sequence.

Although *Sullivan's Travels* is classified as a comedy, it, like *The Great McGinty* (1940), *Christmas in July* (1940), and *Unfaithfully Yours* (1948), contains long stretches of drama. The oppressive atmosphere of the prison camp, heightened by the somber images of beatings, back-breaking labor, and torture, are sufficient to convince the viewer that the film has changed gears and shifted into drama. The lighting of much of the film is also representative of this low-key approach. The sets are more often than not dimly lighted with chiaroscuro shadows. In this manner Sturges telegraphs the melancholy mood for which he is aiming.

One of Sturges' favorite blendings, that of visual slapstick with verbal sophistication, can be observed in action in this film, particularly in the cross-country chase scene early in the movie. A studio trailer carrying a cameraman, secretaries, a doctor, and other studio flunkies is sent out to protect and observe Sullivan during his first foray. Not long after the trek begins, the caravan is forced to take off at top speed after a homemade "tank" carrying the escaping Sullivan. Dishes and pans fly about the kitchen, a motorcycle policeman is splashed with mud, and objects in the road are overturned or nearly missed. The rhythm of the editing is brisk and the shots are timed to the breakneck "William Tell Overture." It is pure, unabashed slapstick of the brand which had steadily lost ground since the advent of sound. The dialogue patterns Sturges had developed in his scripts of the 1930's and refined in the 1940's are also seen at their best here. The opening long take in the studio chief's office lasts more than four minutes and contains some of the fastest dialogue and best-timed performances, in terms of both movement and speech, on film.

James Ursini

SUMMER OF '42

Released: 1971
Production: Richard A. Roth for Warner Bros.
Direction: Robert Mulligan
Screenplay: Herman Raucher
Cinematography: Robert Surtees
Editing: Folmar Blangsted
Music: Michel Legrand (AA)
Running time: 102 minutes

Principal characters:
Hermie .... Gary Grimes
Oscy .... Jerry Houser
Benjie .... Oliver Conant
Dorothy .... Jennifer O'Neill

Summer of '42 delivers a healthy dose of pure schmaltz, but it is to director Robert Mulligan's credit that the film is quite watchable, and even enjoyable. The screenplay, its Academy Award nomination notwithstanding, teeters on the verge of sentimentalism; but Mulligan handles his actors with skill, sets scenes with an eye to humor, and sketches in backgrounds with realism. He flirts with the dangerous morass of sentiment, using highly romantic photography and music, but he uses the best: diffuse soft-focus cinematography by the eminent cinematographer Robert Surtees, and a dreamy score by Michel Legrand. The film that results is what one critic described as "impeccable schmaltz."

The film's theme is the transition from boyhood to manhood. With gentle humor, screenwriter Herman Raucher reminds us of the time in every young man's life when nothing seems so important as the half-dreaded moment when he will lose his virginity. The characterizations are humorous and energetic. Hermie (Gary Grimes), Oscy (Jerry Houser), and Benjie (Oliver Conant) are almost certainly products of Raucher's memory rather than of his imagination; in fact, the film is structured as a memoir with an adult narrator remembering a summer almost thirty years in the past. But just as Raucher's closeness to the subject works in his favor in producing realistic characters and situations, it works against him in his handling of the sentiment. Thirty years have not distanced him sufficiently from Dorothy (Jennifer O'Neill); when he writes about her he is fifteen again.

The story unfolds on an island off the Eastern seaboard where the three boys' families are spending the summer. There are reminders that a war is going on and that brothers and cousins are off fighting. There is a sense, as the three while away the long summer days, of their frustration and lack of fulfillment. They are not yet adults but they are no longer quite children.

Their major interest is sex, and since they inhabit a time when sex education was not yet an academic subject, they are dependent on their own ingenuity to uncover its truths. Oscy, the leader, spends virtually all his waking hours contemplating and discoursing upon the tactical difficulties of making physical contact with a girl. Hermie, the sensitive hero, falls in love at a distance with the lovely image of a neighbor, Dorothy, who—at twenty-two and married—seems completely unattainable. Benjie, the least mature of the three (he bolts when Oscy tries to arrange a date for him), is primarily the butt of Oscy's jokes, but he does achieve a degree of stature when he reveals that he has discovered a medical text in his parents' house with a whole chapter on sex.

In a series of humorous vignettes Raucher's script captures the boys' eagerness and confusion at crossing the threshold to adulthood. Especially memorable is a scene in which Oscy and Hermie and their young dates watch *Now, Voyager* at the movies while the boys' hands gradually explore. As Bette Davis and Paul Henreid on the silver screen discuss why they cannot go to bed together, Hermie spends long, passionate moments caressing his date's arm in the mistaken notion that it is her breast. After studying the sex manual to learn the twelve steps to sexual intercourse and making a trip to the drugstore to buy condoms, Oscy and Hermie feel the moment is at hand to establish their sexual prowess. They plan a marshmallow roast on the beach.

In all these escapades, Oscy has been the leader. It is he who copied out the twelve-step list from the sex manual and instructed Hermie to carry a copy of it at all times. It is he who bullied and coached from outside the store while Hermie faced the druggist over condoms. It is he who invites the girls to the marshmallow roast. And it is he alone who is successful in his conquest. Hermie is hopelessly in love with Dorothy by now, but since she is unattainable, he accepts as part of the inevitable Oscy's preparations for his initiation into manhood. Yet when his big chance comes at the marshmallow roast with a willing young girl, he cannot go through with it. He puts his cold hand on her skin, she squeals, and he gives up.

Raucher's screenplay up to this point has been tightly constructed, and his characterizations fresh, energetic, and thoroughly enjoyable. Hermie's relationship to Dorothy has been gradually developed as a counterpoint to the Hermie-Oscy relationship. Their scenes together—with Hermie being awkward and Dorothy being dreamy—are nicely done despite the fact that Dorothy plays a one-dimensional role. But Raucher loses his control as Hermie and Dorothy grow closer, and an overly sentimental ending threatens to destroy what he has so far achieved.

At first Hermie watched from a distance as Dorothy sent her handsome husband off to war. He offered his assistance in several matters when she needed a man's help (to carry groceries, to take boxes up to the attic). Now, emboldened by the friendly reception he has had so far at her home, he asks her permission to drop by in the evening. When he arrives, the lights are very dim, Dorothy is nowhere to be seen, and the needle on the record player is still going around, making a scratchy noise, although the record has ended. Things are in disarray—a glass and bottle of booze, an ashtray full of cigarette butts. Hermie glances around in confusion and catches sight of a telegram informing Dorothy of her husband's death in combat. Dorothy drifts into the room looking soft, feminine, and in need of comfort. She and Hermie dance a slow, sad dance, tears welling in their eyes. Then they go to the bedroom and, in wordless sorrow, to bed. The room is bathed in soft, moody light and shadow as Hermie leaves behind his boyhood forever.

The film could easily have foundered in these syrupy waters, but it does not; it manages to be appealing and affecting in spite of its implausible ending. Saving it are several entities that have been at work over the course of its first ninety minutes, establishing believability and winning the audience's sympathy. First, there is Mulligan's skill at drawing convincing performances from young people, an ability he demonstrated in some of his earlier films including *Up the Down Staircase* (1967) and *To Kill a Mockingbird* (1962). By the time Hermie and Dorothy go to bed, we know him as a complex character, and in spite of the shadows falling across his face, we can read his feelings. We know he is sad, sympathetic, manly, comforting, frightened, excited, and worried. Another factor that wins our credence is Mulligan's careful attention to background details that create a mood and re-create a time in a wholly believable and authentic manner. The humor serves a similar purpose in balancing the unabashedly romantic mood of the photography, with its sweeping views of seascape and sky, the music, and the story of lost innocence. Even the structure of the film which contains an opening and closing comment by the adult Hermie looking back on that fateful summer is dangerously sentimental, but the humor again undercuts the sentimentality, giving us more than we expect.

Summer of '42 was released to generally good critical comments and to excellent success at the box office. Part of its success depended on timing. It was released in 1971 when public sentiment against the Vietnam War made American audiences ripe for appreciating a tale of simpler times and lost innocence. Nostalgia was an important theme that year, and the Mulligan-Raucher film manipulated that theme masterfully. The director-writer team presented a view of a secluded world on the verge of being shattered, but far from shattering it, they turned it into something funny and beautiful that had just slipped out of reach—Hermie's reach or America's reach. There is implicit hope and promise in such a premise.

Julie Barker

SUNSET BOULEVARD

Released: 1950
Production: Charles Brackett for Paramount
Direction: Billy Wilder
Screenplay: Charles Brackett, D. M. Marshman, Jr., and Billy Wilder (AA)
Cinematography: John F. Seitz
Editing: Doane Harrison and Arthur Schmidt
Art direction: Hans Dreier and John Meehan (AA)
Set decoration: Sam Comer and Ray Moyer (AA)
Music: Franz Waxman (AA)
Running time: 111 minutes

Principal characters:
Norma Desmond .... Gloria Swanson
Joe Gillis .... William Holden
Max Von Mayerling .... Erich Von Stroheim
Betty Schaefer .... Nancy Olson
Artie Green .... Jack Webb
Cecil B. De Mille .... Himself

In *Sunset Boulevard*, writer-director Billy Wilder provides us with a "behind the scenes" investigation into Hollywood. While Wilder's caustic wit is apparent throughout, the investigation is a serious one. As such, *Sunset Boulevard* can be seen as an influence on many subsequent films about Hollywood. With the notable exception of *A Star Is Born* (1937), films about Hollywood prior to *Sunset Boulevard* had tended to be light comedies and musicals. These films served to demonstrate that Hollywood people had plenty of heart and were basically "just plain folks." But *Sunset Boulevard* was made during a period in which Hollywood was reevaluating itself, and audiences were reevaluating the Hollywood product they had been accustomed to. Hollywood was steadily losing its audience, partially as a result of television, but more crucially, as a result of government antitrust action and a Supreme Court decision which forced a restructuring of studio distribution and exhibition policies. *Sunset Boulevard* was also made during a period when audiences were being exposed to films from Europe which were more realistic in approach, as well as independently produced American films which strived for social relevance.

Sunset Boulevard responded to these shifts in the film industry by demystifying star mythology and exposing the more cold-blooded aspects of the studio system. In doing so, it purports to be "realistic," but because the film is a commercial Hollywood product, it ultimately equates star mythology with transcendent and larger-than-life qualities, and reveals that decency does exist beneath the corruption induced by working in the studio system. It is this opposition between exposing Hollywood's "dirty laundry" and reaffirming the value of Hollywood itself that influenced later films such as *The Bad and the Beautiful* (1952), *A Star Is Born* (1954), and *The Barefoot Contessa* (1954). Like *Sunset Boulevard*, these films show movie people who are creative but also obsessed, ruthless, or deeply troubled as a result of making movies. Once having detailed these various personal problems, however, the films stress that movies and what the stars do *in front* of the camera—and the public—are what really matters in the final analysis. The simple message is, "The show must go on."

What makes *Sunset Boulevard* truly unique among these films is its blend of fact and fiction. For the role of Norma Desmond, the legendary star of the silent screen who has deluded herself into attempting a comeback, Wilder cast Gloria Swanson. Absent from the screen for nine years, Swanson was attempting a comeback of her own. While she had made several sound films (including 1934's *Music in the Air*, coscripted by Wilder), her career had never attained the heights she had reached during the silent era, when her name was synonymous with Hollywood glamour. As Norma's faithful butler as well as former director and husband, Wilder cast Erich Von Stroheim, who in 1943 had appeared in Wilder's *Five Graves to Cairo*. As a director, Von Stroheim was among the truly great innovators of the silent screen, and in 1928 he had directed Swanson in *Queen Kelly*, a film that was never released. At one point in *Sunset Boulevard*, Norma shows a scene from *Queen Kelly*. Norma also dresses up in a "Bathing Beauty" outfit, another reminder of Swanson's career since she made her first screen appearances as one of Mack Sennett's "Bathing Beauties." To complete his casting, Wilder used several Hollywood figures as themselves. Cecil B. De Mille appears as one of Norma's directors from the silent days; De Mille had directed Swanson in such films as *Male and Female* (1919) and *Don't Change Your Husband* (1919). Columnist Hedda Hopper also appears, as do Buster Keaton, Ann Q. Nilsson, and H. B. Warner, all of whom were silent era stars who did not make a successful transition to sound, Wilder furthers the sense of verisimilitude by setting many scenes at Paramount Studios.

These legends from Hollywood's pioneering days are clearly opposed to the new Hollywood, represented by a down-on-his-luck young screenwriter named Joe Gillis (William Holden). When Joe pulls into a driveway in an exclusive residential section off of Sunset Boulevard to elude two men who intend to repossess his car, his luck takes a fateful turn; the driveway leads to Norma's decaying mansion. Norma first mistakes Joe for an animal undertaker, but when she learns his occupation, she tells him of her plans to return to the screen in a version of "Salome," which she has scripted herself. Joe finds the script unbearable, but he sees an opportunity to make the money he so desperately needs. He tells Norma that the script has potential, but needs the kind of contemporary slant that he can provide. Norma hires him and soon moves him into the mansion, making him her "kept man." Joe lets Norma pick up the bills while he fuels her delusions of a comeback and makes love to her.

It is significant that Norma mistakes Joe for an undertaker, for his presence at the mansion will eventually lead to his death by her hand. The mansion itself intensifies the foreshadowing of doom. Its gothic ambience is established by rats in the empty swimming pool, the midnight burial of Norma's chimpanzee, and the eerie organ music that punctuates the musty night air.

Joe's death is a result of his romantic involvement with Betty Schaefer (Nancy Olson), a Paramount script girl. The relationship induces Joe to reach beneath his cynical veneer and draw upon his innate decency. Joe's admission to Norma that he has been lying to her and his attempt to make her face reality only serve to make her mind snap. Ever the prisoner of inescapable self-delusion, Norma shoots Joe, and he falls into the now-filled swimming pool, a symbol of filmland status providing Joe with a watery grave.

Wilder continually points out that both Joe and Norma are victims of Hollywood. We are told that Joe has talent, but the studio doors are closed to him because he refuses to turn out hack work. A Paramount producer and Joe's agent, representatives of Hollywood business practices, are both callous individuals. The power structure is presented as unfeeling, while those who toil in the ranks, such as Betty Schaefer and Joe's friend Artie Green (Jack Webb), are depicted in positive terms. Norma's victimization results from her refusing to leave the Hollywood past behind. She believes that her legion of fans are still anxiously waiting her return, but we later discover that the fan letters she has received over the years have been forged by Max (Erich Von Stroheim), her butler. A call from Paramount convinces Norma that her comeback is assured.

The call leads Norma to visit Paramount, and this constitutes the most poignant scene in the film. When Norma enters a soundstage to visit her mentor Cecil B. De Mille (played by himself), she is mobbed in adoration by the technicians and extras who worked with her during the old days. But even here her victimization is suggested, as the mike boom on the set continually casts a shadow over her. It finally swings down to her, and she pushes it away as if it were a pesky insect. Yet Norma cannot get rid of what the mike boom represents—the progress made by Hollywood. Certainly, Norma is one of the inevitable victims that progress must leave in its wake. After Norma leaves, we learn that Paramount had called her to request the use of her vintage automobile in a film. De Mille demonstrates the decency of the Hollywood pioneer when he orders that Norma is never to be told the reason for the call.

Norma leaves the studio convinced of the imminent production of *Salome* and prepares for her triumphant return. Even when she finally lapses into madness, she holds onto her conviction. After Joe's murder and the arrival of the police and reporters, she believes that the newsreel cameras are there to film her comeback. She then descends the stairway for her final close-up. But this close-up is not directed at the filmers of the newsreel, but rather at the audience, as Norma walks past the newsreel cameras and directly toward the offscreen camera filming the scene. The texture of the image then blurs, giving her a transcendent and illusory appearance. It is supremely fitting that Norma, who has been unable to distinguish illusion from reality, should take on such an appearance. Her walking past the fictional characters and toward the audience finally establishes her as a mythic figure.

Like *Double Indemnity* (1944), the events of *Sunset Boulevard* are related through a flashback structure narrated by the male protagonist. But in this instance Wilder adds a gimmick to the structure—the narrator is Joe, who is seen floating in the pool at the beginning. In other words, it is a tale told by a dead man. This gimmick was not an original idea in itself, as evidenced by Charles Chaplin's *Monsieur Verdoux* (1947), which begins with Verdoux's voice-over as a shot of his headstone is seen. But unlike *Sunset Boulevard*, *Monsieur Verdoux* is not bracketed by this narrative device, nor does it contain continual voice-over narration. Actually, Wilder had originally filmed a different dead narrator device, in which Joe sits upright in a morgue and tells his story to the other corpses; but the director scrapped this footage when audiences laughed during a sneak preview.

As it is, the device is audacious enough. What makes it work is Holden's deft reading of Wilder's crisp, cynical dialogue. Despite the publicity surrounding Swanson's return to the screen and her undeniably powerful presence, it is Holden who provides the film with its central source of tension. The look of revulsion on his face when he gets ready to make love to Norma is chilling, and it is one of the many expressive resources Holden draws on to make his dilemma touching. Holden plays Joe as more than a callow manipulator. Indeed, his fleshing in of the character earned him recognition as a serious actor and enabled him to move away from the bland leading roles he was known for prior to *Sunset Boulevard*. Under Wilder's direction in *Stalag 17*, Holden won an Academy Award as Best Actor of 1953, and the actor would later appear in two subsequent Wilder films, *Sabrina* (1954) and *Fedora* (1979). Without Holden, *Sunset Boulevard* might have been a merely a unique collection of old Hollywood relics; with him, the film becomes poignant in its delineation of the past against the present.

Wilder has often been quoted as saying that many Hollywood moguls reacted adversely to the film, but the 1950 Academy Award nominations show that *Sunset Boulevard* was highly regarded within the film industry. The film won Oscars for Best Writing (story and screenplay), Best Score of a Dramatic or Comedy Picture, and Best Art Direction/Set Direction (black-and-white). It was also nominated in several major categories: Best Motion Picture, Best Director, Best Actress, Best Supporting Actress (Olson), and

Best Cinematography (black-and-white). (Ironically, the film honored as Best Motion Picture, Joseph L. Mankiewicz's *All About Eve*, was another exposé of show business with a unique flashback structure in which the narrative is connected by the "unconscious" thoughts of three of its principals.)

In addition to these industry accolades, *Sunset Boulevard* earned far-reaching critical acclaim. The Hollywood press awarded "Golden Globe" Awards to the film as Best Drama, Best Director, Best Actress in a Drama, and Best Score. The National Board of Review honored the film as Best American Film and Swanson as Best Actress, and also included it on its ten best films list, as did the *New York Times* and *Time* magazine. While the film was only moderately successful at the box office, its popularity with audiences—as well as its stature—has increased over the years. In a 1977 survey conducted by the American Film Institute, *Sunset Boulevard* was listed forty-fourth on the list of the fifty most popular films of all time. The film's reputation is richly deserved, for it provides us with a look at an introspective Hollywood and an insight into the mind of its genius creator.

Charles Albright, Jr.

SUPER FLY

Released: 1972
Production: Sig Shore for Warner Bros.
Direction: Gordon Parks, Jr.
Screenplay: Philip Fenty
Cinematography: James Signorelli
Editing: Bob Brady
Music: The Curtis Mayfield Experience
Running time: 98 minutes

Principal characters:
Youngblood Priest .... Ron O'Neal
Eddie ....Carl Lee
Georgia .... Sheila Frazier
Scatter .... Julius W. Harris

Although the characterization of Youngblood Priest was not the first black superhero to appear on the American screen (John Shaft had beat him to it a couple of years earlier), he was the first with strikingly original characteristics. The film *Super Fly* was made by a black director and crew and was produced entirely with black money, not being purchased by Warner Bros. until after completion. Its hero is a successful cocaine dealer whose profession does not disqualify him from getting the girl, the money, or the audience's sympathy; and despite having been heaped with abuse by most reviewers and having received minimal prerelease publicity from the studio, *Super Fly* became a runaway hit, predominantly among black audiences. Only eight weeks after its first showing at Loew's State Theater in New York City (August 4, 1972), *Variety* announced that it had done $1,000,000 in business in New York alone and $5,000,000 throughout the rest of the country, and would soon open in one hundred more locations.

In other words, *Super Fly* is a phenomenon as well as a fine, exciting thriller, with excellent performances, skillful direction, and a disarming portrayal of the black community to which both liberal Hollywood and the NAACP (who protested theaters showing the film) objected. As with most superhero films, *Super Fly* deals in dreams, but dreams more nearly the black community's own than those of the white community adapted for blacks. The film's star, Ron O'Neal, told the *New York Times*, "Here's a picture where a black man finally manages to beat the system."

Super Fly is an action movie whose fairly simple plot allows for extensive thematic development, and for the statement and resolution of issues through its action rather than through dialogue. It has action scenes of fights and car chases, but they are more than mere special effects and stunts; they are the vehicle through which the story is told. Youngblood Priest (Ron O'Neal) is a successful cocaine dealer who wants out of the business. He calculates that by using $300,000 he has accumulated with his partner Eddie (Carl Lee), they can buy enough cocaine to gross $1,000,000 in four months, and then retire. Through his former dealer and mentor, Scatter (Julius W. Harris), now retired and in the restaurant business, he scores the cocaine, but the plan runs into trouble when the police learn of the ring and begin to round up dealers. Before he is killed, Scatter tells Priest that the city's biggest supplier is the Deputy Commissioner of Police, who plans to pick up Priest, relieve him of his drugs and profits, and dump him in the East River. Priest responds in kind by taking out a murder contract on the Deputy Commissioner and his family which is to be carried out if anything happens to him. He also arranges for information about the Commissioner's dealing activities to be made public. Once captured, Priest dispatches most of the police with a display of karate but then is confronted by the Commissioner himself, armed with a gun. Priest simply outlines the precautions he has taken to save his life, especially those matters concerning harm to the Commissioner's family, and drives away from the confrontation free and a rich man.

Initially, *Super Fly* has the structure of a classic crime movie—the more Priest tries to achieve his dream and get out of the business forever, the more tightly he gets caught in his own web. The ending destroys this structure: Priest turns the tides both physically, since the criminal beats the system, and morally, since the criminal seems superior to the system. The screenplay and direction portray Priest as an operator whose methods are equally as violent as those of the system. He has similarly adopted all the values of the contemporary world, but with a cynical awareness of their limited worth. He describes his apartment as "the American dream: color TV and eight-track stereo in every room." In fact, it is through a combination of ironical camera set-ups (predictably dismissed by critics as flashy and pretentious); intentionally overplayed scenes (he makes love to his girl friend in a foam-filled bath); and a surprising recourse to longshots at key moments, that Parks's direction adds a critical extra dimension to the action of *Super Fly* which was spotted by the movie's black audiences. Priest's activities may be wish fulfillment, but they are clearly identified as such.

Shot on location on New York's Lower East Side, *Super Fly* is, in every way, a black movie, with a black subject, director, producer, and crew. Philip Fenty's screenplay was, he claims, based on the career of a successful New York drug dealer whom he had long admired; and the nonmoralizing treatment of drug dealing is one of the film's main virtues. Drugs are and always have been a part of life on the Lower East Side; it was only when they spread to the white middle-class suburbs that they became a subject for major social concern. However, the refusal of *Super Fly* to condemn Priest's livelihood by having him win in the end accounts for much of the hostility which greeted the film upon its release. Jay Cocks of *Time* magazine called it a "crummyboppers little movie," insulting to blacks (all portrayed as "diddy-boppers or street-corner hustlers"); to whites ("drooling, craven criminals"); and to women ("whimpering sex machines"). Kathleen Carroll of the New York *Daily News* thought it should be banned, and Pauline Kael attacked Warner Bros. for peddling this kind of "seditious junk" for profit. There were a few exceptions to the hostility. Roger Greenspun in the *New York Times* admitted that the film had its faults, but found *Super Fly* a "very good movie," particularly praising Parks's "brilliantly idiomatic" direction; and Stuart Byron in *Rolling Stone* was even more enthusiastic, describing it as "one of those rare occasions when art and commerce meet."

Youngblood Priest is a character more mythic than real, a super dude who, with his looks, his clothes, his car, his apartment, and his women (even including an uptown white), not only survives on the Lower East Side but also, unlike Eddie and Scatter, wins. In this respect, the screenplay is a bit schematic: Eddie is a Priestlike character who is too weak to win, and Scatter is like Priest except that he thinks he can get out without winning first. Priest himself is a kind of warrior who cannot succeed and also stay clean in a dirty environment. If he were a white cowboy with the same moral code (and Parks's use of slow motion in the violent scenes is inevitably reminiscent of Sam Peckinpah's Western films), he would not have met with the same outrage. However, he is condemned because he deals in cocaine rather than bullets. The film extols the pleasures of cocaine and portrays contented customers in a series of close-up stills. The legality or safety of its use is a moot point in *Super Fly*; the fact is that cocaine is part of the life-style of the world in which the film is set as is Curtis Mayfield's superb score (predictably, the only thing that most critics praised), and such facts as police collusion in the dope market. All these things are portrayed, without comment, as realities. *Super Fly* is a movie about power, the power of a superhero who takes on authority and wins. It is a fine action movie, more hip than naïve, which deals with the dreams of the Lower East Side a great deal less exploitatively than many more "respectable" black-oriented movies.

Nick Roddick

SUSPICION

Released: 1941
Production: RKO/Radio
Direction: Alfred Hitchcock
Screenplay: Samson Raphaelson, Joan Harrison, and Alma Reville; based on the novel *Before the Fact* by Francis Iles
Cinematography: Harry Stradling
Editing: William Hamilton
Score: Frank Waxman
Running time: 99 minutes

Principal characters:
Johnnie Aysgarth .... Cary Grant
Lina McLaidlaw .... Joan Fontaine (AA)
General McLaidlaw .... Sir Cedric Hardwicke
Beaky .... Nigel Bruce
Mrs. McLaidlaw ....Dame May Whitty

When Francis Iles wrote the novel *Before the Fact*, from which *Suspicion* was drawn, it had a fascinating ending. While the film was in production, Hitchcock must have been aiming toward that same ending since the shooting title of the film remained *Before the Fact*. The picture was then previewed with several conclusions before one was decided to be best for film audiences, and the film was released as *Suspicion*, because that is what the story line is about. Originally, the heroine, becoming convinced that her husband, whom she adores, is going to murder her, drinks the poisoned milk he offers her; for even though love has betrayed her, she will not betray that love. Thus, she becomes an accessory before the fact to her own murder.

Such an ending, of course, would be unsatisfactory for the average filmgoer, especially since the star of the film is Cary Grant, who was, by the time he filmed *Suspicion*, one of the greatest film idols of the time. To portray him as the murderer of his own wife, especially when that wife was played by Joan Fontaine, would have been to invite audience displeasure. Changing the ending, however, meant that the whole theme of the story would have to change. Without the twist of making the husband appear guilty only circumstantially, the theme becomes one in which the obligation of mutual trust in any love affair is mandatory: a wife must not suspect her husband of the worst when she loves him because her love is then not complete. The ending switch involves so many moral turns that it puzzled many a film writer; one critic reported that a large percentage of trade reviewers must still be sitting in the projection room after the previous day's showing, waiting for the story to end.

Suspicion is an intriguing film and one of Hitchcock's best; it is beautifully made and perfectly played, Joan Fontaine as the loving heroine Lina McLaidlaw, a wife forced to doubt her husband, won her an Academy Award as Best Actress. It was a well-remembered year, especially since she was in competition with her own sister, Olivia de Havilland, who was nominated for *Hold Back the Dawn*. Fontaine had been one of the nominees the previous year for *Rebecca*, her first big role, but she had lost the Oscar to Ginger Rogers for *Kitty Foyle*. Some maintained that she won for *Suspicion* the following year because she should have won the year before; but Fontaine handles her role in *Suspicion* with remarkable sensitivity and assurance. Her victory was an honest one in an Oscar race for Best Actress that was even closer than before, for her competition involved not only her sister, but also Bette Davis, Greer Garson, and Barbara Stanwyck.

The role of Lina McLaidlaw is not unlike that of the nameless heroine of *Rebecca* (1940). Lina is a shy, self-effacing, repressed English girl, the daughter of a retired general (Cedric Hardwicke) and his respectable wife (Dame May Whitty). Nothing exciting or adventurous has ever happened to her, and she is almost resigned to ending her days as an unwanted spinster with a sheltered existence. Then she encounters Johnnie Aysgarth (Cary Grant), a lovable scoundrel, and is swept head over heels into romance. She cannot believe that Johnnie returns her love, but when he woos her boldly and asks her to marry him, she blindly consents, knowing little about him and turning a deaf ear to her parents' disapproval of him.

In order to prove his love, Johnnie takes a job when he learns that his wife's monthly income is not sufficient to support them both, but he bets on the races with his earnings and is soon driven to stealing from his employer to pay his gambling debts. Gradually, the evidence against him builds. He is exposed as a liar and a thief, charming but completely irresponsible, and little by little Lina begins to suspect him of the worst.

Johnny has a drinking buddy, a jovial, well-meaning friend named Beaky (Nigel Bruce). One night, as Lina plays anagrams with them, her thoughts are clouded by her gathering suspicions about Johnnie. As her thoughts drift from the men's conversation, she rearranges the letters on the blocks before her, and they spell out the word "murder." Immediately she leaps to the conclusion that Johnnie intends to kill Beaky. Soon after, Beaky is found dead, and, in Lina's mind, circumstances point to Johnnie as the killer. The suspense and sense of dread builds slowly but inevitably.

When Lina learns that her husband could benefit by her death, and when she is driven ill to her bed and he waits on her, she is more certain than ever that he intends to kill her. He brings her the fateful glass of milk to aid her in sleeping, and the suspense Hitchcock achieves during this sequence is maddening. Will she remain silent and drink the milk? Does she subconsciously desire to be the willing victim of her husband's villainy? Will she plan an accident and upset the glass, at least postponing the moment of death?

Or is the whole pattern of suspicion a false one, a web that she herself has spun in her mind? Could it be that Johnnie is utterly innocent, a victim of circumstances?

In the film's last reel, Hitchcock proves himself to be the ultimate master of suspense. He builds on every clue, every plot turn. In the final confession scene, he is dependent upon Cary Grant's skill as an actor, just as he was dependent on Laurence Olivier's in the confession he made to Joan Fontaine in *Rebecca*.

Hitchcock has been accused of making the same picture over and over again, and, in effect, this may be true. However, it must be remembered that there are only so many elements to be used in building a suspense story pictorially. The central character must either run away from damaging evidence, or he must blindly run toward it. He is either in danger himself, or he is creating danger for another. Ultimately, it is Hitchcock's penchant for minor detailing in the development of each film that persuades the audience that this time the situation is truly different, and there is always that certain Hitchcock twist which could make it seem so.

Actually, it is only when one examines the full Hitchcock catalogue that one realizes how very different each Hitchcock film is from the others. The best ones are those which fall, in part, into the gothic romance class: *Rebecca*, *Suspicion*, *Notorious* (1946), *Shadow of a Doubt* (1943), *Strangers on a Train* (1951), *Vertigo* (1958), and *Psycho* (1960). Yet, all have only one characteristic in common: the suspense is gained by honest cinematography, with the camera used as a reflection of the mind of the audience. Hitchcock knows his use of the camera well, and he always tells his tale with it. This is true even when he presents his most un-Hitchcocklike story: *The Wrong Man* (1957), based upon a true story of a miscarriage of justice, in which the wrong man has been accused circumstantially of a crime, and is found guilty. In all his films, Hitchcock's sense of humor always takes an impudent turn; drollery, audacity, and mockery are integral parts of his method. In addition, no one knows better than he how to achieve the most from a stunning moment of shock, or even horror.

Since he favored such stunning blondes as Madeleine Carroll and Grace Kelly as heroines, Hitchcock has been accused of prejudice in favor of the stylish but icy blonde. Yet in some of his best accomplishments, nonblond heroines such as Joan Fontaine and Ingrid Bergman have been warm, compassionate, and moving. Cary Grant is considered the definitive Hitchcock hero; he effectively plays against adventure and melodrama with a becoming tongue-in-cheek disbelief of what is happening to him in such films as *Notorious*, *North by Northwest* (1959), and *To Catch a Thief* (1955), in addition to *Suspicion*. But Hitchcock has been as compatible with other actors quite unlike Cary Grant. James Stewart, for example, responded to the Hitchcock spell in such films as *Rear Window* (1954), the remake of *The Man Who Knew*

Too Much (1955), and *Vertigo*, a rare masterpiece for both Hitchcock and Stewart.

Suspicion, however, was the real challenge, and early proving ground for Hitchcock. Selznick had brought him to Hollywood from England, and his first picture in Hollywood, *Rebecca*, was an overwhelming success. His next two films, *Foreign Correspondent* (1940) and the unlikely *Mr. and Mrs. Smith* (1941), had almost been enough to brand him as a one-time success in this country. But *Suspicion* proved his talent anew, and from this film forward he has seldom erred; no other director has been so consistently successful. He has been admired and imitated, but he remains uniquely Hitchcock, "master of suspense." He has made films his primary interest in life, and *Suspicion* is an important title in any list of his work.

DeWitt Bodeen

A TALE OF TWO CITIES

Released: 1935
Production: David O. Selznick for Metro-Goldwyn-Mayer
Direction: Jack Conway
Screenplay: W. P. Lipscomb and S. N. Behrman; based on the novel of the same name by Charles Dickens
Cinematography: Oliver T. Marsh
Editing: Conrad A. Nervig
Running time: 121 minutes

Principal characters:

Sydney Carton	Ronald Colman
Lucie Manette	Elizabeth Allan
Miss Pross	Edna May Oliver
Stryver	Reginald Owen
Marquis de St. Evremonde	Basil Rathbone
Madame DeFarge	Blanche Yurka
Dr. Manette	Henry B. Walthall
Charles Darnay	Donald Woods
Monsieur DeFarge	Mitchell Lewis

David O. Selznick proved himself to be one of Hollywood's finest producers at other studios, notably Paramount, RKO, and M-G-M, before he formed his own company in Culver City where the most memorable Selznick productions of *Gone with the Wind* (1939) and *Rebecca* (1940), among others, were made. During his term as an M-G-M producer, he favored film versions of classics. The greatest stories of world literature had a special meaning for him, and he wanted to supervise their adaptation to the motion picture medium. In 1934, at M-G-M, he produced Dickens' *David Copperfield* with George Cukor directing, and in 1935 he produced Tolstoy's *Anna Karenina* with Clarence Brown as director. That same year he produced what is regarded as the definitive production of Dickens' masterpiece of life in London and Paris during the French Revolution, *A Tale of Two Cities*, which Jack Conway directed.

Selznick was a martinet for historical accuracy and hired men who could oversee and confirm the backgrounds of his productions. He engaged two outstanding writers, W. P. Lipscomb and S. N. Behrman, to write his screenplay, for which Val Lewton, his story editor, doublechecked every word in every scene for correctness. Lewton, with Jacques Tourneur, also directed the second unit company for the thrilling Fall of the Bastille sequence. *A Tale of Two Cities* justifiably remains a screen classic.

The story line involves a revenge that took a lifetime to bring about. Years before the revolutionary spirit arose in France, the seeds for rebellion were sown. The malicious Marquis de St. Evremonde (Basil Rathbone) had been attracted by the charms of a young peasant girl and had brutally seduced her. The girl was the sister of a young Madame DeFarge (Blanche Yurka), and the aid of Dr. Manette (Henry B. Walthall) was sought in treating the unhappy dying girl. Upon her death, Manette was falsely accused of crimes by the Marquis, the death of the girl was hushed up, and for eighteen years Manette was imprisoned in the Bastille, his mind slowly fading, his only pleasure found in making shoes at a cobbler's bench.

Manette's release from the Bastille is finally gained by Monsieur DeFarge (Mitchell Lewis), who keeps him in the rooms over his wineshop, where Manette's daughter Lucie (Elizabeth Allan), now a young lady, comes to take her father safely home to London.

Meanwhile, the haughty Marquis de St. Evremonde, hastening to Paris in his coach, gives no orders for slowing down as he passes through a provincial village. A child crossing the narrow street is struck down by the horses and killed by the carriage wheels passing over him. It is the child of Madame DeFarge. St. Evremonde makes no apology, shows no remorse; in his view the child should not have been playing in the streets. He gets back into the carriage and orders the driver to make haste for Paris. Madame DeFarge looks after him with angry tears, as she presses the body of her dead child to her breast, swearing lasting vengeance, not only upon Evremonde but everyone in his house and all those allied to him. Her sister and now her child are both dead because of the accursed St. Evremonde.

That night when St. Evremonde has returned to his chateau and is sleeping, he is slain in his bed for his crimes against the citizens of France.

In London lives a once-gallant soul, now defeated through an eternal thirst for alcohol. He is Sydney Carton (Ronald Colman), a lawyer's clerk who gets nowhere in life because of his obsession for drink. He looks enviously upon Lucie Manette, who is now betrothed to Charles Darnay (Donald Woods). Darnay is actually the nephew of the Marquis de St. Evremonde, but he despises his uncle for the evil he has done and refuses to be known by his family name.

Lucie and her father live together in London, under the care of a maid, Miss Pross (Edna May Oliver). Darnay and Carton become frequent visitors, and Darnay's uncanny physical resemblance to Carton is remarked. Both men have proposed marriage to Lucie, but she loves Darnay and has accepted him, not suspecting that he is in reality Charles St. Evremonde, nephew to the evil, and now murdered, marquis.

Lucie gives birth to a child, and the little family is supremely happy until Darnay gets a letter from Paris, supposedly from a onetime family retainer who is now imprisoned by the Revolutionaries. The letter is actually a ruse ordered by DeFarge, who has discovered that Charles St. Evremonde and Charles Darnay are one and the same man. Darnay goes to France, where he is immediately arrested and held for the tribunal. Dr. Manette and Lucie also hurry to Paris to help him, but to no avail. Darnay is sentenced to die on the guillotine, supposedly accused by both Manette and DeFarge, although Manette is only confused and guiltless and has been trapped into making a false accusation.

Sydney Carton becomes a man of desperate action. He hurries to Paris, gets to Darnay in his cell, and secretly drugs him. Darnay is carried by the guards from the prison wearing Carton's garments, and Carton, having deliberately assumed the identity of Darnay, now waits to die in his name.

Meanwhile, Madame DeFarge goes to the Parisian lodgings of Lucie and Dr. Manette to denounce them; but they are on their way with the disguised Darnay to Calais and thence by boat to London. Only Miss Pross is in the apartment. A fierce physical struggle takes place between Miss Pross and Madame DeFarge, who pulls out a pistol and tries to shoot Miss Pross; but the gun goes off early and Madame DeFarge is slain by her own weapon.

In the prison the name of Charles St. Evremonde is called, and Sydney Carton takes his place in the guillotine cart. Riding with him, also falsely condemned, is a little seamstress who begs Carton to hold her hand as they ride through the streets of Paris, lined with citizens laughing and jeering, calling for death to the aristocrats. The little seamstress finds strength in Carton's proximity and goes bravely to her death.

Then it is Sydney Carton's turn, and he mounts the stairs to the guillotine. Before he places his head upon the block, he looks up to the sky over Paris, and the camera zooms upward and over the roofs of the city, as Carton's voice is heard on the sound track speaking his immortal last words: "It is a far, far better thing I do now than I have ever done; it is a far, far better rest I go to than I have ever known."

A Tale of Two Cities is an M-G-M production in the grand style, a faithful screen dramatization of a well-loved book. The film benefits from Colman's performance. Like Laurence Olivier, Colman in real life hailed from Surrey, and Surrey men are renowned for their beautiful voices. His Sidney Carton is droll yet entirely heroic; it is the kind of role that could easily have become pathetic, but Colman makes Carton's sacrifice a noble, believable, and very moving one. In order to play Carton accurately, he shaved off his moustache, as he had also done for *Clive of India* (1935), because a moustache would have been an anachronism for those times. In the midst of the gayest scene, his eyes take on a look that is sad and hurt; he projects a bittersweet quality without a trace of self-pity.

Edna May Oliver was a marvelously heroic comic figure as Miss Pross, who does more than a little sacrificing herself, and Blanche Yurka as the vengeance-mad Madame DeFarge is frightening. Elizabeth Allan does as much as she can with the role of Lucie, and Isabel Jewell's exquisite cameo at the end of the picture as the little seamstress who is afraid to die alone is memorable. The role of the seamstress had previously been the first step toward highly successful careers for at least two other actresses: Norma Talmadge, who played the scene with Maurice Costello in 1911 for Vitagraph; and Florence Vidor, who rode to the guillotine with William Farnum in Twentieth Century-Fox's 1917 production.

DeWitt Bodeen

THE TALK OF THE TOWN

Released: 1942
Production: George Stevens for Columbia
Direction: George Stevens
Screenplay: Irwin Shaw and Sidney Buchman; based on a screen story by Sidney Harmon
Cinematography: Ted Tetzlaff
Editing: Otto Meyer
Running time: 118 minutes

Principal characters:

Leopold Dilg .... Cary Grant
Nora Shelley .... Jean Arthur
Michael Lightcap .... Ronald Colman
Sam Yates .... Edgar Buchanan

The romantic comedy is a staple of the Hollywood film. In this type of film a woman usually chooses between two men, and she virtually always chooses the more romantic and unconventional of the two after getting to know him through some unusual circumstance. This is the basic outline for many films which are merely mindless fluff, but it is also the outline for such fine films as *It Happened One Night* (1934) and *Holiday* (1938) (though the latter finds a man choosing between two women). An outstanding example of what can be done in this genre is *The Talk of the Town*. Not only does it have a schoolteacher having to choose between a law school dean and an escapee from jail but also all three are fully developed, interesting characters and a serious theme is explored—the value of the intellectual life as opposed to the practical. *The Talk of the Town* is both thought-provoking and highly entertaining.

The film is built around an ideological opposition which also becomes a romantic triangle: Leopold Dilg (Cary Grant) represents the unintellectual, even antiintellectual, position; Michael Lightcap (Ronald Colman) the purely intellectual one; and Nora Shelley (Jean Arthur) a middle ground between them. The three come together one night in the house owned by Nora which she is preparing for Lightcap, a law school dean who is renting the house for the summer and is scheduled to move in the next day. First Dilg, a local political activist who has escaped jail just before his trial for murder, comes to the house to hide. Though she knows him somewhat and does not seem to think he is dangerous, Nora does not welcome him, but she does consent to his staying the night in the attic. Minutes later, Lightcap arrives one day early. The next day when Dilg's lawyer, Sam Yates (Edgar Buchanan), tells Nora to keep Dilg there and take care of him, Nora, to make the best of the situation, gets the job of cook and secretary to Lightcap, and Dilg comes out of hiding to pretend to be the gardener. Three quite different people are now forced to spend quite a great deal of time together. Romance develops, but more important is the effect they have on one another's ideas.

At the beginning Lightcap thinks that law is a theoretical matter and that he cannot concern himself with individual cases. Dilg, being an individual case himself, takes the opposite position that the law has no soul, that it needs human qualities.

Dilg is accused of starting a fire in which a man was killed. He knows he is innocent, but he is unwilling to risk standing trial because a very powerful man in the town, Andrew Holmes, does not like him or his ideas and has enough influence to ensure that the trial will go the way he wants. Yates, Nora, and Dilg begin a campaign to convince Lightcap of Dilg's innocence and the impossibility of his getting a fair trial. Lightcap, who has taken the house for the summer so he can write a book, at first resents this intrusion of the real world on the time he was planning to spend on scholarship, but he is gradually convinced as Nora uses such tactics as taking him to a baseball game where they "happen" to sit near the judge who would try the case and Lightcap hears how biased the man is.

Events begin moving quickly as Lightcap discovers that the gardener is actually Dilg, and Nora and Lightcap discover that no one was killed in the fire—the supposedly dead man, Clyde Bracken, is merely hiding out. Lightcap gets so involved in the intrigues that when he finds out that Bracken has a girl friend in town, he takes her dancing merely to get information from her. He finds that Bracken is in Boston getting his mail at the general delivery window and takes Nora and Dilg to Boston to capture him though he has to lie to the police to get them to release Nora and also has to knock out Dilg in order to get him to come along on the trip. Thus Lightcap, having begun the film as the standard ivory-tower intellectual, is so changed by his experiences that by the end he has lied to the police, refused to turn in a wanted person, and used force to achieve his goals—all things he would not have countenanced before, but all things done in the interest of true justice.

Even though Lightcap is told the first day he is in town that he is to be appointed to the Supreme Court and should keep his name out of the newspapers, once he gets involved in the case he insists on seeing it through. The culmination of the change in his thinking comes when he uses a gun to capture Bracken and take him to the courtroom, which is being stormed by an angry mob threatening to lynch Dilg. He gives an impassioned speech in which he says that the law must be "engraved in our hearts," and that both those who want to ignore the law completely and those who think of it as a set of abstract principles are wrong. Even though this speech might sound platitudinous in another context, the fact that it comes out of Lightcap's experience makes it effective and moving. As Dilg says after Lightcap is appointed to the Supreme Court, he is a better Justice for his experience.

These changes in Lightcap's ideas are not the only changes that occur. A suggestion of a romance begins to develop between Nora and each of the men. Neither openly admits his own feelings, but instead each talks to Nora about the other man. Dilg, for example, tells Nora that Lightcap is in love with her and adds, "I know just how he feels." Each man seems inhibited by his respect for the other as well as his uncertainty about the choice she will make.

In romantic comedies a woman usually has to choose between two men or a man between two women, and the choice is nearly always quite predictable. For example, though the film *It Happened One Night* is quite good, there is little doubt that in the end Claudette Colbert will prefer Clark Gable over Jameson Thomas. In *The Talk of the Town*, however, both men are played by actors who were frequently romantic leading men. When Nora has to choose between the two, it is a difficult choice that cannot be so easily predicted, especially since Lightcap has changed so much during the film. In fact, the choice between the two men is so close that the filmmakers shot two endings and made the choice themselves only after previewing the film.

The decisive moment comes on the day Lightcap takes his place on the bench of the Supreme Court. Nora goes to see him in his chambers where he suggests that she choose her "reckless friend." A few minutes later she sees Dilg, who recommends Lightcap because of his "position, dignity, and place in life" and tries to walk away, but Nora, saying she is tired of people trying to make up her mind, kisses him. He then leaves but immediately comes back to take her with him as the film ends.

Although *The Talk of the Town* is a film which deals with ideas, its characters are not always engaged in heavily philosophical discussions. The film's humor runs from the near-slapstick as Nora attempts to keep Lightcap from seeing Dilg at the beginning to such little touches as Dilg seeing his picture on a wanted poster and remarking, "No one would recognize me from that—doesn't catch the spirit." Indeed, it is a comic scene in which the discussions between Dilg and Lightcap begin. The morning after Lightcap's arrival he is dictating to Nora, but she has trouble concentrating on the work because she can see Dilg sneaking into the kitchen to get something to eat. As Dilg is getting food out of the refrigerator, he hears Lightcap describe law as "an instrument of pure logic" and casually walks out to argue with him, much to the consternation of Nora. She quickly explains, however, that Dilg is the gardener and they are able to keep his true identity secret for a little longer.

The screenplay by Irwin Shaw and Sidney Buchman is excellent, but the actors deserve a good portion of the credit for creating such interesting characters. Michael Lightcap seems at first to be merely an intelligent but emotionless man who thinks of everything outside of his work as merely a distraction, but as the film progresses, we learn more about his background, and we see him discover more about himself and about the rest of the world.

He tells Nora that he first grew his beard because he was one of the youngest ever to graduate from Harvard Law School and wanted to look older and more professional. He admits, however, that he began to hide behind that reserved appearance; it became his fortress. The beard, therefore, is emblematic of his detached outlook both for him and for others; it is more significant than it might seem when he shaves it off. Colman, with his usual cultured voice and demeanor as well as his considerable acting ability, perfectly brings to life this complex character. Leopold Dilg and Nora Shelley may be somewhat less complex than Lightcap but are no less interesting, and certainly the performances of Grant and Arthur are equal to Colman's; they are amusing without letting the comedy overshadow the serious side of their characters. Edgar Buchanan also does a fine job in the important supporting role of Sam Yates, Dilg's lawyer who sometimes comments on the action and sometimes keeps it going.

George Stevens ably directs with a lighter touch and quicker pace than in some of his other films, and the efforts of all involved were rewarded. *The Talk of the Town* was a critical and commercial success.

Timothy W. Johnson

TARZAN, THE APE MAN

Released: 1932
Production: Metro-Goldwyn-Mayer
Direction: W. S. Van Dyke
Screenplay: Cyril Hume and Ivor Novello; suggested by the tales and novels of Edgar Rice Burroughs
Cinematography: Harold Rosson and Clyde DeVinna
Editing: Ben Lewis and Tom Held
Running time: 99 minutes

Principal characters:
Tarzan .... Johnny Weissmuller
Jane Parker .... Maureen O'Sullivan
Harry Holt .... Neil Hamilton
James Parker .... C. Aubrey Smith

The character of Tarzan, Edgar Rice Burroughs' famed lord of the jungle, has been a screen personality since 1918. Through numerous actors from Elmo Lincoln to Ron Ely, the noble jungle lord has been portrayed by an army of ex-athletes and body-builders. However, to a great many people the actor who most epitomized Tarzan was Olympic champion swimmer Johnny Weissmuller. So completely did he capture the public's imagination as Tarzan that he played the role through twelve feature films spanning a fifteen-year period. In film after film Weissmuller would rise to the occasion as hero supreme, an embodiment of strength, courage, and virtue on the purest level.

Tarzan, the Ape Man was a first not only because of Weissmuller's portrayal of Tarzan, but also because it introduced the lord of the jungle to the "talking cinema." This spectacular 1932 M-G-M production was the first sound version of Burroughs' famed creation. The plot is derived from a variety of sources. Using Burroughs' tales and novels to create a functional background, *Tarzan, the Ape Man* becomes the blueprint for a series of jungle epics which tried to emulate the success of the original.

In the beginning of the film, Tarzan comes upon a safari headed by James Parker (C. Aubrey Smith). This group of travelers is shocked at the presence of a white man living in the jungle in barbaric fashion. Tarzan befriends this safari and becomes attracted to Parker's daughter, Jane (Maureen O'Sullivan). In order to protect the safari, Tarzan fights many beasts barehanded and concludes each victory with a wild, animalistic cry. He is able to communicate with many of the animals in the jungle, and he uses this ability to gather useful information and eventually rescue the safari from a village of hostile African tribesmen. The intrigues which develop in the course of the safari are of little real consequence to Tarzan, who perceives the world in a very precise way. To him there are no explanations; there is only good, which he defends, and evil, which he battles. He trusts man as he trusts animals, but man, unfortunately, is not always as honest as the denizens of the jungle. His triumph against overwhelming odds at the end of the film and his desire for Jane to remain in the jungle as his mate form a touching conclusion to the film.

The authenticity of the jungle scenes depicted in *Tarzan, the Ape Man* is easy to explain. The film was directed by W. S. Van Dyke, who had served in the same capacity a year earlier on the epic adventure film, *Trader Horn*. That film, starring Harry Carey, was the first to be shot entirely on location in Africa. *Tarzan, the Ape Man* utilized out-takes from Van Dyke's earlier film and blended them with remarkable skill to match the Hollywood sets constructed for his new motion picture. Weissmuller did many of his own stunts in the film. Although his acting may seem stiff at times during *Tarzan, the Ape Man*, Weissmuller appeared totally natural swimming through rivers teeming with crocodiles or wrestling with huge jungle cats.

The sequel to Weissmuller's first film is regarded as one of the most beautiful adventure films ever made. *Tarzan and His Mate* (1934) is a lyrical film which expresses the beauty and danger of the jungle; it is a romance of the highest order. Remarkably, Weissmuller somehow lost whatever awkwardness he had as an actor, and played Burroughs' character with grace and charm. He *became* Tarzan, even if his characterization was completely at odds with Burroughs' original intelligent hero.

The cinema tended to characterize Tarzan as the embodiment of the noble savage, a man freed from the constraints of civilization whose goal is to live life to the fullest. Burroughs had a different character in mind when he wrote his Tarzan novels. His creation was a king of the jungle, rich, powerful, and intelligent, a man of complex goals and desires. He was in control of a vast empire. This characterization was never captured on film except in a serial produced by Burroughs himself entitled *The New Adventures of Tarzan*, released in 1936 and starring Herman Brix (Bruce Bennett) as the jungle lord.

As Weissmuller continued his role as Tarzan, the plots became more fantastic, and a sense of humor and self-parody crept into his later films. The use of character actors and wildly improbable plots centering around lost civilizations and hidden jungle treasures tended to obscure the believability of Tarzan's simplicity. The series reached its ultimate expression of fantasy in *Tarzan's New York Adventure* (1942). In this film Tarzan's "son," known as Boy (Johnny Sheffield), is kidnaped by unscrupulous circus entrepreneurs and taken to New York City to perform as a sideshow attraction. Tarzan goes to New York where he must present his case in court. Realizing the inequity and corruption of society, Tarzan takes matters into his own hands and swings from one towering building to another in order to rescue his son.

The impact of the Tarzan films on the overall process of film history is arguable. They presented no major innovations; they were simply entertainments with basic plots and fast-paced action. Their impact was more cultural than substantial. In the 1930's Tarzan provided an escape, and by the 1940's these films reflected the exoticism that had invaded Hollywood. *Tarzan, the Ape Man* and its sequel *Tarzan and His Mate* are a fascinating reminder that life was once much simpler and more exciting.

Carl F. Macek

TAXI DRIVER

Released: 1976
Production: Michael Phillips and Julia Phillips for Halo-Judeo; released by Columbia
Direction: Martin Scorcese
Screenplay: Paul Schrader
Cinematography: Michael Chapman
Editing: Tom Rolf and Melvin Shapiro
Running time: 113 minutes

Principal characters:

Travis Bickle	Robert De Niro
Betsy	Cybill Shepherd
Iris	Jodie Foster
Sport	Harvey Keitel
Charles Palantine	Leonard Harris
Wizard	Peter Boyle

Taxi Driver is a frightening *tour de force*, a nightmare vision of New York City as one of the middle levels of Dante's Inferno. It is a thoughtful and disturbing study of a psychotic cab driver who, unable to come to terms with his own sexual feelings, becomes so alienated from himself and others that only violence will serve as a catharsis. Writer Paul Schrader provided the story, and director Martin Scorcese brought it to the screen with harrowing results.

The film opens with a shot of the streets of Manhattan at night as seen through the window of a taxicab. Bilious vapors rise slowly from the bowels of the city, colored by the harsh glare of flashing neon. The scene suggests some hellish netherworld and effectively foreshadows the tone of the movie.

Travis Bickle (Robert De Niro), the protagonist, is an ex-Marine in his mid-twenties who is plagued by insomnia. He takes a job as a taxi driver to put his wakeful hours to some use (he works twelve- to fourteen-hour days, six days a week), ferrying passengers through the seamiest sections of New York. He lives in a world of drifters and grifters, of child prostitutes and all-night porno films. Though he professes disgust at his sleazy surroundings—"all the animals come out at night," he says—he cannot seem to dissociate himself from them; he spends most of his free time in the porno houses. Thus Scorese and Schrader give us the first clue that Travis is a schizoid personality.

While driving his cab through this moral miasma one day, Travis first encounters Betsy (Cybill Shepherd), a worker in the Palantine for President campaign. Tall, blonde, and dressed in white, she looks like an angel to Travis. For awhile, he is content to drive by the campaign headquarters and stare at Betsy. Finally, however, he summons the courage to approach her, and, in front of her coworkers, he calls her "the most beautiful woman I've ever seen." Amused and flattered, she agrees to have coffee with him. Up to this point in the film, Travis has spoken mostly to himself. Now he pours his heart out to Betsy, saying that he senses that she is a very lonely person, that their mutual loneliness could become a very strong bond between them. A bit taken aback by his fervor, Betsy nonetheless agrees to go to a movie with him later.

Incredibly, Travis takes his angel in white to a 42nd Street porno house; evidently he is so out of touch with reality that he sees no connection between the images on the screen and the moral decay against which he continually rails. Betsy flees the theater in a rage, and when she rebuffs Travis' subsequent attempts to contact her, he concludes that she was one of the animals all along. This "date" occupies a pivotal position in the film. It is surely the least credible scene in the movie; most critics doubted that Travis or anyone else could be so divorced from reality that he would take his cherished symbol of purity to a dirty movie. Yet this scene, or one like it, was probably necessary if the filmmakers were to separate Travis from the only normal person in his existence, thus leaving no one to break his slide into homicidal insanity.

Back in his cab, Travis encounters the next person who will play a significant part in his life: Iris (Jodie Foster), a fourteen-year-old girl. Iris leaps into his cab, only to be dragged out by an older man who appears to be her boyfriend. Scorsese and Schrader use the character of Iris as a counterpoint to that of Betsy. Both are blonde and pretty, but there the resemblance ends. Betsy is a symbol of the purity of womanhood, whereas Iris is precisely the opposite. She is a child prostitute, and the older "boyfriend" is Sport (Harvey Keitel), her pimp.

Travis' mental condition continues to deteriorate. He tells Wizard (Peter Boyle), a fellow cabbie, that he has "really bad ideas" in his head, and he imagines that he has stomach cancer. As his mental condition worsens, however, his physical condition improves, as he exercises fanatically in an attempt to purify himself. He also buys an arsenal of illegal handguns. One of the film's most chilling scenes occurs as Travis practices his quick draw with a spring-loaded holster in front of a mirror, asking his imaginary antagonist over and over again "You talkin' to me?" The audience is thus prepared for a violent denouement. The only question that remains is who will be the object of Travis' homicidal fury. One possibility is soon suggested as Travis begins stalking candidate Palatine (Leonard Harris). Twice he has brief run-ins with the security force at Palatine rallies, once blocking a nearby road with his cab before moving on, and once sidling up to a Secret Service agent to talk of guns and assassination. Neither encounter, however, leads to his arrest.

Meanwhile, Travis meets Iris on the streets. She claims not to remember the incident with Sport in Travis' cab, and says that she is content with her life. Trying to keep their conversation going, Travis negotiates with Sport for fifteen minutes of Iris' time. When she discovers that he really is not after sex, she is touched, but responds to his suggestion that she return to her parents by saying only "I got no place to go." Like Betsy, however, she agrees to have coffee with him the next day. Over coffee, Travis again urges Iris to leave Sport, telling her that her pimp has no respect for her. This bit of news disturbs Iris, and she accepts money from Travis to buy a ticket home. The streetwise Sport senses Iris' unhappiness, however, and coaxes her into staying.

Travis then resumes his pursuit of Palatine. Travis' abortive assassination attempt is handled effectively. The scene begins with the camera focusing on the torsos of the crowd at a campaign rally. When the camera reaches Travis, it slowly pans upward to his head, revealing first the ferocious gleam in his eye, and next his hair, which he has cut and shaved so that only a single "mohawk" strip across the middle of his scalp remains. It is a clear indication that Travis has slipped over some final edge, and the image is truly shocking. The rest of the scene is a bit anticlimactic, as Travis is spotted by the Secret Service man to whom he had spoken earlier before he can kill Palatine. His plans disrupted, Travis flees, eluding his pursuer.

His blood lust, however, must be satisfied, so he goes looking for Iris—whether to kill her or her enslavers, we do not know. Finding Sport, he picks a fight with him and shoots him; he then heads for Iris' hotel room, and, in a slow-motion gun battle, kills both Iris' customer and the manager of the hotel who profits from renting out rooms to prostitutes. Travis is wounded and near death by the time the police arrive. Unable to speak, he raises a bloody finger to his head and mimics pulling a trigger; then he loses consciousness.

Ironically, Travis is acclaimed as a hero for rescuing Iris, who is returned to her grateful parents. Recovered from his wounds, Travis resumes his work as a taxi driver, and, as the film ends, Betsy is his passenger. More than a little awed by Travis, she reveals that Palatine has won the presidential nomination. When she attempts to pay her fare, Travis declines her money, driving off cooly into the night, a quiet smile playing on his face.

In *Taxi Driver*, director Martin Scorcese and writer Paul Schrader have made a chillingly uncompromising film about sex and sexual repression (which is all the more effective because none of the sex is on the screen, though it is everywhere implicit). In doing so, they have deliberately chosen to approach their subject from a psychological, rather than a sociological, point of view. They avoid every opportunity to comment on the role of assassination in American electoral politics, for example, or to sermonize about the readjustment problems of Vietnam veterans. Instead, they concentrate on showing the viewer what the world looks like when seen through the eyes of a dangerous psychotic.

The acting in the film is excellent throughout. Cybill Shepherd is a convincing Betsy, the overprivileged and slightly bitchy young woman who is initially titillated by Travis' rough exterior, only to recoil in horror when she gets a hint of what is under the surface. Jodie Foster earned an Academy Award nomination for her portrayal of Iris. With her rough, flat voice and world-weary eyes, she betrays not a hint of cuteness that would have marred the characterization in the difficult part of the child prostitute. In the smaller parts, Harvey Keitel is appropriately sleazy as Sport; and Peter Boyle is amusing as Wizard, the cabbie philosopher who has seen it all and learned to live with it.

Nonetheless, the film belongs to Robert De Niro, who also earned an Academy Award nomination. Travis Bickle is a demanding part—virtually the entire film, save for the scene between Sport and Iris, is seen through his eyes—and De Niro meets the challege, making Travis seem not only believable, but, frighteningly, almost reasonable. Surrounded by sex in its most degraded forms, Travis cannot find his way out. De Niro effectively communicates the inarticulate puritanical energy that eventually finds its only outlet in mayhem.

Because it was so uncompromising in its refusal to step outside the world view of its protagonist, *Taxi Driver* was inevitably a controversial film. Though is was nominated for an Academy Award for Best Picture, some critics complained because Scorcese and Schrader refused to moralize, either about Travis or the world which he inhabits. Also, many viewers were bothered by the film's graphic scenes of violence. Nonetheless, *Taxi Driver* is an undeniably powerful film, containing finely honed portrayals of the underside of contemporary urban life. Although it is not an easy film to like, it certainly merits our study and respect.

Robert Mitchell

TEACHER'S PET

Released: 1958
Production: William Perlberg for Paramount
Direction: George Seaton
Screenplay: Fay Kanin and Michael Kanin
Cinematography: Haskell Boggs
Editing: Alma Macrorie
Running time: 120 minutes

Principal characters:

James Gannon	Clark Gable
Erica Stone	Doris Day
Dr. Hugo Pine	Gig Young
Peggy DeFore	Mamie Van Doren

Teacher's Pet is a delightful and witty romantic comedy. The principal characters are a tough city newspaper editor who has never been to college, a psychology professor who has written dozens of books, and an attractive woman journalism instructor. In a lesser film the tough editor would make a fool of the professor and win the woman on his own terms. Fay and Michael Kanin, however, have written a story with deeper meaning in which the newsman changes his ideas about intellectuals and education. Yet the film is not merely what the newsman would call a "think piece." Under the direction of George Seaton, Clark Gable, Gig Young, and Doris Day have fully realized the comic aspects of the story so that *Teacher's Pet* is both intelligent and funny.

Jim Gannon (Clark Gable), the city editor, does not believe journalism can be learned in school. He has nothing but contempt for education and has hired a Phi Beta Kappa in a menial position "for laughs"; then one day he is forced by his boss to visit a college journalism class. When Gannon goes to the college, he sees a frumpy older woman going into the classroom and assumes that she must be the instructor. When he finds that the teacher is instead a young attractive blonde, Erica Stone (Doris Day), he decides to sit in on the class, but without revealing his identity. He quickly becomes her star pupil but tries without success to change the relationship to a romantic one. He finds that he has a rival for Erica's affections, a psychology professor named Hugo Pine (Gig Young). Gannon immediately has his staff at the newspaper do some research on Pine and finds that he has written two dozen books, all with titles like *Symptoms and Syndromes*, and has held many prestigious positions, such as that of a consultant on psychological warfare for the Army.

We see that these credentials do not impress Jim Gannon because he does not like "eggheads," and he assumes that Professor Pine is a dried up old man whose knowledge has nothing to do with real life. Gannon is therefore encouraged about his chances with Erica. The scriptwriters have thus carefully prepared us for the inevitable meeting of Gannon and Pine.

The two men meet accidentally at a nightclub; Gannon is there with a date, Peggy DeFore (Mamie Van Doren), who is a singer at the club. Pine comes in with Erica, and before the evening is over, Pine destroys all of Gannon's preconceptions about intellectuals. For one thing, he is goodlooking (Gannon's date says, "He's dreamy—must be from Hollywood"). After Gannon mutters that Pine probably doesn't know anything outside his specialty, he finds that Pine knows more about baseball and has better war stories than he himself does. Pine can also mambo and beat out a tribal rhythm on the bongo drums. He can even outdrink Gannon, but finally passes out because Gannon has bribed the waiter to give him triple-strength drinks. Erica then confesses that Pine is so good at everything that it is quite a strain on her because she keeps wanting him to miss—"just once."

The next day Gannon visits Pine and seemingly is impressed by his mixture of intellect and hangover. He says, "I'm beginning to think something of the education bit," and back at the newspaper he advises one of the young employees to go back to school so he will not be like Gannon, knowing only newspapers and nothing else. Also, Gannon begins having his writers do more interpretive pieces, to give the readers more to think about. And at the end of the film he is delighted with the idea that he can get faculty status at the college.

Meanwhile, the romance between Erica and Gannon continues its up-and-down course. Gannon's fortunes go up when Erica says she is not romantically interested in Pine; she is just collaborating with him on a book. They go down dramatically, however, when she discovers who Gannon is and assumes he has been playing a trick on her. At this point Pine becomes Gannon's helpful confidant and gets him and Erica back together for the happy ending.

As Gannon and Erica, Clark Gable and Doris Day play quite well together despite the more than twenty-year difference in their ages. Gable had, of course, been playing such roles since the early 1930's, and was still good, but the romantic comedy was new territory for Day. She had been in twenty-one previous films, but chiefly in musical roles. The box-office receipts for *Teacher's Pet* proved that she could be as popular a comedienne as she was a singer, and she went on to make an immensely successful series of romantic comedies with Rock Hudson. Day did sing the title song for *Teacher's Pet* off camera, however, and it became a hit record.

Gig Young is engaging in the role of Dr. Hugo Pine, and Mamie Van Doren is suitably unrefined and voluptuous in the small role of Peggy DeFore, whose main purpose in the film is to embarrass Gannon in the nightclub scene. Many of the newspaper reporters are played by actual newspapermen in what was more a publicity gimmick than an attempt at realism.

Much of the humor of this comedy comes from its turning upside down the popular stereotype of the intellectual. Jim Gannon expects any woman teacher to be old and unattractive and any male professor to be old, stuffy, and so full of "book learning" that he knows nothing else. Since the film is generally presented from Gannon's viewpoint, the audience shares his surprise when he meets Erica Stone and Hugo Pine. The overall view of *Teacher's Pet* indeed seems to be that the intellectual does have something to contribute to the "real world," and that no matter what his virtues, he inevitably is going to lose Doris Day to the fifty-seven-year-old, charismatic Clark Gable.

Though chief credit for the success of a film usually goes to the director or an actor or actress, in the case of *Teacher's Pet*, it is the scriptwriters, Fay and Michael Kanin, who deserve that honor. They gave to the director and actors and actresses a strong story, witty dialogue, and a fine mixture of thought and humor.

Timothy W. Johnson

THAT HAMILTON WOMAN
(LADY HAMILTON)

Released: 1941
Production: Alexander Korda for United Artists
Direction: Alexander Korda
Screenplay: Walter Reisch and R. C. Sherriff
Cinematography: Rudolph Maté
Editing: William Hornbeck
Interior decoration: Vincent Korda and Julia Heron
Special effects: Lawrence Butler, William H. Wilmarth, and Edward Linden
Sound: Jack Whitney (AA)
Running time: 125 minutes

Principal characters:
Lord Nelson .... Laurence Olivier
Emma, Lady Hamilton .... Vivien Leigh
Sir William Hamilton .... Alan Mowbray
Mrs. Cadogan-Lyon .... Sara Allgood
Lady Nelson .... Gladys Cooper
Captain Hardy .... Henry Wilcoxon

One of the great love stories of all time is that of Lord Nelson and Lady Hamilton. Alexander Korda chose the right moment to produce it in 1941, when war was clouding the world, for there is a similarity in the wars between England and Napoleon's France and those between England and Hitler's Germany. On both occasions the isle of Great Britain was fighting for its very existence against invasion, and both times it was the sea that aided England. After the overwhelming success of Vivien Leigh in *Gone with the Wind* (1939) and Laurence Olivier in *Wuthering Heights* (1939) and their romance in real life, Hollywood producers were alert to the box-office value of combining their talents in a great romance, and Korda had a good script by Walter Reisch and R. C. Sherriff, which proved to be the right one to present them as costars.

Unfortunately, war made it impossible even to contemplate production in Europe and England, using the actual backgrounds for their romance, and Korda was forced to shoot the entire film in Hollywood, creating late eighteenth century and early nineteenth century backgrounds on the United Artists lot and utilizing top special effects resources for the stirring battles at sea, including that of Trafalgar, where Napoleon's forces were defeated, and Nelson, in command of the British fleet, was struck by a French bullet and died aboard his ship. The special effects scenes were remarkable, and the sound throughout is astounding and beautifully recorded, meriting its Academy recognition. Eye-satisfying, too, were the extraordinarily beautiful interior scenes with their simple, gracefully classic decor.

The story begins sometime after the end of the Napoleonic Wars in Calais, on a foggy night, when a besotted, aging woman (Vivien Leigh) stumbles into a wine cellar and manages to steal a bottle of wine. She does not get any farther than the street before her theft is discovered and she is accosted by gendarmes; she struggles with them like a common, disheveled street harridan. She is thrown into the women's prison, where she tells her companions that she is what is left of the woman who was once the idol of her nation, the loving mistress of the great Lord Nelson, who, even as he died, begged that his Emma be cared for; she was his bequest to a nation that not only ignored her but had suffered her to exist in Calais because in her downfall at home she shamed her native land.

In her youth, she was the daughter of a common, uneducated, but aspiring mother, and her father had been a blacksmith; but Emma was blessed with such a radiant beauty that painters competed to have her sit for them, and one of them, Romney, painted her on at least forty different occasions. Charles Greville, nephew of the British ambassador to Naples, Sir William Hamilton (Alan Mowbray), takes her as his mistress, and she plainly adores the profligate young man. But Charles is debt-ridden, and when he gets a chance to wed an heiress, he makes a secret deal with his uncle, who agrees to take on Emma and her common mother, known as Mrs. Cadogan-Lyon (Sara Allgood), at the same time paying off his nephew's debts so that the boy may marry.

Emma believes that her mother and she are being sent to Naples in order for Emma to study music and languages and further educate herself, with Sir William's help, in being a proper lady. It does not take her long to discover the truth, and she is so angered and hurt that at first she intends to desert the beautiful villa, with all the gracious hospitality accorded her. But the luxurious environment in Sir William's Neapolitan embassy soon persuades her to change her mind, and when Sir Willam not only is kind to both her mother and her, but also shows that he is openly infatuated with her, she realizes the position and power she might have, and so responds to his advances. He marries her and, as Lady Hamilton, she soon reigns over Naples as its leading beauty, and becomes the daily confidante of the Neapolitan Queen.

Emma is leaving the embassy one morning for her regular visit to the Queen when her husband introduces her to Captain Horatio Nelson (Laurence Olivier), who has brought news of England's immediate declaration of war on France. Nelson also hopes that he can obtain assistance from Naples in securing ten thousand Italian soldiers to seal in Napoleon's fleet at Toulon. Emma offers her help, and not only gets aid from the Queen, but is instrumental in the Queen's doubling the amount of men offered to twenty thousand.

Nelson is deeply grateful, but before they can meet again, years of battle have passed, and the year is 1798. Hounded by the French fleet, Nelson has taken refuge in the Bay at Naples, and desperately tries to get assurance from the Neapolitan monarchs that he may use the bay for his men-of-war. Once again Lady Hamilton comes to his aid with permission gained from the King and Queen of Naples. When Emma brings him the official notice, being rowed out to his ship, she sees him at first only in shadow, but then as he comes forward jubilantly, she sees in the candlelight that he has lost one arm and the sight of one eye in battle. She is at first stunned, but the attachment between them grows all the stronger, and he sails away for the Nile and the great Egyptian campaign, remembering her.

Sometime later, Nelson learns that revolution and terror have broken out in Naples, and the lives of the King and Queen are in danger. Against all orders, he sails for the Neapolitan port, ostensibly to lend protection to the King and Queen, but in fact to make sure that Emma is safe. She is not only safe, but she takes him as her lover, and Sir William, knowing this, deliberately ignores it.

The Admirality, however, is angered because Nelson has disobeyed orders, and, aware of the scandal of his liaison with Lady Hamilton, commands him to return to London. Obediently, he does so, and enemies try to have him relieved of his command, but the situation is critical in Denmark, and Lord Nelson is sent to Copenhagen.

Sir William returns to London with Emma and dies there, leaving Emma beset with debts and pregnant with a child by Nelson. In great secrecy she gives birth to a daughter, Horatia, who is sent to live with a family in the country. When Nelson returns from success in Denmark, he resigns his command and retires with his beloved Emma to a house of their own in the country.

Only for a brief time do they enjoy life together as lovers, and then he is prevailed upon to accept reappointment to his command, and Emma, although it breaks her heart, persuades him to leave her, for she knows that only he can lead the British men-of-war in a sea battle against Napoleon and the French navy. Nelson departs. The Battle of Trafalgar is fought, and Napoleon is ignominiously defeated. But even in the last hour before victory, a bullet from a French gun strikes Nelson, and he is carried below to die. With his last breath, he entreats his men to look after Emma, whom he loves in life and death. At home alone, Emma is conscious of what has happened, that she has lost her hero, her protector, and lover. The rest for her is solitude, ignominy, and degradation—and she knows it.

That Hamilton Woman is an epic romance, told with great taste and sympathy. Nelson provides Laurence Olivier with a magnificent role, allowing him to go from the strikingly handsome admiral with whom Emma first falls in love to a battle-scarred, crippled fighting man who can no longer even stand tall. It is easy to see how Lord Nelson, as Olivier plays him, inspires loyalty and devotion in the hearts of the men he commands, and how the mere sight of him inspires faith and love in the free heart of Lady Hamilton. They are as beautiful and sympathetic a pair of lovers as graced the screen in those first years of the troubled 1940's. Emma Hamilton remains one of Vivien Leigh's most treasured performances. Not only is she beautiful but the resemblance between her and the portraits of the real Emma is remarkable.

Gladys Cooper lends great dignity to the role of the Lady Nelson who was abandoned by her husband, just as Sara Allgood, as Emma's mother who is in constant attendance of her errant, willful daughter, is properly vulgar and very funny. Alan Mowbray has one of those thankless roles as Sir William Hamilton, the cuckolded husband who acquired more of a treasure than he bargained for in the acquisition of the most beautiful and desirable woman in England at that time, Emma Hart.

In these war years there was to be no grander display of the extent to which art decorators and special effects men could go than was allowed those serving the production of this film. The set for the British Embassy at Naples covered an entire sound stage, with a marble gateway and a spacious paved courtyard graced by covered loggias in which beautiful statues, borrowed from museums, were conspicuously placed. Everything was lavish-looking on land, and the battles at sea were as effective and stirring as any ever actually shot on location. The film's budget was not large; in fact, it was spartan, allowing none of the filmmaking values indicative of a Korda production. But Korda utilized an almost stark simplicity in all things, and the story provided a setting for two of the handsomest stars of the English stage and screen at a time when they were deeply in love and beautiful to look upon. It was the final and most resplendent of the three films Olivier and Leigh played in together as lovers; they had only married in the year preceding the picture's release, and some of the wonder of their first love is captured in the moments they share as Lord Nelson and his Emma.

DeWitt Bodeen

THEATRE OF BLOOD

Released: 1973
Production: John Kohn and Stanley Mann for United Artists
Direction: Douglas Hickox
Screenplay: Anthony Greville-Bell
Cinematography: Wolfgang Suschitzky
Editing: Malcolm Cooke
Running time: 104 minutes

Principal characters:

Edward Lionheart	Vincent Price
Edwina Lionheart	Diana Rigg
Peregrine Devlin	Ian Hendry
Trevor Dickman	Harry Andrews
Miss Chloe Moon	Coral Browne
Oliver Larding	Robert Coote
Solomon Psaltery	Jack Hawkins
George Maxwell	Michael Hordern
Horace Sprout	Arthur Lowe
Meredith Merridew	Robert Morley
Hector Snipe	Dennis Price
Mrs. Psaltry	Diana Dors

The film career of Vincent Price spans more than four decades and over one hundred film roles. During his years as a contract player with Twentieth Century-Fox, Price garnered critical acclaim for a string of sturdy supporting roles in films including *Laura* (1944), *Keys of the Kingdom* (1944), and *Leave Her to Heaven* (1945). It is the horror genre and to a lesser extent the science fiction film, however, that have brought Price his fame as an actor. In fact, he is acknowledged to be America's reigning "master of horror."

Price starred in his first horror film in 1940. It was *The Invisible Man Returns*, a film which utilized Price's rather commanding voice—an understandable ploy, considering that Price was "invisible" throughout much of the film. Some thirteen years later, Price returned to the horror format with the three-dimensional film, *House of Wax* (1953). Price spruced up his role as a mad wax sculptor by playing the part broadly and adding a dash of Grand Guignol. By hamming up the part somewhat, Price created a kind of trademark for his future roles in horror films, and followed up *The House of Wax* with *The Fly* in 1958. Since that period he has concentrated mostly on horror film roles. Among his credits is a particularly well-made group of films based on the tales of Edgar Allan Poe, and directed by Roger Corman for American International. Although Price's films have received mixed critical reaction, they have generally been popular at the box office, and today they are the subject of a considerable cult following. Neither Price nor his films, however, have garnered any Oscar nominations.

This lack of critical recognition makes Price's romp through *Theatre of Blood* (also known as *Much Ado About Murder*) all the more enjoyable to watch. Cast as a mad Shakespearean actor, Price enjoys a clever story line and witty, often campy dialogue, which finds him gruesomely doing away with the critics who have panned his work. In *Theatre of Blood*, Price portrays Edward Lionheart, an actor who prides himself on his performances to a greater extent than the critics do. After finishing a repertory season of Shakespearean plays in London, Lionheart is enraged to learn that he has been denied the prestigious Critics Circle prize for 1970. A year after the awards presentation, Lionheart confronts the panel during a penthouse meeting. After declaring his outrage, Lionheart grabs the year's Best Actor trophy which has been awarded to a newcomer and jumps from the balcony into the Thames and, presumably, to his death.

Lionheart's farewell performance is actually the prologue to a mad, detailed scheme which finds the actor murdering his critics one by one. Aided by his supportive daughter, Edwina (Diana Rigg), Lionheart carries out the grisly murders, true to his profession, in Shakespearean style, killing his victims in ways that duplicate the manner that characters in Shakespeare's plays have died.

The first critic to die, George Maxwell (Michael Hordern), is slain by derelict friends of Lionheart in a manner reminiscent of *Julius Caesar*; another critic, Hector Snipe (Dennis Price), dies as his body is dragged by horses to the funeral of the first slain critic (*Troilus and Cressida*); a third critic, Horace Sprout (Arthur Lowe), has his head sawed off by Lionheart while he is in bed (*Cymbeline*). It is at this point that the chief critic, Peregrine Devlin (Ian Hendry), comes to believe that Lionheart is behind the murders.

Still the murders continue. The panel's only woman, Chloe Moon (Coral Browne), is electrocuted while sitting under a hair dryer, representing a kind of modern-day burning of Joan of Arc at the stake (from *Henry VI, Part I*); another critic, Oliver Larding (Robert Coote), drowns in a pool of wine as Lionheart enacts a scene from *Richard III*; *à la The Merchant of Venice*, a pound of flesh is extracted from Trevor Dickman (Harry Andrews) when Lionheart cuts out his heart; Lionheart seduces the wife of critic Solomon Psaltery (Jack Hawkins) in order to goad him into strangling her (*Othello)*. Rotund actor Robert Morley is cast as critic Meredith Merridew, who gags to death after discovering that he has happily consumed a gourmet meal (cooked just for him on the *This Is Your Dish* television show) made of his beloved pet poodles (in a take-off of *Titus Andronicus*). The ninth and final critic, Peregrine Devlin, survives *Romeo and Juliet*-inspired swordsplay and, in the finale, manages to escape from being blinded in the manner of *King Lear*'s Gloucester. Devlin is saved by the police, who are finally convinced of Lionheart's crimes. In the film's final moments, Lionheart's daughter Edwina is killed. After setting fire to the theater where he had achieved his greatest success, Lionheart climbs to the roof with his dead daughter in his arms, and, after delivering a soliloquy from *King Lear*, he jumps to a fiery death. At this point, critic Devlin notes, "He was madly overacting, as usual, but you must admit he knew how to make an exit."

A black comedy, delivered with wit and brimming with puns, *Theatre of Blood* allows Vincent Price to deliver a *tour de force* performance. He is maniacal, especially in the bloody sequence in which he saws off a head and lascivious when, impersonating a chiropractor, he seduces a critic's wife played by Diana Dors. More importantly, Price manages to make the audience care about his character and believe that his outrage as an actor is justified.

Although the film's murders are often carried out in gruesome fashion, there is no discounting the humor and wit with which they are consummated. The critic who is drowned in a vat of wine happens to have a drinking problem; auspiciously, he meets his end via Chambertin '64. When Lionheart and Edwina carry out the electrocution in the beauty shop, Price is disguised as an effeminate hairdresser. The black humor always surfaces, whether Lionheart is delivering an impassioned Shakespearean scene or committing a colorful murder. The panel of critics, displaying a stiff-upper-lip throughout, never falters. "Nothing you can do will sway me from my original judgment," one of them tells an angered Lionheart, even though his death is imminent.

Price, who is alternately sinister and hilarious throughout, is assisted well by Diana Rigg as Edwina. Rigg came to the role from her television portrayal of Emma Peel, supersleuth of the British series *The Avengers*. Noted for her stage performances of Shakespeare, she is a versatile and beautiful actress; her part allows her to assume a variety of disguises in *Theatre of Blood*.

Despite its admirable supporting performances, however, *Theatre of Blood* remains Price's film. From beginning to fiery end, it is the story of an actor consummed with his work. The opening scenes fittingly establish the mood, showing moments from silent Shakespearean film works, including Emil Jannings' portrayal of *Othello* in 1922.

At the time of the film's release in 1973, critics agreed that Price delivered a superlative performance. A number of them, however, were critical of the film's violence, feeling that too much blood and gore ruined the joke. Obviously those critics could not foresee the tawdry, grisly extremes that the horror genre would reach during the latter part of the decade. Alongside contemporary exploitation efforts, *Theatre of Blood* is a polished, witty piece. The direction is concise, and the supporting cast is excellent.

The story's blend of camp and horror provided a perfect showcase for Price's comedic abilities. In films such as *The Abominable Dr. Phibes* (1971) and *Dr. Phibes Rises Again* (1972), he also displayed an affecting campy style. Price's more menacing screen portrayals occurred during the 1960's, when he teamed with producer-director Roger Corman and American International for a string of atmospheric films based on Poe's writings. Considered among the best of the horror genre, these films include *House of Usher* (1960), *The Pit and the Pendulum* (1961), and *Masque of the Red Death* (1964).

Pat H. Broeske

THESE THREE

Released: 1936
Production: Samuel Goldwyn for United Artists
Direction: William Wyler
Screenplay: Lillian Hellman; based on her play *The Children's Hour*
Cinematography: Gregg Toland
Editing: Daniel Mandell
Running time: 93 minutes

Principal characters:
Martha Dobie .... Miriam Hopkins
Karen Wright .... Merle Oberon
Dr. Joseph Cardin .... Joel McCrea
Mrs. Mortar .... Catherine Doucet
Mrs. Tilford .... Alma Kruger
Mary Tilford .... Bonita Granville
Rosalie .... Marcia Mae Jones
Evelyn .... Carmencita Johnson

These Three is a powerful, deeply moving, and sensitively acted and directed film. Indeed, its mounting tension and culminating tragedy at times make it almost too painful to watch as it explores the effects of malicious gossip on the lives of three people. Although the film has a nominally happy and romantic ending, Lillian Hellman's well-written screenplay leaves no doubt in the viewer's mind that the lives of "these three" have been irrevocably changed. Nothing will be quite the same for any of them again.

Martha Dobie (Miriam Hopkins) and Karen Wright (Merle Oberon), two intelligent and ambitious college graduates, discover that their graduation day is not a happy one because they have no family and friends, no jobs, and little money. On an impulse, Karen suggests to Martha that they open a private girls' school in the old farmhouse she has inherited from her grandmother. Upon their arrival at the farm, they find that the house is completely dilapidated, with holes in the roof, windows boarded up, and the grounds overgrown and neglected. Discouraged, they are preparing to leave when they meet Dr. Joe Cardin (Joel McCrea), who likes to spend his free time from the hospital puttering about the place. He encourages them to stay and repair the old house and offers to help them fix it.

Although the two women first think the task is impossible, they gradually grow accustomed to and finally enthusiastic about the idea. While they are still repairing the house, Karen meets wealthy and influential Mrs. Tilford (Alma Kruger) and her granddaughter Mary (Bonita Granville). Mrs. Tilford offers Karen help in starting the school. By sending her granddaughter Mary to it and also urging her friends to send their children, Mrs. Tilford ensures the initial success of the school. In the midst of the preparations for opening the school, Martha's aunt, Lily Mortar (Catherine Doucet), arrives. An egotistical, insensitive woman, she expects to be given a job at the school teaching elocution because she was once a stage actress. Martha is dismayed but unwilling to turn her away.

While working closely with Martha and Karen in repairing the old house, Joe has fallen in love with Karen and she with him. Both are oblivious of the fact that Martha is also in love with Joe. In fact, no one suspects except Lily Mortar, who uses her knowledge to torment Martha.

For a short time all goes well. The school is successful, and Karen and Martha are tired but happy. As the children study and play, there is no suggestion of the trouble to come, although all the causes of the catastrophe have been established: the dishonesty and selfishness of Mary Tilford, the meanness and meddlesomeness of Aunt Lily, and the unrequited love of Martha for Joe.

One winter evening Joe comes to see Karen, but since she is in town buying supplies, Martha invites him to come up to her room to help her paint a table while he waits. Exhausted after his busy day at the hospital, Joe throws himself down on a couch and goes to sleep; but Martha, not realizing this, begins talking about her unhappy childhood with Aunt Lily and why she became a teacher. Being young was so hard for her that she wants to make it easier for other children, she says. When she sees Joe is asleep, she puts out the light, sits down in an easy chair and gazes sadly and longingly at him. In this crucial scene we realize how deeply Martha feels about Joe. Joe awakens suddenly, knocking over a glass of milk and making enough noise to bring Aunt Lily to the scene. After Joe leaves, Lily makes her usual sarcastic comments designed to hurt Martha, who turns away, sobbing. Unknown to them, however, there is another interested observer of the scene. Young Mary Tilford, Amelia Tilford's granddaughter, is watching and listening from the corner of the stairway.

Mary, a pathological liar and a bad influence on weaker, more malleable girls, is a problem for Karen and Martha, particularly since her grandmother has so much influence in the community. Their problems with her come to a head when Karen confronts Mary with one of her lies. Mary then pretends to have a heart attack and fakes a fainting fit, forcing Karen to call Joe to examine her. When Joe tells Karen there is nothing the matter with the girl, Mary becomes hysterical. Afraid of Mary's bad influence on her roommates, Karen orders them to move out of Mary's room, further infuriating Mary, who decides to return home to her grandmother.

Before leaving, however, she forces her roommates, Rosalie (Marcia Mae Jones) and Evelyn (Carmencita Johnson), to tell her what they heard while eavesdropping at the door when Martha was quarreling with Aunt Lily. Karen had asked Martha to get rid of Lily, fearing her bad influence on the students, but when Martha offered to pay for her trip to England, Lily angrily accused Martha of wanting to get rid of her because she knew that Martha was in love with Joe and did not want him to marry Karen. She also reminds Martha that she once saw Joe leave her room late at night. Lily's angry accusations are overheard by the two girls, who repeat them to Mary.

Mary does not want to return to the school, so when her grandmother insists that she go back, Mary tells her what Lily has said to Martha. Realizing that her grandmother may not believe her, Mary has brought Rosalie home with her to support her story. Having accidentally discovered that Rosalie had stolen another girl's bracelet, Mary is able to force Rosalie to do what she tells her by threatening her with exposure and jail. Mrs. Tilford is at first incredulous at Mary's story, but when Rosalie supports it, she promises Mary she will not have to return to the school. Mrs. Tilford then calls all her friends to tell them the story, and all the pupils are taken out of the school.

Karen and Martha watch the exodus uncomprehendingly, still unaware of what has caused the disaster until a gossipy chauffeur enlightens them. Together with Joe, they decide to confront Mrs. Tilford since both their self-respect and their livelihood are at stake. They persuade Mrs. Tilford to let them see Mary and almost succeed in breaking down her story. At the crucial moment, however, a terrified Rosalie backs up Mary's story, and the three leave, having no further recourse but a libel suit.

They lose the suit and afterwards are mocked and laughed at by the hostile spectators. Their reputations ruined and their lives shattered, Karen and Martha return to the deserted school. Joe has been asked to leave his post at the hospital because of the unsavory publicity and decides to go to Vienna for further study. He asks Karen to marry him and go with him, but the lie has also poisoned their relationship. Despite his protestations that there has never been anything between him and Martha, she no longer believes in him and sends him away alone.

Martha is distraught when she learns what has happened and confesses to Karen that, although she has loved Joe from the first, he has never been interested in her and the rumors are completely untrue. When she is unable to convince Karen, Martha decides to leave with Aunt Lily, who has returned from England, after waiting until the trial ended so she would not have to testify.

On the train, Lily casually mentions the story of the bracelet to Martha, who realizes its significance. Martha gets off the train and goes back to the town where she confronts Rosalie and persuades her to go to Mrs. Tilford and confess. When she hears the confession, Mrs. Tilford offers to make a public apology and to assist Karen and Martha financially, but Martha replies that it is too late to mend the damage to their lives. She tells Mrs. Tilford that her punishment will be the greatest, for she must live with Mary for the rest of her life, not knowing when to believe the girl. Martha merely asks

Mrs. Tilford to carry the message to Karen that she return to Joe, and then leaves. In the final scene Karen and Joe are reunited in Vienna for a nominally happy ending.

The central character in *These Three* is Martha, and an important element of the film, which becomes part of the tragedy, is Martha's concealed and unrequited love for Joe Cardin. Her love is revealed by small but telling details. Early in the film she begins to tell him about an old newspaper story she has discovered while stripping off layers of old wallpaper at the farmhouse, but he leaves her abruptly when Karen calls to him. Martha's face registers her pain and disappointment. In a later scene, she reveals the depth of her feelings as she gazes at him longingly and hopelessly while he is sleeping on a couch in her room. Martha's innate dignity and compassion are seen throughout the film. She does not even turn away Lily although we see from the first that Lily is a selfish, malicious woman who will cause mischief. When the three confront Amelia Tilford, it is Martha who tells her that they are human beings, not paper dolls to be played with.

Besides Martha, the other key character is Mary Tilford, the malevolent child whose lies create such havoc. Not only does she willfully wreck the lives of Karen, Martha, and Joe, but also the lives of her grandmother and Rosalie. At first we see that she is selfish and spoiled; later we realize that she is also evil, vicious, and a compulsive liar. The film does not, however, dwell on the reasons for her behavior but rather on the effect of her lies. The ultimate impact is chilling as we see the destructiveness of Mary's original lie to her grandmother spread in ever widening circles, in the manner of ripples after a stone is dropped in a pool of water, until it overwhelms all it touches. Especially tragic is the lack of defense the others have against Mary's machinations.

The film is based on Lillian Hellman's 1934 hit Broadway play, *The Children's Hour*, in which the two teachers are accused of lesbianism. Producer Samuel Goldwyn knew that the lesbian theme was too daring to be filmed in the 1930's, but he wanted the necessary adaptation to be as good and as faithful to the spirit of the original as possible, so he asked Hellman to adapt her own play. Since she saw the play as being not about lesbianism but about the evil that lies and malicious gossip can cause, she was able to adapt the script so that it retained all its original intensity and was still acceptable to the censors.

Although many critics thought the changes would lessen the dramatic impact of the play, *These Three* was greeted upon release by almost universal critical acclaim and was found to retain its poignancy and power. Further evidence of the intelligence of the adaptation came in 1962 when the play was filmed with the original lesbian theme under its original title. The result was not as powerful as *These Three*, and Hellman herself reportedly prefers the original film version.

Hellman's idea for the play came from an actual trial which took place in Scotland in 1810. Two teachers at a Scottish boarding school were accused of lesbianism by the false testimony of a sixteen-year-old girl whose grandmother believed her and persuaded the parents of the other students to withdraw them from the school. The teachers brought a libel suit which dragged on for ten years and destroyed them both economically and socially. The character of Mary was drawn from Hellman's own childhood experiences. Mary's fainting fit, fake heart attack, and her bullying of other girls were all based on "the world of the half-remembered, the half-observed, the half-understood which you need so much as you begin to write," Hellman has commented.

Under the sensitive direction of William Wyler, the actors all deliver fine performances, particularly Miriam Hopkins as Martha, the most varied role. Hopkins ranges from tense, angry confrontations to relaxed, intimate conversations, and her performance provides beautiful nuances and is expressive throughout. Merle Oberon is also memorable as Karen, particularly in the final scenes, in which her suspicions finally surface. Joel McCrae is appropriately strong and supportive as Joe, and Bonita Granville is credible and generally effective as the vicious, selfish Mary.

These Three is a powerful, intense film whose theme retains all its dramatic impact. The sensitive, carefully constructed script, well-written dialogue, sharply etched characters, and moving performances of the actors, all artfully controlled and balanced by director William Wyler, combine to create an intelligent, complex, and often brilliant film.

Julia Johnson

THEY WERE EXPENDABLE

Released: 1945
Production: John Ford for Metro-Goldwyn-Mayer
Direction: John Ford
Screenplay: Frank Wead; based on the novel of the same name by William L. White
Cinematography: Joseph H. August
Editing: Frank E. Hull and Douglass Biggs
Running time: 136 minutes

Principal characters:
Lieutenant John Brickley .... Robert Montgomery
Lieutenant Rusty Ryan .... John Wayne
Lieutenant Sandy Davyss .... Donna Reed
General Martin .... Jack Holt
Boats Mulcahey .... Ward Bond
Ensign Andy Andrews .... Paul Langton
Admiral Blackwell .... Charles Trowbridge

They Were Expendable is about the Philippine Campaign for Bataan and Corregidor in 1942. Based on the experiences of Lieutenant John Bulkeley, a personal friend of John Ford, the film chronicles the destruction of a PT Boat Squadron as it sacrifices itself in a holding action in the Pacific. A story of defeat and the breakdown of military, social, and even personal structures, *They Were Expendable* was shot in 1944 when the war in Europe was ending and the Allied forces were preparing for an invasion of Japan.

Ford's credit reads, "Captain, USNR," for he had been on active duty in the Navy as Chief of the Field Photographic Branch, a unit of the Office of Strategic Services. He had already made *Battle of Midway* (1941) and *December 7* (1943), stirringly patriotic documentaries about American servicemen overseas. He received an Oscar for both of them and a Purple Heart for wounds received during the Battle of Midway.

Given this context, *They Were Expendable* comes as a surprise. Not only is it not a traditional war genre film of courageous victories and brutal, subhuman enemies, it is fundamentally about the meaninglessness of the war for the people who fought it. Generally in the war genre, themes involve the formation of military relationships and the bond of working toward a common goal greater than any individual could attain. The military provides a structure for both hierarchical and pseudofamily relationships and order in the chaos of war. In *They Were Expendable*, however, that structure is broken down both physically in the losing battles and psychologically through its failure to provide the men with a reason to be fighting.

The film begins in order and regularity. The PT boats cutting through the water are graceful, and Brickley (Robert Montgomery) is established in close-up (though isolated from his background through focus) as the stable commander of the PT boat unit, with the lines of men and generals expressing the chain of command and order of the Navy. Scenes in the officers' club and at a retirement party continue in even lighting, indicating normalcy, with natural shadows and stable compositions. The announcement of war brings the beginnings of chaos and isolation and finally breakdown for the PT units. First Brickley is cut off from the regular chain of command visually by the glass doors of the war room, then he passes through a long corridor alone to rejoin his men. The unit is immediately isolated from the rest of the Navy and the meaningful war effort.

Brickley as commander maintains a degree of distance from all his men. It is a required distance; only through such distance can Brickley make decisions that will cost the lives of an unknown number of his men, and only through the distance of command can the men give the unquestioning loyalty demanded by the war effort. Brickley must become a somewhat removed figure for the men, lacking in the personal dimension and accruing the iconographic significance necessary for giving orders to men who may die for the safety of the unit. This hierarchical, increasingly impersonal structure escalates up through the ranks: Brickley occupies the same relationship to the Admiral (Charles Trowbridge) that his men do to him, and the Admiral is a more remote, lonely figure than is Brickley. General MacArthur is the furthest expression of this distance of leadership: his name alone is awesome to the men, and he is photographed like a mythical figure. We see him only from a distance. He walks in long shot alone while his family walks ahead of him and his men follow behind. It is as though his loneliness and necessary isolation are so great they cannot be bridged at all.

Death in *They Were Expendable* is neither glory-filled nor brutally meaningless, the two extremes with which it is usually depicted in war films, depending on the attitude of the filmmaker toward war. In this film, both possibilities are present, balanced in a way that denies neither. The war is abstracted in such a way as to internalize the battle: there are no enemy soldiers, just planes and boats which fill the sky and sea with action and flame, but never with the sense of a struggle between navies. The sea battles especially are so abstracted they become light shows, sensory experiences of dark boats on glistening water, moving with beauty and grace through the white shining explosions that burst around them, creating patterns of light against a black sky. The Japanese carriers go down in glorious fireworks, and the Americans who die in battle do so in silhouetted low angle against the firelit sky. The sea battles are beauty and light: it is in the hospital that death is a reality. The corridor to the hospital is revealed through dark shadow passages that are strangely lit to create an expressionistic hell. Like the sea battles, the hospital is a highly stylized canvas of light and dark, but it reveals the other side of the battles. The hospital shows the people who deal with the results of the battles—the wounded men, the doctors, the nurses. The hospital scenes are no more realistic than those of the sea battles; they simply express an interior darkness filled with people and pain instead of illuminating the vast night with fire and action. The corridor seems an underground link between the world of the living and the world of the dead, and never more so than when the men visit Andy (Paul Langton), one of their company, as he is dying. His bed is in the corridor itself, curtained off from the others. During the visit, the "small talk" sustains no one, and each man faces death alone in the person of Andy.

Death here is a lonely experience, the final isolation. Ford does not try to romanticize it, but he does stylize it in a way that abstracts its full impact and allows both for the grim reality and for the personal tragedy. The levels of Andy's larger representation for the unit and for the war, and his personal dimension to both the men and his family back home, are permitted through the visual style to exist simultaneously. It is Brickley, in the isolation of his rank, who must face it even more alone than the others as Andy entrusts him with his final thoughts and letters to home. Only with Brickley can Andy stop his comforting banter and confront his death with the honesty that is of comfort to him, but only brings pain to Brickley. He walks alone through the dark corridor to join the silhouetted figures of the rest of the men, isolated from them through light and composition as he was from Andy by the finality of facing his own death while having to go on living.

The funeral in the little Spanish church is another ritualized scene in which the structures of meaning and glory in burial are observed but fall short of their comforting possibilities. Rusty (John Wayne) cannot even stay to observe the ceremony, but runs out to get a drink to sustain him as the religious service cannot.

Like the absence of enemies in the film, the concept of home is abstracted instead of conjured through flashback or misty memory. Home becomes a larger realm than simply "The States" in *They Were Expendable*, as does the military family. The men of the unit constitute a family, and Torpedo Boat Squadron 3 is its home. From the first, the men are displaced, having no specific role to play in the Navy's fight, and the first scene is of a rejection of their possible usefulness. They function as a smooth unit, and the Admiral comments on their maneuverability, but he can see no place for them. Then comes the attack on the base, and their "home" is devastated. The squadron is continually leaving one island and going to another, until it is difficult to keep track of where they are. While it is true that in 1945 audiences had a closer knowledge of the battles of the Pacific than they do today, it seems that this constant upheaval has more to do with the impermanence of any kind of base for the men than with a disregard for details that may have been unnecessary when the picture was released. The family of men disintegrates as well, first with the loss of boats which frees two crews to go fight with the army. Men die and more boats are lost, until all that is really left is Brickley, Rusty, and the small troop of men who will be left behind on the island, certain to be killed by the Japanese. The crew members we know best are the ones who die—Cookie, Slug, and Andy.

Home is more than a place in *They Were Expendable*. It is a condition that they are fighting for and which they cannot maintain. This is the basis of the transcendent failure of meaning that underlies this film. Unlike other war films which depict men becoming a unit or family whose interests are greater than those of any individual or of the country for which they are fighting, in this film the condition of "home" does not even exist structurally, and thus the sacrifices of war cannot affirm it. The war effort becomes a meaningless exercise, with the only possibility for creating meaning existing on an individual level.

The fragile love relationship between Rusty and Sandy (Donna Reed) refers to a concept of home which must always be subordinate to the war. They try to conjure up an image of home that probably never existed when they talk of tall corn and apples, images tied to the primary desire for land and food. The dinner party attempts to establish a feeling of community and home (Sandy's pathetic and touching attempts at femininity in a harsh, hellish world), but the real meaning of the party comes from its proximity to destruction and the maintenance of fragile if schematized normalcy in the face of it. Without the war, Ford suggests, the values represented by "home" would not have such meaning. Only in the face of loss and chaos can these values even be alluded to, although they are not realized. This is the dichotomy upon which Ford so often draws for depth in his films: life can be meaningful only because there have been socially required sacrifices for its continuance through rituals like religion and war, yet that sacrifice fails to return meaning to those who must carry it out, and to whom the film gives the greatest attention and sympathy.

The smooth, graceful beauty of the PT boats performing at the beginning of the film has been destroyed by the end, as the ordering chain of command has been broken beyond recognition. Brickley and Rusty trudge through the dust and dirt, in the unorganized disarray of the Army, Marine, and Navy men and equipment, totally broken down and defeated. The smoke of the battle provides a softening texture which contributes to the utter desolation of the chaotic mass of men without any chain of command or formal order, and it expresses their inner breakdown.

In the last shots, the redeeming effects of formal abstract beauty are recruited to give a transcendent quality to the utterly despairing and hopeless ending of the men being left to die as Brickley and Rusty bitterly fly off to "do their duty." The men are abstracted visually into an emotional entity, first with the close-up of guns, then with shots of two men we do not know, and finally, simply with dark shapes on the beach as the plane flies into the distance. The men and the plane are moving to different destinies, but the beauty and stability of the compositions, along with the abstraction which takes the viewer's emotions out of the realm of response to specific individuals, relates the hopelessness of the film.

It is in the visual expression of the film that the entire concept of value is contained. The dichotomy of the formal beauty and classical composition with soft, romantic lighting of the scenes which allude to home, contrasted to the unstable, harsh, dark world of the hospital and the otherworldly character of the battles, is reconciled in the last scene of the men on the beach. No real point to the struggle is thematically offered in this last scene: the men have "laid down the sacrifice" for no reason that the film will give us; they are simply alone and cut off. The structures of the military family have broken down and all that remains is the dispersing men, who are removed from individuality through lighting. The audience feels the failure of the war on every level, with the loss of human contact and men left behind to die, and simultaneously feels the redeeming effects of the visual beauty. The despair of the film is not mitigated but rather intensified by the visual abstraction, because it generalizes the central theme of lack of meaning while leaving its specific representations intact.

Janey Place

THE THIEF OF BAGDAD

Released: 1940
Production: Alexander Korda for London Film Productions; released by United Artists
Direction: Ludwig Berger, Tim Whelan, and Michael Powell
Screenplay: Miles Malleson
Cinematography: George Perinal (AA)
Editing: Charles Crichton
Art direction: Vincent Korda (AA)
Special effects: Lawrence Butler and Jack Whitney (AA)
Music: Miklós Rózsa
Running time: 106 minutes

Principal characters:

Abu	Sabu
Prince Achmad	John Justin
Jaffar	Conrad Veidt
Princess	June Duprez
Djinni	Rex Ingram
Old Sultan	Miles Malleson
Old King	Morton Selten
Halima	Mary Morris
Storyteller	Allan Jenyes

The Thief of Bagdad (sometimes spelled *Baghdad*) is arguably the best Arabian Nights motion picture ever made, and a strong contender for the best fantasy film ever made as well. The first of all Arabian Nights movies was the silent *The Thief of Bagdad* (1924), produced by and starring Douglas Fairbanks and directed by Raoul Walsh. Although this was one of the most spectacular and imaginative of silent films, the 1940 remake surpasses it on all counts. The only thing the 1940 and 1924 films have in common is the title and a few standard ingredients of Arabian Nights fantasy, such as a flying carpet. Otherwise, the remake is entirely new. In the early version, the thief is a fully-grown man (played by Fairbanks) who defeats numerous aristocratic claimants to win the hand of the princess. In the 1940 version, the thief is a boy (Sabu), and the romantic lead is the Caliph of Bagdad, Prince Achmad (John Justin). Although the story borrows such ingredients as a djinni or genie, a flying horse, and a flying carpet from the classic tales of Sheherezade, the plot is wholly original.

The Thief of Bagdad begins *in medias res* with the ship of the evil magician Jaffar (Conrad Veidt) arriving at the port of Basra. There, the Princess (June Duprez) has been lying in a trancelike sleep from which she can be awakened only by a kiss from her beloved, the Caliph Achmad of Bagdad. Achmad, however, is now a blind, ragged beggar asking for alms in the bazaar, accompanied by a mongrel dog that seems possessed of human intelligence in performing tricks. Jaffar arranges for the blind beggar to be taken to the palace, where the sleeping princess lies. There he tells his story to the palace maidens.

In the beginning, he was the Caliph Achmad of Bagdad, a master of arms and of armies, the husband of a harem of hundreds of wives. Despite his power, he enjoyed nothing, for he knew nothing of the world and was dominated by his cruel vizier Jaffar, who made the caliph hated for the acts of tyranny that Jaffar perpetrated in his name. Achmad looked on reluctantly as a political prisoner was beheaded outside the palace walls, while a soothsayer chanted a prophecy of liberation that would be achieved by a boy flying on a cloud, who would shoot the tyrant with the arrow of justice.

With Jaffar's encouragement, Achmad decided to venture out in disguise among his people, as the great Haroun-al-Rashid had done, to learn for himself how they lived and what they thought of him. No sooner had he left the palace, however, than he was arrested by Jaffar's police and sentenced to death. In prison, his life began anew, for there he met Abu (Sabu), the thief of Bagdad, a boy also condemned to death. Abu behaved hysterically as the guards threw him into the cell, but as soon as they left, he broke into a broad grin and produced the key to the dungeon, which he had stolen. Together, he and Achmad escaped and traveled by boat from Bagdad to Basra. There Abu planned to ship as a sailor aboard Sinbad's ship.

First, however, he and Achmad explored the city. Just as they had finished a stolen breakfast, the Sultan's cavalry galloped through the marketplace, driving everyone indoors and shooting arrows at any unboarded door or window. The princess was coming, and no person could look upon her and live. Achmad was determined to see this forbidden wonder, and he and Abu hid on a rooftop to watch the procession. As the Princess rode by on a pink elephant, Achmad was so smitten by her beauty that he vowed he must see her again and persuaded the reluctant Abu to help him.

That afternoon, as the Princess and her ladies-in-waiting were languishing by a pool in the palace garden, the face of a man appeared reflected in the water. The attendants thought that it was a djinni and fled, but the Princess was drawn to the handsome stranger and remained. Achmad then swung down from the tree where he was concealed; and though they had just met, he and the Princess pledged eternal love.

Meanwhile, Jaffar had arrived on a visit to the Sultan and asked for the Princess' hand in marriage. Her father (Miles Malleson) demurred; but knowing that the Sultan was a fanatical collector of mechanical toys, Jaffar tempted him with the gift of a flying horse. The Princess nevertheless refused Jaffar, saying that she loved another. At that point, guards brought in Achmad and Abu, who had been captured trying to reenter the garden. Livid with rage,

Jaffar used his magical powers to blind Achmad and turn Abu into a dog; the two of them were then cast out into the streets. Upon learning of her lover's fate, the Princess fell into a trance from which not even Jaffar's magic could awaken her.

Thus far has Achmad told his story to the women attending the sleeping Princess. For months, he has been wandering as a ragged beggar and storyteller of the bazaars, until Jaffar found him and brought him to awaken the Princess. Not knowing of Jaffar's presence, Achmad does awaken her with a kiss. Although dismayed at his tragic fate, the Princess still loves him. But their happiness is short-lived, for Jaffar now abducts her aboard his ship and sets sail back to Bagdad. Abu the dog follows her onboard and tries to protect her, but he is thrown overboard. Jaffar persuades the Princess that only if she allows him to take her in his arms can Achmad's sight be restored. With a shudder, she asks Jaffar to take her in his arms. At that moment, Achmad gives a cry of pain and clutches at his eyes, only to stop in wonder as he finds he can see again. Abu the dog clambers onto the pier, shakes himself, and is transformed back into Abu the thief.

He and Achmad immediately take a boat and go in pursuit of Jaffar's ship. The Princess sees them and cries out with joy, but Jaffar raises a storm that sinks the small craft. When the storm subsides, the waves toss the exhausted Abu upon the beach of a desert island. There he bemoans his fate; but as he explores the beach, he finds a bottle. When he uncorks it, smoke pours out, a menacing laugh breaks the silence, and a deep voice cries "Free!" as the smoke consolidates into an immense djinni, or genie. The djinni (Rex Ingram) seizes the theif and threatens to kill him. When Abu pleads that the djinni should be thankful for his freedom, the djinni replies that King Solomon had imprisoned him. For the first one thousand years of his captivity, he promised to lavish rewards upon the person who freed him, but during the second thousand years, he became so frustrated that he promised to kill when he regained his power. The genie is about to crush Abu when the thief expresses disbelief that the immense djinni could be contained in a small bottle. The djinni proves it by dissolving back into smoke and reentering the flask. Abu promptly caps it up again and says he will fling it into the sea unless the djinni promises to behave. The djinni then offers Abu three wishes. While wondering how to use them, Abu realizes that he is hungry and idly wishes he had some of his mother's sausages. Cautiously, without using a second wish, Abu asks where Achmad is. The djinni tells him that the only way to find out is to obtain the All-seeing Eye of the World. To get it, he must fly "to the highest peak of the highest mountain of the world, where earth meets the sky; and there is the temple of the gods; and in the great wall of the temple is the Goddess of Light; and in the head of the Goddess is the All-seeing Eye."

When Abu asks the djinni to take him there, the djinni places him on his shoulder, tells him to hold onto his hair, and soars off into space. They fly over the Himalayas and arrive at the temple. Green-skinned priests, guardians of the temple, look up in fright and flee inside. The djinni opens the temple door for Abu, places him inside, and blows him across the polished floor to the foot of the Goddess. There, a door leads to a tunnel within the immense statue. When Abu enters, the guards move a lever that closes and locks the entrance behind him. Within, he finds immense cobwebs everywhere and a chamber of skeletons. From one of them, he takes a rusty sword and proceeds, whistling to keep up his nerves, along a narrow ramp that leads to a void. Looking down, Abu sees a pit full of sea monsters. The only way out is to climb up a vast cobweb, its cords the size of a ship's rigging.

As Abu ascends, a gigantic spider emerges from a hole in the ceiling and descends upon its prey. It is almost upon Abu when he takes alarm. As the monstrous spider slashes at him, Abu fights it off with his sword. Finally, the spider backs off and then swings at Abu, who severs the cord from which it dangles. The spider plunges into the pit and is devoured by the monsters there. Abu completes his ascent, emerges by the head of the Goddess, and takes the All-seeing Eye, as the accolytes now prostrate themselves in homage. The eye is a giant ruby, in which Abu sees Achmad lost in a desert wilderness. He asks the djinni to take him there, halfway back across the world. When they arrive, Achmad asks to see the Princess.

Meanwhile, the Sultan has promised her that she will not have to marry Jaffar if she does not wish. Jaffar then gives him another present, a mechanical silver maid—a six-armed goddess that performs an Indian dance. In one of her hands, Jaffar has hidden a dagger, and when the Sultan embraces her at the climax of her dance, she stabs him to death. Jaffar then tempts the Princess to inhale the fragrance of a blue rose. She does not know that it will cause her to forget the past and to love Jaffar. She is just about to inhale it when Achmad and Abu see her in the ruby. Engulfed with despair, Achmad blames Abu and wishes he were back in Bagdad. "I wish you were," answers Abu in momentary anger, and the wish is granted. Achmad arrives in the nick of time and nearly succeeds in fighting off the palace guards, but he is finally overpowered. He and the Princess are both sentenced to death and chained at opposite walls of the death cell.

Abu sees all this is the ruby, but he has used up all of his wishes, and the djinni has vanished. In despair, Abu smashes the ruby against a canyon wall. The earth then revolves beneath him, and he is transported to a land of golden tents where a body of white-bearded patriarchs see him as the messiah who can restore their lost childhood. The kindly king tells Abu he can have everything there except a magic carpet, on which the king expects to ride to paradise at the end of his life.

Abu needs the carpet even more urgently, however, so he steals it, together with a magic crossbow with arrows that never miss their target. At Bagdad,

Achmad is tied down on the very beheading block where he watched a prisoner die at the beginning of the story. The same soothsayer is telling the same prophecy of deliverance at the hands of a boy flying on a cloud. Just in time, Abu appears on the flying carpet, fits an arrow to the bow, and shoots the executioner. The crowd then riots against Jaffar's guards, and Jaffar flees upon the flying horse. Abu shoots again, and as the arrow strikes Jaffar in the forehead, the horse disintegrates in midair. At the end, Achmad is once more the ruler in Bagdad, with the Princess as his bride. Abu, dressed uncomfortably in palace attire, is to become vizier when he completes his education. However, like Huckleberry Finn, he wants no part of being a model youth and flies off on the carpet in search of further adventures.

Several years in the making, *The Thief of Bagdad* is a stunning visual spectacle. The beginning of World War II interrupted production in England (the scene with the djinni on the beach had been filmed near Tintagel in Cornwall), and production was resumed in America, with the desert and mountain scenes filmed at the Grand Canyon and Bryce Canyon. Sabu aged two years during the filming, but this was not very noticeable.

Korda had discovered Sabu in India and starred him in *Elephant Boy* (1937) and *Drums* (sometimes called *The Drum*, 1938); Sabu made one more film for Korda, *The Jungle Book* (1942), and then moved to Hollywood for a brief, disappointing career. Conrad Veidt was a veteran of films since *The Cabinet of Dr. Caligari* (1919). He usually played menacing villains; among his notable roles were Louis XI of France opposite John Barrymore in *The Beloved Rogue* (1927) and the lead in Victor Hugo's *The Man Who Laughs* (1928). During the early years of World War II, he played Nazis, most notably in *Casablanca* (1942), the year before his death. June Duprez had starred in 1939 in Korda's *Four Feathers*; she went on to Hollywood and starred in *None but the Lonely Heart* (1944) and *And Then There Were None* (1945), after which her career faltered. As Prince Achmad, John Justin made his screen debut, after which he returned to the stage, playing Shakespeare at Stratford. He reemerged in films in the 1950's, playing supporting roles in *The Sound Barrier* (1952), *Melba* (1953), *Island in the Sun* (1957), and others.

The cast of *The Thief of Bagdad* captured admirably the spirit of legendary adventure and romantic idealism. These qualities were reinforced by the richest color cinematography to date and by William Cameron Menzies' opulent, imaginative sets—gleaming marble palaces, swarming bazaars, the red sails of Jaffar's ship, the busy harbors, and exotic temples. A major merit of the film was the lush score by Miklós Rózsa, which rivals Rimsky-Korsakov's *Sheherezade* in evoking the wonders of the Arabian Nights. Miles Malleson, who plays the old Sultan, wrote the screenplay, which attains the level of prose poetry. The film was nominated for a number of Academy Awards and won three of them— for art direction/set decoration, special effects in sound, and cinematography—more than any other film of 1940.

All in all, *The Thief of Bagdad* succeeds better than any other film in projecting a sense of wonder. It started a rash of Arabian Nights films in the 1940's and early 1950's; the best of these were *Kismet* (1944) with Ronald Colman and *Sinbad the Sailor* (1947) with Douglas Fairbanks, Jr., but neither of these had the magic of *The Thief of Bagdad*. Universal Studios cranked out a series of Arabian adventures starring Jon Hall, Sabu, Maria Montez, and Turhan Bey, but these rarely rose above the level of adult comic strips. In 1945, Rex Ingram got to play a genie again in *A Thousand and One Nights*, a burlesque version of the story of Alladin, portrayed by Cornel Wilde. Thereafter, most Arabian Nights films (many with Maureen O'Hara) were simply desert horse operas, though a series of Sinbad films have the distinction of ingenious special effects (skeleton swordsmen, harpies, assorted monsters and demons) in the "Superdynamation" of Ray Harryhausen. A low-budget Italian film entitled *The Thief of Bagdad* was issued in 1961, starring muscleman Steve Reeves of the Hercules films, with dubbed English dialogue, but it had nothing to do with the 1940 classic. None of the later films is in the same league with *The Thief of Bagdad* of 1940, which remains one of the finest of all fantasy films, perhaps the finest of them all.

Robert E. Morsberger

THE THIN MAN

Released: 1934
Production: Hunt Stromberg for Metro-Goldwyn-Mayer
Direction: W. S. Van Dyke
Screenplay: Albert Hackett and Frances Goodrich; based on the novel of the same name by Dashiell Hammett
Cinematography: James Wong Howe
Editing: Robert J. Kern
Running time: 91 minutes

Principal characters:

Nick Charles	William Powell
Nora Charles	Myrna Loy
Dorothy Wynant	Maureen O'Sullivan
John Guild	Nat Pendleton
Mimi Wynant Jorgensen	Minna Gombell
MacCaulay	Porter Hall
Chris Jorgensen	Cesar Romero
Clyde Wynant	Edward Ellis

From the comfortable retrospect of almost fifty years, Hollywood in the early 1930's looks like a regulated sort of place: Warner Bros. was doing backstage musicals and social pictures, Paramount was producing sophisticated comedies, Universal was making horror movies, and M-G-M was doing dramas set in satin bedrooms and filled with "more stars than there are in the heavens." The reality, of course, was a good deal less straightforward: no studio could afford to rely on formula, and, almost without exception, the movies that now look like the beginning of a new trend turn out to have been seen, at the time, as doubtful commercial ventures into territory that was all but played out at the box office.

So when, as studio legend has it, W. S. Van Dyke—"one-take Woody," the studio's star director who could be relied upon to bring anything in on time, under budget, and looking highly marketable—came to Louis B. Mayer with Dashiell Hammet's novel, *The Thin Man*, the reaction was true to form: not *another* private-eye movie! Things looked even bleaker when Van Dyke announced that he wanted William Powell to play Nick Charles. Powell was too strongly associated in the public mind with the detective Philo Vance, a character whom he had played in a string of films. He had been playing the part so long, claimed one producer, "that theater managers have been putting the name Philo Vance on their marquees instead of William Powell." But Van Dyke persevered, and, with the aid of his usual associate, the veteran producer Hunt Stromberg, *The Thin Man* was shot in a mere sixteen days—about average as far as Van Dyke was concerned—with a good deal of improvisation on the set, a style perfectly suited to Powell and Myrna Loy.

Powell and Loy made an ideal screen couple, one which was to survive for many other films: they brought to the screen something almost unique among the platinum blondes and juvenile romances of the 1930's—a mature, happy, and clearly physical married relationship. Powell and Loy as Nick and Nora Charles may joke about their relationship, but there is a real bond between them. "You let anything happen to him," Nora warns Asta the dog only half-jokingly, "and you'll never wag that tail again." As the movie ends, Nick and Nora (and Asta) are aboard the San Francisco train heading home after their unrelaxing Christmas in New York. "Put Asta in here with me tonight," says Nora as they return to their sleeping compartment for the night. "Oh yeah?" declares Nick. Asta is tossed unceremoniously onto the top bunk where, in embarrassment, he covers his eyes with his paws. What happens next is as unmistakable as it is when the train rushes into the tunnel at the end of *North by Northwest* (1959). What happens next is, of course, the end title.

The Thin Man opened in New York at the end of June, 1934. It was reasonable to expect that it would do brisk business, since Hammett's novel had been a nationwide best seller, serialized in a number of coast-to-coast newspapers and described by Alexander Woollcott as "the best detective story written in America." But public response to the movie exceeded all expectations. Reviews were generally superlative: "an excellent combination of comedy and excitement" (the *New York Times*), and "a picture you simply cannot afford to miss unless you want to cheat yourself" (*World Telegram*).

Few people, it seems, did cheat themselves, and *The Thin Man* swept Powell, Loy, and Van Dyke to the top of the 1934 box-office polls. It also gave birth to quite a dynasty: *After the Thin Man*, directed by Van Dyke in 1936 from a Hackett/Goodrich screenplay based on a Dashiell Hammett story, which picked up Powell and Loy (and Asta) in San Francisco only two weeks after the end of the first movie; *Another Thin Man*, directed by Van Dyke in 1939 from a screenplay by Hammett himself; *Shadow of the Thin Man* (1941), the last movie in the series to be directed by "one-take Woody" (who died in 1943), from a screenplay by Irving Brecher and Harry Kurnitz; *The Thin Man Goes Home*, directed by Richard Thorpe in 1944 from a screenplay by Robert Riskin and Dwight Taylor; and *Song of the Thin Man* (1947), directed by Edward Buzzell from a screenplay by Steve Fisher and Nat Perrin. A television series with Peter Lawford and Phyllis Kirk was first aired in 1957. It was not a bad run for a movie that M-G-M let Van Dyke make almost as a favor.

To a modern viewer, the first movie in the series takes a little getting used to. The screenplay, Van Dyke's direction, and the main performances operate at a staccato pace, and are sometimes a little abrupt for modern tastes. Van Dyke basically devotes his energy to keeping the plot moving along at a pace scarcely less breakneck than that of Hammett's novel. The details of the complex plot are so involved and the plot's development and conclusion so nearly incomprehensible that when asked if his theory about the crime is true during the final summing up, Nick can only answer "I don't know. It's the only way it makes sense." Perhaps the best comment on the plot is that made by Nora Charles at the end of the novel when she has had it all explained to her: "That may be, but it's all pretty unsatisfactory."

The story of *The Thin Man* is as confused, and as intentionally so, as any Raymond Chandler plot. Suffice it to say that it concerns the efforts of former private eye Nick Charles to track down an eccentric inventor, Clyde Wynant (Edward Ellis), who appears to have murdered his secretary/mistress. This search brings him into contact with a wide range of equally eccentric criminals and honest citizens, including Wynant's ex-wife Mimi (Minna Gombell), her second husband, Chris Jorgensen, played with a lazy sycophancy by a young Cesar Romero, and various other odd characters. At the end of a drunken Christmas party, with a tearful thug trying to phone his mother in San Francisco and a group noisily caroling "Tannenbaum, O Tannebaum!," Nora turns to her husband and remarks "Oh, Nick, I love you. You know such *wonderful* people."

The Thin Man is, in its way, a piece of social history, a sweet and sour image of the 1930's with a hero who is almost always drunk, shoots the ornaments off the Christmas tree with a toy air gun, and never goes without his trusty but spectacularly cowardly guard dog Asta. "Don't make a move or that dog will tear you to pieces," he warns one crook as Asta cowers miserably under a nearby table. Complete with montage sequences of headlines spinning out of the background and, in one memorable insert, a net spreading across a map of the United States as the police search for Wynant spreads, *The Thin Man* is never for a moment a movie to take itself more seriously than is absolutely needed. Even when Nick is shot, more or less by mistake, it is little more than the cue for a gag. Looking through the press reports next day, Nora remarks, "I heard you were shot five times in the tabloids." "It's not true," replies Nick, "he didn't come anywhere near my tabloids."

Nick Roddick

THE THING

Released: 1951
Production: Howard Hawks for RKO/Radio
Direction: Christian Nyby
Screenplay: Charles Lederer; based on the story "Who Goes There?" by John W. Campbell, Jr.
Cinematography: Russell Harlan
Editing: Roland Gross
Running time: 87 minutes

Principal characters:

Captain Hendry	Kenneth Tobey
Dr. Carrington	Robert Cornthwaite
Nikki	Margaret Sheridan
Dr. Stern	Eduard Franz
Scotty	Douglas Spencer
Crew Chief	Dewey Martin
The Thing	James Arness

John W. Campbell, Jr.'s "Who Goes There?" appeared in 1938 in *Astounding Science Fiction*. Charles Lederer's screenplay makes the Campbell story more timely by exploiting the widespread interest during the early 1950's in unidentified flying objects or UFO's. The Thing itself becomes an eight-foot anthropomorphic creature composed of vegetablelike matter that lands in a flying saucer at the North Pole near a scientific expedition base. In the original story, Campbell's alien had lain frozen in the ice for millions of years. The scientists and an Air Force group remove the Thing, which has been frozen in ice, to the expedition's base. After inadvertently being thawed out, it proves to be an intelligent adversary of immense strength which subsists on blood. The Air Force men try to destroy it, but their efforts are hampered by one scientist in particular, Dr. Carrington, who is convinced that mankind has much to learn from the extraterrestrial invader. However, despite a fruitless and last effort by Dr. Carrington to strike a peace with the Thing, the Air Force finally burns it to ashes in an electric trap.

The story develops around the battle between the alien (James Arness) and the people who discover it, and the consequent strife arising between the scientists, led by Dr. Carrington (Robert Cornthwaite), and the Air Force men, led by Captain Hendry (Kenneth Tobey). From the beginning of the film, the Thing seems to be a danger of some kind; it comes from another planet and its very size and appearance make it suspect. Ultimately it is freed from its ice block when a nervous guard, bothered by its staring eyes, covers the block with an electric blanket that melts the ice. Once escaped, it survives an attack by sled dogs and the loss of an arm in the Arctic cold. The conclusive proof of its danger, of course, is its vampirism. It not only regenerates its lost arm but reproduces itself asexually and quickly, as Dr. Carrington demonstrates to his incredulous fellows by planting some scrapings from the severed arm in soil fertilized with blood plasma. The Thing's purpose for coming to this populous planet now becomes manifest: Dr. Carrington observes that it views human beings in the same way humans look upon a cabbage patch—merely as sustenance.

Because of his frank admiration for the Thing's intelligence and purpose, Dr. Carrington quickly falls into conflict with Hendry, who is charged with conducting the investigation. Hendry refuses to risk more lives, since two men have already been killed, so that the Thing may be preserved for study. He is a man of common sense, faced on the one hand with a mysterious hostile force and on the other with a fanatic whose dedication to scientific inquiry borders on depravity. Dr. Carrington emphasizes the extent of his dedication to scientific inquiry over social consciousness by growing further specimens of the Thing (which Hendry immediately has burned), nourishing them with scarce plasma while one of Hendry's men, injured by the Thing, must depend on direct transfusions. He elevates knowledge above human life itself, and claims the Thing to be "wiser than us all." The film ultimately can be charged with an antiintellectualism hardly subtle in its workings: the scientist is openly fascinated with the Thing's lack of any feeling or emotion, yet he seems incapable of reckoning with the consequences of that lack. He believes that logic alone suffices in life, and with some ingenuousness, attributes the same conviction to this creature that bellows, drinks blood, and hangs its victims, men as well as dogs, upside down from a rafter after slitting their throats. Thus, in his own way, Dr. Carrington behaves at odds with humane values, while his colleagues meekly follow until the end.

The Thing was the first film directed by Christian Nyby, Howard Hawks's editor for *The Big Sleep* (1946) and *Red River* (1948), and Hawks's influence is evident in such aspects of this film as the character of the loyal, supportive heroine Nikki (Margaret Sheridan). Although Nyby's subsequent work was rather unexceptional, he does intelligently balance two genres in *The Thing*—science fiction and horror—although the film does not square fully with either tradition. Common elements of science fiction film abound: the military and the scientists confront an invasion from outer space; the Thing arrives in a circular craft, a UFO; it comes with the purpose of repopulating the earth with its own kind and thus destroying civilization. Missing, on the other hand, is evidence of the invader's greatly superior intelligence: while it did build the ship that brought it through space, it evinces scanty knowledge of its destination, landing as it did in the frozen, nearly deserted North Pole, and presumably would have lain helpless in the ice had not the expedition found it. Also the Thing wars on its human adversaries by quite ordinary means; it shuts off their fuel supply, and, at the end of the film, attacks with a club, readily allowing itself to be tricked into stepping on the electric trap which ultimately destroys it. Furthermore, rather than delving into philosophical issues in the manner of a science fiction film such as *The Day the Earth Stood Still* (1951), *The Thing* explores no larger question than the conflict restricted to the expedition at hand—one between the rival claims of scientific advancement and immediate survival.

The basic plot of the film may be science fiction but most of its trappings belong to the horror genre, and the screenplay and directing respond best to this emphasis. Sequences of the horrific abound, but are presented with a deliberate matter-of-factness that juxtaposes the naïveté and the destructiveness of the unknown: the long shot of the men forming an almost perfect circle as they determine the shape of the craft visible under the ice; the water dripping steadily from under the electric blanket thrown over the ice block that encases the Thing, juxtaposed against film cuts to the guard, his back to the block unaware of his immediate danger and absent-mindedly reading; the quick (and expected) close-up of the Thing when Hendry opens the greenhouse door. Although the characters naturally show fear and anxiety, they never show terror, and the dialogue remains conversational and low-key throughout. Thus, the characters, in their ignorance of the full potential for destruction at hand, emerge fairly well realized; the Air Force group in particular continually engages in a banter and camaraderie that rests upon instinctive professionalism. The audience shares with Hendry's men a sympathetic interest in their captain's bumpy courtship of Nikki; that courtship becomes a symbol of everyday human concerns still flourishing amidst the chaos caused by an angry invader from outer space.

The film's plot, reminiscent of the political philosophy of America during the early 1950's, depends on an oversimplified division between the heroic actions of the military in protecting commonplace values and interference of a group of impractical, potentially subversive scientists; Dr. Carrington even has a Trotsky-like beard and a noticeably Slavic accent. The idea for destroying the Thing by electricity originates, not in scientific expertise, but in an offhand remark made by Nikki, who, when asked what one does with a vegetable, replies "You boil it, bake it, or stew it."

The intent upon timeliness at the end of the film becomes a major detraction. Scotty (Douglas Spencer), a surviving expeditionary member, delivers to the world, via a short-wave radio broadcast, a newscast full of precious sentiment, concluding both his report and the film itself with the admonition, "Watch the skies! Everywhere. . . . Keep looking. . . . Keep watching the skies!" *The Thing* should be reckoned primarily as a horror film composed of skillfully managed scariness which conveys a message respectable enough: man is not necessarily vulnerable to the irrational dangers from without so long as he can provide a morally alert, united defense.

William H. Brown, Jr.

THINGS TO COME

Released: 1936
Production: Alexander Korda for London Film Productions; released by United Artists
Direction: William Cameron Menzies
Screenplay: H. G. Wells; based on his book *The Shape of Things to Come*
Cinematography: George Perinal
Editing: Charles Crichton
Running time: 96 minutes

Principal characters:
John Cabal/Oswald Cabal .... Raymond Massey
The Boss .... Ralph Richardson
Pippa Passworthy/
Raymond Passworthy .... Edward Chapman
Roxana Black/Rowena Black .... Margaretta Scott
Theotocopulos .... Sir Cedric Hardwicke

Far more than the comic strip exploits of Buck Rogers, *Things to Come* has influenced all the films which have come to constitute the genre of "science fiction." It is a prototype for science fiction movies both in style and content. Even after more than forty years of advancement in film technique, there are few science fiction films which manage to surpass the stylistic achievement of *Things to Come*; and, although its explicit ideological content was (and remains) creaky and bombastic, the film provides an object lesson on the true function of science fiction. Usually, science fiction literature and cinema mask their ideological content in a flurry of technological wizardry, but *Things to Come* is still an important reminder that the creation of a world which might be always implies an analysis of and comment upon the world which is.

The production of *Things to Come* was unusual in view of the fact that the balance of power was shared among three equally creative and forceful individuals: producer Alexander Korda, director/art director William Cameron Menzies, and screenwriter H. G. Wells. In the case of Korda and Menzies, it was a felicitous collaboration; the contribution of Wells's script to the success of the film is dubious (although, obviously, it was his nonfiction work, *The Shape of Things to Come*, which provided the basic structure of the film). Alexander Korda is noted as the producer/director of well-mounted, large-scale history and adventure extravaganzas, such as *The Private Life of Henry VIII* (1933), *The Scarlet Pimpernel* (1934), *Elephant Boy* (1937), and *The Jungle Book* (1942). Through his association with America's United Artists, he was able to provide the financial backing for Britain's first million dollar feature, *Things to Come*; and his skill at assembling first-rate technicians and the artistic expertise of Menzies causes *Things to Come* to look like a million dollar picture, even today.

Menzies is probably best known as the production designer of *Gone with the Wind* (1939). It was through him that the role of production designer came to be defined as the person who is responsible for the overall look of a film, the coordinator of sets, costumes, and art direction to provide a unified style. Among his other cinematic achievements are *The Thief of Bagdad* (1924), *Alice in Wonderland* (1933), and *Around the World in 80 Days* (1956).

H. G. Wells is popularly known as a writer of science fiction works, many of which—*The Time Machine*, *The Invisible Man*, and *The War of the Worlds*—have been dramatized and all of which were written, incredibly, in the late nineteenth century. In later years, however, Wells applied his vision to philosophical speculation about Utopias; in *Things to Come* his skill at predicting the possible development of technology beyond existing reality and his speculation about the logical development of social order from current trends come together in what was a most timely, and hence, popular movie.

The film opens in 1940, at Christmas time in Everytown, with shots of carollers and posters announcing imminent war juxtaposed. Rational men of science gather the generations around them to celebrate the holidays as the sounds of bombers are heard. Everytown and its art deco street scenes are plunged into chaos as the bombs drop and the city is destroyed in a masterful montage of rubble, lined and shadowed faces, panicky crowds, and shadowy marching figures. Images of tanks and troops signal the continuation of the war until 1966, when a new segment begins.

In the second part, against the backdrop of Everytown ruins, a pretechnological, medieval-looking society has emerged. Doctors work with limited supplies to save people from an epidemic of the wandering sickness, craftsmen work with primitive tools, and autos are pulled by horses. A violent bully who shoots the victims of the wandering sickness emerges as the leader, a petty tyrant called "The Boss" (Ralph Richardson). Into this budding Fascist state flies a mammoth, futuristic plane (with propellers), piloted by a representative of "Wings over the World," another form of civilization which has developed in the wake of the thirty-year war. The conflict of ideologies begins. The pilot represents a vaguely socialist, Utopian technocracy in which all citizens are members of the "Brotherhood of Efficiency." They govern themselves by "common sense" and exploit resources for prosperity and world order. The Boss represents an antitechnological, nationalistic, totalitarian state: "who wants books to muddle our thoughts and ideas . . . so what if we can't travel, isn't our land good enough for us. . . ." While the Boss carouses in his ruined castle an escape is engineered; an old plane flies off to return with Wings over the World planes, which drop the gas of peace on the inhabitants of Everytown and disarm them.

In 1936, when the film was released in Britain, audiences laughed at the image of squadrons of planes flying over the white cliffs of Dover to bomb Everytown, and yet this image remains a haunting and powerful prediction of what was in store for England in but a few years.

In the third segment of *Things to Come*, society has reached the year 2036 and the film achieves its full artistic and technical development. Through the use of special effects, miniatures, and vast sets, a world of inventiveness and industry is represented: prefab high-rise apartments, monorails, neon, air-conditioned interior spaces with Plexiglas furniture and inhome film screens, helicopters, spacious Bauhaus-design factories, and people in winged white suits with short tunics and sandals. It is interesting to note that all of the innovations in technology and design, while far-reaching for 1936, are plausible and possible extensions of existing technology; there are no predictive leaps beyond known scientific knowledge, as is painfully obvious at the end of the film.

A rebellion against scientific progress is led by the master craftsman. His target is "the great white world of science and order" as symbolized by a rocket ship scheduled to depart for outer space; his longing is to return to the days when life was "short and hot and merry." The offending rocket ship, invented by designers not privy to the secrets of jet propulsion and nuclear energy, is a gigantic gun, complete with sight and trigger, from which the spaceship bullet will be shot into space. Despite attacks by artisans and aroused citizens, the space vehicle (which contains the descendants of those men who conquered the primitive Fascist state) is launched into space and the future. The ultimate image of the film is not of the earth but the stars, where, through the creation of a technological order, the future lies.

Throughout the film are images of children, from the war-torn streets of Everytown in 1940 to the futuristic scientific world of home-viewing screens. While the images of the material world change radically throughout the film, the continuity of humanity and the notion of the future contained in the present are expressed through these images of children. This notion is further and more explicitly reinforced by the use of the same actors to play their own descendants. The finest actors of the day, among them Raymond Massey, Ralph Richardson, and Cedric Hardwicke, are often constrained from creating three-dimensional characters by the script's preachy dialogue, but, as is the case with all fine and lasting films, the images speak for themselves. Massey's gaunt and haunted face, Richardson's swaggering posture, and Hardwicke's toga-draped demagoguery continue to be intriguing.

Connie McFeeley

THE THIRD MAN

Released: 1949
Production: Sir Carol Reed for London Films
Direction: Sir Carol Reed
Screenplay: Graham Greene
Cinematography: Robert Krasker (AA)
Editing: Oswald Hafenrichter
Music: Anton Karas
Running time: 93 minutes

Principal characters:
Holly Martins .... Joseph Cotten
Anna Schmidt .... Alida Valli
Major Calloway .... Trevor Howard
Harry Lime .... Orson Welles

Apart from his Academy Award-winning *Oliver!* (1968), Sir Carol Reed is best known for his direction of films during the late 1940's and 1950's which usually focus on the man apart, the independent character outside the social norm. In *Odd Man Out* (1947), *Outcast of the Islands* (1951), and *Our Man in Havana* (1959), Reed's work embodies the moral uncertainty, alienation, and anxiety which grew out of World War II and the Cold War. Thus, he began to establish the ambiance for much of modern cinema. However, only in *The Third Man* do all of the major cinematic elements—sound, scene, character, script, and symbol—come together to epitomize the modern sense of increasing artificiality, dying innocence, and irrepressible pain.

From the film's initial moments, an emotional tension is engendered in the audience. This harbinger of the picture's dominant mood comes directly from the sound track, from the only musical backdrop given the picture: the solo zither productions of composer/performer Anton Karas. The relatively unfamiliar, repetitive, twangy, and slightly disconcerting tones of this oddly strung instrument alert the listener to the emotional and moral discomforts that the plot soon will unveil. Thus, the wry and anxious mixture of personalities and actions which will characterize the film are sensed well before they become verbally or visually evident; and as soon as the viewer begins to understand this picture's setting, this tonal impression is reinforced.

We find ourselves in a city divided, postwar Vienna, a city historically and symbolically suggesting the downward movement the plot will take. Occupied Vienna, split into segments by the armies of the United States, Britain, and Russia, graphically shows the fragmentation of postwar society and indicates the distance between Europe's present spiritual, material, and cultural paucity and its august past. During the credits the camera walks through this symbolic arena, constantly glancing at a Ferris wheel in the midst of the gray and shattered city. Thus, a seemingly incongruent and yet appropriate polarity is established between the world of men and children, war and play, experience and innocence.

This architectural urban symbolism quickly finds a protagonist in the person of Holly Martins (Joseph Cotten), a writer of juvenile Western fiction and youthful companion to the dark antagonist of the story, Harry Lime (Orson Welles). Holly enters the picture on a note of bad luck as he walks under a ladder leaning against the front of Lime's hotel. But more than misfortune is implied by this first shot: we are immediately confronted with the imagery (the ladder) of upward and downward progression that is to characterize the movie. We are reminded of the importance of architecture; the hotel is faced with pseudo-Greek statuary and thus implies the break between Vienna's façade of past cultural glory and the corruption, in the person of Lime, at present contained within. The viewer may not fully comprehend all of these symbolic interrelations at first, but repetitions make them more evident throughout the film.

Certainly, the viewer cannot depend upon the narrator, Holly, for any clarification. Indeed, one of the movie's accomplishments is its exploration of point of view. Holly's insights are as juvenile as are his literary productions; thus, from the start, Holly is associated with darkness, innocence, and relative ignorance.

Entering Lime's hotel, he learns from the caretaker that Lime was just run over by a car. While relating this incident in broken English, the caretaker is replacing a burnt-out light bulb. With these actions almost all of the movie's symbolic elements have been introduced: Europe's past, represented by its ancient buildings, has been replaced with the scarcities and destruction of the present. Only in innocent Americans do images of plenty and of moral certainty survive. However, even Holly's blind moralism is threatened by the darkness which surrounds him. Likewise, his mastery of a Western fiction of inexperienced youth is threatened by the "babel" of foreign tongues which further confuses this occupied city.

Opposing Holly in every way is the master of movement and rhetoric, the prince of darkness, Harry Lime. He, who created the illusion of his own death to throw off the police, flourishes on destruction; illness is his milieu. Pursued by the Americans, the Russians, and the British, Harry had stolen penicillin from postwar hospitals, diluted it, and sold it back at an amazing profit. This crime and its disastrous effects on patients using the drug were so heinous that he had to stage his own demise by using the body of a cohort, a hospital orderly, to take his place among the dead. Ironically, Lime's presence at his own accident, observed by his hotel caretaker, creates for Holly the impression of "a third man" who, Holly thinks, must have been responsible for Lime's "death." Thus, Martins' bumbling sense of moral obligation to his dead friend leads him to find instead that this friend was his own fictional murderer and the actual murderer of thousands of drug-dependent war victims. Ultimately, however, Holly's innocence must die.

Eventually, these tangles of plot bring about their own unlikely conclusion. Holly's pursuit of Lime's imaginary killer constantly casts Lime into the spotlight. Thus, in order to defend his dead image, he must at last emerge into the light and meet Holly on that central symbolic icon of the film's changing fates, the black Ferris wheel at the center of the dark city.

It is here that Lime's character becomes completely evident and that Holly's illusions finally die. From the top of this last ride of childhood, both Holly and the audience understand Harry's position. For Lime, people are like the "ants" seen from the height of the ride, and the ride's height itself is no longer a childish thrill but a potential means of executing a possibly uncooperative Holly Martins. Nor is Lime at all embarrassed about this violence, for he recognizes that, despite appearances to the contrary, war and culture, black and white, up and down, and good and evil are complementary concepts: "In Italy for thirty years under the Borgias, they had warfare, terror, murder, bloodshed. They produced Michelangelo, Leonardo da Vinci, and the Renaissance. In Switzerland they had brotherly love, five hundred years of democracy and peace, and what did they produce . . . ? The cuckoo clock!" With this dark ride Holly begins at last to see, and he is now ready to become part of that dark world and to betray his sometime friend.

Working with Lime's long-time pursuer, Major Calloway (Trevor Howard), and against Lime's girl friend Anna Schmidt (Alida Valli), Holly betrays Lime. In the final chase sequence, an incongruous nighttime balloon salesman forces a last children's balloon on a police officer trying to be inconspicuous. With this final ironic gesture, the film descends into the architectural depths of the city, the Hades which is Lime's haunt, the sewer system. Here, in dramatic shadows which no longer seem to impede our protagonist, Holly completes his initiation: he kills Lime.

At the end we return to the beginning. The symbolic circle is drawn into a knot: Lime is buried once again. All of the imagistic, narrative, and plot devices have come back upon themselves. Holly Martins will no longer be able to write a child's Western. Instead, we finally realize, it was he who, in retrospect, narrated his greatest work of art, *The Third Man*. Out of the violence he had previously avoided he found, like Michelangelo and the Borgias, the capacity to create something other than another cuckoo clock narration of virile cowboys on an unspoiled plain.

While Holly Martins may get credit for a growth in sophistication within the film's framework, Graham Greene deserves most of our plaudits once the film ends. His screenplay not only supplied the movie's excellent plot and symbolism but also a torrent of exquisitely ironic dialogue. Nor could he, with Carol Reed, have picked a better pair than Joseph Cotten and Orson Welles to play the opposing poles of his verbal exchanges. Drawing on their mutual experience in *Citizen Kane* (1941), Cotten and Welles are the perfect vehicles for the communication of the dark realizations of the postwar era.

Daniel D. Fineman

THE 39 STEPS

Released: 1935
Production: Michael Balcon and Ivor Montagu for Gaumont-British
Direction: Alfred Hitchcock
Screenplay: Charles Bennett, Alma Reville, and Ian Hay; based on the novel of the same name by John Buchan
Cinematography: Bernard Knowles
Editing: D. N. Twist
Running time: 81 minutes

Principal characters:

Pamela	Madeleine Carroll
Richard Hannay	Robert Donat
Annabella Smith	Lucie Mannheim
Professor Jordan	Godfrey Tearle
Margaret	Peggy Ashcroft
John	John Laurie
Mrs. Jordan	Helen Haye

The 39 Steps is vintage British Hitchcock at its best, and, similar to *The Lady Vanishes* (1938), it manages to blend comedy and suspense to just the right degree. Yet the reason for much of the appeal of *The 39 Steps* lies not in its direction or in the fairly obvious studio-bound production, but in the script. Full credit for this must go to Charles Bennett, who took the original novel by John Buchan and completely rewrote it for the screen, adding not only a romantic interest but also a new story, leaving in essence nothing of Buchan's original but the basic idea. Charles Bennett's contribution to the success of Hitchcock's British films should never be underestimated; he was involved with the director's most famous films of that era: *Blackmail* (1929), *The Man Who Knew Too Much* (1934), *The 39 Steps*, *The Secret Agent* (1936), *Sabotage* (1936), and *Young and Innocent* (1937).

The 39 Steps features Robert Donat, fresh from his success in *The Count of Monte Cristo* (1934), and Madeleine Carroll, who might be described as the first in a long line of classic and cool Hitchcock blondes, a line which was later to include Grace Kelly and Tippi Hedren. The two have the distinction of being starred in a film which Alfred Hitchcock has described as one of his favorites and one of his first major successes in the United States.

Richard Hannay (Robert Donat), a Canadian living in London, is first seen at a London music hall, where an act named "Mr. Memory" is onstage. In the act, Mr. Memory identifies Hannay as a Canadian, and that is about all the audience ever learns of him. Outside the music hall, Hannay meets Annabella (Lucie Mannheim), who has fired some shots in the auditorium; she explains to him that she was forced to do so in order to create a diversion and thus escape from two men who were trying to kill her. She tells Hannay, "I'd like to come home with you," to which he replies, prophetically as it transpires, "It's your funeral." At Hannay's apartment, Annabella tells him of a plot to take military secrets out of England and that her destination is Scotland. Hannay is somewhat unbelieving, again prophetically telling her that the episode sounds like a spy story; but Hannay is rapidly made aware of the reality of the situation when he is literally awakened in the middle of the night by Annabella's staggering into his room and falling dead across his bed, a knife in her back.

Hannay finds himself trapped in his apartment, and is only able to escape by changing places with the milkman. He heads for Annabella's destination, Scotland, with no further clues and pursued not only by her killers, but also by the police, who suspect him of being Annabella's murderer. On the train, there is a brief comic interlude with two traveling salesmen, surely forerunners to Naunton Wayne and Basil Radford in *The Lady Vanishes*; this is one of a series of comedy moments which enliven what has now become little more than a chase film. Another great comedy sequence has Hannay forced, for his own protection, to pretend to be a political candidate addressing a meeting; the speech is so full of double-talk and sounds so much like a genuine political tirade that it warrants a round of applause from the audience in the Assembly Hall.

Back on the train, Hannay is forced to fake a friendship with a woman named Pamela (Madeleine Carroll) to evade the police; however, she identifies him to the law, and Hannay jumps from the train as it crosses the Forth Bridge. Fleeing across the Scottish moors, Hannay takes shelter with a stern, middle-aged Calvanistic crofter named John, magnificently played by character actor John Laurie, and with the crofter's young wife Margaret (Peggy Ashcroft). The wife seems romantically inclined towards Hannay and helps him; but later she suffers a beating from her husband for her interest in him. The crofter directs Hannay to the house of a professor (Godfrey Tearle) who seems to be the most pleasant of the characters in *The 39 Steps*. He is a genial family man, the only character who welcomes Hannay with friendship, but he is also the leader of the spies. Annabella, before she died, had warned Hannay to beware of a man with part of his finger missing, and Hannay recognizes that man as the professor.

Hannay escapes from the professor, locates and again turns to Pamela for assistance, this time during the political speechmaking at the Assembly Hall. He is again turned in by her, this time to the spies who are forced to take Pamela with them; she and Hannay are handcuffed together. Because of the obtrusion of a flock of sheep, Pamela and Hannay are separated from the spies, and, handcuffed together, wander across the moors. The handcuffs obviously have sexual overtones, not only as a form of fetish—symbols of a love-hate relationship—but because they force the couple to spend the night very much together. While Hannay sleeps, however, Pamela manages to slip off the handcuffs since they are a man's and she has a small feminine wrist. She is about to desert Hannay, when she overhears the professor talking of "thirty-nine steps" and arranging a meeting with his fellow conspirators at the London Palladium.

At the Palladium, Mr. Memory's act is again on the bill and all the elements of the plot merge. As the police arrive to arrest Hannay, he shouts out the question to Mr. Memory, "What are the thirty-nine steps?" Mr. Memory, who has been taught all his life to respond with the truth even if that truth means his death, replies before he is shot by the professor, "The thirty-nine steps is a political organization of spies collecting information on behalf of the foreign office of. . . ." We never do discover which foreign government was involved. Unlike John Buchan's novel in which the thirty-nine steps are a place, in the film the designation refers to a group of people. *The 39 Steps* was remade in 1960 and 1978, in versions starring Kenneth More and Robert Powell respectively; both the later versions are dull, tedious affairs, perhaps because they are closer to John Buchan's novel than they are to Charles Bennett's script, and both were only moderately successful, with the 1978 remake not even being released in the United States until 1980.

Anthony Slide

THIS SPORTING LIFE

Released: 1963
Production: Karel Reisz for Independent Artists
Direction: Lindsay Anderson
Screenplay: David Storey; based on his novel of the same name
Cinematography: Denys Coop
Editing: Peter Taylor
Running time: 129 minutes

Principal characters:
Frank Machin .... Richard Harris
Mrs. Hammond .... Rachel Roberts
Weaver .... Alan Badel

The hard-hitting *This Sporting Life* was released in England early in 1963 and in the summer of the same year in the United States. It appeared when the socially committed, realist style of British filmmaking—the so-called "Angry Young Man" school, begun with *Room at the Top* (1959) and continuing with *Saturday Night and Sunday Morning* (1960) and *A Taste of Honey* (1962)—was fully established. Directed by Lindsay Anderson and written by David Storey, the film is set in grimy, smokey, industrialized Northern England and combines a character study of Frank Machin (Richard Harris), a brawny miner hoping to claw his way out of his squalid working-class milieu via the rough rugby playing fields, with the story of his attempt to win the love of his landlady, Mrs. Hammond (Rachel Roberts), a sexually repressed, withdrawn widow with two children.

The film begins in the midst of a bruising rugby match in which Machin's front teeth are bashed in. Carried off to the cheers of the fans, the dazed Machin is attended to in the locker room, then sent to a dentist. Throughout these treatments, while slipping in and out of consciousness as a result of the dentist's anesthesia, Machin relives episodes of his life: his grueling regimen as a miner; his jealousy of the well-paid professional rugby players (a feeling which later turns to pride when he tries out for the team and is accepted and given a check for £1,000 upon signing); and his initial encounters with Mrs. Hammond, who has not recovered from her husband's death (possibly a suicide), but who is drawn to her young roomer out of sexual longing and loneliness.

At this point in the movie, director Anderson abandons the flashback technique he has so expertly utilized and presents his story in straightforward fashion, as Machin, playing the violent sport for the money it brings him, tries to break through Mrs. Hammond's coldness. This happens only once, briefly, at Christmas, as both confess to their helpless loneliness and confide details of their past lives. However, money does nothing to overcome Machin's boorish and brash manner, which offends Mrs. Hammond, and their relationship, still only sexual in nature, deteriorates into a series of increasingly bitter arguments. At the same time, Machin comes to realize that he is only being used by the uncaring, middle-class businessman, Weaver (Alan Badel), who coowns the rugby team as a well-paying "hobby," and whose wife unsuccessfully attempts to seduce Machin.

Machin eventually leaves the rooming house in anger and frustration. When he is unable to stay away and returns to find it dark and empty he is informed that Mrs. Hammond has suffered a brain hemorrhage. As he rushes to the hospital and speaks to her with tenderness and concern, revealing his true feelings and hopes for the future, she dies. Torn by remorse, Machin finally realizes what he has lost. The film fades out as it has opened, on the bloody sporting grounds with Machin playing his customary ruthless game to the bloodthirsty screams of the crowds.

This Sporting Life was judged a superlative blend of acting, directing, and writing resulting in an emotionally direct, thematically concise and realistic treatment of a segment of British life seldom seen on the screen. European critics and mainstream American reviewers were particularly enthusiastic, although the more literary critics in the United States, such as Andrew Sarris and Dwight MacDonald, faulted the script and Anderson's "excessive" directorial mannerisms.

The film served to introduce several important British film artists who went on to achieve prominence. David Storey based his screenplay (the first of his career) on his own popular and prize-winning novel. The effective, mood-enhancing black-and-white cinematography was by Denys Coop, who had worked his way up from the ranks of camera operators. The film was also the first production of Karel Reisz, who had come to prominence by directing the similarly themed and styled *Saturday Night and Sunday Morning*. The movie was the first feature directed by Lindsay Anderson, a former critic and prize-winning documentary filmmaker, who would later direct *If . . .* (1969) and *O Lucky Man* (1973).

This Sporting Life marked the return of Rachel Roberts, who had starred in *Saturday Night and Sunday Morning*, and gave Richard Harris his first important screen role. Then thirty years old, he was favorably compared with Marlon Brando and a young Richard Burton. Harris won the 1963 "Best Actor" prize at the Cannes Film Festival for his performance as well as the Joseph Burstyn Award in the United States, and was nominated for the New York Film Critics Award (as was Storey's screenplay), losing to Albert Finney in *Tom Jones*, a British film totally opposite in nature to the grim, hopeless *This Sporting Life*. Both Harris and Roberts were nominated for Oscars but lost to Sidney Poitier (*Lilies of the Field*) and Patricia Neal (*Hud*), respectively.

This Sporting Life appeared in no fewer than six of the more prestigious American "Best Ten" lists for 1963 releases.

David Bartholomew

A THOUSAND CLOWNS

Released: 1965
Production: Fred Coe for Harrell; released by United Artists
Direction: Fred Coe
Screenplay: Herbert Gardner; based on his play of the same name
Cinematography: Arthur J. Ornitz
Editing: Ralph Rosenblum
Running time: 118 minutes

Principal characters:

Murray Burns	Jason Robards
Nick	Barry Gordon
Sandra	Barbara Harris
Arnold Burns	Martin Balsam (AA)
Albert	William Daniels
Leo (Chuckles)	Gene Saks

The quality which is remarkable about *A Thousand Clowns* and which keeps it a favorite on the cult film circuit is its precocity. Several years before the radical fringe and the liberal body of Americans began to hear the rumblings of a different drummer, playwright Herb Gardner was exalting all sorts of deviant behavior. Long before Americans began to experience mass anxiety over their loss of individualism, their subjugation to corporate power, their mindless addiction to television, and their need for something greater than material success or respectable conformity, Gardner had begun to prod his audiences into an awareness of these issues. In *A Thousand Clowns*—a successful Broadway play that became a somewhat less successful film—a well-employed television comedy writer named Murray Burns (Jason Robards) gives up everything to roam the streets of Manhattan in search of his identity. The conflict is supplied by the intrusion of two do-gooder social workers who profess to be concerned for the welfare of Murray's illegitimate twelve-year-old nephew and roommate, Nick (Barry Gordon). Their message to the wayward Murray is that he must either get a job or lose custody of Nick.

The film follows Murray in a poignant, fun-filled romp through the city, through playful episodes with the precocious Nick, through romance with the wide-eyed female half of the child welfare team, and through painful confrontations with the infantile embodiment of his terror—the Chuckles the Chipmunk character from his television writing days. Throughout, Murray fights to preserve both his individualism and his benignly derelict life-style, abusing his neighbors, frustrating his family and friends, and confounding his detractors.

Murray is presented as an uncommon man, bright, talented, and potentially successful, yet willing to live in meager circumstances, dependent only on a regular unemployment check and a daily delivery of fresh fruit from his successful brother Arnold (Martin Balsam). He spends his time strumming a ukulele, cruising the waters off Staten Island, bidding exuberant bon voyages to nameless travelers on ocean liners, and daring the rest of the world to defy him. Gardner's description of Murray's life suggests that there is an inherent virtue in eccentricity and in one's freedom to express it.

Murray fights to win over Sandra (Barbara Harris), the young child psychologist who would like to turn him into a typical Madison Avenue executive (she brings flowers and lace curtains to his rather dumpy apartment), a sort of corporate Everyman. Yet, she succumbs to the charm and gentle rebelliousness of Murray for what proves to be only a brief flirtation with his world. In the end it is Murray who gives in, but more because of his love for Nick than for Sandra. The last scene of the film shows him marching off, briefcase in hand, to rejoin the world of the nine-to-fivers. The final freeze frame of Murray rushing off to work leaves an ironic, discomforting sadness with the audience.

Jason Robards is a charming if less than satisfying hero in this re-creation of his stage role. His character is unfortunately never given the dimension one might expect of a contemporary knight-errant who wages his own private war against "the system." Although essentially full of warmth and wry humor, his performance sometimes seems contrived and shallow. Conversely, Barry Gordon's abundant earnestness in his role occasionally makes Robard's role seem pale. Gordon's performance suffers, however, from the fact that Gordon at sixteen was playing a twelve-year-old character. Barbara Harris, who made her screen debut in the film, is most convincing as the naïve yet admiring psychologist who offers a balance between the fantasy world in which Murray lives and the one that is real to most people. A strong performance is also given by Martin Balsam, who won an Oscar for Best Supporting Actor for his role as Murray's "straight" brother; he infuses a bemused warmth into his character which makes it likable and sympathetic. Gene Saks as the crazy television clown is also well cast.

If all of the performances lack some depth, it may be because of the problems involved in adapting a small-scale, live stage play to the film medium, rather than because of any fault with the actors. The filmmakers realized that the ingredients which made the play work—the bright dialogue, honest humor, and a worthwhile theme—would have to be modified in order to translate well into film; successful adaptations of plays to film usually demand increased movement and a wider variety of scenes. In the case of *A Thousand Clowns*, the changes made in the film version tend to dilute the plot with a series of camera techniques which detract from the original story idea, yet which, ironically, improve the work as a film.

The innovative use of black-and-white cinematography by Arthur J. Ornitz is a triumph. His use of zooms, jump cuts, and extreme facial close-ups are suggestive of Swedish director Ingmar Bergman. Ornitz's camerawork is enhanced by unusual use of speed, sound, and rhythmic sequences, such as the scene in the automat when a cheese sandwich is produced to the accompaniment of the "Hallelujah Chorus." There are scenes of people marching to work like Druids in fast-forwards, responding to stop lights, horns, and bells, which cinematically illustrate Murray's view of life in a way that mere dialogue cannot. It is an effective and artfully applied technique that is reminiscent of early German documentarians such as Walter Ruttmann.

The film's momentum is uneven, but it is strongest in the interaction scenes between Murray and Nick. The weakest moments, dramatically, although the ones which appeal to many of the film's followers, are the several long, meaningless jaunts through New York during which Murray demonstrates his extravagant *joie de vivre*. These are afterthoughts, it would appear, added to provide some visual relief from the dark enclosure of Murray's cluttered apartment in which most of the action takes place.

Philosophically, *A Thousand Clowns* is based on the position that the only real way to fight the nefarious influence of the corporate world is to "drop out" and take occasional vocal potshots at it. Murray is something of a modern-day Henry Thoreau who withdraws into his own urban apartment. His humor and love of life make the audience aware of a certain aspect of themselves which they usually suppress and which, in the end, Murray does as well.

Sally V. Holm

THREE COMRADES

Released: 1938
Production: Joseph L. Mankiewicz for Metro-Goldwyn-Mayer
Direction: Frank Borzage
Screenplay: F. Scott Fitzgerald and Edward E. Paramore; based on the novel of the same name by Erich Maria Remarque
Cinematography: Joseph Ruttenberg
Editing: Frank Sullivan
Running time: 98 minutes

Principal characters:

Erich Lohkamp	Robert Taylor
Pat Hollmann	Margaret Sullavan
Otto Koster	Franchot Tone
Gottfried Lenz	Robert Young
Alfons	Guy Kibbee
Franz Breuer	Lionel Atwill
Dr. Jaffe	Monty Woolley
Dr. Heinrich Becker	Henry Hull
Dr. Plauten	George Zucco
Local Doctor	Charley Grapewin

Frank Borzage was one of the most underrated directors to come out of Hollywood, and yet recent reappraisals and retrospectives of his work have proved that he was, if not a great director, one of the few American directors with a vision all his own and with the unique talent to turn anything he was working on into a "Borzage film." In the preauteur days of the 1930's and 1940's when Borzage was at his most prolific, American directors were assigned stories to film and often found it difficult to put their own special stamp upon a work. Some succeeded; certainly John Ford did, sometimes Michael Curtiz did, and almost always, Frank Borzage did. A Borzage film was usually melodrama in its purest form, almost in the manner of the films of D. W. Griffith, the director Borzage most closely resembles. What distinguished Borzage, however, was his sense of spirituality. In almost all of his major pictures, his lovers are united by a force that is more than physical, and their love triumphs in spite of adversity.

Borzage made a series of three films that combined this spirituality with an awareness of the specter that was gradually creeping over the world prior to World War II. These three films, which were based on best-selling novels, all told the effect of the rising influence of Nazism on couples in love, and all starred Margaret Sullavan, an actress Borzage used again and again for her blend of wistfullness and vulnerability. The films were *Little Man What Now* (1934), an adaptation of Hans Fallada's influential book about a young couple in Germany during the worst years of the depression; *Three Comrades*

(1938), based on Erich Maria Remarque's novel and adapted by F. Scott Fitzgerald; and *The Mortal Storm* (1940), from the novel by Phyllis Bottome. *Three Comrades* is the middle film of Borzage's anti-Nazi trilogy, and is in many ways the most interesting one. In addition to being the only film for which F. Scott Fitzgerald received a screen credit, the film contains outstanding performances from its all-star cast, which includes Margaret Sullavan (nominated for an Oscar), Robert Taylor, Franchot Tone, and Robert Young. The supporting cast is nearly as impressive; Borzage chose distinguished actors such as Monty Woolley, Guy Kibbee, and Lionel Atwill for even the smallest of roles.

The original screenplay by Fitzgerald was so pessimistic in its outlook that both Borzage and Joseph L. Mankiewicz, the film's producer, made some changes in the basic plot concept and put an additional writer on the project to give the story a stronger romantic base. This tale of doomed love and friendship set against the rise of Nazism in Germany reaches heights of almost painful emotional intensity at times, but Borzage's presence behind the camera stops it from drifting into mindless sentimentality.

The film opens after the Armistice in 1918 when three German soldiers return home to operate a taxi and garage business together. They have come back from the war somewhat disillusioned, especially Otto (Franchot Tone), who only values his friendship with the other two. Gottfried (Robert Young), the most politically oriented of the three, has remained an idealist, while Erich (Robert Taylor), the youngest and least affected, is determined to live his life to the fullest. The three jointly buy a car which they repair and for which they develop a great affection. During a slight road mishap, they meet Pat Holliman (Margaret Sullavan), a beautiful consumptive who was living on the remnants of a family fortune that she lost during the war when she became ill. She is presently keeping company with Herr Breuer (Lionel Atwill), a wealthy Fascist. Erich falls in love with Pat, unaware of her ill health; but because he earns so little, he is reluctant to ask her to marry him. Pat is also deeply in love with Erich, but hesitates to return his affection because of the uncertainty of her condition. Pat becomes a kind of mascot for Otto and Gottfried, and the three men become the most important people in her life causing a rift between her and Herr Breuer.

Otto finally persuades Pat that she must take a chance both for her sake and for Erich's. The two need to learn how to be happy and unafraid. Pat and Erich marry, but on their honeymoon, Pat collapses with a hemorrhage. Her doctor is rushed from Berlin to her bedside by Otto in his car. The doctor tells Pat and Erich that she must spend the following winter in a sanatorium, or he cannot be responsible for her life. The couple go back to Berlin and sadly wait for the cold weather to arrive. Meanwhile, the rumblings of Nazism are being felt throughout Germany. Street gangs are forming and violence is becoming common. Gottfried joins forces with some liberal politicians; he sees what is in store for Europe. When Gottfried becomes increasingly concerned that his political views are ruining their taxi business, however, he tries to sever his relations with the pacifist Dr. Becker (Henry Hull), the man who had been his mentor. Later, however, he sees Becker being mobbed after a street meeting and rushes to his aid. Gottfried is shot and killed, and the assassin is spotted by Otto, who arrives too late to help his companion. Otto keeps the news from Erich at first, and when he finally tells him, he insists that Erich keep out of trouble, that his only job is to keep Pat happy until she is ready to leave for her cure.

After a time of great happiness with Erich, Pat finally goes to the sanatorium; there she is told that she must have a very dangerous operation which, at best, will leave her either a permanent invalid or greatly weakened. The operation is paid for by Otto, who sells his beloved car. While Erich is at Pat's bedside awaiting the results of her operation, Otto tracks down and kills Gottfried's murderer, feeling himself avenged at last. Pat wakes up from the operation and is ordered to lie perfectly still; any sudden movement could prove fatal. After several hours of great internal struggle, she orders Erich out of her room, then deliberately goes to the window to watch him leave, knowing that the act will kill her. As Erich turns around, he sees Pat wave from the window and then fall down in a faint. He rushes upstairs and she dies in his arms; but before she dies, Pat tries to explain that she did not want Erich to keep on making sacrifices for her, and that this way, he would remember their love as something beautiful. Erich is comforted by the only friend he now has left—Otto, who suggests that they both leave Germany for South America and a new life.

The outstanding camerawork by Joseph Ruttenberg lends this film its special quality of luminosity. Margaret Sullavan is often photographed from above in an almost madonnalike manner. The film's theme that love and friendship can ultimately triumph over the evils of a powerful force like Fascism is one that Borzage was to repeat over and over. As in most of his films, the power of love is almighty and can transform a person's life, even if the love is short-lived. *Three Comrades* is Frank Borzage's hymn to universal brotherhood, and a further affirmation of his strong belief that only through love and adversity are souls made great.

Joan Cohen

THREE GODFATHERS

Released: 1948
Production: John Ford and Merian C. Cooper for Metro-Goldwyn-Mayer; released by Loew's Incorporated
Direction: John Ford
Screenplay: Laurence Stallings and Frank S. Nugent; based on the novel of the same name by Peter B. Kyne
Cinematography: Winton C. Hoch
Editing: Jack Murray
Music: Richard Hageman
Running time: 106 minutes

Principal characters:
Bob Hightower .... John Wayne
Pete .... Pedro Armendariz
The Abilene Kid .... Harry Carey, Jr.
"Buck" Perley Sweet .... Ward Bond
Mrs. Perley Sweet .... Mae Marsh
The Mother .... Mildred Natwick

John Ford's *Three Godfathers* uses a form rarely seen in films, and seen even less in the Western genre: that of the religious parable. Although Ford had dealt in religious allegory in a previous film, *The Fugitive* (1947), it is in *Three Godfathers* that he most successfully illustrates the theme of spiritual redemption through individual commitment and sacrifice. The film is dedicated "To the Memory of Harry Carey—Bright Star of the Early Western Sky." Carey, who had died in 1947, starred in Ford's silent Western, *Marked Men*, which was the director's original film version of the same story that serves as the basis for *Three Godfathers*. The story has been filmed a total of five times, including a television version in the late 1970's.

The film begins with three outlaws planning a robbery. Ford encourages us to accept the basic decency of these three "good badmen" by having the leader of the group, Bob Hightower (John Wayne), urge the youngest to consider quitting before he becomes too deeply involved in crime. The Abilene Kid (Harry Carey, Jr.) refuses the offer, and the three men—Bob, the Kid, and Pedro (Pedro Armendariz)—ride into the small Arizona town of Welcome to rob its bank. They stop at a house and talk jokingly with a man leisurely tending his garden. The outlaws prepare to get on with the robbery when they discover that the man with whom they have been amicably chatting happens to be the town marshal. Undeterred by Marshal "Buck" Perley Sweet's hospitality, they rob the bank, but in the escape, the Abilene Kid is wounded, and Sweet and his posse pursue them.

Ward Bond's admirable portrayal of Sweet makes the character a satisfying mixture of adherence to duty combined with a keen understanding of human nature, qualities often shared by other characters in Ford films, such as the priest in *The Quiet Man* (1952) and Captain Clayton in *The Searchers* (1956). Sweet's fulfillment of the obligations of his job do not obscure or diminish his humanity. Although he has an opportunity to shoot Hightower, Sweet shoots the outlaw's water bag instead, declaring, "they ain't paying me to kill folks." Nevertheless, he is a thorough professional. In a move to divert the posse, the outlaws do not go to the railroad watering station as expected, but go into the desert toward a watering hole called Tarapin Tanks. Marshal Sweet is only momentarily deceived by the outlaws' diversionary tactic and correctly assesses what their next move will be. He deftly moves his posse into the desert in pursuit of the three men.

In these scenes of pursuit, Ford's location shooting in the Mohave Desert effectively establishes a needed sense of physical reality in a film that is largely concerned with the spiritual. As he did in *She Wore a Yellow Ribbon* (1949), in which the chance occurrence of a thunderstorm provided him with the opportunity to film one of the most breathtaking sequences in any of his films, Ford uses a natural event, an actual dust storm, to enhance the physical struggle by grounding it in a believable film "reality." The terrible dust storm causes the outlaws to lose their horses and they reach Tarapin Tanks by foot—only to discover that the waterhole is dry.

When the outlaws see a covered wagon perched eerily near the edge of the Tanks, Ford resorts to an effective device that he often uses for important emotional moments. Bob goes ahead to inspect the wagon, but the audience must wait until he returns to his companions to find out what he has discovered. Bob's account of his offscreen experience is similar to Ethan Edwards' report of finding Lucy's body in *The Searchers* and Gil Martin's exhausted retelling of his battle experience in Ford's *Drums Along the Mohawk* (1939). The emotional reaction of each of the characters to his offscreen experience increases the audience's perception of that experience. Bob relates what he found in a poignant, half-literate, half-poetic monologue that reveals his own anger and despair as well as the facts of the discovery. Because a tenderfoot emigrant dynamited the waterhole in a foolish attempt to find water, Tarapin Tanks is permanently ruined. The man, leaving his wife alone in the wagon, went off into the desert to find water. "But that still ain't the worst of it," Bob declares. "She's gonna have a baby. She's gonna have it now."

Pedro goes to care for the woman, and as he approaches the wagon, Ford adds a religious touch to the imagery by framing Pedro in the wagon cover as if he were standing under the archway of a cathedral. The woman bears a son, and, realizing that she is dying, she asks the three men to be her child's godfathers. In a masterful stroke of understatement, Ford never allows the real father to be mentioned again, although the anguish of the mother is communicated in her naming the baby not with the surname of the husband who deserted her, but after the men who found her. In one of the film's most touching scenes, each man takes a solemn oath to care for little Robert William Pedro Hightower. As the mother dies, a gust of wind extinguishes the lantern. The outlaws bury her in a funeral ceremony that echoes those in many other Ford films. Gathered around her grave, they read from her Bible, and the Abilene Kid sings "Shall We Gather at the River?"

The mother's death is significant because it thrusts upon the men the responsibility of her child. Death in *Three Godfathers* is inexorably bound to the necessity of sacrifice. A mother dies, but her hope for her child lives in the sworn promise of three thieves. Later Pedro and the Kid die trying to reach a town called New Jerusalem which they choose as a destination because the Kid reads a passage in the mother's open Bible telling of the journey of the Christ Child and his family to Jerusalem. The Abilene Kid insists on carrying the baby, but he becomes increasingly weak and finally collapses, then dies, deliriously reciting a child's prayer. Pedro steps into a hole, and to avoid falling on the baby in his arms, twists around, breaking his leg. Knowing he is doomed, Pedro gives Bob the child, says his good-byes, and takes Bob's gun, ostensibly to defend himself against coyotes. Bob walks away, and a shot is heard. He stops motionless for a moment, then starts walking again.

Bob's journey is not toward such a sacrificial death, but toward a redemption ensured by the sacrifice of others and by his own acceptance of the responsibility thrust on him by that sacrifice. Of the three outlaws, Bob is shown to be the least religious. He must go through a journey in his own spiritual desert as well as through a journey in the physical one. When, as the only outlaw left alive, he decides to give up and die, Bob turns to the Bible. The passage he reads tells of the Christ Child being carried on a donkey, and the obvious, but spiritually necessary, miracle occurs: a donkey and its colt wander into sight. Using the donkey for support, Bob carries the infant into New Jerusalem on Christmas Day. His commitment to the child is rewarded with survival, but penance is due. Marshal Sweet arrives to arrest him.

Three Godfathers is saved from maudlin religiosity by its balancing of intensely serious moments with the kind of rambunctious comic scenes one comes to expect in Ford films. The opening exchange between the outlaws and Sweet is such an instance, and another occurs when the three godfathers attempt to care for the infant with the aid of a baby book. The end of the film also returns to this lighter tone. Welcome's judge offers Bob his freedom if he will let Mr. and Mrs. Sweet adopt the baby. Bob refuses, and the judge, realizing the sincerity of Bob's commitment to the child, gives Bob the minimum sentence of one year and one day. The town gives Bob an incredibly cheerful send-off. In a final comic irony, the banker's daughter gives him a warm farewell that seems to promise Bob a future married life when he returns from prison to rear his godson.

Three Godfathers presents an effectively controlled expression of Ford's themes of responsibility to community, commitment to others, and unashamed need for home and family. Robert Marmaduke Sangster Hightower's journey to spiritual redemption ends with Ford's optimistic assurance that the values he expounds in *Three Godfathers* are surely worth waiting one year and a day for.

Gay Studlar

TIGHT LITTLE ISLAND (WHISKY GALORE)

Released: 1949
Production: Michael Balcon for J. Arthur Rank-Ealing Studios; released by Universal-International
Direction: Alexander Mackendrick
Screenplay: Compton Mackenzie and Angus McPhail; based on the novel of the same name by Compton Mackenzie
Cinematography: Gerald Gibbs
Editing: Joseph Sterling
Running time: 82 minutes

Principal characters:

Captain Paul Wagget	Basil Radford
Peggy Macroon	Joan Greenwood
Dr. MacLaren	James Robertson Justice
George Campbell	Gordon Jackson
Joseph Macroon	Wylie Watson
Mrs. Waggett	Catherine Lacey
Mrs. Campbell	Jean Cadell
Sergeant Odd	Bruce Seton
Farquharson	Henry Mollison
Catriona Macroon	Gabrielle Blunt
Narrator	Finlay Currie

Along with *Passport to Pimlico* (1949) and *Kind Hearts and Coronets* (1949), *Tight Little Island* (British title *Whisky Galore*) was one of three comedies produced by Britain's Ealing Studios in 1949 that scored a tremendous hit on the world film market and sparked the vogue for British comedies that lasted throughout the 1950's. Ealing's policy was to produce films that could earn back their entire cost on rentals from the British release, which meant that director Henry Cornelius and screenwriter T. E. B. Clarke were free to look for humor (in a film like *Passport to Pimlico*) in the special problems of British society after World War II. In the United States, the appeal of these films was strongest on the burgeoning art house circuit; but in recent years the appeal of the more strictly topical and local comedies has waned even for this relatively sophisticated audience. Director Alexander Mackendrick's *Tight Little Island* is one of the handful of postwar British and/or Ealing comedies (the terms are almost, but not quite, interchangeable—other British studios produced their own "Ealing" comedies) still frequently revived today. Like *Kind Hearts and Coronets*, with its turn-of-the-century setting and universal themes of sex and money, or Mackendrick's *The Man in the White Suit* (1952), about the role of scientific research in an industrial economy, *Tight*

Little Island survives because the filmmakers looked for comic inspiration beyond the immediate concerns of British audiences in 1949.

Compton Mackenzie got his idea for the novel on which the film was based from a true incident that occurred during World War II. In 1943, a British cargo ship carrying whisky for export to the United States ran aground off the Scottish island of Eriskay. The resourceful islanders, languishing under a whisky famine created by wartime rationing, organized a salvage operation to rescue as much of the precious cargo as they could before the ship went under. Mackenzie's story is set on the mythical island of Todday in the Outer Hebridies. Like the people of Eriskay, the people of Todday have been hard hit by the whisky famine.

Joseph Macroon (Wylie Watson) is having problems with his two marriageable daughters, Peggy (Joan Greenwood) and Catriona (Gabrielle Blunt). Peggy is being courted by a Londoner, Sergeant Odd (Bruce Seton), a career army man assigned to Todday to assist in training the Home Guard. Catriona, at least, is engaged to an island boy, the local schoolmaster George Campbell, who is played by Gordon Jackson, best known to American audiences for his role as the butler Hudson in the *Upstairs, Downstairs* television series. George lives with his sternly Calvinistic mother (Jean Cadell), who so dominates her only son that she locks him in his room rather than let him participate in a Home Guard exercise on Sunday, which would be breaking the Sabbath. Naturally, she disapproves of Catriona, who wears lipstick and smokes cigarettes, and she forbids George to marry her.

Captain Waggett, the well-intentioned but hopelessly Blimpish commander of the Todday Home Guard, is unable to deal with the islanders' un-English refusal to see that there is a war on. He complains to Odd that so long as there was an apparent threat of an invasion the men were keen enough, but that now they regard the drills he puts them through as a waste of time. Even the island doctor (James Robertson Justice) refuses to support him and angrily insists that Waggett's men remove a practice roadblock they have constructed so that he can drive past to get some sleep after staying up all night delivering twins. Waggett is played by Basil Radford, a portly actor with a neatly trimmed mustache and military bearing who became one of the screen's outstanding exemplars of the stereotyped English gentleman. He first attracted notice in this role when he and Naunton Wayne (with whom he was teamed in many subsequent films) played the two British tourists abroad in Hitchcock's *The Lady Vanishes* (1938). *Tight Little Island* gave him the only real starring role of his career before his death in 1952.

Waggett's greatest ordeal begins one foggy night when a freighter (whose bearded captain is played by Compton Mackenzie himself) bound for America runs aground off the island. As soon as the thirsty Toddayers discover that the ship is carrying fifty thousand cases of whisky, they begin laying plans to salvage what they can before it all goes down. Waggett's sense of honesty is outraged by this affront to the inland revenue (the whisky has been marked for export only); and he tells Odd that, since none of the Home Guard can be trusted, the two of them will have to stand watch themselves to prevent the islanders from reaching the freighter. When Mrs. Waggett (Catherine Lacey) timidly asks why it would be so terrible if the islanders did rescue a few bottles, her husband explains that once you let people take the law into their own hands you have anarchy. Fortunately, it is Sunday morning and the Presbyterian Toddayers can be counted on to do nothing about the ship during the twenty-four hours of the Sabbath. But Odd will have to stand the first watch beginning at midnight Monday morning until Waggett relieves him four hours later.

Macroon, mindful of Waggett's determination to thwart the islander's plan, explains to Odd the old Scottish custom of the *reiteach*, a traditional betrothal feast for which a seven-gallon jar of whisky must be provided. Odd is desperately eager to marry Peggy; and Macroon gives him his ultimatum: "You can't have a wedding without the *reiteach*, and you can't have a *reiteach* without the whisky." When the islanders arrive on the beach after midnight to find Odd on guard, they decide to overpower him using some of the commando tactics he has taught them. Their version of the panther crawl fails completely to take him by surprise; and Odd insists they do it over again until they have him properly bound hand and foot.

The freighter is listing badly by the time the islanders have rowed out to its side; but the men of Todday load about two hundred cases of whisky into their boats before it capsizes and sinks. They hide their precious treasure in a cave at the north end of the island, agreeing that each man will take only what he needs for now and return for more later. Waggett arrives to relieve Odd promptly at 0400 hours and learns of his ambush by a party of unknown islanders. When Waggett telephones his commanding officer, Colonel Linsey-Woolsey, he is horrified to hear the colonel ask if a few bottles of the stolen whisky can be set aside for him. "I shall never understand the professional military mind," Waggett tells his wife, and makes plans to recover the whisky himself. In the meantime, the owner of Todday's only public house has finally received his legal quota of four bottles of whisky. Angry that his customers no longer need him, he tells Waggett where the whisky is hidden.

Waggett calls the colonel again, requesting permission to visit him on the mainland for a talk about Home Guard affairs. He will have to be gone at least two days; and the Macroons joyfully prepare to celebrate a double *reiteach* in his absence. Not only are Peggy and the sergeant to be wed; but George Campbell, who participated in the salvage operation and got gloriously drunk for the first time in his life, has at last stood up to his mother and announced his determination to marry Catriona whether the old woman approves or not. Waggett has not gone to the mainland, however, but to the excise office on a neighboring island. On the night of the *reiteach*, with most of the islanders assembled in Macroon's Post Office for a merry celebration, Waggett is on his way back in the excise launch with a party of officers headed by a man named Farquharson (Henry Mollison). Waggett suggests they head straight for the cave; but Farquharson, who has had run-ins with Macroon before, wants to conduct a house-by-house search of the village first to uncover any bottles the islanders may already have hidden in their homes.

The excise launch is spotted by an elderly islander as Waggett and Farquharson and his men are coming ashore. A warning is quickly telephoned through to the celebrators in the Post Office; and, in a lightning and superbly orchestrated effort, the islanders hide every bottle before the excise men reach the village. When Farquharson and Waggett knock on Macroon's door, they are greeted by a bathrobe-clad Peggy who sleepily tells them that the Post Office is closed. Farquharson tells her that he has business with her father; and Macroon comes down in his night shirt to talk with them. He gives permission for Farquharson's men to search his house; but they are unable to find a single bottle. When they have gone, Macroon thoughtfully turns on the kitchen tap an pours himself a tumbler full of whisky from the *reiteach* jug hidden in the cistern.

The officers' search of the other houses in the village proves equally fruitless, and Farquharson and his men climb into Waggett's car to be driven to the cave a few miles away. The islanders mobilize to keep them from reaching the whisky before they have a chance to move it to a new hiding place. Again making use of the commando tactics Waggett and Odd have drilled into them, they erect roadblocks, post sentries, and even try a little diversionary sniper fire with their blank training ammunition. By the time Waggett's car finally gets through to the cave, the islanders have managed to load the remaining cases of whisky onto a truck and drive away. The heavily loaded truck has left a clear trail in the sand, however; and the excise men jump back into Waggett's car and set out in hot pursuit. The truck runs out of gasoline just as Waggett crashes into a barbed wire roadblock about a hundred yards behind. With four flattened tires, the car creeps slowly toward the stalled truck. At the last possible minute, one of the islanders breaks the top off a whisky bottle and pours the contents into the truck's tank. The ancient vehicle comes to life with a roar and disappears into the night and a new hiding place, leaving Waggett and the excise men to cut their way out of the barbed wire as best they can.

The next morning, Farquharson receives a telephone call from the excise office while he is recuperating at Waggett's house. He informs the exhausted Waggett that he will have to go back with him to headquarters: it seems that six bottles of the stolen whisky turned up hidden in a case of ammunition that Waggett had Macroon send back to the mainland under his personal authority, and now Farquharson's superiors want to question Waggett as a suspected smuggler. When she hears this, Mrs. Waggett, who has followed her husband's misadventures with grave misgiving, breaks into hysterical laughter which merges on the sound track with the joyful laughter of the Toddayers as they resume the interrupted *reiteach*.

The triumph of Dionysus (or of Macroon, his chief disciple on the island) is complete: all of the characters who tried to hold out against the understandable, but patent, dishonesty of the whisky thieves have either compromised their principles (like Sergeant Odd, who allowed himself to be tied up during the salvage operation, or Mrs. Campbell, who so far unbends as to have a glass herself at the *reiteach*), or, like Farquharson, have joined Wagget in defeat. Actually, Farquharson, who is portrayed as an island man himself, enjoys Waggett's discomforture as much as the Toddayers. When, during their mad drive to the cave, he and Waggett crash into the first roadblock the islanders have erected, Waggett asks exasperatedly: "Now, how did *that* get there?" "It's the fairies. They're very active in these parts," is Farquharson's laconic reply. However, the basic conflict in the story is not between the law (sobriety, order) and dishonesty (drunkenness, anarchy), but between the English (or Saxon) and Scottish (or Celtic) temperaments. The accommodation the English characters have to make with the islanders is foreshadowed in an early scene when Odd is courting Peggy. She teasingly tells him that she will only listen to his proposal if he asks her in Gaelic; and he painfully pronounces a few words he has memorized for the occasion. The reason that Waggett has so much trouble with the people of Todday is that, at bottom, they do not speak the same language.

Mackendrick has revealed that he grew more and more depressed while the film was being shot as he realized how deeply he sympathized with Waggett's honest principles. If this was true, perhaps he derived some consolation from Mackenzie's brief epilogue. By the time the Toddayers' private stock was exhausted, legal whisky was once again plentiful. The price went up and up, however, until no one on the island could afford so much as a dram. The only people unaffected by this new calamity were Peggy and the sergeant, who were not whisky drinkers and so lived happily ever after. "And if that isn't a moral story," concludes the Scots-accented narrator (Finlay Currie), "I don't know what is."

Charles Hopkins

TO BE OR NOT TO BE

Released: 1942
Production: Ernst Lubitsch for Alexander Korda Productions; released by United Artists
Direction: Ernst Lubitsch
Screenplay: Edwin Justus Mayer; based on a screen story by Ernst Lubitsch and Melchior Lengyel (uncredited)
Cinematography: Rudolph Maté
Editing: Dorothy Spencer
Production design: Vincent Korda
Running time: 100 minutes

Principal characters:

Maria Tura	Carole Lombard
Joseph Tura	Jack Benny
Lieutenant Stanislav Sobinski	Robert Stack
Greenberg	Felix Bressart
Rawitch	Lionel Atwill
Professor Alexander Siletsky	Stanley Ridges
Colonel Ehrhardt	Sig Rumann
Bronski	Tom Dugan
Dobosh	Charles Halton
Wilhelm	Peter Caldwell

When *To Be or Not to Be* opened in March of 1942, audiences were understandably melancholy about this satire of Germany's occupation of Poland. America's participation in World War II was just three months old, and star Carole Lombard's death was still fresh in moviegoers' minds. The film was released two months after the beautiful thirty-two-year-old star and her mother had been killed in a plane crash after completing a war bond drive. Just as Charlie Chaplin's comedy *The Great Dictator* (1940) had paved the way in ridiculing Hitler, Ernst Lubitsch's film showed in a similarly humorous fashion how an occupied country coped with Nazism. Significantly, both films can be appreciated more in retrospect. In particular, the black comedy aspects of *To Be or Not to Be* are much funnier forty years later when the horrors of World War II are far behind. Jokes based on concentration camps and bombing raids were simply too stinging to be humorous in 1942.

To Be or Not to Be was one of the Hollywood productions made by British film magnate Alexander Korda in the early 1940's after he emigrated from war-torn England. Producer-director Lubitsch also wrote the original story for the film with Melchior Lengyel (who, received no screen credit for his writing). The screenplay was written by Edwin Justus Mayer. The European influence on the film is evidenced by the craftsmen and the international cast connected with it. German actors are cast in German parts, Englishmen play the roles of Englishmen, and a varied combination of performers from different countries portray the Polish patriots. Most of the latter are actually actors playing actors, performing play-within-a-play sequences and masquerading as different characters throughout.

One of the principals of the film, Jack Benny, while not usually remembered as a screen star, had actually been in twenty films between 1929 and 1945. This is undoubtedly the best of all of his screen roles, although his acting career is recalled more vividly by the film *The Horn Blows at Midnight* (1945), which Benny turned into a standing joke to explain the abrupt end of his film career. Benny's portrayal of the archetypal ham actor Joseph Tura, who is more concerned with his own stature than the fate of his native land, calls for a comic skill which is fully realized here. As Maria Tura, Carole Lombard has less of an opportunity to display an emotional range, being called upon mainly to project her beauty and allure, which was considerable. Robert Stack as her would-be lover is suitably boyish and naïve, although his performance is not particularly noteworthy. Others in the cast, such as Lionel Atwill and Sig Rumann, are competent in their character roles, while German actor Felix Bressart as the Jewish actor who always wanted to play Shylock, and American Tom Dugan as the Hitler imitator, are exceptional. Lubitsch had a particular fondness for "character" actors, often giving them the best lines and scenes of his films. One example of this is a scene between Rumann and Lombard in which Rumann is given all of the close-ups in preference to the beautiful Lombard.

The film begins with a narrator describing Warsaw in August of 1939 (still a month before the German invasion). After a brief description of the city, we see the shocked citizens staring at Adolf Hitler. The action then shifts abruptly to Berlin, where a Nazi youth named Wilhelm (Peter Caldwell) is given a toy tank by a Gestapo officer (Jack Benny) for his exemplary behavior. While attempting to persuade the boy to inform on his father for telling a joke about Hitler which likens him to cheese, Hitler himself enters, topping his subordinates' salutations of "Heil Hitler" with "Heil Myself." The entire scene is revealed to be a rehearsal for a play when the director, Dobosh (Charles Halton), takes the actor portraying Hitler, Bronski (Tom Dugan), to task for his ad libbing. Then his star, Maria Tura, enters wearing a dazzling evening dress which she insists would be perfect for the concentration camp scene. She and her husband, Joseph, argue over who should have the spotlight. Amidst the backstage arguing, when Dobosh tells Bronski that he does not resemble Hitler, the actor goes out into the street to prove that he does. At this point the story line and the narration come together. While Dobosh frightens most of the people on the street, a little girl shyly approaches him and asks for his autograph, addressing him as "Mr. Bronski."

These scenes, while not an integral part of the plot, add much to the satire of the film. The tension built up by the war is released in the scenes where characters and situations are exposed as ridiculous. The reality of the Nazi occupation is brought back into the plot when an officer tells the theatrical troupe that the government is afraid of offending Hitler with their play *Gestapo*, and so they must continue with their current production of *Hamlet*.

During the following night's performance, when Joseph begins his soliloquy with "To be or not to be," a young Polish flyer, Lieutenant Stanislav Sobinski (Robert Stack), walks abruptly out of the audience. He has been sending Maria flowers for the past three nights, and she is intrigued and flattered enough to invite him to her dressing room during her husband's longest scene. While Joseph is left on stage flustered and angry that someone should leave during his masterful performance, Stanislav and Maria meet. He professes his devotion to her, saying that he has seen all of her plays and that he wants to see her again.

The next night when Joseph begins with the words "To be or not to be," Stanislav exits again, which prompts the actor to repeat the lines louder and more angrily. Stanislav wants Maria to tell her husband that they are in love and will retire to his farm. Despite her lack of enthusiasm, he promises that he will wait for her until she is free. At just that moment, the news comes to the theater that war has broken out, and Stanislav leaves, vowing to return to her. An air raid sequence follows which leaves Warsaw in ruins and Nazi Colonel Ehrhardt (Sig Rumann) in charge of the city.

When Poland falls to the Nazis, Stanislav, along with other Polish pilots, goes to Britain to fight with the R.A.F. When a group of the Poles learn that a Professor Alexander Siletsky (Stanley Ridges) is shortly to return to Poland on a secret mission, they ask him to contact their relatives in Poland. Stanislav becomes suspicious of the professor when Siletsky fails to recognize the name of Maria Tura, something which any Pole would know because of her widespread fame as an actress. In order to investigate the professor, the British fly Stanislav into Poland to follow and, if necessary, kill him.

Siletsky contacts Maria for Stanislav via their "To be or not to be" code. The actress and her husband are now living in small quarters which make Siletsky feel that she might entertain the possibility of a romance with him to better her somewhat reduced circumstances. Stanislav hides in the Turas' apartment where he, Maria, and Joseph plan to destroy the information about the Polish fliers' families which Siletsky possesses. The three lure Siletsky to "Gestapo headquarters," actually a vacant stage where Joseph poses as Colonel Ehrhardt. In his attempt to sound authentic, Joseph is reduced to inane small talk with Siletsky, repeating the rhetorical question "So they call me Concentration Camp Ehrhardt, Eh?" in a scene which attempts, but fails, to be as humorous as the filmmakers had intended it to be. When Siletsky realizes that Joseph is a fake, he runs into the theater, where he is shot. Bleeding on stage, he dies with a defiant "Heil Hitler."

In a fast-moving final sequence, Joseph poses as Siletsky to obtain the information which is locked up in a trunk in his hotel. He finds Maria there, waiting for Ehrhardt, who is smitten with her. Pretending not to know Maria, he convinces Ehrhardt that he is indeed Siletsky, but he cannot pass up the opportunity to ask the Colonel if he knows of that great Polish actor, Joseph Tura. Yes, he does, answers Ehrhardt; "What he did to Shakespeare, we're doing now to Poland." Later, when Siletsky's body is found and put into Ehrhardt's office, the still-disguised Tura "proves" that Siletsky has a false beard and continues his pose. His friend, actor Rawitch (Lionel Atwill), masquerades as a German officer who exposes Tura, and thereby actually saves him. A final plan is evolved, designed to get the troop safely out of Poland. Hitler is to appear at a theater, so the actors dress as Gestapo officers. They divert attention from their friends by pretending to apprehend a would-be assassin, played by Greenberg (Felix Bressart), who is led away reciting Shylock's speech from *The Merchant of Venice*. Bronski, again dressed as Hitler, leads the soldiers out of the theater, which is then dynamited. He goes to pick up Maria, prompting Ehrhardt to shoot himself for daring to be interested in his *Führer*'s woman.

The actors fly to Scotland, and in a final scene which serves as a sort of epilogue, the audience sees Tura onstage reciting Hamlet's soliloquy once again. As he says "To be or not to be," a young naval officer abruptly leaves the audience.

For all of its attempts at satire and black humor, the real comedy of *To Be or Not to Be* comes from standard backstage or romantic triangle material. There are a few funny lines based on the Nazis, but on the whole the best parts of the comedy concern Tura's pomposity and Maria's cuckolding of him. Maria justifiably feels dominated by the bombastic Joseph, who takes top billing and all of the credit for their success. Their interplay provides most of the film's humor, but the real sympathies of the audience lie with some of the minor characters, such as Bronski and Greenberg, who finally prove their merits as actors by fooling the Nazis and saving their friends.

John Cocchi

TO CATCH A THIEF

Released: 1955
Production: Alfred Hitchcock for Paramount
Direction: Alfred Hitchcock
Screenplay: John Michael Hayes; based on the novel of the same name by David Dodge
Cinematography: Robert Burks (AA)
Editing: George Tomasini
Running time: 97 minutes

Principal characters:
John Robie .... Cary Grant
Frances Stevens .... Grace Kelly
Jessie Stevens .... Jessie Royce Landis
Bertani .... Charles Vanel
Danielle .... Brigitte Auber
H. H. Hughson .... John Williams

By 1955, when he made *To Catch a Thief*, Alfred Hitchcock had long since established his reputation as a master of suspense. From *The Man Who Knew Too Much* (1934) and *The 39 Steps* (1935) to *Dial M for Murder* (1954) and *Rear Window* (1954), Hitchcock's admirers reveled in the tension for which his films were justly famous. Some of these admirers were, therefore, taken aback somewhat by *To Catch a Thief*, a lush comedy. Not that the film is entirely devoid of suspense—there is a mystery to be solved, after all. But *To Catch a Thief* finds Hitchcock in a playful mood, and the film never generates any real tension. However, a relaxed Hitchcock is still Hitchcock, and *To Catch a Thief* is a richly rewarding cinematic experience.

The film's title is derived from the old proverb "Set a thief to catch a thief," and Hitchcock populates the film with thieves and manipulators of all sorts. Some of them are reformed thieves; at least one of them is an active jewel thief; some of them are merely expense account padders; and some are manipulative lovers. As the film opens, they have at least one thing in common—none knows which of the other characters fits into which category. Indeed, one of the director's themes (although he never presses his case to the point of didacticism) is that the moral implications of theft are, if not entirely subjective, frequently dependent upon the perspective of the observer.

The film opens with a typical Hitchcock shock, this time laced with humor. The credits roll as the camera first focuses on the window of a travel agency and then pans to a sign that reads "If you love life, you'll love France." As the camera pulls in on the sign, Hitchcock suddenly cuts to a close-up of a woman screaming, "My jewels! I've been robbed." In one fell swoop, Hitchcock has established both the film's location and its subject—jewelry theft. The scene continues with a montage of similar screams, intercut with shots of a black cat running across a series of tiled roofs; the obvious association is that of a cat burglar.

Hitchcock introduces us to a real cat burglar (albeit a retired one) in the next scene. John Robie (Cary Grant) strides into Bertani's Restaurant on the French Riviera with a grim look on his face, a look which the restaurant's staff reciprocates. He walks back to the glassed-in kitchen, where he stands for a long moment peering through the transparent door. As the camera moves in for a close-up of Robie's face, Hitchcock delivers his second visual shock of the film—a raw egg splatters against the glass in front of Robie's face.

An explanation is soon forthcoming. Robie is an American who had fought alongside Bertani (Charles Vanel) and most of his kitchen help in the French Resistance during World War II. After the war, he remained in France and became a famous, and for a time successful, jewel thief, growing rich at the expense of those who could afford the losses he inflicted ("I never stole from anyone who would go hungry," he remarks at one point). Long since retired from the burglary business, Robie nevertheless finds himself under suspicion, both from the police and from his former Resistance comrades, for the latest string of thefts, all of which seem to bear his mark. Robie's assertions of innocence are met with skepticism by all concerned; some are angry, a few are amused, and Danielle (Brigitte Auber), the young daughter of the wine steward, is obviously smitten with Robie.

Robie realizes that the only way he will be able to prove that he is telling the truth is to apprehend the new cat burglar himself. To do so, he must set a trap for the "Cat," and he asks Bertani's help to do so. The pair are interrupted by the police, however, who are hot on Robie's trail. Danielle helps him to escape. Eventually Bertani puts Robie in touch with a man named H. H. Hughson (John Williams), an insurance adjuster from Lloyd's of London. Robie again protests his innocence and outlines his plan to Hughson. In return for a list of Lloyd's of London's most prominent insurees, who will, therefore, likely be the thief's next victims, Robie will undertake to apprehend the new Cat. The two men engage in some intense verbal sparring. Hughson, a proper Briton, is puzzled by Robie's cheerful, guiltless acknowledgment of his past crimes. Robie responds by forcing Hughson to admit that he occasionally pads his expense account and takes towels from hotels as souvenirs; thus, the boundaries of morality are blurred a bit. "You're a thief," asserts Robie. Hughson gives in and provides the American with a detailed list of his clients and their jewels.

Most prominent on the list are Jessie Stevens (Jessie Royce Landis), a rich American widow, and her beautiful blonde daughter, Frances (Grace Kelly). Robie contrives to meet them, and, as "Mr. Burns," ingratiates himself quickly. Mrs. Stevens is a blunt, humorous woman who is open and outgoing; Frances is almost the exact opposite. Cool and virginal, she hardly says a word all night. Thus it comes as a surprise, both to the audience and to Robie, when she kisses him passionately at the end of the evening.

With the introduction of Jessie and Frances Stevens, Hitchcock's cast is virtually complete. He then sets about complicating their lives, much to the audience's delight. Hitchcock presses the theme of the hunter hunted, as the depredations of the new Cat continue, and Robie, who is pursuing the Cat, is himself pressed by both the police and his former friends in the Resistance, who vow to kill him for discrediting them. Meanwhile, Danielle and Frances quarrel bitchily over which of them has the right to pursue the bemused and befuddled Robie, who wants as little as possible to do with either of the young women.

Two long scenes between Robie and Frances demonstrate the playful mood that Hitchcock was in while making *To Catch a Thief*. He even relaxes enough to permit his characters some witty double entendres (both verbal and visual)—a rarity for the moralistic director. The first of these scenes involves a high-speed car chase in which a calm Frances helps a nervous Robie elude the police once again. She is driving, and Hitchcock shows their contrasting moods by focusing on their hands. Hers rest lightly on the steering wheel, even as she careens around curves; his hands clench and unclench helplessly as he wonders whether capture by the police might not be preferable to death in an automobile accident on a remote French road. Having successfully eluded the police, the two banter a bit. When Robie calls her "a rich, headstrong young girl," she replies challengingly, "the man I want doesn't have a price." "That eliminates me," Robie chuckles. Then Frances reveals that she knows that "Mr. Burns" is actually John Robie, the jewel thief. Far from being shocked or offended, she is thrilled; it makes him all the more attractive to her. She pulls off the road to a secluded picnic area and offers him some fried chicken: "Do you want a leg or a breast?" she inquires meaningfully. When she announces that she plans to join him on his "crime spree," he groans in dismay. "Don't say it," he pleads, but she does anyway: "The Cat has a new kitten."

The second of Hitchcock's playful scenes occurs back at the hotel. Frances decides to force Robie into admitting his passion; but whether for her or for the glittering jewels she is wearing, Hitchcock leaves an open question. The director intercuts some marvelously photographed shots of exploding roman candles with the sexual fireworks provided by Frances and Robie. The double entendres fly, as Frances seduces Robie by extolling the beauty of either (or both) her diamonds or her breasts. The evening proves eventful; Frances loses her virginity and her mother loses her jewels. Frances tearfully accuses Robie of being the thief. Mrs. Stevens believes Robie's denials—like her daughter, she finds his former career more than a little intriguing—but Frances calls the police, and Robie is on the run again.

Hitchcock has one more shock scene up his sleeve. Robie is once more on the track of the Cat. Quite suddenly, he is jumped from behind. The figures grapple in the darkness on a cliff near the water's edge, and one man—we do not know who at this point—plummets over the side. For a moment, we fear that Robie has been killed, but the dead man turns out to be Danielle's father, the wine steward. The wine steward is immediately branded as the jewel thief, but Robie knows otherwise; the old man lacked sufficient agility to prowl the rooftops like the Cat. The mysterious sequence does tip the real thief's identity to him, however, and he begins to set his trap.

Robie springs the trap at a delightful costume ball on the Côte d'Azur. With the help of Jessie and Frances Stevens, who play along, and Hughson, who surreptitiously slips into Robie's nubian slave costume and holds the attention of the police by dancing the night away with Frances, Robie is free to track his Cat. He stations himself on the roof of the villa, where he awaits his victim. As the party is breaking up, the thief emerges, and a rooftop chase is on. Dodging bullets from the police below, Robie unmasks the Cat—who turns out to be Danielle. She breaks Robie's grip, but trips as she turns to run. Robie grabs her hand to keep her from falling off the roof, but threatens to drop her unless she confesses, and loudly enough for the police to hear. Trapped, she admits her guilt, and implicates Bertani, the restaurateur, as well.

Hitchcock ends the film on what he humorously calls "a pretty grim note." Back at Robie's villa, Frances and Robie stop sparring long enough to realize that they love each other. They kiss, and Frances remarks "So this is where you live. Oh, mother will love it up here!" A brief look of undisguised dismay crosses Robie's face as Hitchcock brings the film to a close.

Neither Cary Grant nor Grace Kelly were strangers to Alfred Hitchcock by 1955, Grant having appeared in *Notorious* (1946) and *Suspicion* (1941), and Kelly in *Dial M for Murder* and *Rear Window*. Hitchcock melded their talents expertly. It is difficult to imagine anyone other than Grant as John Robie; his sophisticated charm and his genius for light comedy make him perfect for the role. Kelly, too, is superb; she brings talent as well as beauty to the role of Frances Stevens, and she works exceptionally well with Grant. Jessie Royce Landis also deserves special mention for her supporting role as Frances' mother; her irreverent, wisecracking portrayal of Jessie Stevens stands out, even in the company of Grant and Kelly.

The direction, of course, is up to the usual high standards of Hitchcock. The film is expertly paced, with just enough jolts interspersed with the comedy to remind the audience that it is, after all, viewing an Alfred Hitchcock film. As Hitchcock himself has admitted, *To Catch a Thief* is a "lightweight story," at least compared to such thrillers as *Strangers on a Train* (1951), *Rear Window*, or *Psycho* (1960), to name a few of the film's approximate contemporaries. But a lightweight story in the hands of Alfred Hitchcock does not necessarily make for an inconsequential film. *To Catch a Thief* is an outstanding comedy, highlighted by the acting of Grant, Kelly, and Landis, and the Academy Award-winning cinematography of Robert Burks, all guided by the incomparable hand of the master, Alfred Hitchcock.

Robert Mitchell

TO HAVE AND HAVE NOT

Released: 1944
Production: Howard Hawks for Warner Bros.
Direction: Howard Hawks
Screenplay: Jules Furthman and William Faulkner; based on the novel of the same name by Ernest Hemingway
Cinematography: Sid Hickox
Editing: Christian Nyby
Running time: 100 minutes

Principal characters:

Harry Morgan (Steve)	Humphrey Bogart
Marie Browning (Slim)	Lauren Bacall
Eddie	Walter Brennan
Cricket	Hoagy Carmichael
Captain Renard	Dan Seymour
Johnson	Walter Sande
Paul de Bursac	Walter Molnar
Mme. Hellene de Bursac	Dolores Moran
Gerard (Frenchy)	Marcel Dalio

To Have and Have Not is perhaps best known as the film that introduced a new young actress named Lauren Bacall to the screen. At the age of only nineteen, she starred with Humphrey Bogart and managed to do more than a creditable job. Bogart's role as a tough, self-reliant individual plays best when it is up against a tough, self-reliant woman, and Bacall as Slim is perfect for the part. Their scenes together crackle with chemistry and fire and some of film's most memorable dialogue. The plot further engages the viewer's sympathies because it involves a classic struggle against infringement of personal liberty.

To Have and Have Not, however, is not generally considered a classic. In a catalogue of Bogart's films, it is not as admired as *The Maltese Falcon* (1941), *High Sierra* (1941), or *Casablanca* (1942). Likewise, in a catalogue of director Howard Hawks's works, this film is not as well known as Westerns such as *Rio Bravo* (1959) or *Red River* (1948), or screwball comedies such as *Bringing Up Baby* (1938) and *Ball of Fire* (1941). Even *The Big Sleep* (1946), which followed *To Have and Have Not* and reunited Hawks, Bogart, Bacall, and writers Furthman and Faulkner, is generally better regarded and remembered, although *To Have and Have Not* is arguably the better movie.

One of the problems faced by the makers of *To Have and Have Not* was that the film followed close on the success of *Casablanca*; in fact, Warner Bros. wanted it to be another *Casablanca*. The plot of the Hemingway novel was manipulated to include French resistance fighters and the women who support their work. Most of the interior action takes place in a bar much like Rick's Café Americaine. And there is even the ubiquitous pianist, now named Cricket and played by Hoagy Carmichael. But the film is essentially upbeat, a restrained comedy rather than melodrama. It is *Casablanca* as Howard Hawks would have made it.

To Have and Have Not is a highly appealing movie. In a role perfectly suited to his film *persona*, Bogart plays Harry Morgan, an expatriate American living in Vichy-controlled Martinique who is menaced by the war and women and who struggles to retain his freedom and individuality. Morgan owns a fishing boat and hires it out by the day to tourists. When he is approached by a group of French patriots who want to hire the boat to rescue a fellow resistance fighter from Devil's Island, Morgan refuses to get involved at any price, saying that he has no politics, nor any use for them. "What are your sympathies?" he is asked at one point. "Minding my own business" is his answer.

Bogart meets Bacall in a rather familiar looking tropical bar. The action, however, is not so typical. Morgan has been sitting at the bar watching the pianist, Cricket, and the group gathered around him, which includes Marie Browning (Lauren Bacall). She has just arrived in Martinique, a drifter who makes her way from place to place by practicing petty larceny and accepting small presents, such as plane tickets, from admirers. As she gets up to leave the room, Morgan follows and accuses her of lifting the wallet of the gentleman who was buying her drinks. Morgan has an interest in recovering the wallet because the man, Johnson (Walter Sande), is his client, and owes him more than $800 for sixteen days of fishing. Although Johnson has promised to pay him the next day after he has a chance to go to the bank, Morgan finds more than enough travelers checks in the wallet to cover the fee. Also in the wallet is a ticket out of Martinique on that night's plane. From this Morgan deduces that Johnson had intended to leave without paying. This makes allies of Morgan and Slim, as he calls Marie, since she has done him a favor by lifting Johnson's wallet.

But Morgan's luck does not hold out. Although he confronts Johnson with the evidence and asks him to start signing over the checks, they are interrupted by a raid by the Sûreté who had recognized the resistance members leaving the bar. In the ensuing struggle, Johnson is killed by a stray bullet before he has signed over the checks. This incident sets up the rest of the action. Both Morgan and Slim are now broke. They are hauled down to the headquarters of the Provisional government where they are slapped and mistreated by a surly and contemptible officer named Captain Renard (Dan Seymour). Eventually, it is Renard's authoritarianism even more than Morgan's need for money that leads Morgan to accept the offer of the resistance fighters. However, he still refuses to be emotional about their cause. Asked why he has suddenly changed his mind, he says simply, "Maybe because I like you, and I don't like them."

The rescue from Devil's Island is an atmospheric scene involving fog and shadows, flashes from far-off lanterns, and the monotonous drone of the boat's motors. Stowed away on board is Morgan's pal Eddie (Walter Brennan), an alcoholic who is no longer any good as a ship's mate, but whom Morgan keeps around because he is loyal. The relationship adds a dimension to Morgan's character; although independent and unemotional, he is shown to value friendship and loyalty. At Devil's Island, two passengers are taken on board. They turn out to be a man and wife, Paul and Hellene de Bursac. She travels with her husband, Hellene de Bursac tells Morgan, because without her, he would be useless to the cause. He would be always worrying about having to leave her behind, wondering if she had been approached by the authorities and made to talk. This exchange expands upon the theme that a man is at his strongest when he allows himself to feel emotion.

Heading back to port, Morgan spots a government boat. He takes a shot at its searchlight and prepares to make a run for safety, telling everyone to stay down. Bursac, however, panics. Standing up, he catches a bullet in his shoulder. The Bursacs are then hidden in the basement of the hotel where Morgan and Slim both are living. The two team up to nurse Paul de Bursac back to health. Morgan acts dispassionately. He does not like Hellene de Bursac and he does not believe in their cause, but he knows how to care for a bullet wound. Slim helps out because she likes Morgan.

The relationship between Slim and Morgan, whom she calls Steve although his name is Harry, develops in a series of scenes highlighted by fast-paced dialogue, pointed enough to reveal both characters. Hawks is said to have created the character of Slim because the only way the romance could bridge the age gap between Bogart and Bacall was to have Bacall dominate and to have Bogart enjoy her extravagant performance. (Interestingly, Bogart and Bacall actually did fall in love during the making of the film.) Sexual repartee and a somewhat cynical assessment of each other's pasts give way to a partnership based on mutual understanding. Gradually, we sense, a respect grows. In a showdown scene with Renard and his thugs, the understanding between Slim and Steve is crucial to the action. "Anyone got a match?" asks Morgan, echoing a phrase Slim had used in their first meeting. He directs her to open a drawer where the matches, and a gun, are kept. With Slim's help, Morgan is able to turn the tables on the police and take control of the situation. The movie ends with Steve and Slim, accompanied by Eddie, setting off, suitcases in hand, to enjoy the future together.

Besides bringing together Bogart and Bacall, *To Have and Have Not* joined Bogart and Hawks. Harry Morgan is the perfect realization not only of the Bogart character but also of the Hawks hero. Loosely based on Hemingway's novel, the movie is more Hawks than Hemingway. The two collaborated on a treatment using the character of Harry Morgan from the novel, but almost everything else was changed. Instead of Cuba and Florida, the setting is the French West Indies island of Martinique. Morgan has been changed from a down-and-out loser to a strong, upbeat hero, and Marie, the wife, is now the single and footloose Slim (Hawks's nickname for his own wife).

Hawks preferred comedies to melodramas and action to issues. Thus, although Harry Morgan is a classic Bogart hero, tough and seemingly without loyalties other than to himself, Hawks's influence makes him more appealing than many of Bogart's other tough roles. He is a loner, not an outlaw. He makes his own decisions out of choice, not because he is pursued. The role is made compellingly believable both because of what film lovers already know of Bogart and because of what is now revealed. It adds a new dimension to the Bogart *persona*. He is softened and given humor, without losing any of his strength. Hawks can be given much of the credit for having achieved a new characterization. Unlike Hitchcock, for instance, who insists that his movies are all but made before shooting begins, Hawks leaves room for invention; he is very much a collaborative director. Hawks was also fortunate in filming *To Have and Have Not* to be surrounded by people who thought very much as he did. For the man who made *Red River* and *Rio Bravo*, a Hemingway novel was a perfect vehicle, and for the man who made *Bringing Up Baby* and *His Girl Friday* (1940), Bogart and Bacall were a perfect team of costars. Hawks also reaped the benefit of having Jules Furthman, a long-time collaborator and top-notch dialogue writer, and William Faulkner, an excellent developer of character and scene, work on the screenplay.

Hawks has often been underrated by American film critics because he was not particularly daring in his interpretation of a script. Whether he was making a comedy, a Western, an action film, or a musical, he always worked within the conventions of the genre. With what he had to work with in the case of *To Have and Have Not*, and with vigorous directing and the talent and collaboration of his writers and stars, Hawks produced a memorable, enjoyable film.

Julie Barker

TO KILL A MOCKINGBIRD

Released: 1962
Production: Alan J. Pakula for Universal
Direction: Robert Mulligan
Screenplay: Horton Foote (AA); based on the novel of the same name by Harper Lee
Cinematography: Russell Harlan
Editing: Aaron Stell
Art direction: Alexander Golitzen and Henry Bumstead (AA); set decoration, Oliver Emert (AA)
Running time: 129 minutes

Principal characters:

Atticus Finch	Gregory Peck (AA)
Scout	Mary Badham
Jem	Phillip Alford
Dill	John Megna
Tom Robinson	Brock Peters
Mayella Ewell	Collin Wilcox
Boo Radley	Robert Duvall

When *To Kill a Mockingbird* was released in 1962, it received acclaim on three different levels. First, it was a resounding critical success on the basis of the fine performances it contained and the modest, coherent technique by which its story unfolded. Second, the film was literally beloved by audiences. This popular response was notable in view of the fact that people were bringing with them dangerously high expectations created by deep loyalty to the best-selling, Pulitzer Prize-winning novel by Harper Lee from which the film was adapted. Third, the film was given several awards for its "decency" in the presentation of racial injustice in the South; in the heightened climate of the Civil Rights Movement, *To Kill a Mockingbird* was taken primarily as a moral exposition of the plight of blacks in America. It is evident now that "decency" is very much at the heart of this motion picture, but its qualities of decency are more complicated and enduring than was generally realized in 1962. The film endures because its direction, screenplay, cinematography, and performances all serve to sensitize the viewer less to a specific injustice than to the problem of injustice as a fact of life, and to how dignity, sensitivity, and moral courage are maintained in the face of human irrationality.

The film reveals its vision of these fundamental problems by presenting them from a child's perspective. The viewer is invited to see the complicated interplay of good and evil as it dawns on energetic and innocent minds. The story begins with and centers on two children and their widowed father in a small Alabama town during the Depression. In the midst of the slow, apparently simple life of this place and time, Scout (Mary Badham), a six-year-old tomboy, and her ten-year-old brother Jem (Phillip Alford) weave the fantasies and fears of childhood, operating inside their own private and elaborate reality. These fears and fantasies revolve around Boo Radley (Robert Duvall), the supposedly mad son of their mysterious neighbors. Boo has not been seen since his family locked him in years ago, but rumors of his fearsome habits and appearance provide ample material upon which childish imaginations can expand. In this youthful myth-making process, Scout and Jem are aided over the long summer days by their summertime neighbor, the small, eccentric Dill (John Megna).

Gently presiding over the dreamworld of his children is Atticus Finch (Gregory Peck), a lawyer of quiet but firm bearing and dry wit. Called "Atticus" by Scout and Jem, he behaves toward his children with a no-nonsense tenderness, always appreciating the seriousness of their childhood crises and never talking down to their awakening intelligences. It is through Atticus that a more ambiguous, contradictory reality is suddenly introduced into the lives of Scout and Jem. In a plot paralleling that of Boo Radley, Atticus is asked to defend a black man, Tom Robinson (Brock Peters), accused of raping a "white-trash" girl, Mayella Ewell (Collin Wilcox). By agreeing to defend a black man against a white woman Atticus exposes himself and his children to the hostility of the white townspeople. In the course of events precipitated by this situation, Scout and Jem experience revelations about their father's character, about the implacable tyranny of societal codes, about the differences between one human being and another, and about the myriad angles from which life can be viewed. They watch as Atticus patiently withstands threats and compassionately attends to his client's family. They follow him one night as he goes to stand guard outside the jail to which Tom has been moved during the trial. In this, one of the most quietly powerful scenes on film, a lynch mob has gathered, and Jem, understanding the danger, refuses to leave at his father's command. Scout, innocent of the danger, "disarms" the crowd by humanizing them with her uninhibited chatter at one of the potential lynchers whose son she knows from school.

The Boo Radley plot develops along with the plot of the rape trial. Jem, Scout, and Dill sneak up to the Radley house one night hoping to catch a glimpse of Boo. When a large shadow appears they run in terror. Jem, who discards his overalls when they get tangled in a fence as he flees, goes back later to find them neatly folded, waiting for him. The mystery is compounded as he begins to find little gifts left in the knothole of a tree at the edge of the Radley property. Both as a result of these developments and of his father's role in the rape case, Jem's understanding of the world is being altered. Scout too suffers growing pains as she must give up her overalls for a dress to start school, and, once in school, must fathom a world in which her natural candor backfires.

It is at the explosive trial of Tom Robinson that Scout and Jem are dramatically affected. They witness simultaneously the tangible reality of injustice as well as the possibility of moral courage embodied by Atticus. Although Atticus skillfully and eloquently demonstrates Tom's innocence and argues convincingly that, in fact, Mayella made sexual advances to the black man and was beaten by her father, Tom is convicted by the white jury. As Atticus leaves the courtroom in defeat, the black people in the upper gallery, Scout and Jem with them, stand in his honor. Tom is later shot to death as he supposedly attempts to escape.

The two plots of the film are brought together at the conclusion. Bob Ewell, Mayella's father, after having been disgraced by Atticus, takes drunken revenge upon him by attacking Scout and Jem as they are walking home through the woods at night. Boo Radley, who has obviously watched lovingly over the children all along, kills Ewell and saves them. In the final scene, the injured Jem, whose important revelation came at the trial, lies asleep, watched over by Atticus. Scout, whose revelation is now occurring, walks the pale, gentle Boo Radley home, then stands on his porch to view the world from his perspective, and to understand what Atticus has told her—that you do not understand a person until you see things from inside his skin.

The most obvious strength of *To Kill a Mockingbird* lies in the performances shaped by director Robert Mulligan. Mulligan confidently cast two children from Alabama with no acting experience in the roles of Scout and Jem, and managed to elicit from them precisely the riveting naturalness so essential in this story told from the children's perspective. Mary Badham's performance as Scout, the small girl both sustained and burdened by the honesty of her responses, stands as one of the most astonishing portrayals of a child's consciousness ever put on film. She is relentlessly touching and unsweet. Phillip Alford as Jem, through whom the viewer is sensitized to the moral nature of Atticus, evokes a perfect late-childhood seriousness. Mulligan skillfully orchestrates the interaction of these performances to underline the difference in the stages of childhood being dramatized. Gregory Peck's performance as Atticus, for which he received an Academy Award for Best Actor, demonstrates a thorough understanding not only of the character but of the overall design and ambition of the film. It is evident in the power of Atticus' verbal and physical reticence that Peck understands the extent to which the definition of dignity as a form of tender and exquisite modesty makes all the delicate perceptions of the film more available. The supporting acting in the film is notably strong and affecting. While the uniform quality of performance points to the considerable skills of director Mulligan, the Academy Award-winning script by Horton Foote deserves particular mention for establishing the principles of eloquent silence and effective understatement.

The major virtue of *To Kill a Mockingbird* that has emerged over time is Robert Mulligan's original understanding of the truly powerful elements in the story. Though the issue of racism slanted the perception of the film in 1962, it is clear now (as it was then to critic Arthur Knight) that Mulligan directed in such a way that the children's coming to terms with life's ambiguities is the real story. The film's pace, as the camera pauses on Atticus listening from the front porch to his children talking in bed about the mother they barely remember, or as the viewer is shown Jem's intensity as he watches his father in court, is designed to provoke complex awareness rather than simple indignation. Both Mulligan and screenwriter Foote realized the story's capacity for delicate statement about the relationship between parent and child, and about the critical reconstructions a child's understanding must pass through. Under Mulligan's direction, the restrained pace of Foote's script, the modesty of Russell Harlan's black-and-white cinematography, the low-key quality of the art direction by Alexander Golitzen and Henry Bumstead and of Oliver Emert's set decoration, and the poignant score by Elmer Bernstein, all converge in a single, coherent vision.

The film may be criticized for its rather melodramatic and possibly self-righteous treatment of Tom Robinson's plight (which, ironically, is the thing for which it was praised in the early 1960's) and for its contrived ending. Yet in this the film is especially faithful to the Harper Lee novel, and both of these elements appear to be the result of conscious decisions by Foote and Mulligan. In any case, *To Kill a Mockingbird* endures on the strength of its quieter truths.

Virginia Campbell

TOM JONES

Released: 1963
Production: Tony Richardson for Woodfall; released by United Artists (AA)
Direction: Tony Richardson (AA)
Screenplay: John Osborne (AA); based on the novel of the same name by Henry Fielding
Cinematography: Walter Lassally
Editing: Antony Gibbs
Music: John Addison (AA)
Running time: 128 minutes

Principal characters:

Tom Jones	Albert Finney
Sophie Western	Susannah York
Squire Western	Hugh Griffith
Miss Western	Dame Edith Evans
Lady Bellaston	Joan Greenwood
Squire Allworthy	George Devine
Mrs. Waters	Joyce Redman
Molly	Diane Cilento
Blifil	David Warner
Lord Fellamar	David Tomlinson

Tom Jones is a lusty, rollicking comic masterpiece. For more than two hours of invention and comic incident it tells the story of the adventures and misadventures of a robust, fun-loving young man. It is a maxim of film criticism that a good film cannot be made from a good book, but *Tom Jones* is a glorious exception. Based on the eighteenth century novel by Henry Fielding, it uses twentieth century cinematic equivalents of Fielding's distinctive style. The novel is so full of incident that the film has to maintain a breakneck pace simply to cover the main features of the story line. Although it cannot show every scene from the novel, it remains remarkably faithful to the spirit of the book; yet a viewer who has never heard of the novel can also completely enjoy and appreciate the film.

The film uses myriad cinematic devices: accelerated action, off-screen narration, silent film titles, actors directly addressing the camera, wipes, and freeze frames. These devices are perfectly appropriate to the adaptation of a book in which the author often addresses the reader directly and uses such chapter headings as "Containing what the reader may, perhaps, expect to find in it." In their artful translation of the novel to the screen, director Tony Richardson and scriptwriter John Osborne have produced a film in which both the story and the manner in which it is told are continually delightful.

The mood of the film and the background of its story are established in the opening sequence, which occurs before the main title credits. The sequence is treated like a silent film with titles instead of dialogue, slightly speeded up action, and—since it takes place in the eighteenth century—harpsicord music corresponding to the piano music which accompanied silent films. Squire Allworthy (George Devine) returns to his manor house to find a baby boy left in his bed. A servant, Jennie Jones, is accused of being the mother and sent away from the house. Allworthy decides to call the boy Tom Jones and bring him up himself. Then, after the title and credits and a flip of the screen, we pick up the story some twenty years later.

Allworthy is now rearing not only Tom (Albert Finney) but also Blifil (David Warner), his widowed sister's child. Tom has grown into a handsome, robust young man whose frequent escapades with the ladies the camera must avoid, the narrator tells us, "where taste and decorum and the censor dictate." A neighboring landholder, Squire Western (Hugh Griffith), thinks Tom a great sporting companion. Yet when his daughter Sophie (Susannah York) and Tom fall in love, he is infuriated. Both Western and his sister (Dame Edith Evans), who is visiting, insist that she marry Blifil, whom she detests. Blifil causes Tom to be banished from Allworthy's house, and Sophie escapes from her father and her aunt. Tom and Sophie both go to London, but not together. In London Tom becomes entangled with Lady Bellaston (Joan Greenwood), who is ostensibly helping him find Sophie. Sophie has her problems also in resisting the advances of Lord Fellamar (David Tomlinson). After many adventures and Tom's near-hanging, they are reunited. In a whirlwind finish it is revealed that Tom is actually the illegitimate son of Allworthy's sister, and the union of Tom and Sophie is blessed by both Allworthy and Western. Indeed, the pace of the final scenes becomes so fast that one character, Mrs. Waters (Joyce Redman), has to turn to the camera and explain to us all that is happening.

On one level the film is a commentary on eighteenth century England, with Squire Western the chief representative of the excesses of the time. To say he lacks refinement is an understatement; he eats with less decorum than the swine in his barnyard, gnawing meat off the bone and then wiping his hands on his wig only to drink himself into a stupor as he sits before the fire with his dogs. He is lecherous toward any available woman and applauds Tom's wenching; but we find that he has a double standard. When he learns that his daughter, Sophie, is in love with Tom, he is enraged. Tom is a great friend and hunting companion, but being illegitimate and without wealth he is not fit for the Squire's daughter. Instead he tries to force her to marry Blifil, chiefly because Blifil is Allworthy's heir and the marriage would unite their estates. The fact that neither he nor Sophie likes Blifil has no bearing on the matter. Also revealing of Western and of eighteenth century landed gentry as a whole is the stag hunt—one of Western's favorite sports. Magnificently photographed from all points of view, including overhead shots taken from a helicopter of the party at full chase, the sequence portrays both the excitement and movement of the hunt and also its brutal and bloody side. Horses fall, farm animals are trampled by the hunters, spurs seen in close-up bring blood spurting from the flanks of the horses, and Western's triumphant display of the bloody stag which the dogs have ripped apart is not a pretty or inspiring sight.

If the country squire as personified by Western is depicted pejoratively, London and its society, particularly Lady Bellaston, receive no better treatment. Our first view of the city is Tom's view as he walks through the squalor of the dirty, crowded streets in a scene reminiscent of the paintings and drawings of Fielding's contemporary, the caricaturist Hogarth. But Tom soon finds in Lady Bellaston a totally different side of London life. Rather than helping him find Sophie, she appropriates him for herself and introduces him into her world of expensive clothes, elegant manners, and lack of sincerity. For example, when Lord Fellamar is unable to persuade Sophie to accept his advances, Lady Bellaston advises him to rape her.

In addition to the social comment depicted through such characters as Squire Western and Lady Bellaston, there is a basic moral opposition between Tom Jones and Blifil. Tom has all virtues except prudence and self-discipline while Blifil has only those two virtues. Tom is generous, open, and virile while Blifil is mean, deceitful, and effete. We perceive this contrast initially in their appearance. Tom is frequently dirty and disheveled while Blifil is always formally and correctly dressed. An early scene further reveals the nature of each. Tom has brought a bird as a gift for Sophie Western, and Blifil surreptitiously lets it escape from its cage. Tom, through a victory of zeal over prudence, climbs a tree by a pond to recapture the bird. He gets the bird but also falls in the pond.

Tom is seldom able to restrain his impulses, especially his amorous ones. Early in the film he is seen tumbling in the bushes with Molly (Diane Cilento), daughter of Squire Allworthy's disreputable gamekeeper, and even later, when he is seemingly consumed by his passion for Sophie, Molly is still able to entice him very easily. On the way to London, he is seduced by Mrs. Waters in the film's most famous scene. As they begin to eat their meal at an inn, Tom is intent on the food and Mrs. Waters is intent on Tom. She begins eating her food lasciviously, fixing her eyes always on Tom. He begins to respond in kind until they are each opening lobster claws, swallowing oysters, gnawing drumsticks, and biting into fruit with undisguised passion for each other rather than for the food. Not a word is spoken, but no one in the audience has any doubt where they are going when they leave the table.

Tom's undisciplined nature, however, frequently gets him into trouble and certainly leaves him vulnerable to the conniving of Blifil. Not only does Blifil get Tom banished from the house and the affections of Allworthy, but he also has him framed on a charge of robbery in London. Only a last-minute rescue by Squire Western keeps him from being hanged. But in the end Blifil's villainies are exposed, and Tom is triumphant. In fact, Western's last-moment rescue of Tom from the gallows is the only major deviation from the novel. In the book Tom was sentenced to hang, but was freed before being taken to the gallows.

It does not slight the fine achievement of Albert Finney as Tom Jones to say that the most memorable performance is that of Hugh Griffith as the outrageous Squire Western. Never calm, he throws himself physically and emotionally into everything he does. And, if only for the eating scene, Joyce Redman should be singled out of the excellent cast for her portrayal of the lustful Mrs. Waters.

The artistry of *Tom Jones* was rewarded with huge returns at the box office, awards from many countries, including the Academy Award for Best Picture as well as Academy Awards for Tony Richardson as director, John Osborne as scriptwriter, and John Addison for his original musical score.

Timothy W. Johnson

TOP HAT

Released: 1935
Production: Pandro S. Berman for RKO/Radio
Direction: Mark Sandrich
Screenplay: Dwight Taylor and Allan Scott
Cinematography: David Abel and Vernon Walker
Editing: William Hamilton
Art direction: Van Nest Polglase
Costume design: Bernard Newman
Dance direction: Hermes Pan
Song: Irving Berlin
Running time: 101 minutes

Principal characters:

Jerry Travers .... Fred Astaire
Dale Tremont ....Ginger Rogers
Horace Hardwick .... Edward Everett Horton
Madge Hardwick .... Helen Broderick
Alberto Beddini .... Erik Rhodes
Bates .... Eric Blore

Between 1933 and 1939, Fred Astaire and Ginger Rogers appeared in nine films for RKO, beginning with *Flying Down to Rio* and ending with *The Story of Vernon and Irene Castle*. The fourth of these, *Top Hat*, epitomizes their legendary elegance, charm, sophistication, and dancing style. Indeed, if one film is more often associated with their names than any of the others, and if one film crystallized their screen personalities, it is *Top Hat*, the most popular and arguably the best. The film has achieved the status of a classic and has endured as one of the great dance musicals.

The film continues the mood and tone of the previous Astaire-Rogers musicals with its spontaneity, smooth integration of the musical numbers into the plot, and use of the songs and dances to deepen and enhance the emotions and moods expressed in the story. In a typical Astaire-Rogers musical, the two usually play strangers who meet by accident. Astaire almost always falls in love with Rogers immediately, but she is antagonistic to him or annoyed by his advances and tries to escape or evade him until finally, persuaded by a romantic dance number, she succumbs. In their films the dances communicate the romantic interludes depicted in the stories surrounding them, revealing the nuances of the characters' relationship more dramatically than words. Through the dances the audience can identify the moods of the characters played by Astaire and Rogers and the depth of their involvement with each other.

Top Hat opens with the credits superimposed over a top hat which turns out to belong to a gentleman about to enter the stately Thackeray Club in

London. The quiet, hushed atmosphere inside is so profound that the crackle of a newspaper disturbs the elderly members. The noisy newspaper belongs to the American dancer, Jerry Travers (Fred Astaire), who is waiting for his friend, Horace Hardwick (Edward Everett Horton), the producer of his London stage show. Before leaving the club with Horace, Jerry turns and delivers a staccato burst of taps that awakens all the members.

Back in his hotel room, Horace tells Jerry that his wife, Madge (Helen Broderick), who is vacationing at the Lido, a seaside resort near Venice, expects Jerry to fly over with him for the weekend. Horace says Madge wants him to meet a young woman, and he suspects that Madge feels it is time for Jerry to marry and settle down. Jerry scoffs at the idea, telling Horace, "in me you see a youth who is completely on the loose. No yens. No strings. No connections. No ties to my affections," breaking into song in midsentence as he smoothly and easily begins the first song, "No Strings," in which he proclaims his independence and unwillingness to settle down. The song deftly establishes the character of Jerry Travers, and the exuberant dance that follows cleverly brings about the meeting of Jerry and Dale Tremont (Ginger Rogers).

Jerry's dance carries him all around the sitting room of Horace's hotel suite in a series of complicated steps, during which he kicks his heels together while airborne. Unable to contain his high spirits, he dances about the room unaware that he has awakened Dale Tremont, who is staying in the room below. Furious, she telephones the hotel manager, who in turn telephones Horace's room. Not understanding the message, Horace goes down to the lobby to investigate, and after he leaves, Jerry, still dancing, answers a knock on the door. It is Dale. As he stares at her, immediately smitten, she glares at him and icily informs him that she is trying to sleep. He can only reply bemusedly that "Every once in a while I suddenly find myself dancing." After she leaves, he scatters sand on the floor and does a delicate sand dance to help her go to sleep, gently patting the floor and finally collapsing into a chair, yawning sleepily. Though almost never seen in films, the sand dance was popular among black tap dancers in the 1920's and 1930's.

The next morning Jerry has all the available flowers in the hotel flower shop sent to Dale's room with a card reading "From your Silent Admirer." When he encounters Dale, dressed in riding clothes in the lobby, he offers to drive her to the stables, but she declines his offer, saying she has a hansom cab waiting outside. As the cab leaves, we see that Jerry is driving it, but Dale does not discover this until she hears him tapping his feet on the roof of the cab. She is slightly amused, but when the cab arrives at the stables she simply gives him a coin and tells him to buy himself a new hat. Later, a rain shower forces her to seek shelter in a deserted bandstand. Jerry drives up in the cab, offering to rescue her, but she persists in being antagonistic. "No thank you, I prefer being in distress," she replies. A sudden clap of thunder, however, sends her scurrying into his arms. She recoils immediately, but he begins a whimsical explanation of thunder to soothe her fears, and when the next burst of thunder begins the music, he sings, "The weather is frightening, the thunder and lightning seem to be having their way, but as far as I'm concerned it's a lovely day." Seemingly impervious to his musical blandishments, she nevertheless listens with a sparkle in her eye. After the song is over, he walks casually away, whistling. She then accepts his tacit challenge by following him, copying his steps and gestures exactly, thus beginning the dance.

The dance starts slowly, with a few simple steps which Dale mimics, but soon she adds variations of her own as she enters more and more into the spirit of the dance. Another thunderclap begins an acceleration in the tempo of the music. The two freeze and look at each other, the music stops and starts and stops again. When it starts again he seizes her in an exuberant embrace and they whirl joyously around. At the end they perch on the edge of the bandstand, smiling and shaking hands in silent acknowledgment of what has happened between them.

After Dale returns to her hotel she receives a telegram from her friend Madge Hardwick requesting her to look up Madge's husband, Horace, who is staying at Dale's hotel. When Dale inquires at the desk, the clerk tells her that Horace Hardwick has the room above hers and points him out as he crosses the mezzanine. Looking up at the mezzanine, Dale sees Jerry, and since she does not know Jerry's name she mistakes him for Horace. Furious because she thinks that her best friend's husband has been pursuing her, she slaps Jerry's face when he comes up to her in the lobby, creating a scene. Dale is supposed to go to the Lido, both to accompany Alberto Beddini (Erik Rhodes), the dress designer whose clothes she models, and to visit Madge, but she is uncomfortable at the idea of facing Madge after what has happened. Ironically, Madge has invited Dale in order to introduce her to Jerry. It is Beddini who finally persuades Dale to make the trip.

Jerry is disconsolate when he finds that Dale has left until a telegram from Madge to Horace accidentally reveals Dale's whereabouts. Preparing for the opening night of his London show, he tells Horace to charter an airplane, and bounds jauntily onstage, the telegram still in his hand, and begins the song "Top Hat, White Tie and Tails" with the line, "I've just got an invitation through the mail." The song will forever be associated with Fred Astaire, and the dance that follows is an Astaire classic. Performing with a few simple props and a male chorus, Astaire varies not only the tempo but also the mood of the dance. What begins as a straightforward routine with a male chorus becomes an eerie, mysterious mood piece with Astaire creating all the effects. At first he taps in rapid circles around his cane, then the music slows and stops, the chorus disappears, the lights are lowered, and suddenly he is a man afraid, startled by shadows, looking uneasily behind him. He crouches as if menaced by some unseen presence. Then the lights come up, the chorus reappears, and Astaire uses his cane to mime shooting them, at first singly, then in two's and three's, then in a rapid burst of machine gun fire, using taps to represent the gunfire. The last dancer wavers but refuses to fall until Astaire mimes using his cane as a bow and arrow to bring him down.

As the theater orchestra reprises "Top Hat, White Tie and Tails" the scene dissolves to a gleaming white art moderne set with white gondolas and bridges representing the Lido. There Madge is assuring Dale that Horace's attentions to her mean nothing—he flirts with any pretty girl. Madge, of course, does not realize that Dale has mistaken Jerry for Horace.

Later that evening Dale has to face Jerry again when he joins her and Madge at their table. Since Madge does not know of Dale's mistake, she urges the two to dance. Trying to shrug off her confusion, Dale says, "Well, if Madge doesn't care, I certainly don't." "Neither do I," Jerry replies. "All I know is that it's Heaven, I'm in Heaven," he says, breaking into song in the middle of the sentence, and he proceeds to describe the joys of dancing "Cheek to Cheek." When he finishes singing, he dances Dale across a bridge, away from the crowd, and they perform a romantic dance. At the end of their dance he asks her to marry him. She is outraged at his impudence and slaps him, exclaiming angrily, "How could I have fallen in love with anyone as low as you." But Jerry is overjoyed because she has admitted she loves him.

Seeing no possibility of her relationship with Jerry working out because she thinks he is married to Madge, Dale agrees to marry Beddini. The rest of the film is spent in straightening out the mistaken identities and untangling the complications of Dale's marriage to Beddini. Jerry finally manages to get Dale alone in a gondola to explain to her that he is not married and is not Horace. She is contrite but upset because she is now married to Beddini. While Beddini is searching for them, they return to the hotel for a champagne supper.

As they dine they watch a parade of white gondolas which are followed by a troupe of dancers performing "The Piccolino." A medium-sized production number, "The Piccolino" uses a variety of camera angles, including some overhead shots of the dancers to create intricate patterns in a manner somewhat reminiscent of Busby Berkeley, but is relatively restrained, with Astaire and Rogers as the scintillating centerpiece of the dance. First Rogers turns to Astaire and sings the lyrics to him, then they skip onto the floor to do their own inimitable version of the dance. At the conclusion they dance back to their table and raise their champagne glasses in a silent toast to each other.

The denouement of the film reveals that the man who married Dale and Beddini was actually Horace's valet, Bates (Eric Blore), posing as a clergyman, so they are not really married at all. The film ends on a buoyant note as Astaire and Rogers do a brief reprise of "The Piccolino" before whirling out of the picture.

Irving Berlin reportedly regards his score for *Top Hat* as the best he has ever written. He attended all script conferences for the film with the result that the songs develop specific plot points or illuminate the characters' feelings. Indeed, the songs are such an integral part of the film that none of them except "The Piccolino" could be eliminated without substituting dialogue scenes in their place.

The thoughtfully conceived and beautifully executed dances in the film give resonance and meaning to the slender plot surrounding them, not only dramatizing the characters' moods and the depth of their involvement with each other, but also often developing the story line and giving the film added momentum. Although he did not receive screen credit for choreographing or directing his dance numbers, Astaire was largely responsible for them and the way they were filmed. He disliked the idea of using reaction shots (showing other people watching the dancers), unusual camera angles, or close-ups showing only the head or feet of the dancer. His method was to film a dance straight through, keeping the full length of the dancer in the camera frame and the flow of the dance intact. He felt that in any dance, even tap, the movement of the upper part of the body was as important as the feet. Always trying to keep the audience from being aware of the camera, Astaire placed it at eye level and seldom changed angles. Thus, the flow of the dance was never interrupted, and, since film presents the dance from the ideal perspective, the audience can follow intricate steps that would be lost on a theater stage. It was not only with the camera that Astaire concerned himself, however. He also supervised every stage of the development of a dance number from the orchestration through the final recording and editing of the sound and picture for it.

"No Strings" both defines the character played by Fred Astaire—exuberant, footloose, fancy free, ready for romance—and provides the mechanism for his meeting with the character played by Ginger Rogers. (She is awakened by his dancing and goes to his room to complain.) The dance in the rain to "Isn't This a Lovely Day?" is the crucial one in the development of their relationship. She is cold and distant, determined to maintain her haughty reserve. He breaches her defenses by first singing to her, then by shrewdly challenging her to join him in an increasingly joyous and complicated tap duet. She cannot resist the challenge and not only copies him but also varies his steps with original twists of her own. It is the dance equivalent of an argumentative, increasingly flirtatious conversation. At first the movements are tentative as the two test each other, but they pick up speed and intensity until the two whirl each other around in an enthusiastic embrace, no longer trying to hide or to contain their feelings. Their acquaintance, courtship, and romance is vividly dramatized in this one brief dance, the kinetic equivalent of several dialogue scenes.

In "Cheek to Cheek" the lyrics express Jerry's joy at dancing with Dale again, and their dance displays their emotional harmony and perfect teamwork. It is only afterwards that reality and common sense reassert themselves as Dale remembers that Jerry is, as she mistakenly believes, married to her best friend Madge.

The songs and dances in the film are supported by the able comic performances of Erik Rhodes as ineffectual Alberto Beddini, Eric Blore as the stately valet Bates, Edward Everett Horton as fussy Horace Hardwick, and Helen Broderick as sardonic Madge Hardwick. Their adroit handling of comic lines and scenes adds to the fun of *Top Hat*.

Top Hat has a special quality which goes beyond the excellence of the dancing, singing, and acting. It lies in the affinity of the screen personalities of Fred Astaire and Ginger Rogers. Neither technical proficiency nor talent alone is enough for a film performer to reach audiences successfully. In both Astaire and Rogers we find not only talent but also a distinctive screen presence. Together they create a style and a mood which is still remembered and, many would say, unequalled.

Julia Johnson

TOPPER

Released: 1937
Production: Hal Roach for Metro-Goldwyn-Mayer
Direction: Norman Z. McLeod
Screenplay: Jack Jevne, Eric Hatch, and Eddie Moran; based on the novel *The Jovial Ghosts* by Thorne Smith
Cinematography: Norbert Brodine
Editing: William Terhune
Special effects: Roy Seawright
Running time: 98 minutes

Principal characters:

Marion Kirby	Constance Bennett
George Kirby	Cary Grant
Cosmo Topper	Roland Young
Mrs. Topper	Billie Burke
Wilkins	Alan Mowbray
Casey	Eugene Pallette
Elevator Boy	Arthur Lake
Mrs. Stuyvesant	Hedda Hopper

Unlike the creatures which terrified the audiences of many movie houses in the 1930's, ghosts were thought to elicit only laughter. As a result, the ghost became a comic device long before Dracula, the Frankenstein Monster, Wolfman, or the Invisible Man came to the screen. In 1937, Hal Roach, who is best known for the Laurel and Hardy and Our Gang comedies, produced *Topper*. Based on *The Jovial Ghosts* by Thorne Smith, the film features Roland Young as Cosmo Topper, a wealthy, conservative banker with a domineering, straightlaced wife (Billie Burke). In contrast to Topper are George and Marion Kirby (Cary Grant and Constance Bennett), an uninhibited, sophisticated young couple who are the principal stockholders in his bank.

While rushing from good time to good time, the Kirbys are killed one evening in an automobile accident. Not the types to let death interfere with their fun, they set out to accomplish one last redeeming act—the emancipation of Cosmo Topper. Unfortunately, Topper does not want to be freed of the inhibiting bonds which limit his existence; he is quite content to remain the dull, boring man he has always been. The Kirbys, however, will not hear of it. He is their project, and whether he likes it or not, they are now a part of his life.

For a man not subject to flights of fantasy, the sudden appearance and disappearance of ghosts can be quite disconcerting and at times embarrassing. The Kirbys constantly pop up at the most inconvenient times, and the ribald ways that defined their earthly existence have now taken on even greater dimensions. Teaching the ways of hedonism to a man who not only has never experienced them, but who is also fighting the lessons at every turn, can be very difficult. Nevertheless, George and Marion are very qualified teachers, and their invisibility gives them a slight advantage. Cosmo is given the unenviable choice of either going along and trying to maintain his dignity or blaming his circumstances on the intervention of ghosts. Since seeing ghosts is an unacceptable excuse for most people and completely unforgivable for a banker, he is forced into many situations which require fast thinking and equally fast talking.

Eventually, the complications become more difficult, and fights, panics, and general upheaval are blamed on Cosmo. Along the way, however, he also experiences a little of the fun he has forsaken for so many years and even begins to appreciate his corruption. Nevertheless, the conservative businessman is forever manifesting itself, forcing him to make excuses for himself which make others wonder if Cosmo Topper has "flipped his wig." By the end of the film, Topper has regained his self-respect. His wife has repented and given up many of her shrewish tendencies. Life, in general, looks more promising for him. George and Marion, having accomplished their goal, go off to what is assumed to be their final destination at some "great cocktail party in the sky."

Topper is a successful blend of fantasy and screwball comedy. Cary Grant is perfect as the impeccably dressed but impish George Kirby. Constance Bennett is equally charming as his beautiful and mischievous wife Marion. Roland Young is also perfectly cast as the respectable banker who must deal with ghosts.

The film was a success and spawned two sequels, *Topper Takes a Trip* (1939) and *Topper Returns* (1941). In the first of these two films, Topper, again played by Roland Young, is harassed by Constance Bennett while vacationing on the Riviera. In *Topper Returns*, Young as Topper gets involved in a murder mystery. He is assisted by his two ghostly friends, this time played by Joan Blondell and Dennis O'Keefe. In 1953 *Topper* found its way to television with Leo G. Carroll in the title role of the successful series.

All in all, without the aid of witty dialogue and lively performances, *Topper* would have fallen into the category of "one joke" films. The misadventures of a person besieged by floating ashtrays and unseen kicks on the behind have been witnessed on far too many occasions. Furthermore, the exasperated attempts of a man trying to explain this phenomenon to a scrutinizing observer gets boring in a hurry. Fortunately, in *Topper* this is not the case. Cary Grant and Constance Bennett are far too sophisticated and stylish to become clowns, and they bring an air of class to the story. Without Cary Grant, the sequels, while entertaining, did not measure up.

The screwball period of comedy in the 1930's consisted of films which combined sophisticated, bright, witty dialogue with highly energetic and violent slapstick action. These films usually teamed a male and female star who provided both the comic and romantic interest for the film. In addition, the leads were aided by the best supporting players in Hollywood. *Topper*, for example, featured Billie Burke as Topper's wife, Alan Mowbray as his forever scrutinizing butler, and Eugene Pallette and Arthur Lake as a harassed hotel detective and an elevator operator. The heroes of screwball farces are usually wealthy, like the Kirbys, and oblivious to the problems of the Depression; their sole purpose is to be humorous. *Topper* is an excellent example of the screwball genre. Considering all the films which attempted to utilize the various aspects of screwball cinema, it is amazing how few have retained a freshness over the years. *Topper* is worthy of recognition as one of the best.

James J. Desmarais

THE TREASURE OF THE SIERRA MADRE

Released: 1948
Production: Henry Blanke for Warner Bros.
Direction: John Huston (AA)
Screenplay: John Huston (AA); based on the novel of the same name by B. Traven
Cinematography: Ted McCord
Editing: Owen Marks
Art direction: John Hughes
Sound: Robert B. Lee
Music direction: Leo F. Forbstein
Music: Max Steiner
Running time: 126 minutes

Principal characters:

Fred C. Dobbs	Humphrey Bogart
Howard	Walter Huston
Curtin	Tim Holt
Cody	Bruce Bennett
McCormick	Barton MacLane
Gold Hat	Alfonso Bedoya

The Treasure of the Sierra Madre is a powerful film, which, although it can take its place unblushingly among the best that Hollywood has made, is nevertheless a difficult movie to classify. At the time of its release in 1948, some critics labeled it a masculine adventure and some a Western, while a number of trade publications reported that in more than a few instances audiences had responded to it as a comedy. John Huston, who wrote the screenplay and directed the film, adapted it from a novel by the mysterious author B. Traven. As a written piece, it was a sardonic and intensely realistic fable masquerading under the guise of an adventure story. Huston's screen adaptation transformed it into a bitingly cynical character study dealing with the corrosive effect of greed on a trio of down-and-out prospecting bums.

During the writing of the script for *The Treasure of the Sierra Madre*, Huston was in constant correspondence with its illusive and mysterious author. Novelist Traven had an enormous following in Europe, but little was known of him except that he had lived invisibly somewhere in Mexico for many years. Traven made numerous suggestions for the film treatment that were so intelligent and knowledgeable that Huston was fascinated and wanted to meet him. One day in the Hotel Reforma in Mexico City, Huston was confronted by a thin little man who presented his card. He was Hal Croves, a translator who claimed to be Traven's old friend and to know the author better than Traven himself did. Huston hired him at $150 a week as technical adviser for the film. By the time Croves had done his job and disappeared, the director was almost certain that the uneasy little man was indeed Traven himself.

Set in Mexico in 1920, the riveting story concerns three dirty, unshaven, penniless Americans: Fred C. Dobbs (Humphrey Bogart), the most fanatic and avaricious of the trio; Curtin (Tim Holt), who is relatively stable and decent; and Howard (Walter Huston), the philosophical old-timer who is the most experienced of the group. After Dobbs wins some money in a lottery, the three pool their limited resources, leave their Tampico flophouse, and head toward the Sierra Madre Mountains in search of gold. Despite old Howard's warnings of what the lust for gold can do to a man's soul, Dobbs and Curtin dismiss the notion of any possible dangerous consequences. In the midst of the hostile environment of the mountainous jungles, however, the surface friendship of the three men begins slowly to crumble. When they do uncover a gold field and strike it rich in the Mexican wilderness, distrust and suspicion erupt; rather than setting up a common treasury, each character hides his own share of the gold in greedy self-preservation. In the tension of the dark and lonely nights, emotions become more and more strained; Dobbs begins to accuse the others of trying to steal his share of gold.

Following an attack by bandits led by the malevolent Gold Hat (Alfonso Bedoya), the three decide that they have enough gold. Approached by a group of friendly Indians who ask Howard's aid for a dying child, the old-timer goes off and saves the small boy. Meanwhile, the other two partners move onward. Because of their exhaustion and the tension caused by distrust, a quarrel ensues, whereupon Dobbs shoots and wounds Curtin and steals his share of the gold. Howard finds and saves Curtin, but Gold Hat's Mexican bandits ambush Dobbs, rob him, and slay him.

With the men's feverish greed the film's tone becomes cynical, violent, and macabre. The heart of the story is its simple revelation of three types of human character altering in the presence of the sinister catalyst, gold. The tale is told with humor, wisdom, and suspense. It is by turns exceedingly funny and completely terrifying. In the film's final shot, the gold is mistaken for sand and tossed away; as the gold dust is scattered by the whirlwind, the bitter but wise Howard cries out to Curtin, "Laugh, Boy, it's a joke played on us by the Lord or Fate or whatever. . . . The gold's gone right back where we got it."

The performances are uniformly excellent. Humphrey Bogart cannot completely eliminate the existence of his own screen *persona* as established by such films as *Casablanca* (1942) or *To Have and Have Not* (1944), but he makes a noble effort here to alter that image and the result is arguably the best work of his career. As the unkempt, unsavory Dobbs, he creates a well-developed character. At the peak of his popularity in 1948, he could afford to eschew more romantic roles to play an unscrupulous character.

Yet it is the character of Dobbs as written or interpreted that constitutes the only fundamental weakness in the film. Although the story is about gold and its effects on those who seek it, it is also a fable about all human life and about the essence of good and evil. A number of the possibilities inherent in this idea are treated but some of the most telling implications are missed. Because the Dobbs character is so undisciplined and troublesome from the beginning, it is impossible to demonstrate or even hint at the ultimate depth of the problem; instead, his character dominates much of the film. Since a bit of Dobbs is realistically a part of every human being, it would have made a much more dramatic tragicomedy if the character had been more restrained. In that way the demonstration of the effect of gold upon men could have been more neatly rendered as the fanatical side of Dobbs's character slowly and believably emerges and establishes its universal implications.

At the other extreme is the character of Curtin, the youngest member of the trio. Tim Holt is perhaps less an actor than a presence, but he is a powerful presence. Not nearly as base as Dobbs, the essentially moral Curtin, who plans to use his money to settle on a farm, is sympathetically portrayed by Holt in a role originally intended for John Garfield. The most memorable performance of the film, however, is that of veteran character actor Walter Huston. As the grizzled and toothless old prospector who learns true wisdom from the peaceful life of the Indians, Huston is both charming and eccentric. He totally submerges himself in the role to the extent that he appears short and stocky, even though he appeared tall and lanky when he played Abraham Lincoln in an earlier film. Although the character is extremely well-conceived and competently written, it is still the actor who lends the character its charm and wisdom. In spite of the significant amount of other talent involved in the picture, Huston carries the entire film as deftly and easily as he handles his comedy lines.

Like John Huston's other films, *The Treasure of the Sierra Madre* deals with a harsh, masculine environment and is concerned with men under pressure. Often presented in a romantic context, the films involve violence and danger in exotic locales: Mexico in this case, Revolutionary Cuba in the 1930's in *We Were Strangers* (1949), and India in *The Man Who Would Be King* (1975). Huston has little patience with theories of aesthetics or matters of style; his sharp, crisp directing is intuitive. He has a coldly intelligent aptitude for how much to leave free within the frame and the true artist's passion for the possibilities inherent in his medium. He has been quoted as saying that in any given scene, "I have an idea of what should happen but I don't tell the actors." Instead, he lets them go ahead and do it and sometimes they do it better. "Sometimes they do something accidentally which is effective and true. I jump on the accident."

Huston's most remarkable single achievement is that he focuses all of the symbolic elements as finely as light rays through a magnifying glass. All that is evident to the viewer is a story told so masterfully and realistically that the picture's most ideal, and, in fact, most knowledgeable audience is one made up of the kind of man the film is about. Yet this single accomplishment is the result of many components. The film is one of the most masculine in style ever made and displays a strikingly true cinematic understanding of character and of men. The bums depicted in the film seem real, and their lives and circumstances are as a bum's would be. Also, the city is presented as a bum would see it; it is not glamourized.

The film is, on several levels, a cruel presentation of an almost absolute desolateness in nature and its effect on men. The hardship, labor, and exhaustion of the gold-seeker's existence is skillfully sketched and also enhanced by the introduction and expert handling of amateur and semiprofessional character actors; significantly, Alfonso Bedoya in the role of Gold Hat gives the film a frightening realism. Huston's starkly depicted scenes of violence or those that build toward it combine with his treatment of location and scenery to unfold gradually the film's perspectives on human nature.

The perfect blend of actors and scenery is sustained throughout by the superb camerawork of Ted McCord. There is not one superfluous, arty, or self-conscious shot in the film. The camera is always in its proper position and never exploits or dwells too long upon its subject. Instead, there is a sense of leanness and vigor in every scene without any sacrifice of sensitivity. There is, for example, a shot of Gold Hat reflected in muddy water which is so subtly photographed that, although the film is shot in black-and-white, his hat seems to shed a golden light. McCord's style is so delicate as to be almost invisible and yet he effectively conveys the symbolism of the scene. The film's studio exteriors offer a jarring and unfortunate contrast to the location shots, however, and detract from the overall effect of the film. The score by Max Steiner is also, at times, intrusive, and perhaps unnecessary.

The Treasure of the Sierra Madre marked the first time in Academy Award history that a father and son both won an Oscar for the same film in the same year. Walter Huston won an Oscar for Best Supporting Actor, and his son John (who has a bit part in the film as the American in the white suit) won Oscars for Best Screenplay and Best Direction. The film is indeed an outstanding motion picture and a true representation of Huston's fine work, as well as that of Humphrey Bogart and Walter Huston.

Leslie Taubman

THE TROUBLE WITH HARRY

Released: 1955
Production: Alfred Hitchcock for Alfred Hitchcock Productions; released by Paramount
Direction: Alfred Hitchcock
Screenplay: John Michael Hayes; based on the novel of the same name by Jack Trevor Story
Cinematography: Robert Burks
Editing: Alma Macrorie
Music: Bernard Herrmann
Running time: 99 minutes

Principal characters:

Captain Albert Wiles	Edmund Gwenn
Sam Marlowe	John Forsythe
Jennifer Rogers	Shirley MacLaine
Miss Gravely	Mildred Natwick
Mrs. Wiggs	Mildred Dunnock
Calvin Wiggs	Royal Dano
Arnie Rogers	Jerry Mathers

For Alfred Hitchcock, *The Trouble with Harry* is an eccentric film. Although it relies little on the particular techniques of suspense usually associated with his work, it does have a subtle tension of its own. It is an uncharacteristically mellow film in which Hitchcock makes considerable use of his very droll English sense of humor, while at the same time demonstrating his gift for using real locations as counterpoint to his fanciful ideas. The exteriors of *The Trouble with Harry* were made in Vermont during the autumn, and the camera captures beautifully the reds, oranges, and yellows of the changing leaves and the tranquility of a peaceful countryside.

In the midst of this beauty, a corpse is discovered; three people believe themselves responsible. Captain Wiles (Edmund Gwenn), a kindly retired seaman, believes he has accidentally shot the man while hunting. Miss Gravely (Mildred Natwick), a prim spinster who believed the man meant to attack her, has struck him on the head with her hiking shoe. The man's estranged wife, Jennifer Rogers (Shirley MacLaine), has hit him with a bottle, which has resulted in his staggering away into the woods in a stupor. A fourth person, Sam Marlowe (John Forsythe), conspires with the three guilty parties to hide the corpse. For the entire length of the story, these four people find themselves burdened with the dead man as a result of their indecisiveness about what to do with him. Finally, they hit upon the idea of having Jennifer's son, Arnie (Jerry Mathers), whose understanding of time is totally confusing, rediscover the dead man at his original resting place.

This is admittedly a slim premise for a film, but for Hitchcock it is only a premise and not the substance of the realized work. The director troubles the audience by making death amusing and by showing no sentiment for Harry, who is unlamented even by his wife and son. More perversely, he uses Harry's death to bring together two couples, Sam and Jennifer and the Captain and Miss Gravely. The film clearly shows that death may be beneficial to the living, since these characters do not know one another before Harry's death, and develop deep mutual affection through their common cause. All four characters refute the mistaken view that Hitchcock is only able to take an interest in mentally unhealthy relationships and psychopathic murderers. Each member of this group may be a bit eccentric in some way, but each has an attitude toward life that is essentially healthy and positive.

The character of Sam is unique in the fact that he is the only major character in a Hitchcock film who is an artist. He is a young man whose talent is unrecognized; all of his paintings are unsold, although his fortunes change at the end. John Forsythe is ideally cast as Sam, who alone does not share in the imagined guilt of his companions, but who assumes the role of leader in all of their schemes by virtue of his quick mind. Forsythe conveys the charm and intelligence necessary to make Sam's manipulation of the others credible.

The other characters are equally well realized. Shirley MacLaine, in her first film, makes an uncommon Hitchcock heroine, and there is no question that she was chosen for the qualities which set her apart from other actresses. Rather than the pathos associated with MacLaine's most celebrated roles (*Some Came Running*, 1958; *The Apartment*, 1960), Hitchcock brings out her comic flair and ability to project sexiness in an amusing way, qualities also evident in her next film, *Artists and Models* (1955). Edmund Gwenn and Mildred Natwick, both endearing character players, make an unusual romantic couple. They take full advantage of the film's rich possibilities for humor, and are unexpectedly touching in the courtship scenes, evoking the combination of shyness and bravado more commonly associated with romance between adolescents.

The Trouble with Harry was made in Hitchcock's richest period. Robert Burks, a constant collaborator for over a decade, had already photographed a number of Hitchcock films, and his work in VistaVision and Technicolor is entrancing, especially in the attractive scenes of New England which are visually unlike those in any other film. Bernard Herrmann, another valuable collaborator in this period, composed his first Hitchcock score for *The Trouble with Harry* and expressed regret in later years that he had not been able to score more comedies. His music for the film is alternately wistful and whimsical. John Michael Hayes was scenarist for four consecutive Hitchcock films; these four screenplays abound in verbal wit and are easily Hayes's best work. Hayes deserves special praise for the dialogue in the first meeting between

Sam and Jennifer, in which they sit on the porch drinking lemonade as Jennifer talks matter-of-factly about her marriage to the ill-fated Harry. This sequence is one of the most outrageous boy-meets-girl episodes on film and would by itself be enough to justify Hitchcock's high opinion of *The Trouble with Harry*, which he always cites as a personal favorite.

Blake Lucas

TRUE GRIT

Released: 1969
Production: Hal B. Wallis for Paramount
Direction: Henry Hathaway
Screenplay: Marguerite Roberts; based on the novel of the same name by Charles Portis
Cinematography: Lucien Ballard
Editing: Warren Low
Costume design: Dorothy Jeakins
Music: Elmer Bernstein
Running time: 128 minutes

Principal characters:
Rooster Cogburn .... John Wayne (AA)
Mattie Ross .... Kim Darby
La Boeuf .... Glen Campbell
Emmett Quincy .... Jeremy Slate
Lucky Ned Pepper .... Robert Duvall
Tom Chaney .... Jeff Corey
Moon .... Dennis Hopper

By 1969, the year of *True Grit*, the Western was beginning to enter a period of revisionism in which its myths and archetypes would be treated either with glibness (*Little Big Man*, 1970) or contempt (*McCabe and Mrs. Miller*, 1971). Yet in retrospect, revisionist Westerns seem pathetic replacements for their classic predecessors. *True Grit* is one of the last Westerns to tell vividly a story which is concerned with positive values. John Wayne gives an Oscar-winning performance as Rooster Cogburn, a fat, one-eyed U.S. Marshal who drinks too much but dispatches all villains with a steady trigger finger. The film is a picturesque and homespun account of a girl's adventure in which Cogburn initially serves as comic relief but becomes in the end a noble and moving figure whose relationship to the girl, Mattie Ross, has unexpected meaning.

Henry Hathaway is not noted for rapid exposition, and it is necessary to accept a leisurely pace for most of the film's length to be rewarded by its exciting concluding reels. Hathaway's willingness to take time to give substance to the characters ultimately works in his favor, as he has established considerable interest in what happens to them when they are faced with a host of villains.

The opening of the film brings into focus the complex character of Mattie Ross (Kim Darby). Her admirable courage and determination, which the male characters in the story initially find amusing, are presented as exceptional qualities in a young woman of Mattie's time and place. Prim, well-bred, and a bit naïve in the more rugged ways of the West, she is forced into action by a cruel act of fate, the unmotivated shooting of her father by a man of low character, Tom Chaney (Jeff Corey). She allies herself with Cogburn and a well-groomed Texas Ranger named La Boeuf (Glen Campbell), and against the protestations of the two men, rides out into dangerous country to bring Chaney to justice. La Boeuf and Cogburn have more mercenary reasons to apprehend the obscure killer—La Boeuf because Chaney is wanted in Texas and Cogburn because Chaney is riding with a gang led by the notorious Ned Pepper (Robert Duvall); but both men ultimately prove that self-interest is not the motivating force in their characters. In the climactic sequences, Mattie lies in a pit bitten by a rattlesnake and the mortally wounded La Boeuf dies in the process of helping to save her, while Cogburn heroically carries her to civilization in time for her to be treated.

Yet Mattie also has a morbid streak which is perverse in a character whose actions are so positive, and she is associated with images of death in several key scenes. Early in the film, for example, she somberly witnesses a hanging, while in another, which is extremely tender and touching, she holds her late father's watch to her cheek and cries. As the story progresses, her dual nature is revealed in other memorable moments. In one sequence, she demonstrates her spirit by riding her horse, Little Blackie, across a river in order not to be left behind by Cogburn and La Boeuf; on the other hand, there is the image of her in the snake pit, trapped and helpless with a grisly skeleton at her side.

Producer Hal Wallis is responsible not only for giving Hathaway a subject ideal for his talents, but also for providing him with collaborators whose participation makes the film perhaps the finest of the director's career. Lucien Ballard contributes cinematography of a kind very different from that found in his work on *The Wild Bunch* (1969). Where Sam Peckinpah calls for a harsh look, Hathaway calls for a romantic one, and Ballard imbues *True Grit* with glowing colors and clear, direct imagery. Warren Low, a close associate of Wallis over the years, is responsible for the graceful editing which assures that Hathaway's relaxed pacing will seem neither unduly lethargic nor falsely hurried. Dorothy Jeakins also deserves to be singled out for her imaginative, character-defining costumes, especially those for Mattie.

The cast includes a memorable gallery of villains, notably Robert Duvall as the amusing Lucky Ned Pepper, totally bewildered by Mattie, and Dennis Hopper as the hapless Moon, a victim of the first shoot-out midway through the film. Kim Darby's performance as Mattie, in spite of her much publicized conflicts with Hathaway, is a very special characterization, which she has not subsequently had the opportunity to equal. Her unusual looks and her ability to convey an endearing sweetness while at the same time projecting Mattie's repressions result in one of the great heroines of the genre.

As for Wayne, his theatricality in the earlier scenes, which accounts for the long-overdue recognition of his acting when the film was released, is balanced by the final scenes, in which he demonstrates what are truly his best qualities: restraint in conveying strength and subtlety in expressing emotion, qualities both notably evident when he has brought Mattie to the doctor and the camera moves to capture him standing quietly in a doorway. Whether he is being amusingly raucous or calmly gallant, Wayne unfailingly personifies the Westerner. Cogburn is a totally life-affirming individual. He may not be very genteel or ceremonious, but he is almost invariably warm and cheerful. The irony of this old man's pleasure in being alive contrasted to the girl's denial of her capacity for joy enriches the story considerably, and something remains in reserve about this aspect of the relationship which is not revealed until the very last sequence.

Hathaway's singular contribution is to bring to the film a certain magic which this kind of story needs if it is to capture the imagination. The director's enchantment with adventure is revealed in his flair for staging action; the quick shoot-out in the cabin, for example, involving Cogburn, Emmett Quincy (Jeremy Slate), and Moon is as impressive as the more famous one in which Cogburn rides across a clearing with the reins in his teeth shooting it out with the entire Pepper gang. The heroic journey which is the true climax of the film is thrilling. Throughout this part of the narrative, which finds Cogburn first wearing down Little Blackie, then carrying Mattie on foot when the horse dies, and finally commandeering a wagon, Hathaway expertly alternates close shots of the grim protagonists as they race across the plains with serene long shots which show Mattie and Cogburn to be vulnerable figures in an untamed land.

The beautiful locations used in the filming contribute to defining the characters and the meaning of the story. Most of the film takes place amidst the greens, russets, and yellows of nature at the peak of autumn. In the final sequence in which Cogburn visits Mattie in a graveyard, winter has come and the landscape is covered with snow. Mattie speaks of death, but Cogburn affectingly tries to persuade her to look forward to her life, movingly demonstrating that he continues to treasure his own. In this final exchange, there is a warm note as we perceive that what Mattie really wants to convey is her love for Cogburn. She will always feel close to him since they shared together what will remain the most vivid experience of her life, a great adventure now frozen in memory.

Blake Lucas

TWELVE ANGRY MEN

Released: 1957
Production: Henry Fonda and Reginald Rose for United Artists
Direction: Sidney Lumet
Screenplay: Reginald Rose; based on his teleplay of the same name
Cinematography: Boris Kaufman
Editing: Carl Lerner
Running time: 95 minutes

Principal characters:

Juror #1	Martin Balsam
Juror #2	John Fielder
Juror #3	Lee J. Cobb
Juror #4	E. G. Marshall
Juror #5	Jack Klugman
Juror #6	Edward Binns
Juror #7	Jack Warden
Juror #8	Henry Fonda
Juror #9	Joseph Sweeney
Juror #10	Ed Begley
Juror #11	George Voskovec
Juror #12	Robert Webber

The 1950's are often referred to as the "Golden Age" of television because of the abundance of live television drama during that period. Unfortunately, many of the programs of that decade are lost. However, one of the best, "Twelve Angry Men," which was initially broadcast as a Studio One presentation in 1954, was later remade as a film in 1957. The film version of this Reginald Rose teleplay was largely a result of the influence of Henry Fonda, who was its star as well as its coproducer (with Reginald Rose). Director Sidney Lumet, a man experienced in television, had never directed a feature film before. The remainder of the cast was made up of some of the best actors in television, including E. G. Marshall, Ed Begley, Lee J. Cobb, Jack Warden, and Martin Balsam.

The film centers on one of democracy's most sacred myths: the jury system. While not exactly an attack, the film questions the ultimate fairness and reliability of such a system. With the exception of a short introductory scene inside the courtroom and one closing scene outside the court building, the film centers entirely on what happens within the closed jury room. It is the process that these twelve jurors go through in determining the defendant's guilt or innocence which makes the film so engrossing.

The Constitution of the United States guarantees everyone a fair and speedy trial before one's peers. Screenwriter Reginald Rose, however, questions both the practicality and feasibility of such a jury through his script.

The defendant is an uneducated, teenaged Puerto Rican slum dweller. The "peers" who compose his jury are white, generally middle-aged, middle-class males. Nevertheless, these men have been chosen to decide whether he lives or dies. The script further suggests that these men, in addition to being socially, culturally, economically, and racially divergent, are, more importantly, indifferent.

Fortunately, there is one man (Henry Fonda) who instinctively feels the young man may be innocent. When the first vote is taken, he alone votes for acquittal. He does not do so because he is sure he is right but because he alone fears he may be wrong. The others, eager to help him reach the "right" decision, decide to review the case against the boy. Finally, Fonda agrees not to stand in the way if no other juror feels there is a possibility that the boy is innocent. However, if anyone wavers, then the others must agree to see it through to the end. Another vote is taken, and this time another juror votes for acquittal. Angered and frustrated, the jury begins the process of debating the case.

Initially, the case against the youth looks strong, but step by step Fonda introduces a question of doubt. Since the law states that this is all that is necessary to acquit a defendant, convincing the other members of the jury that there is such a question becomes the focus of the remainder of the film. Fonda must overcome the prejudice and personal hatred held by each of the members of the jury. Nevertheless, each piece of evidence is examined and questioned until slowly each member begins to accept the possibility of innocence. Finally, when evidence no longer supports a guilty verdict, a few members must face the reality that their personal prejudices have overtaken their reason. Eventually, the initial vote of guilty is reversed, leaving only one man in favor of that verdict. However, after a heartrending display of personal frustration, he, too, reverses his vote to make it unanimous for acquittal.

While the film ends on a positive note, the process leaves questions. What if there had been no Henry Fonda? How many juries have allowed deep-seated prejudices to interfere with their judgment? What chance of an unbiased decision has a defendant who is racially, socially, ethnically, religiously, or politically deviant? The film has retained its emotional impact over the years because it raises these questions.

Cinematically, the film effectively captures the claustrophobic atmosphere of the jury room. The characters complain incessantly about the humidity and stifling lack of air. The tension and irritation generated by the proceedings further help to create an uncomfortable environment. The room becomes a pressure cooker ready to burst from the pent-up energies inside.

The film is a powerful and emotional experience. As is often the case when a teleplay is transferred to film, the strengths remain with the writers and actors. Live television was a writer's medium. Because the plays were broadcast live, visuals were kept simple. Television was not afforded the luxury of making mistakes. Therefore, the thrust was on performance of the written word.

In the transition of *Twelve Angry Men* from television to film little was changed, and as a result, the film is often accused of appearing staged. However, considering the environment in which the story takes place, the film can be excused for not being visually diverse. The emotional outbursts which punctuate the story serve as reminders that decisions are not always made by the brain but often by the emotions. This is what makes the film ultimately so unsettling. It becomes clear how close these men came to committing a grave error, and we see that it is quite possible that they and others like them might err in the future. The experience has been one of consequence for these men. Some have been affected in such a way that it seems impossible for them ever to be the same. Nonetheless, one wonders if they really have learned from the experience. They have been persuaded for today, but what about tomorrow? One suspects that their experience might simply become a memory they choose to forget.

In many ways, the film is an indictment of the American thought process in the 1950's. The jurors in *Twelve Angry Men* are initially very confident in their decision to find the man guilty. However, after being forced to think and reconsider the evidence against the youth, it becomes apparent that they have not put as much thought into their decision as one might hope. Their confidence in the American system of justice has blinded them to the possibility that it may have inherent weaknesses which affect the ability of some citizens to receive a fair trial. Nevertheless, because one man has the courage of his convictions, justice prevails. Idealistic optimism suggests that as long as there are good men, the system will succeed. This may ultimately be the film's message.

James J. Desmarais

TWELVE O'CLOCK HIGH

Released: 1949
Production: Darryl F. Zanuck for Twentieth Century-Fox
Direction: Henry King
Screenplay: Sy Bartlett and Beirne Lay, Jr.; based on their novel of the same name
Cinematography: Leon Shamroy
Editing: Barbara McLean
Sound: Thomas T. Moulton (AA)
Running time: 132 minutes

Principal characters:

General Frank Savage	Gregory Peck
Major Harvey Stovall	Dean Jagger (AA)
Colonel Davenport	Gary Merrill
Lieutenant Colonel Ben Gately	Hugh Marlowe
Captain "Doc" Kaiser	Paul Stewart
General Pritchard	Millard Mitchell
Major Cobb	John Kellogg
Sergeant McIllhenny	Robert Arthur
Lieutenant Bishop	Robert Patten

Henry King made some notable silent films (*Tol'able David*, 1921; *Stella Dallas*, 1925) before becoming, in the early 1930's, a mainstay at Twentieth Century-Fox. There, he sporadically turned out amiable, usually sentimental projects such as *In Old Chicago* (1938) and *The Song of Bernadette* (1943) amidst an embarrassing amount of studio hack work. Nonetheless, *Twelve O'Clock High* reveals King's talent for a bleak, forceful account of men in combat. This film—its title is a term used by the Air Force during World War II to mean "bombers over target"—details the resignation of a disillusioned bomb group in the hands of Brigadier General Frank Savage (Gregory Peck), on the surface a strict disciplinarian with minimal regard for human shortcomings. His character owes much to the famous Major General Frank A. Armstrong, Jr., who in fact led the first daylight raids that the Flying Fortresses made on the Continent. In *Twelve O'Clock High* (and in *The Gunfighter* the next year, again with Gregory Peck as star), King evidences an impressive grasp of human motivations and of the price exacted by heroism. By keeping his people in a series of confrontations, he focuses on the various tensions and rivalries generated in combat situations.

The story is framed in a simple flashback. In 1949, a middle-aged American attorney, Harvey Stovall (Dean Jagger), buys an old Toby jug in a London antique shop and, his memories awakened, bicycles out to Archbury Field, where he wanders among the ruins of a large American air base. The flashback is to the fall of 1942, and he is, once again, Major Stovall, group adjutant for the weary, loss-ridden 918th Bomb Group. General Pritchard (Millard Mitchell) replaces Colonel Davenport (Gary Merrill) as commander of the group with General Savage, who begins enforcing impersonal, down-the-line discipline. At the first briefing he so antagonizes the pilots that shortly afterwards they all request transfers. Savage and Stovall conspire to delay these requests while Savage continues putting the group in top form, leading it on low-altitude daylight missions with negligible losses. When the Inspector General's office investigates the missing transfers, the pilots to a man withdraw their requests. Not long after the 918th begins bombing targets in Germany itself, Savage, like Davenport before him, gives way before the strain of his responsibilities; but he has finished his job.

Although *Twelve O'Clock High* centers on the fortunes of the 918th Bomb Group, it becomes the story of the man who rescues the group from further deterioration: General Savage. After the opening minutes of the film he appears in almost every scene, and his presence is strong even in those in which he does not appear. Practically all of the other characters are defined in relation to him. He remains at odds with his pilots until the end; they appear as a defeated, resentful lot, convinced that their problems are a matter of hard luck. Savage understands, therefore, that he must restore morale while building up leadership in the group, at whatever cost. One of his first casualties is Lieutenant Colonel Ben Gately (Hugh Marlowe).

As a punishment for his unauthorized absence from his command, Savage publicly humiliates Gately by demoting him from air executive and renaming his plane "The Leper Colony." All of the incompetents and misfits go to Gately—any navigator who "can't find his way to the men's room," any bombardier who "can't hit his plate with a fork." The other pilots immediately rebel against the bloodless way in which Savage harangues them, first about their own self-pity and then about the necessity for redoubled efforts, no matter how much they have done in the past. The best way to survive, he tells them, will be to "consider yourselves already dead." They elect for their representative their most visible member, Lieutenant Bishop (Robert Patten), a man recently nominated for the Congressional Medal of Honor; but, his well-documented bravery aside, Bishop can muster only such vague, noncommittal responses to Savage's probings as "I just know I want out." Although the attitude of the pilots obviously distresses Savage, he remains the iron man, never giving them a glimpse of his sensitivity.

Some in Savage's command do support him. The man closest to Savage is Harvey Stovall, a veteran of World War I and an attorney who now takes the general as his "client." He has the experience and perceptiveness to grasp immediately what Savage wants to do, recognizing beneath the martinet a conscientious, humane leader with an overly developed notion of responsibility. He aptly defends his part in the illegal delay of the pilots' applications for transfers by reminding Savage that he has never heard of a jury convicting the lawyer. "Doc" Kaiser (Paul Stewart), the flight surgeon, disapproves somewhat of Savage's first encounter with the pilots, calling it insensitive to the strong personal bond that they had with Davenport. But he backs Savage while trying to make him appreciate the terrific strain of "maximum effort" on the men as well as on himself. Major Cobb (John Kellogg), who replaces Gately as air executive, shows deep respect for Savage, and, like Stovall and Doc Kaiser, sees beyond Savage's brusqueness.

All the while Savage bullies his men, disciplining minor infractions and putting the crews back through training procedures. They slowly begin to be proud of the group's accomplishments. Then Savage enjoys a major victory over the Germans and over the hostility of his men as well. On one mission that he leads, the 918th is the only group not to turn back as ordered because of bad weather. It reaches the target and destroys it. General Pritchard, officially but half-heartedly, reprimands Savage for insubordination while the office staff listens on the other side of the door. Not long after the pilots withdraw their requests for transfers, the group's *esprit de corps* is greatly heightened when the order comes down to bomb Wilhelmshaven, the first target on German soil.

For that mission many of the group personnel stow away on various planes, among them Harvey, Doc Kaiser, Savage's orderly, the sometime Sergeant McIllhenny (Robert Arthur), and even the chaplain. This incident furnishes the best comedy in the film. When Savage discovers that McIllhenny had flown as a gunner on his plane, he promptly demotes McIllhenny to private (again). But Cobb tells him that McIllhenny has been credited with two German planes destroyed and one probable; furthermore, demoting McIllhenny means that he must do the same to Stovall, the flight surgeon, and a chaplain, among others. Savage accepts that in this case, any attempt to enforce discipline would be pointless. Lest anarchy thrive, however, he berates Stovall and the chaplain like a father who has caught his two small boys with a package of cigarettes. He impresses upon the sheepish chaplain that his combat days are over, that his business is sin, and that in the future he will restrict his activities to that theater of operation. Stovall proudly owns that although his glasses were fogged, he thinks he got "a piece of one," to which Savage counters with the inevitable question, "Theirs or ours?"

As Savage, Gregory Peck is in his best form. He credibly shows a man warring not only against the enemy and many of his subordinates, but against his own limitations. In time he goes the way of his predecessor, identifying himself too closely with his men and flying too many missions himself. He lets the men become more and more dependent on him. Stovall observes to Cobb that the only difference between Savage and Davenport is, as he indicates three or four inches with his fingers, that Savage stands just that much taller than Davenport. General Pritchard also sees the danger signals in Savage's behavior but reluctantly grants him more time as group commander. Presumably Savage's breakdown at the end spares him the embarrassment of having another replace him, as he had done Davenport. Merrill plays Davenport with just the right contrast to the rigid Savage, remaining close to this old friend who has taken his job. A fine man although a poor leader, Davenport has given his all. He has overextended his sense of responsibility, as evidenced in the beginning when he tries to take the blame for an error made by his navigator that contributes to the loss of five planes and fifty men. The film's finest performance is by Jagger as the wry, methodical, and fiercely loyal Harvey Stovall; the role earned him the Academy Award for Best Supporting Actor. It is through Stovall's nostalgic perspective that the story unfolds. Stovall is an anomaly: he works smoothly within the military hierarchy while managing to remain always without, a true old soldier, but finally a civilian lawyer who simply has a different kind of case now that he has returned to uniform.

Twelve O'Clock High gives a restrained, joyless view of war, strengthened through actual combat sequences shot by both American and German cameramen. It avoids such prevalent clichés in war films as studied, glamorized heroics, elaborately drawn battle scenes, and the girl left back home or somehow acquired along the way (one woman appears briefly in the film, a nurse who exchanges a few words with Savage and with Gately at the hospital, even though at that time field hospitals had no women nurses). King presents heroism quietly, never attractively, within the context of overcast skies and steamy interiors, where it translates into feats of debilitating, nerve-shattering endurance. Lieutenant Bishop, in line for his country's highest citation, is a confused, bitter young man. Gately continues to fly with a fractured vertebra until he passes out from the pain after returning from a later mission. Savage succeeds where Davenport cannot; after Savage collapses, Davenport comments that he saw something in the kids' faces at briefing that morning he had never put there himself. Nonetheless, Savage has had to endure the humiliation of not being able to climb into his plane, the feeling of shame and defeat that comes with being led away from the field.

The thesis of the film is that exacting discipline, carried out for a common cause, taps the best to be found in men. The once discredited Gately takes over the lead when Savage collapses, then returns with nineteen of the twenty-one planes sent out. Savage himself becomes a model of unselfish heroism. Yet *Twelve O'Clock High* departs from most of the other films about World War II done at this time, such as Walsh's *Fighter Squadron* (1948) or Dwan's *Sands of Iwo Jima* (1949), in which war emerges a deadly and still adventuresome business. If *Twelve O'Clock High* never disclaims the rationale of war, or, for that matter, never transcends a basic sentimentality, it modestly asserts the staggering cost of bravery and courage to the human psyche. Savage's tough-minded yet scrupulous campaign against the decay of his group's morale finally strips him of his own physical and spiritual reserves. His actions, like those of many of his men, leave scars that most likely will be permanent. At the end, when Savage is returned to his quarters, speechless and barely mobile, Doc Kaiser explains his condition to Davenport and to Stovall by saying simply, "I think it's called 'maximum effort.'"

William H. Brown, Jr.

TWENTIETH CENTURY

Released: 1934
Production: Howard Hawks for Columbia
Direction: Howard Hawks
Screenplay: Ben Hecht and Charles MacArthur; based on their play of the same name, adapted from the play *Napoleon on Broadway* by Charles Bruce Milholland
Cinematography: Joseph H. August
Editing: Gene Havlick
Running time: 91 minutes

Principal characters:

Oscar Jaffe	John Barrymore
Lily Garland	Carole Lombard
Oliver Webb	Walter Connolly
Owen O'Malley	Roscoe Karns
Max Jacobs	Charles Levison
Clark	Etienne Girardot
Sadie	Dale Fuller
George Smith	Ralph Forbes
Mr. McGonigle	Edgar Kennedy

According to her second cousin, Howard Hawks, Carole Lombard was blessed from childhood with a vibrant, energetic personality; but this lively spirit had been largely absent in her motion pictures prior to 1934. As Hawks bluntly stated, she was a "lousy, phoney" actress, but one nevertheless with a potential for greatness that lay dormant within her, a greatness that he was determined to uncover. Hawks prevailed upon Columbia's obstinate president, Harry Cohn, to secure Lombard's services, and before long, the twenty-five-year-old starlet was contracted to appear opposite the brilliant John Barrymore in Ben Hecht's and Charles MacArthur's adaptation of the Broadway hit, "Twentieth Century," to be directed by Hawks himself.

As the first day of filming progressed, everyone on the set could plainly see that the young actress was in deep trouble. Her performance was miserable, and Barrymore was so appalled at the prospect of playing opposite such a poor performer that he began to make rude faces behind her back. During a short break, Hawks took his struggling relative aside. After reassuring her that she was indeed working very hard, Hawks asked, "How much do you get paid for this picture?" Lombard answered that her salary for *Twentieth Century* was $5,000. Hawks then said, "That's pretty good. What do you get paid for?" "Why, acting, of course," came the confused reply. "Okay," Hawks continued, "supposing I tell you that you've earned all the money. You don't owe anything." The director then asked, "What would you do if a man said 'so and so' to you." The plain-spoken Lombard told Hawks that if any man dared to call her those horrible names, she would kick him in the groin. "Well," said Hawks, "Barrymore said that to you. Why didn't you kick him?" He then told her that if she failed to kick her costar in the pants during the next scene, he would fire her from the picture and hire another actress.

Filming resumed with Barrymore unaware of the nature of Hawks's conversation with Lombard, and Hawks playfully decided to keep him in the dark a while longer. The director placed three cameras on the set to be assured of catching every bit of what was about to unfold and called for action. When Barrymore started in on Lombard, she let out a vicious kick, catching the startled actor completely off guard. However, consummate performer that he was, Barrymore continued his dialogue without missing a beat, punctuating it by jabbing his fingers at Lombard, and dancing around the set like a boxer. She in turn, kept up the pace, lashing out with both feet while Barrymore jumped to and fro. The scene finally concluded with Barrymore's exit; he returned to the set in amazement. "She's magnificent," he told Hawks. "Were you fooling me all this time?" Then, both men looked towards Carole Lombard, who was emotionally drained and sobbing in a corner of the set, and each realized that he had been privileged to witness the birth of a star.

The plot line of *Twentieth Century* has its parallels to the true tale recounted above. It also involves the process of molding a beautiful, innocent, untrained, and unpolished actress into a star, its Pygmalion/Galatea overtones overshadowed only by the more sinister ones of a Svengali/Trilby relationship. The film is a frenetic, farcical romp that has been a pleasure to behold for over forty years. Barrymore plays Oscar Jaffe, a near-legendary theatrical figure who seems to run everything, although his exact occupation is left unclear. A combination of producer, author, director, and talent coordinator, Jaffe is an imperious, egotistical tyrant who commands his underlings as a feudal lord would his serfs. His capriciousness baffles everyone. Actors, press agents, managers, and secretaries all follow his every whim.

Jaffe decides, seemingly on the spur of the moment, that a novice actress named Mildred Plotka will, after being renamed Lily Garland (Carole Lombard), become his next star, his biggest discovery. Against all advice he sets out to mold the frightened new "Lily" into a thespian. In one of the film's most memorable sequences, Jaffe shows Lily exactly how to move on the stage, indicating every few paces where and how a line is to be delivered, drawing a maze of chalklines on the floor to help her remember, and finally poking her with a pin to get the proper scream at the proper time.

Jaffe's plot succeeds and Lily is an opening-night sensation—an instant star. The scene then quickly shifts ahead three years. We see that Lily has reached the top of the theatrical world, and has become, in the bargain, her mentor's mistress. Jaffe endeavors to control every aspect of her life, from her stage career to her day-to-day activities. Lily has endured this domination for three long and frustrating years, but finally she can stand it no longer. Her breaking point is reached when she discovers that Jaffe has tapped her telephone and has hired a detective to follow her every move. Furious, she packs her bags and leaves Jaffe once and for all.

She heads West to Hollywood. Once there she singly conquers the movie world. Before long her photograph graces the cover of every fan magazine; her name appears in lights on every movie-house marquee. During this time, however, Jaffe has fallen upon hard times. Unable to produce a decent play without his longtime star, the one-time theatrical wizard watches in stunned horror as flop after flop closes on opening night. After his last-ditch comeback attempt, "The Bride of Bagdad," fails also, he appears at the end of his financial and emotional rope. Thoroughly disheartened, he takes a train to New York only to discover that Lily is also onboard. The final results of the film now involve Jaffe's frantic attempts to win his former star and lover back onto his stage and into his arms. He miraculously accomplishes both goals as the picture ends, although he has to fake a heart attack to do so.

A Svengali/Trilby motif runs throughout *Twentieth Century*, serving as the film's underlying theme. Jaffe constantly makes reference to the "gold" and the "diamond" inside Lily which are just waiting to be mined by some Svengali. Lily is, in turn, quite aware of the unnatural nature of their relationship. At one point, she screams out, "I'm no Trilby," while behind her Jaffe enters the room in the manner of Svengali, a malevolent presence in his dark hat and unfurled cape. Jaffe creates Garland's career and her public image, but is ultimately unable to control what he has wrought. While a reconciliation is finally achieved, one gets the impression that Lily will no longer be as pliable as before. She has matured enough to realize that she can make it on her own, and he, at last, has become aware of her true strength and character.

Twentieth Century is loaded with satirical barbs aimed at the theater and its denizens. This is not surprising since screenwriters Hecht and MacArthur were among the elite of New York's theatrical society. They enlarged the scope of the film to include long scenes of rehearsals and backstage life, in contrast to the stage production in which the action was confined entirely to the transcontinental train from which the play and the film take their name. The film's characters are largely stereotyped caricatures of theatrical people. Jaffe is the archetype of the pompous, arrogant producer whose artistic vehicles are merely corny melodramas with titles such as "The Heart of Kentucky" and "Desert Love." Walter Connolly plays the much-suffering manager with a bad heart, and Roscoe Karns plays the perpetually inebriated press hack. Lily herself typifies the frightened waif-turned-obstinate prima donna, her intransigence matched only by that of her mentor.

The movies *per se* are also subject to frequent jibes. When Jaffe learns that

Lily has left him and the theater for Hollywood, he moans, "Oh, Lily. How could you do it?," meaning, on the one hand, how could she ever leave him, and on the other, how could she stoop so low as to appear in movies. The filmmakers—Hawks, Hecht, MacArthur, and Barrymore—are all poking fun at themselves and their profession when they employ these little jokes, demonstrating that while they may be getting rich by making films, and while they always try to do the best job they can, they do not take their lofty positions very seriously.

Hawks's direction of *Twentieth Century* is characteristically unobtrusive. Camera movement is minimal, with long takes serving as the dominant visual strategy. He prefers to let his players create the kinesthetics as they roam about the small sets, constantly in motion, their lines delivered at a rapid-fire pace that has become the hallmark of Hawks's comedy. Hawks steps aside to allow the performers to stand out, and as always, he draws exceptional performances from his ensemble. Lombard's emergence as a brilliant comedienne was a surprise to everyone except her director, who, like Oscar Jaffe, knew that she had vast reserves of talent buried within her, abilities that required a firm guiding hand to bring them to the fore.

Barrymore relished his role as Jaffe since it gave him the opportunity, as Hawks told him, to play "the world's second greatest ham," Barrymore himself being the world's foremost, and he played the part with great enthusiasm, allowing his comedic range to flow naturally. He is a whirlwind of energy all through the film, and even during slow moments his imagination and verve propel the film forward. His hilarious facial contortions, double and triple takes, and pompous gesturings are a marvel to watch, a perfect combination of uncontrolled slapstick and split-second timing.

The supporting players, in particular Connolly, Karns, Etienne Girardot, and Edgar Kennedy, all have their excellent moments. Seeing them in action, one cannot help mourning the passing of the days of the great character players. These secondary actors and actresses graced and enlivened countless films of the 1930's and 1940's, and too often were the only high points of a bad picture.

Finally, due credit must be given to Howard Hawks, who chose his cast with impeccable taste and care and directed the film with unassuming style and grace. Last but by no means least, he acted as Lombard's Svengali: a benign one to be sure, but nevertheless a master manipulator who played a large role in the creation of one of America's most loved comediennes and enduring personalities.

Daniel Einstein

20,000 LEAGUES UNDER THE SEA

Released: 1954
Production: Walt Disney for Walt Disney Productions; released by Buena Vista
Direction: Richard Fleischer
Screenplay: Earl Felton; based on the novel of the same name by Jules Verne
Cinematography: Franz Planer and Till Gabbani
Editing: Elmo Williams
Art direction: John Meehan (AA)
Set decoration: Emile Kuri (AA)
Special effects: John Henchy and Josh Meador (AA)
Running time: 126 minutes

Principal characters:

Ned Land	Kirk Douglas
Captain Nemo	James Mason
Professor Aronnax	Paul Lukas
Conseil	Peter Lorre

The fantastic tales of Jules Verne have been brought to the screen countless times and by many filmmakers, but it is Walt Disney who gave cinema its most memorable and best-executed production based on Verne's work. *20,000 Leagues Under the Sea* has all the right ingredients. Characterizations, though held to only a handful, are nonetheless rich. The brilliant-but-mad Captain Nemo, who refuses to share his intelligence and scientific advances with the world, epitomizes cinema's classic archvillain. Handsome Ned Land, Nemo's adversary and prisoner, stands for all that is right with society—so much so that he even risks his own life to save Nemo. Superlative special effects, the key to any convincing science fiction or fantasy effort, are in abundance here, and range from the fantastic submarine *Nautilus* to the monstrous giant squid. There is even thrown in for good measure and to enchant the youngest viewers a charmer of a seal, who does a "duet" with the musical Land.

In terms of box-office and critical acclaim, *20,000 Leagues Under the Sea* is one of the most successful films to come from the Disney creators, and in many ways it marks a departure from the standard Disney product. For the first time in its history, the studio brought in big names—names not generally associated with a Disney production—for the starring roles. Kirk Douglas, James Mason, Paul Lukas, and Peter Lorre all contributed to making the film a special piece, as did an especially superb production crew. When *20,000 Leagues Under the Sea* first went into production, the Disney studio's emphasis was on animation. Because Disney did not have a live-action crew, he solicited the work of some of Hollywood's most skillful artists, including art director

John Meehan, an Oscar winner for *The Heiress* (1949) and *Sunset Boulevard* (1950), who went on to take an additional Oscar for his work in this Disney film. Among the highlights of his work was the lush main lounge of the *Nautilus*, complete with pipe organ and fountain as the crowning glory to the detailed Victorian decor.

Directed by Richard Fleischer, *20,000 Leagues Under the Sea* is set in the year 1868. Harpooner Ned Land (Kirk Douglas), Professor Arronax (Paul Lukas), whose specialty is sea creatures, and his assistant, Conseil (Peter Lorre), are aboard the armed frigate *Abraham Lincoln* in the Pacific. The ship is investigating reports of a gigantic sea monster which reportedly attacks ships, when the *Lincoln* itself suffers an attack and sinks. Land, the Professor, and Conseil are rescued by what appears to be a monster but is, in actuality, a submarine. The film's submarine design carefully follows Verne's descriptions, and Disney had his artists build the ship to scale—some two hundred feet long. Its exterior is covered with "scales" and it possesses headlight-type "eyes."

Captain Nemo (James Mason), who commands the submarine *Nautilus*, is an embittered man; artistic and brilliant, he is also sadly deranged. He tells his three waterlogged prisoners that he is not what is called a civilized man; that he has forsaken society entirely for reasons that seem to him good. Nemo and his men cruise the waters in the atom-powered submarine, attempting to purge the seas of all warships. The current destination of the *Nautilus* is the island Vulcania, where Nemo's headquarters are located.

Although contemptuous of mankind, Nemo is also a lonely man who seems to delight in showing his "guests" the wonders of his underwater world. Among his innovations are seaweed cigars and octopus fillets. Excited over Nemo's discoveries, the Professor actually relishes being onboard the vessel, and is hopeful that he can convince Nemo to use his advanced discoveries to help mankind. Harpooner Land, however, sees little glory in Nemo's world. He wants only to escape, and enlists the support of Conseil to that end. Resentful that he is being kept aboard the *Nautilus* against his will, Land nevertheless comes to the aid of the nefarious Nemo, who later is caught in the grips of a monstrous squid.

The squid attack is one of the film's most eventful scenes, and also its most famous sequence. A cannon shell from another ship has damaged the *Nautilus*, which submerges for safety, but in the process the ship is attacked by a giant squid. Nemo, caught in the clutches of the monster, is rescued only after Land manages to harpoon it. It took twenty-eight technicians to operate the film's giant squid. The mechanical creation—which had forty-foot tentacles—initially caused problems, so the sequence with it was shot a second time in order to please Fleischer and, of course, Disney.

Once Land saves his life, Nemo's attitude towards the three men softens. At last, because of the Professor's encouragement, he agrees to share his secrets of atomic energy and other marvels with society. However, an earlier move by Land results in destruction for Nemo and the *Nautilus*, for when Land was determined to escape, he had tucked messages into a batch of bottles, which he had released into the sea. Upon arriving at the island of Vulcania, therefore, the *Nautilus* is surrounded by warships-in-waiting. In anger, Nemo decides that he will no longer share his discoveries. After planting a bomb on the submarine, Nemo, who has been shot by the warships, takes the vessel down for a final voyage. Ned Land, the Professor, and Conseil are able to escape just before the bomb explodes.

With special effects in the true starring role, *20,000 Leagues Under the Sea* required a budget of five million dollars. Filmed in ultra widescreen CinemaScope, at the time a new process, the film took Oscars for Best Art Direction (Color) and Special Effects. In the Special Effects category for the year, the Disney film beat out *Them!*, the classic science fiction film about giant ant mutants.

Peformances are good, with Kirk Douglas as an amiable Ned Land who even sings the jaunty "Whale of a Tale." It is James Mason, however, as the deranged Nemo, who dominates, and his is a compelling figure encompassing both nobility and tragedy. Several years following *20,000 Leagues Under the Sea*, Mason went on to star in *Journey to the Center of the Earth* (1959), another film based on a Jules Verne tale.

Until *20,000 Leagues Under the Sea*, the Disney studio had concentrated on lavish animation efforts. Live-action features were inexpensive and mostly period productions, such as *Treasure Island* (1950), *Rob Roy: The Highland Rogue* (1953), and *The Sword and the Rose* (1952). The success of the Disney-Verne film would ultimately encourage the studio to tackle other ambitious live-action projects, most notably *Swiss Family Robinson* (1960) and *The Black Hole* (1979). Director Richard Fleischer would also move on to other films within the science fiction-fantasy genre, including *The Fantastic Voyage* (1966), as well as garnering acclaim for his direction of crime drama pieces, such as *The Boston Strangler* (1968). It should be noted that Fleischer is the son of Max Fleischer, a filmmaker who got his start in short subjects and was, at one time, considered to be a Disney rival when he created cartoon characters Betty Boop and Popeye in the 1930's.

Pat H. Broeske

2001: A SPACE ODYSSEY

Released: 1968
Production: Stanley Kubrick for Metro-Goldwyn-Mayer
Direction: Stanley Kubrick
Screenplay: Stanley Kubrick and Arthur C. Clarke; based on the short story "The Sentinel of Eternity" by Arthur C. Clarke
Cinematography: Geoffrey Unsworth
Editing: Ray Lovejoy
Special effects: Stanley Kubrick and special effects team (AA)
Music: Richard Strauss, Johann Strauss, Aram Ilich Khachaturyan, and György Ligeti
Running time: 141 minutes

Principal characters:

David Bowman	Keir Dullea
Frank Poole	Gary Lockwood
Dr. Heywood Floyd	William Sylvester
Moonwatcher	Daniel Richter
HAL 9000	Douglas Rain

Stanley Kubrick is known as one of the most creatively independent writer-producer-directors in the film industry. His works from *The Killing* (1956) on have produced both lavish praise and extensive controversy. Although he has not made many films—less than a dozen in his twenty-five year career—those which he has made have been either critically or commercially successful, and usually both. Such diverse films as *Lolita* (1962), *Dr. Strangelove* (1964), *Barry Lyndon* (1975), and *A Clockwork Orange* (1971) are illustrative of his diversity and creative genius.

Of all of the films with which Kubrick has been associated, however, none has been as commercially successful as *2001: A Space Odyssey*, which *Variety* magazine lists among its top fifty moneymaking films of all time. Additionally, the film has received great attention from the critics since its initial release and continues to provoke interest and controversy. It is a very unusual film. Adapted from a short story by science fiction author Arthur C. Clarke, who coauthored the screenplay with Kubrick, it was also one of the first films to generate a novel from its screenplay which was also highly successful.

The film opens in the prehistoric past as the audience sees a relatively peaceful group of apes managing to scrape together a meager life from the semidesert environment they share with other apes and assorted animals. One morning the colony awakens to find a large, black, rectangular monolith in their midst. After inspecting and eventually touching the monolith, the leader of the apes (named Moonwatcher in Clarke's novel based on the film), develops the capacity to use bones and sticks as tools and weapons. A brilliant cut follows the ape sequence which associates a flying chip of bone with a spacecraft in the year 2001. The spacecraft is carrying Dr. Heywood Floyd (William Sylvester) on a secret mission to the moon from earth, via an orbiting space station. It seems that a monolith has been discovered buried beneath the surface of the moon at Clavius crater. After Floyd's arrival on the moon, while he and other scientists are having their photographs taken, tourist-style, in front of the monolith, it is struck by sunlight for the first time. This triggers the transmission of a highly powerful radio signal toward the planet Jupiter.

The United States then decides to send a nine-month, one-half-billion-mile expedition to Jupiter to find out what is causing this unexplainable transmission. The voyagers on this mission are astronauts David Bowman (Keir Dullea), Frank Poole (Gary Lockwood), three comrades kept in cold-storage hibernation until they are needed at the end of the mission, and a HAL 9000 computer. HAL (voice of Douglas Rain), as the computer is known, is programmed to operate as a sixth member of the crew and can talk and listen just like a human being. In fact, HAL is in many ways the most human of the characters in the film. The problem is that only HAL knows the real reason for the trip, but he has been programmed to withhold the information from Bowman and Poole until the spacecraft is almost to Jupiter. Partway through the mission, HAL detects an impending failure of a component on the ship. After comparing the same data, a twin HAL on earth indicates that there is no problem with the unit and that HAL on the spaceship *Discovery* is in error. While Poole is outside the ship, HAL murders him by ordering a small space pod to cut his lifeline. Bowman immediately rushes out in another pod to try the impossible task of rescuing Poole. While he is gone, HAL cuts off the life support systems of the three hibernating members of the crew. When Bowman returns to the Discovery, HAL refuses to let him back onboard. Bowman uses the explosive bolts on his pod to force his way back onto the *Discovery* through an escape hatch. He then proceeds to the machine room and disconnects HAL's higher logic functions, reducing the computer to a mechanical shipkeeper.

The disconnecting of the computer automatically triggers the playback of a tape which tells Bowman the true purpose of the mission. After completing the flight to Jupiter alone, Bowman sees another monolith among the moons of Jupiter. Setting off in one of the spacepods to investigate, he is immediately drawn into a vortex of strange sensations. After what seems like an eternity, the pod finally lands. Bowman finds himself in a light-green Louis XIV-style suite lit by an eerie glow. The rapidly aging astronaut leaves the capsule for the last time. Then, after several jumps in the aging process, Bowman is seen as a withered old man lying in bed. A fourth monolith is seen at the foot of the bed, and as Bowman slowly raises his arm toward it he is enveloped in a strange glow. He is then seen transformed, or perhaps evolved, into a wide-eyed star-child floating above the earth. The evolution from ape to angel is now complete.

Although it attracted large crowds from the beginning, many of the first reviews of *2001: A Space Odyssey*, were negative. The critics complained about the lack of plot and the weak characterizations, emphasizing that the most sympathetic character in the film is the computer. *2001: A Space Odyssey* was not intended to be a traditional drama, however, but rather a work of visual communication. There are only forty minutes of dialogue in the film, and the first words are spoken almost thirty minutes into the picture. Kubrick wanted to have the nonverbal elements of the film tell the story. *2001: A Space Odyssey* is one of the few motion pictures in history to rely so heavily on the nonverbal aspects of the film art, and the only one to be so commercially successful.

The background music is an important part of the film, as music is in many of Kubrick's efforts. The use of Johann Strauss's "On the Beautiful Blue Danube" accompanying the initial space scenes provides a feeling that would be difficult to achieve by other means. The distorted voices of Ligeti's "Atmospheres" gives the viewer an added feeling of unreality when the space pod lands in the strange suite after the ride through the star gate. Perhaps even more dramatically significant is the use of Richard Strauss's "Thus Spake Zarathustra," which became the virtual theme music of the film, and since the film's release, this composition has become exclusively associated with it in the minds of many filmgoers.

Another example of Kubrick's emphasis on the nonverbal aspects of the picture is the almost documentary quality of the special effects. The Oscar-winning team of Wally Veevers, Douglas Trumbull, Don Pederson, and Tom Howard provided the film with its magnificent technical achievements, but it was Stanley Kubrick's insistence on accuracy which paved the way for their work. Kubrick consulted with some of the most qualified scientists in the space field in an attempt to make both spacecraft and space "locations" as accurate as possible.

Possibly the most important aspect of the film, however, and one which caused some of the initial displeasure on the part of the critics, is that Kubrick refused to provide pat answers to the many questions raised in the film. One could argue that he intended the film to be an essay on intelligence. It raises questions which the viewer must answer, for the filmmaker does not. It portrays the trend of men to become more like machines, while machines become more like men. The fact that HAL is in many ways the most sympathetic character in the film is by no means accidental.

The ability of Kubrick to produce a film which raised such questions, while providing an enjoyable entertainment for such a wide audience makes *2001: A Space Odyssey* one of the most outstanding pictures of all time, and it is regularly cited as such by critics all over the world.

Steven D. Robertson

THE UNINVITED

Released: 1944
Production: Charles Brackett for Paramount
Direction: Lewis Allen
Screenplay: Dodie Smith and Jack Partos; based on the novel *Uneasy Freehold* by Dorothy Macardle
Cinematography: Charles Lang
Editing: Doane Harrison
Running time: 98 minutes

Principal characters:
Mary Meredith .... Betty Farrington (voice)
Stella Meredith .... Gail Russell
Roderick Fitzgerald .... Ray Milland
Pamela Fitzgerald .... Ruth Hussey
Commander Beech .... Donald Crisp
Miss Holloway .... Cornelia Otis Skinner

The Uninvited is a ghost story with Freudian overtones which lingers in the mind long after one has seen it. While by no means a perfect film, it has a resonance to it which makes the story more than just one of the coming of age of a young girl and the defeat of the dark forces which seek to deprive her of her emotional heritage. The real story takes place seventeen years before the events we see on the screen, but the essential facts are kept from the audience until the last ten minutes of the film. This story involves the search for the true identity of the heroine, Stella Meredith (Gail Russell), a sheltered young girl whose grandfather has made her past a barrier to her full emotional development. The phantoms, real or imaginary, which haunt her life are exorcised only after his death; the loving relationships which his tutelage denied her are then restored to her.

The action of the film begins as Pam (Ruth Hussey) and Roderick Fitzgerald (Ray Milland), a sister and brother on vacation from London, stumble upon Windward House, an abandoned mansion which broods high on the edge of a cliff overlooking the Cornish coastline. They are enchanted by the place and decide to buy it, not knowing that twenty years before it was the home of the Meredith family.

While all the facts about the tragic emotional history of the Merediths are not revealed in the denouement, the basic outline of their story is clear. The bride, Mary Meredith, is a lesbian who agrees to marriage only out of respect for her father's sense of propriety. Her sexual choices seem to stem from her hatred of life, and she delights in torturing her husband, a gentleman artist, by denying him a chance at fatherhood. Her husband therefore seeks solace in the arms of his Spanish model, Carmel Casada. When Carmel becomes pregnant, the Merediths take her to Paris for the birth of her daugher, Stella; they then buy Stella from Carmel and return to Windward to rear her as their own child.

A Miss Holloway (Cornelia Otis Skinner) is hired as the child's nurse, but she also becomes Mary's lover. Thus a household is established in which all normal relationships have been perverted; neither the husband, wife, nurse, nor child are what they seem to be, and yet appearances are maintained. The stability of this group is threatened three years later by Carmel's return. Mary is driven to a murderous rage by Carmel's request to have her daughter back. She attempts to hurl Stella off the Cliff, but Carmel's attempt to stop her results in Mary herself dying by a fall to the rocks. Carmel contracts pneumonia from being out in the rain that night, and thanks to Nurse Holloway's leaving the window open in the sickroom at night, Stella's real mother dies two weeks after her false one.

Stella's father leaves England never to return, and the three-year-old girl is turned over to her maternal grandfather, Commander Beech (Donald Crisp). He attempts to turn her into a carbon copy of his daughter. In his eyes, this means to be respectable, God-fearing, and conformist, repressing most natural emotions. He does not know, however, that not a trace of the blood of his family flows in Stella's veins. The rebellious gypsy blood of her mother makes her revolt against his attempt to keep her away from Windward House, and to repress the memory of the few caresses her real mother was allowed to give her, the kisses which live in her subconscious as the only real love she has ever known.

Stella therefore tries to talk her grandfather out of selling the old house to the Fitzgeralds, but the old man is only too happy to part with the property, since it has proved impossible to rent. Former tenants have complained of being annoyed by the sound of a woman sobbing in the night, a sound which seems to come from everywhere and yet nowhere in the house. On the day the Fitzgeralds move in, they see Stella standing on the cliff's edge, staring at the house with the wistfulness of an exiled princess. Their arrival allows her to return to her kingdom, and her repressed sexuality finds an outlet in Rick, who is fascinated by this mysterious girl who seems to come from another age, who tells him that she has never known a person who laughs as much as he does.

Yet Rick Fitzgerald is not exactly a carefree person. A London music critic by profession, he allowed himself to be talked into buying Windward by his sister's argument that the house would be a perfect place for him to pursue his own career as a composer. While there is no hint in the film of any sexual dimension between the brother and sister, they form yet another of the sterile relationships which seem to be attracted to the house.

Rick turns the artist's studio where Stella's father worked into his office. He could not have made a worse choice, for the room is dominated by Mary's spirit. The air is noticeably chilly, and fresh flowers brought into it wilt within minutes. Rick himself feels a flattening of his self-confidence and creativity as soon as he enters the room. He manages to overcome this, however, and composes a piano piece which he calls "Stella by Starlight," but the night he plays it for Stella, she passes out right beside the piano, and then makes an unconscious attempt to jump off the cliff.

The coldness in the studio is but the physical manifestation of the emotional frigidity which is the central concern of the film. As Rick describes it at the beginning of the picture, this coldness is "the draining of warmth from the vital centers of the living." It is created by a lack of something, and cannot be creative or productive. It represents the loveless life which Commander Beech has tried to impose on Stella. It is opposed by the scent of Mimosa which occasionally drifts through the downstairs rooms of Windward. This was the perfume favored by Carmel, and it represents love, life, and the possibility of fruitful relationships between people.

Cornelia Otis Skinner's masterful interpretation of the pivotal role of Miss Holloway is the audience's first clue to the fact that there was something more radically wrong with the Meredith household than the fact that its mistress died in a fall from the cliff. At the time the action of the film occurs, she is operating the Mary Meredith Retreat, a sinister rest home where the motto inscribed over the entrance is "Health through harmony." Dressed in robes reminiscent more of a high priestess than a doctor, she receives visitors in an office dominated by the portrait of her dead lover, of whom she speaks in reverent tones. It is no accident that Miss Bird, one of the crazed "guests" at the Home (beautifully portrayed in a cameo appearance by Dorothy Stickney), brings her rocks instead of flowers that she gathers in the garden. At least they will not wilt in her presence the way that the flowers which Pam earlier took into the studio at Windward did. Holloway intervenes when Commander Beech tells her that Stella is again visiting Windward, not out of any concern for the girl, but because she is afraid that the truth about Mary will come out, besmirching the saintly reputation she so jealously guards, much in the manner of Mrs. Danvers in Du Maurier's *Rebecca*.

Gail Russell luminously portrays Stella as a frightened yet heroic figure. She was only eighteen when she made this, her third film, but her strong performance is no small part of the effectiveness of the picture. Stella seems to look at the world from beyond the tomb, her limpid eyes seeming to conceal the mysteries of life and death. The strange happiness which steals over her in the house along with the mimosa scent awakens her intuitive recognition that "somebody loves me with all her heart." She refuses Rick's offer to move to London with him, confident that the love Windward holds for her will triumph over its evil forces. Her faith is rewarded at the seance which Pam arranges to be held at Windward. When the spirits are asked why they stay at the house, the reply is "I guard." Carmel is there to prevent

Mary from driving Stella into throwing herself off the cliff, something she tries to do twice in the film. At the end of the film, Miss Holloway arranges for Stella to be returned to the empty house so that Mary can finish off what she began seventeen years before, to tie up this loose end which Stella represents. Commander Beech has stationed himself in the studio to warn her away, but manages only to deliver his warning before he dies as Mary's wraith appears before the terrified Stella. Rick saves the girl just as she is about to fall off the cliff.

At this point, Carmel intervenes by turning the pages of the village physician's journal to a passage which indicates just who Stella's mother was. This knowledge liberates Stella from her terrible heritage as Mary Meredith's daughter; as she says, "I can be myself now." The conflict between her instincts and her heredity is now put into proper perspective; she no longer needs to repress her own emotions. This transition is beautifully symbolized at the film's conclusion, when Rick confronts Mary's wraith alone and exorcises her by laughing at her, before descending the great winding staircase of Windward to throw open the great double doors so that the first rays of the rising sun can fill the hallway with light, forever banishing the dark forces which have lived in Stella's psyche.

Rodger Nadelman

AN UNMARRIED WOMAN

Released: 1978
Production: Paul Mazursky and Tony Ray for Twentieth Century-Fox
Direction: Paul Mazursky
Screenplay: Paul Mazursky
Cinematography: Arthur J. Ornitz
Editing: Stuart H. Pappe
Running time: 124 minutes

Principal characters:

Erica Benton .... Jill Clayburgh
Martin Benton .... Michael Murphy
Saul Kaplan .... Alan Bates
Charlie .... Cliff Gorman
Patti Benton .... Lisa Lucas
Tanya .... Penelope Russianoff

Although the women's movement was creating numerous changes in the social, political, and cultural patterns of the United States in the 1970's, the film industry largely ignored the trend. Few of the films produced in the first half of the decade had any female roles of significance. By 1977, however, this trend was ending as Hollywood reacted to the demand for meaningful movies about women. Several films featured women as the central character; among them were *Julia*, *The Turning Point*, *Looking for Mr. Goodbar*, and *An Unmarried Woman*. Nominated for three Academy Awards, including Best Picture and Best Actress, Paul Mazursky's *An Unmarried Woman* is a very successful study of a 1970's woman facing the emotional upheaval of divorce.

Mazursky has gained the reputation of being a satirical commentator on the American middle class and its problems. His previous works include *Bob and Carol and Ted and Alice* (1969), *Blume in Love* (1973), and *Harry and Tonto* (1974). In *An Unmarried Woman* the characteristic satire is missing, but he continues his pattern of commenting on the middle class. While divorce is certainly not restricted to one strata of society, this film is only concerned with its effect on the comfortably affluent, established segment of the population. As such, the main character, Erica, is not concerned with financial settlements or establishing credit, and the audience is involved only with her emotional and psychological development.

The setting is New York City. Erica (Jill Clayburgh) and Martin (Michael Murphy) Benton have been married sixteen years. She works part-time in a Soho art gallery and he is a successful stockbroker. Their fifteen-year-old daughter, Patti (Lisa Lucas), has an easy, warm relationship with her parents. Everything appears to be going well. Then, suddenly Martin tearfully announces he is leaving Erica for a younger woman. Without warning, Erica's world has collapsed as the man around whom she has built her life and identity walks out. The rest of the movie follows Erica through the painful, lonely, and frightening transition from Mrs. Martin Benton to Erica, an unmarried woman. The screenplay, written by Mazursky and nominated for an Academy Award, portrays this transition with skill and subtlety. Erica's growth and development is witnessed by the audience through her relationships with the other characters. With few exceptions, the dialogue and characterizations are truly believable throughout the movie.

Central among Erica's relationships are her three friends. Their frequent consciousness raising sessions reveal them as hard and cynical in contrast to Erica's gentle refinement. The contrast is so striking that Erica's friendship with them is not truly understood. However, they do represent various stages in the survivor syndrome, as reflected in their advice given to Erica. In return, Erica relies heavily on their friendship and finds that it fills a need in her life.

Another key figure in Erica's life is her daughter. The mother-daughter relationship is a strong, warm, and nurturing one for both. Although often outspoken, Patti appears genuinely sensitive to her mother's emotions and does her best to be supportive while undergoing emotional traumas of her own. In very believable performances, the audience sees them laughing, crying, singing, and fighting, all of which reiterates the importance of the relationship to Erica and reveals another facet of her personality.

Continuing his tradition, Mazursky uses a therapist in *An Unmarried Woman* as he has in previous works; in this case, the result is not completely successful, and the scenes between Tanya, played by real-life therapist Penelope Russianoff, and Erica are possibly the weakest of the film. The dialogue is very loosely developed, and while some insights into Erica's character are revealed, the scenes are generally long and uncomfortable.

Following Martin's departure, Erica's encounters with men only serve to increase her distrust and scorn of the male sex. On the advice of Tanya, she decides to take a chance and meet some men. Her first sexual encounter is with Charlie (Cliff Gorman), a somewhat likable male chauvinist whose philosophy centers on work, food, and sex. Having slept with him, Erica leaves immediately with no intention of repeating the episode. This segment of the film is especially well done; both Clayburgh and Gorman give excellent performances.

Charlie, however, is definitely not worthy of the Erica the audience has come to know. Her real love interest arrives in the person of Saul Kaplan (Alan Bates). Almost too good to be true, Saul is a charming, witty, intelligent, and successful artist. Their affair begins as another of Erica's experiments, though it soon develops into something much stronger. As a result, Erica grows stronger. Two specific instances show the positive effect Saul's love has had on Erica's self-confidence. The first example comes in a meeting with Martin, who woefully explains that his girl friend has left him and asks to come back. Erica says no. Later with Saul she again shows her independence. While discussing the future, Saul says he approves of her need to be on her own; Erica angrily states she does not need nor seek his approval. She has come a long way from the woman who cried from fear of being alone.

The film closes with a final act of courage and independence. Saul has asked her to spend the summer in Vermont with him. It would be easy for Erica to agree. She would be with a man who loved her, would protect her, and around whom she could build her world. Instead, she declines. She has now come full circle from the woman who needed a man to complete her life. The final scene is symbolic of Erica's new attitude. As she struggles down the street carrying a huge canvas Saul has left her, she is jostled by passersby and buffeted by the wind, but undaunted, she continues on her way.

Jill Clayburgh's portrayal of Erica is definitely worthy of the Academy Award nomination it received although she lost the award to Jane Fonda for *Coming Home*. Her range of emotions and expressions, and the pathos blend to create a character with whom the audience can easily relate. She is, of course, helped in her performance by the script and direction of Paul Mazursky, who has used his diverse talents to present a meaningful drama about a modern woman and an excellent commentary.

Elaine Raines

THE UNSINKABLE MOLLY BROWN

Released: 1964
Production: Lawrence Weingarten for Metro-Goldwyn-Mayer
Direction: Charles Walters
Screenplay: Helen Deutsch; based on the musical play of the same name by Richard Morris and Meredith Willson
Cinematography: Daniel L. Fapp
Editing: Fredric Steinkamp
Choreography: Peter Gennaro
Music: Meredith Willson
Running time: 128 minutes

Principal characters:

Molly Brown	Debbie Reynolds
Johnny Brown	Harve Presnell
Shamus Tobin	Ed Begley
Mrs. McGraw	Audrey Christie
Christmas Morgan	Jack Kruschen
Buttercup Grogan	Hermione Baddeley
Grand Duchess Elise Lupavinova	Martita Hunt
Prince Louis de Laniere	Vassili Lambrinos
Monsignor Ryan	George Mitchell

The Unsinkable Molly Brown is loosely based on the life story of Margaret ("Molly") Tobin Brown, who won a place in history for her heroism in the aftermath of the disastrous sinking of the *Titanic*. Based on the hit Broadway play of the same name, the film is considered the last of the large-scale M-G-M musicals, although it is not in the same league as such classics as *Singin' in the Rain* (1952) and *An American in Paris* (1951).

The historical Molly Brown is portrayed as feisty, spirited, and adventursome in the film's opening scene, which shows six-month-old Molly in her cradle, being buffeted about by the rapids of the Colorado river flood and having the time of her life. When she is next seen, she has grown into a backwoods tomboy who can hunt and fish but who has no formal education. She wrestles fiercely with neighbors when they pick a fight, and when pinned down and told to capitulate, she retorts that she will never say she is down. In the rousing anthem "I Ain't Down Yet," Molly (Debbie Reynolds) pours out her hopes and desires—to learn to read and write, to see some of the world, to become somebody, and most of all, to live in a red house with a big brass bed.

Molly leaves home to seek her fortune, thanking her foster father Shamus (Ed Begley) for rescuing her from the flood and promising to send for him after she has married a millionaire. On the way to Leadville, a town where she plans to earn enough money to be able to live in Denver, Molly meets

Leadville's Johnny Brown (Harve Presnell), a rough-hewn miner who expresses, in the ballad "Colorado, My Home," his only desires in life—the Rocky Mountains, fresh air, a cabin, and a wife. Theirs is a meeting of opposites: an ambitious woman who aspires to wealth and a simple man who finds contentment in lesser needs. In Leadville, Molly finds work as a bar girl and entertainer in a saloon owned by Christmas Morgan (Jack Kruschen). During one scene in the bar, she leads the miners in the boisterous showstopper, "Belly Up to the Bar, Boys." Settling into life and work, Johnny teaches her to read and write, falling in love with her in the process. In the ballad "I'll Never Say No," he asks her why she cannot settle for the happiness of his love and devotion instead of her previous desire for wealth; he builds her a cabin with a brass bed and Molly, even knowing that he is far from the millionaire whom she has planned on, follows her heart and marries him anyway.

In order to prove his love to Molly, Johnny sells a portion of his goldmine claim for $300,000. For safe keeping, Molly hides the money in their stove until an unsuspecting Johnny lights a fire in it, burning the money. Johnny's mine, however, strikes gold that very night. With the discovery of gold in the Little Johnny mine, the Browns become instant millionaires and move to Denver. However, they are woefully out of place. Molly aspires to become an accepted member of the "Sacred Thirty-Six," Denver's inner-society circle, but her extravagance, friendliness, and backwoods mannerisms are viewed as crude and vulgar by the socialites. Led by Gladys McGraw (Audrey Christie), they openly snub her. Only Buttercup Grogan (Hermione Baddeley), Mrs. McGraw's earthy mother, and the Monsignor Ryan (George Mitchell) accept her. The latter suggests to her that she could benefit from a European trip to acquire polish and learn about the arts.

While in Europe, the Browns acquire not only culture but also a circle of royal friends, particularly Prince Louis de Laniere (Vassili Lambrinos) and Grand Duchess Elise Lupavinova (Martita Hunt). Molly's earthiness and enthusiasm are considered as a breath of fresh air, and she becomes the toast of European society but Johnny, totally out of his element, turns sullen and depressed. Johnny and the "new" Molly return to Denver, now accompanied by titled heads of Europe, and give a lavish party to impress the Sacred Thirty-Six. Their Leadville friends crash the party, and Johnny, the "old" Molly, and even the royalty all join in the spirited song-and-dance, "He's My Friend." The party, however, ends in a brawl, leaving the Browns in disgrace.

Louis and the Grand Duchess persuade Molly to return to Europe, but this time Johnny refuses to leave his beloved Colorado. In Europe and with the world at her feet, Molly nevertheless finds that she cannot be happy without the man she loves. When Johnny writes, telling her to remove her wedding ring, she capitulates for the first time in her life, and does so; but, discovering a loving inscription inside the ring, Molly decides she "ain't down yet," and sails for home on the *Titanic*. When the ship strikes an iceberg and sinks, leaving Molly and other passengers in lifeboats, she takes charge, barking commands, giving her clothes to others for warmth, and keeping spirits high. When a woman cries out that they will sink, Molly replies, "Not with Molly Brown onboard. That ship may be down, but not me. I'm unsinkable!" The lifeboat passengers survive, and Molly becomes an acknowledged heroine, internationally famous and decorated for bravery. Members of the Sacred Thirty-Six—even Mrs. McGraw—receive her graciously, and her triumphant homecoming is complete when she finds Johnny and the brass bed from Leadville waiting for her. The film ends as they are reunited in a tearful but joyous embrace.

The Unsinkable Molly Brown is a prime example of Broadway's and Hollywood's penchant for taking the truth and embellishing and romanticizing it to create a story far more interesting and enjoyable than the mere facts would allow. The real Molly Brown, while as colorful, ambitious, and unmannered as her film counterpart, differed in several ways from that characterization.

Rather than being an illiterate orphan, she was part of a large family and received a public school education. Her husband was not Leadville Johnny, indeed an owner of the Little Johnny, but Jim Brown, the mine's superintendent; it was Jim's share in the mine as reward for striking gold there which made possible the Browns' move to Denver. Losing $300,000 in the stove is pure myth—Jim did unwittingly burn money, but only $75 in coins, which were recovered when the fire was extinguished. And it was not in Europe, but Newport, Rhode Island, that Molly made her social hit. Perhaps most important of all, when Molly and Jim separated, they never reconciled.

The film's director, musical veteran Charles Walters, whose previous credits include *Easter Parade* (1948) and *Good News* (1947), once again demonstrates his expertise in the staging of musical numbers, aided by artful and unobtrusive camerawork (the film's cinematography was nominated for an Oscar). Walters elicits strong performances from his cast, the star being, of course, Debbie Reynolds as Molly. Reynolds begged M-G-M to let her have the part, even offering to pay $5,000 for a screen test (the studio wanted Shirley MacLaine). Fortunately, she won out, and was rewarded with an Academy Award nomination for Best Actress. Debbie Reynolds is perfect as Molly Brown; she is utterly convincing, both as an unschooled tomboy and as a polished sophisticate. Harve Presnell in his film debut as Johnny, repeating the role he created on Broadway, plays well against Reynolds and has a rich, full tenor voice which greatly enhances his musical numbers. Ed Begley, Jack Kruschen, and Hermione Baddeley provide colorful supporting performances; Vassili Lambrinos and Martita Hunt are suitably aristocratic and Audrey Christie properly stuffy.

The musical numbers, by Meredith Willson, contribute greatly to the film's success. Several of the Broadway tunes were dropped and a new song, "He's My Friend," was added. The film's musical highlights are the lively song-and-dance productions—"I Ain't Down Yet," "Belly Up to the Bar, Boys," and "He's My Friend"—which feature Peter Gennaro's athletic and inventive choreography. All of the musical numbers are well integrated into the plot and arise logically from the action and dialogue preceding them. Besides being entertaining, each number serves the purpose of having the audience learn something about the character and/or situation with which it is involved. The effective scoring garnered an Oscar nomination.

Helen Deutsch's screenplay is stronger in comedic elements than dramatic ones; indeed, the film succeeds better as comedy than as drama. While there are many sharply etched humorous vignettes—Molly's reading lessons, for instance, or the money-burning episode—the script somehow never reaches a comparable dramatic level.

The film has several technical flaws. In one scene, for example, Molly speaks without moving her lips. Also, although shot mostly on location, certain mountain scenes are obviously backdrops. The most glaring error, however, occurs during the musical number, "I Ain't Down Yet," when Molly, who has already sung of living in a house that is red and has "a big brass bed," sings quite unmistakably, ". . . a big brass *bell*." It is surprising that the scene was not reshot correctly.

Production values in general, though, are excellent; the movie also received Oscar nominations for Costume Design, Art Direction, and Sound, as well as Cinematography, Musical Score, and Best Actress—a total of six nominations, but no wins. The film was well received by critics and audiences alike, becoming the third-highest-grossing picture of 1964. Highlighted by Debbie Reynolds' outstanding performance and a rousing musical score, *The Unsinkable Molly Brown* successfully combines elements of the film musical to create a product well representative of that genre.

Libby Slate

VIVA ZAPATA!

Released: 1952
Production: Darryl F. Zanuck for Twentieth Century-Fox
Direction: Elia Kazan
Screenplay: John Steinbeck; based on the novel *Zapata, the Unconquerable* by Edgcumb Pinchon
Cinematography: Joe MacDonald
Editing: Barbara McLean
Music: Alex North
Running time: 112 minutes

Principal characters:
Zapata .... Marlon Brando
Josefa .... Jean Peters
Eufemio .... Anthony Quinn (AA)
Fernando .... Joseph Wiseman
Pancho Villa .... Alan Reed
Soldadera .... Margo
Pablo .... Lou Gilbert
Huerta .... Frank Silvera
Madero .... Harold Gordon
President Diaz .... Fay Roope
Don Nacio .... Arnold Moss

Sometime in the late 1940's, Elia Kazan approached John Steinbeck with the idea of collaborating on a film about the great Mexican revolutionary, Emiliano Zapata. At the time, both men considered themselves basically politically left while at the same time antiauthoritarian, and they wanted to create a work which confronted this dilemma. Essentially they were dealing with Albert Camus' theory of Rebel (a man who acts spontaneously against injustice) *versus* Revolutionary (someone willing to purge the unorthodox individual for an abstract Good). The notion appealed to Steinbeck; it was something he had been grappling with for years in his novels, such as *In Dubious Battle* and *The Grapes of Wrath*. From late 1948 until 1950 he worked diligently on the Zapata screenplay, while Kazan, fresh from his successes with such unorthodox films as *Gentleman's Agreement* (1947) and *Pinky* (1949), plus the enormous triumph of *A Streetcar Named Desire* (1951), convinced Darryl Zanuck and Twentieth Century-Fox of the salability of a film about Zapata. What finally emerged was a highly entertaining film which not only captured the sweep and contradictions of the Mexican Revolution, but also wove into the rich fabric of the work a strong warning against abuse of power and the dangers of legitimate rebellion turning into intractable totalitarianism.

The film opens in 1909 when a delegation of peasants from the state of

Morelos arrives in Mexico City at the palace of President Diaz (Fay Roope), once an ardent fighter with Juarez and now the corrupt absolute dictator of Mexico. The peasants have come, much as did our own founding fathers, to petition for redress of grievances. Their land has been confiscated by the large landowners backed by the armed might of the Rurales. They ask Diaz for aid, but he offers only platitudes and the suggestion that they check their boundary stones to make certain the land is indeed theirs. Zapata (Marlon Brando), until now only a face in the crowd, steps forward, stating that the peasants do not have time to wait; their crops must be planted and harvested. Diaz, enraged, demands Zapata's name and draws a circle around it. Zapata's lack of servility has made him a marked man.

When the farmers return home and attempt to find the markers which would prove their ownership of the land, a machine gun opens fire on them, but Zapata, riding his white horse, Blanco, lassos the gun and leads the peasants to safety.

Retreating to a mountain hideout with his brother Eufemio (Anthony Quinn) and his friend Pablo (Lou Gilbert), Zapata is sought out by a young itinerant revolutionary, Fernando Aguirre (Joseph Wiseman), who suggests that Zapata join in an alliance with Francisco Madero (Harold Gordon) and lead a revolt to overthrow Diaz. Zapata is reluctant; he only wants to marry Josefa (Jean Peters), the daughter of a local merchant, and live a quiet, untroubled life. He agrees to send Pablo to Texas, where Madero resides in exile, and then busies himself with his interrupted courtship. Considered unworthy of Josefa by her father, Zapata enlists the influence of Don Nacio (Arnold Moss), a benevolent landowner, to have the charges against him for his opposition to the Rurales dropped, and he goes to work appraising horses for his new patron.

Zapata's instinctive hatred of injustice, however, continues to thwart his dreams of peace. Seeing a child being whipped, he knocks down the overseer. Later, witnessing an old farmer being dragged by Rurales, he cuts the rope. This action proves unpardonable and Zapata himself is captured and dragged through the streets by the Rurales. However, he has established himself as a leader among his people, and, by sheer force of numbers, they stop the Rurales and free Zapata. At the urging of Fernando he orders Eufemio to cut the telegraph wires. This act brands him once and for all as an outlaw and a revolutionary at war with Diaz and oppression.

In the brief flurry of battles which follow, the corrupt regime of Diaz is toppled and Madero is welcomed back to Mexico as a liberator. Josefa and Emiliano, overjoyed by the end of the fighting, are married. On his wedding night, a restless Zapata confesses to his bride that he is terrified of his coming meeting with Madero because he has never been taught to read. Patiently, the two sit on the edge of the bed, and she begins to teach him to read in one of the most touching moments of the film.

Once in the capitol, Zapata urges Madero to begin immediate land reform, but Madero, steeped in the law, is hesitant. Everything, he says, must be done correctly; changes take time. Angered at this response and at Madero's suggestion that he order his men to stack their arms, leaving the keeping of the peace to the regular army (recently aligned with Diaz), Zapata returns to Morelos. Pablo sees the new President as a good man and urges him to meet with Zapata again. Fernando, however, regards Madero as an ineffectual leader and has already begun to plot with General Huerta (Frank Silvera) to stage a *coup*.

The *coup* coincides with Madero's second meeting with Zapata. Once again the country is plunged into war. Madero is placed under house arrest by Huerta, who eventually orders his murder. Zapata, joined with the forces of Pancho Villa (Alan Reed) in the north, wages a bloody struggle which ends in Huerta's defeat. The allied Generals enter Mexico City in triumph.

Villa wants no part in governing Mexico, having had enough of politics and war. He delegates this thankless task to Zapata, who accepts under protest, while insisting that he be referred to as General rather than President Zapata. At his side, acting as his aide, is the treacherous Fernando.

Not long after he has taken power, Zapata is confronted by a delegation from his home state. History has repeated itself, for these men are his neighbors and former comrades-in-arms. Zapata finds himself mouthing the words of Diaz, and, as before, a young zealot steps forward stating that the farmers cannot wait for the gradual change Zapata suggests. Angered, Zapata demands the man's name and begins to circle it. This is the pivotal scene of the film. With the shadow of Fernando looming over Zapata, one hand on his shoulder, there is a Satanic quality to the moment. Zapata, however, remains a rebel, refusing to be corrupted by the power which has been handed him. Taking only the belongings with which he entered the city, he leaves with his countrymen and returns home.

Back in Morelos, Eufemio has allowed his status as "liberator" to transform him into a tyrant. He has taken another man's wife. His brother attempts to reason with him, but Eufemio, drunk, chooses instead to shoot it out with the woman's husband, and both men are killed. Zapata, grief-stricken, speaks to the delegation which has followed him home, saying "You've looked for leaders. For strong men without faults. There aren't any. There are only men like yourselves. . . . There's no leader but yourselves." Zapata's abdication brings more bloodshed, and Fernando, now aligned with Carranza, plots the murder of his former ally.

Zapata is lured into a supposedly abandoned garrison stacked with enough ammunition and weapons to allow the Zapatistas to continue their guerrilla war for another year. In the garrison he finds his lost horse, Blanco, and buries his head in her mane, for a brief moment unaware of danger. The horse bolts, but it is too late. A fusillade from the parapet cuts Zapata to ribbons, although Blanco escapes the carnage. At Fernando's insistence, the bullet-riddled body of Zapata is dumped in the village square as a lesson to the people of Morelos.

As Emiliano earlier explained to Josefa, however, the people no longer require a leader. They express disbelief at Zapata's death ("shot up like that it could be anybody!"), declaring that even if he were dead, they, the people (echoing the words of Ma Joad in *The Grapes of Wrath*), cannot be vanquished. One man says that Zapata is in the mountains and that if they should ever need him again he will return. The peasants look up toward the mountains and the final shot is of Blanco, the spirit of Zapata, which cannot be destroyed.

Viva Zapata! is a stirring work. The performances are brilliant. Brando's Zapata is a complete change from his Kowalski and confirmed him as one of the finest actors of his generation. Anthony Quinn, long relegated to thankless roles as Indians and small-time gangsters, won a Best Supporting Actor Award for his portrayal of the impetuous Eufemio, and Joseph Wiseman is perfect as Fernando, a man obsessed with revolution for the mere sake of it.

It was unquestionably Kazan's most cinematic work to date, and he drew heavily on the imagery of Sergei Eisenstein (most particularly on the Russian director's aborted masterpiece *Que Viva Mexico*). Alex North's score was stirring, both in its use of original music and in its skillful integration of folk tunes and revolutionary ballads of the period.

The political climate in America did not help the film on release. Liberal and left-wing critics felt that Kazan and Steinbeck had betrayed Zapata, reducing him from revolutionary hero to a more wavering, uncertain figure. Worse, they felt that through the character of Fernando, the film was somehow reduced to an anti-Communist tract. On the other side, any film which voiced more than mild concern over injustice was branded Communist propaganda by right-wing critics. Also, while the film had been made before Kazan's testimony before the House UnAmerican Activities Committee, some interpreted the film as an attempt on the director's part to cater to the Committee and salvage his career.

Viva Zapata! finally found its audience and its place as a film of power and integrity; indeed, Kazan has said that it has become as much a cult film as has *The Battle of Algiers* (1966). While never stooping to the level of obvious propaganda, the film suggests that permanent vigilance, indeed, permanent revolution, is necessary to avoid the tendency toward corruption inherent in individuals and the social systems by which they live.

Michael Shepler

A WALK IN THE SUN

Released: 1945
Production: Lewis Milestone for Comstock; released by Twentieth Century-Fox
Direction: Lewis Milestone
Screenplay: Robert Rossen; based on the novel of the same name by Harry Brown
Cinematography: Russell Harlan
Editing: W. Duncan Mansfield
Running time: 117 minutes

Principal characters:

Sergeant Tyne	Dana Andrews
Rivera	Richard Conte
Friedman	George Tyne
Windy	John Ireland
Sergeant Ward	Lloyd Bridges
McWilliams	Sterling Holloway
Porter	Herbert Rudley
Archimbeau	Norman Lloyd

Director Lewis Milestone adapted Erich Remarque's book *All Quiet on the Western Front* in 1930 and produced a landmark in cinema history. The film, showing World War I from the point of view of the German soldier, was a bitter indictment of the use of force as a means of solving disputes between nations. In 1946, Milestone completed *A Walk in the Sun*, an adaptation of a book by Harry Brown, and the result was another notable film. Unlike its predecessor, however, this movie, which concerns World War II, makes no overt judgments at all, and consists simply of the record of a day in the life of a platoon of soldiers. Yet, while it is no less a social document than the earlier film, it represents a tempering and broadening of earlier positions that had placed Milestone squarely in the pacifist camp. *A Walk in the Sun* is an antiwar film, but it reflects the complexities of the world at midcentury. It is thus less of a negation of that world than was *All Quiet on the Western Front*, and becomes more of a quiet exhortation that the brutality and misery of war must be justified by a better world in peace. Milestone recognizes that war is evil but he now recognizes that it is not the only evil or any longer the lesser evil in a world that was entering the Cold War and the nuclear era.

A Walk in the Sun also reflects a broadening in the techniques of production over *All Quiet on the Western Front*, which was laid out upon relatively conventional lines. Since the latter film was produced comparatively early in the era of talking pictures, the mechanics were admittedly clumsy and the photographic reproduction crude in comparison to contemporary sophisticated standards. Yet the director's work reflected the wealth of pure cinema techniques that carried over from the days of silent films, techniques which would be temporarily lost in the flurry of experimentation with sound. By the 1940's, the cycle had rounded out with dialogue and sound effects being placed in their proper perspective in relation to visual cinematic values. The result was that the knowledgeable director's scope became immeasurably broadened by the sensitive use of the new dimension. Lewis Milestone, among the most adept of American directors, made best use of these techniques, and in *A Walk in the Sun* he has structured an intricate web of dialogue and pictures within a provocative time scheme.

The film, extraordinarily faithful to Harry Brown's novel, is the story of an all but leaderless platoon of United States infantrymen of the Texas Division who land at Salerno and march six miles inland from the Italian beachhead to capture a Nazi-infested farmhouse and destroy a strategic bridge. The story is told in a series of alternate conversation and action sequences. This is not a typical Hollywood interpretation of a cross-section of American men. It is true that the "types" are there, but character is revealed as it is in life, bit by bit, until at the finale we know these men, individually and as a group.

By design, the picture is static: the viewer sees only what the men see, and through the paced slowness of Milestone's direction, the suspense mounts. The film opens with the shivering men in the dark, aboard a landing craft which advances toward the beach. Wonderful close-up shots of watching faces in the shadows establish that the war "is nothing but waiting." Suddenly the lieutenant is hit by a shell and dies on the beach after the landing. The sergeant who takes command breaks down, becoming a mental casualty on the march inland. A nervous and insecure Corporal Tyne (Dana Andrews), who is promoted to sergeant, then takes over the platoon.

The film moves forward through small talk as the men walk in the hot sun. We meet Rivera (Richard Conte), the gunner who is always bumming a cigarette, and his sidekick Friedman (George Tyne); McWilliams (Sterling Holloway), the slow-witted medic; Porter (Herbert Rudley), the frightened sergeant; Archimbeau (Norman Lloyd), who had all the facts and foresaw the battle of Tibet in 1958; and Windy (John Ireland), who is always mentally composing an unwritten letter to his sister.

Milestone misses no chance for action or accumulative suspense in this foot-slogging odyssey from barge to beach to bridge and farmhouse. En route the platoon encounters enemy planes, armored cars and tanks, and the even deadlier things that happen in a soldier's mind when he has fought one battle too many. Yet the camerawork is almost second in importance to the sound track, as the film records the infrantrymen's talk and the thinking aloud at zero hour. There is chatter about *Saturday Evening Post* covers, work in war plants, the disgrace of being an infantryman, and the probable source of krations (the sewers of Hoboken). The sergeant, formerly a farmer, desperately longs for an apple and devotes a moment of pity to the poor Italian soil, which is no good because too many soliders have been walking on it. The men tell the story of the battle largely in their own words through their banter, their work talk, their reminiscences, and their articulated dreams for the future. Although the dialogue is excellent, it is occasionally marred by the persistent use of repetitive phrases as devices to add to its realism.

When the men are faced with any military problem, they chant an ironic G.I. litany, "Nobody dies," and make up the best solution they can, often meaning death for many of their comrades. Although the scope of their problems is small in comparison to the whole war, their encounters with a handful of strafing planes, a couple of tanks, and an armored car are full of shrill excitement. Stumbling about and wondering what actually is going on, the soldiers agree with McWilliams the medic who remarks, "That's the trouble with wars—you've got to fight 'em by ear." There are no great battles here and no one higher in rank than the sergeants who take over when their lieutenant is killed in the landing operation. When the farmhouse is captured by noon, we have come to know all of these men, the casualties as well as those who survive. *A Walk in the Sun* is a highly charged capsule of war that epitomizes all war.

Most of Harry Brown's pungent and colorful dialogue is used in the film, only slightly altered for the purposes of the medium. The effect is one of realism although the talk sometimes more closely approaches poetry than G.I. prose. A ballad written by Earl Robinson and Millard Lampell introduces and ends the film, and provides throughout the film a musical commentary on the story in the manner of a Greek chorus. Whenever it occurs, it forcibly severs the viewer's identification with the action; this can be deemed useful or destructive depending on the viewer's need to participate in the film. The cinematography by Russell Harlan is well integrated into Milestone's scheme and projects all of the gradations of light that lie between the black of night and the blinding white of the Mediterranean sun. The gradual increase of daylight opening the film is technically well done, and the subsequent manipulation of bright and cloudy light adds to the motion and vitality of the film's progress.

A Walk in the Sun comes alive because of the performances of several of its players. Dana Andrews as the sergeant who commits himself to the command of the platoon is notable for his quiet, forceful performance, and Herbert Rudley in his role as the sergeant who mentally collapses is utterly convincing. Although Robert Rossen does an excellent and subtle job of translating the dialogue of the novel into the screenplay, if the film has a major fault, it is that the opening half bogs down in static literary patterns. The written words, stretched out into spoken dialogue, seem at times too many or too much the same, and the literary preoccupations become so strong as to destroy the sense of reality at times.

On the whole, however, *A Walk in the Sun* is a notable achievement in filmmaking, as an experiment by Milestone which emphasized sound in a primarily visual medium to present a realistic picture of the soldier's war. Its antiwar flavor is not heavy-handed and relies upon its microcosm of an isolated platoon on an average day to make a universal statement. Milestone fights his war by ear in this film and it is a brave effort. Released in 1946 to a world tired of war, *A Walk in the Sun* opened to favorable reviews, but was disappointing at the box office.

Thomas A. Hanson

WATCH ON THE RHINE

Released: 1943
Production: Hal B. Wallis for Warner Bros.
Direction: Herman Schumlin
Screenplay: Dashiell Hammett, with additional scenes and dialogue by Lillian Hellman; based on her play of the same name
Cinematography: Merritt B. Gerstad and Hal Mohr
Editing: Rudi Fehr
Running time: 114 minutes

Principal characters:

Kurt Muller	Paul Lukas (AA)
Sara Muller	Bette Davis
Fanny Farrelly	Lucile Watson
David Farrelly	Donald Woods
Teck de Brancovis	George Coulouris
Marthe de Brancovis	Geraldine Fitzgerald
Joshua	Donald Buka
Bodo	Eric Roberts
Anise	Beulah Bondi
Joseph	Frank Wilson

Watch on the Rhine was a great stage success on Broadway in April, 1941, before America entered World War II. By 1943, with the United States thoroughly involved in the fighting, playwright Lillian Hellman's warning that Fascism threatened all the free world became an urgent and topical message.

Warner Bros. purchased *Watch on the Rhine* in a double *coup*; the patriotic feather in the studio's cap was also an award-winning success of the day. Wisely deciding not to tamper with a winning combination, Warner Bros. engaged the services of the play's director, Herman Schumlin, and five members of the original stage cast: Paul Lukas, Lucile Watson, George Coulouris, Eric Roberts, and Frank Wilson. They work together as a faultless ensemble. Dashiell Hammett, a close companion of Hellman, wrote the filmscript, for which he received an Academy Award nomination. The dialogue remains almost unchanged from that of the play. Hellman herself added additional scenes and dialogue chiefly to augment the major portion of the play, which takes place in the Farrelly family's Washington drawing room.

These additions do not make *Watch on the Rhine* excellent cinema; it remains a filmed stage play, a drama of words punctuated by a single action, guaranteed to shock the American audience into awareness about the war in Europe. The film's opening scenes are deceptively low-key. The Muller family crosses into the United States at a hot and dusty Mexican border station and begins a long train ride to Washington, D.C. The three children are hungry but uncomplaining; they look after one another. Sara Muller

(Bette Davis) is weary and apprehensive; she has not seen her prominent Washington family since she married a German engineer eighteen years before. Her husband Kurt (Paul Lukas) is worn and ill. We know Sara is American, but she and her family all have the tired look of European refugees.

The scene shifts to Washington where Fanny Farelly (Lucile Watson), Sara's mother, is preparing for the arrival of the Mullers. Fanny is in a frenzy of anticipation and anxiety; she orders her French housekeeper, Anise (Beulah Bondi) and the butler, Joseph (Frank Wilson), about in a whirl of activity. Throughout the film the cheerful banter between these two employee/friends and Fanny serve to define her character: she is a strong-willed, opinionated, but very likable autocrat devoted to the memory of her dead husband; determined to mold her son, David (Donald Woods), in his image; and much given to outrageous statements and impertinent questions. Lucile Watson repeats her stage success and makes the character of Fanny Farelly at once larger than life and completely believable.

Fanny confides her nervous anticipation of the Mullers' arrival to her houseguests, Count Teck de Brancovis (George Coulouris), a destitute Romanian nobleman, and his American wife, Marthe (Geraldine Fitzgerald). The Count and Marthe are not favorites of Fanny and have overstayed their welcome, but they remain at David's request. David is not above using it to assure himself a soft billet while watching for his main chance. Not an attractive character, George Coulouris is an excellent villain as he re-creates his stage role.

The Mullers arrive early and a joyous homecoming ensues; it is marred, however, by Fanny's probing questions about her daughter's frequent changes of address over the years and her present financially strapped circumstances. Sara bristles in defense; but Kurt quietly responds to the interrogation, explaining only that he no longer works as an engineer but is an anti-Fascist. When Fanny asks him what kind of work that entails, he answers, "Any kind, anywhere." Fanny stops her barrage of questions; she is afraid of answers.

The Mullers settle in for a rest, and Sara confides that Kurt has been ill but will return to Europe when he has recovered his strength. It is through such asides from Sara and the Muller children that we begin to see Kurt as other than a gentle German engineer, much in love with his wife and devoted to his children. We discover that he has fought in Spain, has been tortured by the Gestapo, and still continues his fight as part of an underground anti-Nazi movement. He has brought his family to safety but intends to return to Europe himself.

Fanny and David cannot understand why Kurt has exposed his family to such dangers for six years, being on the run all over Europe. Kurt's fight, however, is for more than his hearth and homeland. He says, "I love my children, but they are not the only children in the world." He is a true visionary, fighting for his principles and for all peoples. He quotes Luther:

"Here I stand. I can do nothing else. God help me. Amen." Aside from Hellman's dramatic expertise, much of the credit for the success of this film must be accorded to Paul Lukas, whose characterization of the quietly heroic Kurt Muller is a flawless artistic triumph.

Although Fanny and David shelve their questions, the Count's curiosity continues unabated. He forces open Kurt's luggage and finds a large amount of American currency; through his contacts with the German Embassy, he picks up additional bits of information until he correctly deduces that Kurt is the lieutenant of a recently captured underground leader. At this point, the Count plans to sell Kurt to the Germans if he is not paid off. Marthe denounces her husband and leaves him, but he carries on with his blackmail. If Kurt has not used the money donated to the underground to feed his children, he certainly will not buy his life with it. David and Fanny offer to pay him off, but Kurt knows that the Count will only take the money and then double-cross them with the Germans anyway.

In the film's climactic scene Kurt shoots the Count. Up to this point, the story has been one of noble speeches; now Kurt has taken a dramatic action. Without fanfare he has murdered the Count so he can return to Germany to seek the release of his comrades. He tells Fanny and David what he has done, and Sara implores them to give her husband time to get away before they report it to the police. Fanny and David, finally shocked out of their American complacency, agree. Kurt bids his family a tearful farewell and leaves for Germany. Months pass with no word from Kurt; finally all realize that he is not coming back. The film ends with Sara's eldest son, Joshua, mapping a route to Germany, planning to carry on his father's work.

It is seldom that ideals are dramatized with such intelligence on the screen. Hellman's brilliant play remains just that. As cinema, *Watch on the Rhine* is nothing spectacular; as drama it is a powerful statement that has remained vital and effective since its release.

Cheryl Karnes

WAY OUT WEST

Released: 1937
Production: Stan Laurel for Hal Roach and Metro-Goldwyn-Mayer
Direction: James W. Horne
Screenplay: Charles Rogers, Felix Adler, and James Parrott; based on a story by Charles Rogers and Jack Jevne
Cinematography: Art Lloyd and Walter Lundin
Editing: Bert Jordan
Running time: 65 minutes

Principal characters:
Stan .... Stan Laurel
Ollie .... Oliver Hardy
Mickey Finn .... James Finlayson
Lola Marcel .... Sharon Lynne
Mary Roberts .... Rosina Lawrence

Way Out West ranks with *Sons of the Desert* (1934) and the three-reel short *The Music Box* (1932) as the best showcase of the comic talents of Stan Laurel and Oliver Hardy. Among the most prolific of the classic screen comedians, the duo made their share of mediocre films. Their career bridged the gap between silent films and talkies, and their cinematic contemporaries ranged from Charlie Chaplin and Buster Keaton to W. C. Fields and the Marx Brothers.

Much of the duo's comedy was physical, and the humor started with the physical contrast between the two men. Stan Laurel was a scarecrow, tall, thin, and angular, while Oliver Hardy was a rotund three hundred pounds. Laurel's hair sprouted from the top of his head in an unruly shock; Hardy's was slicked down over his forehead. Their screen personalities were likewise a study in contrast. Hardy played a pompous egomaniac, eternally convinced of his own superiority and perpetually annoyed by reality's failure to live up to his expectations—a failure which he invariably blamed on the hapless Laurel. Laurel's character was awesomely, almost supernaturally, stupid, a quality matched only by his meekness. If the quintessential Hardy expression was an exasperated scowl, the quintessential Laurel expression was an uncomprehending blink.

Way Out West finds Stan and Ollie on their way to the town of Brushwood Gulch, where they are to deliver the deed to a goldmine to Mary Roberts, the daughter of their late partner. The pair enter to the sound of "The Cuckoos," their theme song. Stan leads Dinah, their mule, who is pulling Ollie on a makeshift sled. Ollie is roused from his contented nap when Stan blithely leads Dinah into a stream. Annoyed, Ollie begins to wade across—only to step into a deep, hidden hole.

Stan salvages the situation by flagging down a passing stagecoach—he bares his legs *à la* Claudette Colbert in *It Happened One Night* (1934)—which takes them into town. His composure recovered, Ollie attempts to make small talk with a lovely female passenger. "A lot of weather we've been having lately," he remarks suavely. Alas, the unwilling object of Ollie's attentions turns out to be the wife of Brushwood Gulch's sheriff who angrily orders the two out of town on the next stage. As Stan and Ollie hurry off to complete their appointed rounds, they are captivated by the sound of music emanating from the steps of Mickey Finn's Saloon. As the Avalon Boys (featuring Chill Wills) sing "Commence to Dancin'," Stan and Ollie break into a charmingly impromptu soft shoe routine.

Inside the saloon, the plot begins to thicken. The proprietor, Mickey Finn (James Finlayson), overhears the boys asking for Mary Roberts, one of his barmaids, and immediately rushes to their side. Stan blurts out the reason for their interest in Roberts, and an exasperated Ollie sighs "Now that *he's* taken *you* into *our* confidence, you'd better know the rest." The larcenous Finn's eyes light up as he hears about the gold mine, and when Ollie admits that neither he nor Stanley has ever seen Mary Roberts, Finn hatches a plan. He rushes upstairs, where he briefs his wife, Lola Marcel (Sharon Lynne), on the plan: she is to play the grieving Mary. When Stan and Ollie are ushered into her room, she tearfully asks if it is true that her dear daddy is dead. "I hope he is. They buried him," replies Stan, who is always full of helpful remarks. "Now that you've got the mine, I'll bet you'll be a swell gold digger," he says.

The boys hand the deed over to the fake Mary Roberts and repair downstairs to the bar, where they join the band for another song, "In the Blue Ridge Mountains of Virginia," with Ollie taking the lead and Stan furnishing the high harmony. Suddenly, however, Stan breaks into a gutteral bass. Exasperated once more by his partner's antics, Ollie grabs a mallet and beats him over the head, making an instant soprano out of poor Stan. The song finished, the two prepare to leave the saloon, only to run into the real Mary Roberts (Rosina Lawrence). Stanley recognizes their error: "That's the first mistake we've made since that guy sold us the Brooklyn Bridge," he says. They rush back upstairs and snatch the deed back; whereupon Lola pursues Stan into the bedroom. In a comic reversal of most similar scenes, Lola chases Stan around the bed, finally forcing him to give up the deed by tickling him into hysterics.

The men are foiled, but not for long. They regroup for their final assault on the Finn stronghold. The film's climax is also its longest sustained slapstick sequence, a sequence particularly well conceived and executed which contains the film's funniest bits of physical comedy. The plan is for Stan to raise Ollie to the saloon's upstairs window by means of a rope and pulley. As Stan arranges the rope around Ollie's ample girth, Ollie casts the audience a meaningful glance from the corner of his eye. The glance presages disaster. Having hoisted the corpulent Ollie halfway up to the second floor, Stan pauses to spit on his hands, and the horrified Ollie plummets to the ground. They try again. This time Dinah the mule, with Stan aboard, hauls Ollie skyward. Stan inexplicably dismounts, however, and Ollie, who evidently outweighs the mule, once again falls to earth, sending Dinah flying onto the saloon's second floor balcony.

The racket awakens Finn, who scrambles into the street, his gun cocked. In the confusion, Stan and Ollie dash inside, where, after a lengthy game of hide and seek, they recover the deed and present it to the real Mary Roberts. The trio leaves town together, and the film ends much as it began—with Ollie stepping into that same pot hole in the stream outside Brushwood Gulch.

Laurel and Hardy have yet to achieve the complete critical acceptance of Chaplin, the Marx Brothers, and some of their other peers. Whereas Groucho Marx and W. C. Fields were perceived as genuinely witty, Laurel and Hardy were often considered to be merely silly, perhaps because they made so many films, and because so many of those films seemed, to the uninitiated, to be interchangeable. For this reason, *Way Out West* is an excellent introduction to the underrated duo.

Although at sixty-five minutes *Way Out West* is one of the pair's longer features, there is not a wasted moment in the film. Critics of the Laurel and Hardy style have accused the two of developing their routines at a snail's pace and of resorting to physical mayhem (almost always directed towards each other) for laughs. In *Way Out West*, the action moves along briskly, and physical violence is kept to a minimum. In addition, that bane of classic screen comedy, the extraneous musical interlude (which brought many an otherwise wonderful Marx Brothers film to a grinding halt while the romantic leads warbled pointlessly for several minutes) is here avoided entirely. All of the music in the film is directly related to its comedy. In James W. Horne, Laurel and Hardy found a sympathetic director, and writers Charles Rogers, Felix Adler, and James Parrot keep the plot moving right along. The result is a Laurel and Hardy film that shows off these unjustly ignored comedians at their best, and their best is good enough to rank them with any of the giants of screen comedy.

Robert Mitchell

WEST SIDE STORY

Released: 1961
Production: Robert Wise for Mirisch Productions in association with Seven Arts Productions; released by United Artists (AA)
Direction: Robert Wise and Jerome Robbins (AA)
Screenplay: Ernest Lehman; based on the musical play of the same name by Arthur Laurents
Cinematography: Daniel L. Fapp (AA)
Editing: Thomas Stanford (AA)
Art direction: Boris Leven (AA); set decoration, Victor Gangelin (AA)
Costume design: Irne Sharaff (AA)
Choreography: Jerome Robbins (AA Special Award)
Sound: Fred Hynes for Todd-AO Sound Department and Gordon E. Sawyer for Samuel Goldwyn Sound Department (AA)
Music: Saul Chaplin, Johhny Green, Sid Ramin, and Irwin Kostal (AA)
Song: Leonard Bernstein and Stephen Sondheim
Title design: Saul Bass
Running time: 155 minutes

Principal characters:
Maria .... Natalie Wood
Tony .... Richard Beymer
Riff .... Russ Tamblyn
Anita .... Rita Moreno (AA)
Bernardo .... George Chakiris (AA)

By the end of the 1950's, the heyday of the Hollywood musical had passed. The elaborate studio system which had included musicals as a staple—and had maintained the necessary talent under contract—had undergone radical changes due to the advent of television. Much of the musical entertainment, whether good, bad, or indifferent, which the movies had provided throughout the 1930's and 1940's, was now available in abundance on television variety shows. With the exception of those films which began to focus on rock 'n' roll (whose excessively sensual pleasures, such as Elvis Presley's torso, were denied by the more prudish television medium), the production of original screen musicals came almost to a halt. More and more from the mid-1950's on, the movies looked to Broadway for proven source material. Most major musicals of this period had already been smash hits on stage—including *South Pacific*, *Oklahoma!*, *Carousel*, *Silk Stockings*, and others. Technological advances such as CinemaScope and stereophonic sound merely underscored the fact that musicals were getting bigger, but not necessarily better. Nowhere in evidence was the cinematic stretching of the musical form which had distinguished the work of Busby Berkeley in the 1930's and Vincente Minnelli, Stanley Donen, and Gene Kelly in the 1940's and early 1950's. In addition, the screen's increasing emphasis on realism and social relevance made the traditional type of musical seem more and more dated. Symbolic of the state of the musical film as the 1950's drew to a close was the fact that its major figures—Fred Astaire and Gene Kelly—abandoned it to essay their first major dramatic roles (in *On the Beach*, 1959, and *Inherit the Wind*, 1960, respectively). Quite simply, they had no choice; the film musical was clearly a dying art form, and only a radical change in direction could revitalize it.

Still looking to Broadway for material, Hollywood discovered *West Side Story*, which had opened on September 26, 1957. It had been hailed as a revolutionary musical largely because of its subject matter: it was a modern-day reworking of the Romeo and Juliet theme, set amidst the radical and social tensions of street-gang rivalry in New York City. The story (as it appears in the film) concerns Maria (Natalie Wood), a young Puerto Rican girl newly arrived to the slums of Manhattan's Upper West Side. Maria's brother, Bernardo (George Chakiris), is the leader of a neighborhood gang, The Sharks. Despite the warnings of Bernardo and his fiery girl friend Anita (Rita Moreno), Maria falls in love with Tony (Richard Beymer), a young Polish boy who was once leader of The Jets, the hated enemies of The Sharks. Tony is trying to leave the gang life behind following a stretch in jail, but is still linked by association to The Jets; the love affair between him and Maria fans the radical tensions at the root of the two gangs' enmity. Events lead eventually to a showdown "rumble." Encouraged by Maria, Tony attempts to intervene and prevent bloodshed, but he fails; the Jet leader, Riff (Russ Tamblyn), is stabbed to death by Bernardo. Tony, overcome by passion, stabs and kills Bernardo. Running to Maria, he begs her forgiveness and pleads with her to go away with him. Before they can escape, however, Tony is cornered and killed in a neighborhood playground by one of The Sharks. Maria and the remaining members of the two gangs discover the body, and, stunned by the tragedy of the three deaths, join together to carry the dead Tony away.

Given the prevailing trends, *West Side Story*'s relevance (and its phenomenally successful Broadway run) ensured that it would eventually be produced as a film. Jerome Robbins, who directed and choreographed the stage production, and Hollywood veteran Robert Wise were engaged to co-direct, and the book by Arthur Laurents was adapted for the screen by Ernest Lehman. The filmmakers believed that in order to translate the play's realism, which had necessarily been stylized on stage, effectively to the film medium, it would be necessary to photograph much of the film on location in the streets of Manhattan. The dances were adapted by Robbins, who choreographed them for free movement in the street, and plans were made for shooting in New York City. Robbins and Wise disagreed early in the shooting, and Robbins quit the production after having choreographed all but two of the dance numbers; he still, however, shared direction credit and the Oscar for Best Direction with Wise.

It is fair to say, without necessarily implying that more credit belongs to Robbins than to Wise, that *West Side Story*'s most successful moments are the dance sequences. The spontaneous opening street ballet by The Jets is beautiful and exhilarating, as are most of the other dances, particularly "Dance at the Gym" and "America." Leonard Bernstein's music and Stephen Sondheim's lyrics are quite good, including such favorites as "Maria," "Tonight," and "I Feel Pretty"; the singing is excellent, even though the singing voices of the stars, Natalie Wood and Richard Beymer, are not their own; they were dubbed by Marni Nixon and Jimmy Bryant, respectively.

But as good as the music and dancing may be (and this is by no means a universal opinion), the rest of the film, and ultimately the film as a whole, is another matter. Much of the charm of the traditional movie musicals—and *West Side Story*, for all its revolutionary and experimental posturing, is structurally quite a conventional musical—was based on their general lack of serious purpose. Their plots may have been silly and inconsequential, but they never pretended to be anything else. *West Side Story*, on the other hand, is fairly bursting with self-importance. In challenging established notions of movie musical content by daring to tackle social issues such as juvenile delinquency and racial tension, *West Side Story* goes melodramatically overboard. The most glaring problem is simply the inconsistency of styles, a reflection of the film's schizophrenic nature and of the apparent indecision on the part of the filmmakers to concentrate on fantasy or realism. For example, although much was made at the time about the film being shot on location "in the streets," in fact most of the film is quite obviously studio-bound, and the preponderance of artificiality and stylization makes a mockery of the film's "realistic" pretensions.

The nonmusical sections of the film are uneven in quality. The romantic interludes are often mawkish, the drama is overly schematic, and the sociology is pretentiously moralistic. In a sense, *West Side Story* is simply a "message" picture, of the type common to that period, masquerading as a revolutionary musical. Even this pose is something of a fraud: *West Side Story* represents no stylistic advancement over its direct antecedent, *On the Town* (1949), ironically an earlier Bernstein-Robbins collaboration.

The direction of Robert Wise, although technically accomplished, particularly in such action-oriented scenes as the rumble between the two gangs, is also obvious and heavy-handed. Wise has never been a master of understatement, and his style merely serves to emphasize the film's melodramatic content. Fortunately, the direction is unable to submerge a number of excellent performances, especially those of George Chakiris as Bernardo, Russ Tamblyn as Riff, and Rita Moreno as Anita. The latter easily steals whatever scene she appears in, and the three together provide much of the energy which fuels the film. In a sense, Bernardo and Riff are the film's most important characters; they are the leaders of their respective gangs, and the stark contrast in their appearances (the dark and fiery Chakiris and the curly-blonde Tamblyn) serves as a handy and effective visualization of the racial conflict at the core of the drama. Their importance becomes somewhat abruptly apparent in the latter portion of the film; after both are killed, one realizes that Natalie Wood and Richard Beymer, although pleasant and capable as the romantic leads, simply do not have the charisma necessary to carry the film on their own. With the deaths of Riff and Bernardo, the film seems to lose an almost palpable energy, and the remainder of the proceedings seem dragged-out and somewhat anticlimactic.

West Side Story, with its overwhelming sense of its own importance, was swallowed whole by many critics and by the film industry itself. It garnered ten Academy Awards, including Best Picture, Direction, Color Cinematography, and Supporting Actor and Actress (Chakiris and Moreno). It did not, however, revolutionize the musical film as many had believed it would. It has become more apparent with the passage of time that the triumph of *West Side Story* was largely that of the stage original; yet although its film version is neither a great film nor as important a milestone as was claimed at the time, it is by no means an insignificant achievement. Whatever its failings as film art, *West Side Story* is a cunningly structured entertainment which often transcends its specious content through sheer theatrical exuberance. It is to these qualities that audiences continue to respond enthusiastically today.

Howard H. Prouty

THE WESTERNER

Released: 1940
Production: Samuel Goldwyn for United Artists
Direction: William Wyler
Screenplay: Jo Swerling and Niven Busch; based on a story by Stuart N. Lake
Cinematography: Gregg Toland
Editing: Daniel Mandell
Art direction: James Basevi
Music: Dmitri Tiomkin and Alfred Newman (uncredited)
Running time: 100 minutes

Principal characters:

Cole Hardin	Gary Cooper
Judge Roy Bean	Walter Brennan (AA)
Jane-Ellen Mathews	Doris Davenport
Caliphet Mathews	Fred Stone
Southeast	Chill Wills
Wade Harper	Forrest Tucker
Chickenfoot	Paul Hurst
Teresita	Lupita Tovar
Lily Langtry	Lillian Bond
Hod Johnson	Dana Andrews

The Western had flourished in silent films with such stars as William S. Hart, Tom Mix, and the young Gary Cooper, and with epic productions such as James Cruze's *The Covered Wagon* (1923) and John Ford's *The Iron Horse* (1924), and it continued to do well through the earliest years of sound films. For some unaccountable reason, however, it fell into a decline between 1931 and 1939, during which time the genre lapsed into B-class productions or serials. During that interval, only four major studio productions were Westerns: King Vidor's *The Texas Rangers* (1936), Cecil B. De Mille's *The Plainsman* (1937), Frank Lloyd's *Wells Fargo* (1937), and James Hogan's *The Texans* (1938). But in 1939, the genre underwent a spectacular revival with such big-budget films as *Jesse James*, *Stagecoach*, *Dodge City*, *Union Pacific*, and *Destry Rides Again*. In that year, John Wayne finally became a star, and Henry Fonda, Errol Flynn, James Stewart, and Tyrone Power each made his first Western. The Western continued to flourish until World War II, when war dramas preempted almost all other action films.

After the blockbuster success of 1939's Westerns, most studios and stars were eager to get into the act, and in 1940, Samuel Goldwyn made *The Westerner*, his sole talking Western and only his second film in the genre. Goldwyn's only previous Western, *The Winning of Barbara Worth* (1926), was Gary Cooper's first featured film. Although Cooper made an impressive debut, Goldwyn let him go, observing that his studio did not make Westerns and Cooper seemed typed as a Western star. Cooper then moved to Paramount, and Goldwyn did not get him back until 1935.

Actually, although Cooper is the quintessence of the Western star, he did not play primarily in Westerns. From 1926 to 1931, eight of his films were Westerns, but during the next nineteen years, he made only four Westerns (in addition to playing a cowboy in *The Cowboy and the Lady*, 1939, which is not a Western) and played a great diversity of roles.

Nevertheless, the Western and Cooper put an indelible stamp on each other. Lean, laconic, soft-spoken, steely-eyed, wryly humorous, quick on the draw, and a superb horseman, Cooper epitomizes the image of the Westerner. He starred in *The Virginian* (1929), the prototypal Western novel and the first talking Western made, and entered legend with his portrayal of Wild Bill Hickok in *The Plainsman*. He was therefore the only possible star for a film called *The Westerner*. No other actor, not even John Wayne (who at that time had just emerged from a decade of B pictures), could qualify for that title.

Though Cooper is the star, *The Westerner* is primarily the story of Judge Roy Bean (Walter Brennan), a scruffy Confederate veteran who is self-appointed judge and boss of the scratchy, sun-baked hamlet of Vinegaroon, Texas. Bean runs the saloon, which doubles as a kangaroo court where he dispenses vigilante-type justice as the only law "west of the Pecos." (The actual town, on the Mexican border, is only about ten miles west of the Pecos River.) A hanging judge, Bean is less interested in evidence, legality, and justice, than in the cash in his victims' possession or the value of their horses and outfits. To be accused is to be convicted, and Bean confiscates the victim's money and possessions for "court costs." Into his lair comes Cole Hardin (Gary Cooper), a rootless drifter captured by Bean's men and unjustly accused of stealing a horse. This is a hanging offense, and the undertaker gallops up with his hearse, ready like a vulture for its prey. During the jury's deliberations, Jane-Ellen Mathews (Doris Davenport), daughter of a homesteading farmer, comes to town to denounce the judge for having his cattlemen harass the homesteaders in the area. She condemns Bean's travesties of justice and sympathizes with Hardin's plight, but believes he is as good as dead.

Meanwhile, Hardin discovers Bean's one soft spot, an idolatry of Lily Langtry (Lillian Bond), the British actress known as the "Jersey Lily" and the reigning beauty of the day. In her honor, Bean has renamed the town "Langtry." Hardin persuades Bean that he knows Lily personally and that he has a lock of her hair, which he will give to Bean, but that he unfortunately does not carry the lock with him. Accordingly, although the "jury" has convicted him, Bean postpones the execution. Sizing up each other, the two men develop a grudging admiration for each other, and Bean celebrates their temporary alliance with a bottle apiece of a local rot-gut whiskey called "Rub of the Brush." The next morning, they are horribly hungover, but Hardin manages to get up first and ride off. Fearful of being betrayed and losing

Lily's lock, Bean gallops after him, leaps onto Hardin's horse, and knocks him sprawling into the sand. Fortunately, Hardin has taken the precaution to steal Bean's revolver, and he persuades him that he has merely gone to get the lock of hair, though his real plan is to move on to California.

Hardin's first stop is at the Mathews farm, where Jane-Ellen is startled to see him alive. Her father induces her to persuade Hardin to join the farmers in their fight against Bean's cattlemen. She is embarrassed to have to flirt with him, but they are genuinely attracted to each other. Wade Harper (Forrest Tucker), her frustrated suitor, denounces Hardin as a spy for Bean and forces him into a fist fight, which Hardin wins. He agrees to help the farmers and rides back to town to reason with Bean. Baited once more by the lock of hair, Bean promises to have the cattle rounded up and removed from the homesteaders' farms. Pretending he wants it for himself, Hardin snips off a lock of Jane-Ellen's hair and gives it to the Judge. Bean, however, breaks his promise and has his men burn the farmers' homes and fields. While trying to put out the fire, Jane-Ellen's father is killed, and the men turn against Hardin for allegedly deceiving them with false promises of peace.

Realizing that Bean must be stopped, Hardin has himself deputized, gets a warrant for the Judge, and goes to arrest him. He discovers that Bean has gone to Fort Davis to see Lily Langtry, who is there on tour. Wanting Lily all to himself, Bean has bought out the entire house. He is dressed in his Confederate uniform, takes the best seat, and waits eagerly for the show to begin. After the overture, the curtain rises to reveal Hardin on stage with his guns drawn. "I'm coming for you, Judge," he says. "Come a-shootin'," says Bean. As the orchestra dives for cover, the two men shoot it out in the empty theater. Bean is mortally wounded, but before he dies, Hardin takes him backstage to meet Lily Langtry. Bean kisses her hand, falls to the floor, and dies happy, his last vision being of the Jersey Lily.

Except for the conflict between the homesteaders and the cattlemen, *The Westerner* avoids most clichés of the genre. Most previous Westerns were shoot-'em-up action films designed for the adolescent mentality. Goldwyn and director William Wyler were determined to make a sophisticated, adult, psychological Western for a change. *The Westerner*, therefore, stresses characterization rather than action; the fist fight, the burning fields, and the final shoot-out provide some excitement, but audiences looking for another slam-bang adventure were disappointed. Director William Wyler had done his share of two-reel silent Westerns during his apprentice days, but *The Westerner* was his first major work in the genre (his only other Western was *The Big Country* in 1958). He directed at a deliberate pace, maintaining tension in the relationship between Hardin and Bean. René Jordan says Cooper was discouraged by his initial look at the screenplay, in which he would merely have been providing star assistance to Walter Brennan, who indisputably had the central role as the fabled Judge Roy Bean.

Brennan congratulated himself on having the juicier part, for which he won his third Academy Award as Best Supporting Actor. It is a mistake, however, to dismiss Cooper. Not only is his role the longer of the two, but also in *The Westerner*, he gave one of his most subtle performances. What makes the film work is the chemistry between Cooper and Brennan. Cooper underplays with a wry sense of humor that provides a necessary foil to the more flamboyant Judge. Without his contrasting role, the story becomes merely the history of a colorful but insignificant eccentric. When John Huston made *The Life and Times of Judge Roy Bean* in 1972 with Paul Newman in the title role, the project misfired, largely because Bean was magnified into a mythological figure. There was no normal protagonist for balance, and there was no central plot to hold his career together; instead, the narrative consisted of a series of vignettes spanning a generation. Newman's Bean became a symbol of authentic justice and of a West when there were giants in the earth. By contrast, William Wyler opted for an unglamorous realism. Brennan's Bean is a whiskey-voiced, stubble-bearded, vinegary old goat who spends most of the time in a flannel undershirt and baggy pants held up by suspenders. What passes for justice in his saloon-court is of the vigilante variety. He is more than a little mad, and there is a manic gleam in his eye. His redeeming traits are a crackerbarrel sense of humor, a feistiness, and his devotion to Lily Langtry. The latter has all the quality of courtly love; like a knight-errant with his lady's scarf on his helmet who challenges all comers to concede that she is the fairest in the world, Bean adores the "Jersey Lily" with a platonic purity and hangs anyone who dares suggest the slightest disrespect towards her. The incongruity of knightly veneration from such a scruffy source is part of the humor which makes up a good deal of the film.

Cooper likewise contributes a more quietly humorous characterization; the scene in which he snips a lock of hair from the farmer's daughter and the later one in which he reluctantly parts with it to the eager Judge are masterpieces of comic underplaying. If Brennan's Judge Roy Bean is a legendary figure, so too Cooper's Cole Hardin is an archetypal Western hero—like Shane, he has no past, comes from nowhere, owns only his horse and outfit, and becomes involved only reluctantly with the settlers who are trying to put down roots. Cooper plays Hardin with consummate assurance; a decade later, when Clifton Webb was to do a Cooper imitation in *Dreamboat* (1952), he asked Cooper what film to study, and Cooper advised *The Westerner*.

Cooper and Brennan made such an effective team that they did six films together; the others are *The Cowboy and the Lady* (1938), *Meet John Doe* (1940), *Sergeant York* (1941), *Pride of the Yankees* (1942), and *Task Force* (1949), but they were at their best together in *The Westerner*, where Cooper's quiet reserve and perceptive understanding of human nature balanced Brennan's garrulous and basically childish Judge. It is the combination of appealing and appalling traits in Bean and the friendship/antagonist relationship between him and Hardin that gives the film its tension and provides a richly ambiguous texture. The Old West itself was simultaneously colorful, adventurous, dangerous, dingy, and dull; and *The Westerner* captures this paradox as few films have done.

William Wyler's direction constructs an authentic blend of legend and unglamorous realism. The secondary players lend admirable support. Stage actor Fred Stone and newcomers Forrest Tucker and Dana Andrews are in their movie debuts; and as Jane-Ellen, Doris Davenport (in her only film role) is appealing, with a mixture of wistful shyness and spunky indignation. In too many Western films the heroines were spoiled by wearing thick lipstick, elegant gowns, and fancy coiffures; for instance, Calamity Jane in *The Plainsman* never has her lipstick smeared, even when being tortured by the Cheyenne Indians. Doris Davenport, however, is refreshingly free from makeup and is dressed like a working farm girl. None of the men wears a fancy costume; they are all dressed in working clothes that show hard wear. The details throughout were so authentic that James Basevi's art direction was nominated for an Academy Award. Stuart N. Lake was also nominated for his original story. Gregg Toland contributed strikingly artistic cinematography, but Wyler was dissatisfied with Dmitri Tiomkin's score and had Alfred Newman rewrite it, though Tiomkin received sole credit. Perhaps because of its minimal action and offbeat humor, *The Westerner* was less successful than the big-budget Westerns of 1939, but it holds up better and is one of the most durable classics in the genre.

Robert E. Morsberger

WHAT PRICE HOLLYWOOD?

Released: 1932
Production: David O. Selznick for RKO/Radio
Direction: George Cukor
Screenplay: Jane Murfin, Gene Fowler, Rowland Brown, and Ben Markson; based on a screen story by Adela Rogers St. John
Cinematography: Charles Rosher
Editing: Jack Kitchin
Running time: 91 minutes

Principal characters:

Mary Evans	Constance Bennett
Maximilian Carey	Lowell Sherman
Lonny Borden	Neil Hamilton
Julius Saxe	Gregory Ratoff

Hollywood has always liked to portray itself on the screen; the mood of such self-portraits ranges from the nostalgic *Singin' in the Rain* (1952) to the sardonic *Sunset Boulevard* (1950). Affectionately satirical, *What Price Hollywood?* falls somewhere between these two extremes. Its theme, the contrast between two careers, is a popular one, but seldom has it been so well realized.

While working as a waitress at the Brown Derby Restaurant, Mary Evans (Constance Bennett) meets Max Carey (Lowell Sherman), a famous and successful movie director. While he is tipsy he invites her to accompany him to a Hollywood premiere, and afterwards she sees him safely home. As a reward he gives her a bit part in one of his films. Though she has only one line of dialogue ("Hello, Buzzy, you haven't proposed to me yet tonight"), her performance is seen by an important producer, Julius Saxe (Gregory Ratoff), who realizes she has some talent and decides to make her a star. As Mary's career blossoms (she is publicized as "America's Pal"), Carey's declines because of his alcoholism. Saxe has tried to persuade him to quit drinking and has given him jobs but now he can no longer rely on Carey's work. Finally, Saxe's patience is exhausted, and despite Mary's pleading, he refuses to hire Carey again. Through all this Mary remains loyal to him, remembering that it was he who gave her a chance for stardom.

Meanwhile, Mary meets a wealthy polo player, Lonny Borden (Neil Hamilton), and after a stormy courtship, they are married despite Carey's gloomy prediction that a movie star's marriage never lasts. Saxe sees the wedding as a chance for more publicity for Mary and arranges for it to be a big media event. As a result, Mary is mobbed by the crowd as she and Lonny attempt to leave the church, and she has to be rushed back inside, torn and disheveled. Lonny and Mary are tired and overwhelmed by the photographers, the reporters, and the crowd, but Saxe is happy because the wedding "broke all house records for this church." He then tells Mary that her honeymoon will have to be postponed to film more scenes for her latest picture.

During the shooting of Mary's film we see a busy set with every member of the cast and crew active. Only Lonny, sitting on the sidelines reading a magazine, has nothing to do. When Carey finds Mary talking to Lonny instead of listening to his directions, he becomes very irritated and tells him to "let me direct Miss Evans, and you be Mr. Evans." At a script conference Lonny is again the outsider. His advice is ignored, and as Saxe, Mary, and Carey argue heatedly, he walks away from the group, unnoticed.

In the most effective satirical scene in the film, a gossip columnist comes to interview Mary and Lonny about their marriage. Mary has to cajole an embarrassed and uneasy Lonny into talking to the columnist, who overhears their heated argument. As Mary clings closely to Lonny, the columnist asks them several impertinent questions about their love life—"Do you have separate bedrooms?" "How far should a wife go to keep her husband's love?" Lonny is outraged and he replies sarcastically to all of her questions, finally stalking out of the room.

The film deftly but affectionately mocks Hollywood, yet makes it plain that its inhabitants are loyal, compassionate, and kind. These qualities are contrasted with those of Lonny's friends, whom Mary calls "stuffed shirts" (although we never see any of them). Lonny, on the other hand, thinks Mary's professional friends are cheap and vulgar and does not want her to associate with them socially.

Mary and Lonny's marriage slowly disintegrates, and its end is hastened by the appearance one night of a drunken Carey at their house. Upset and disgusted by this intrusion into their private life, Lonny wants Carey to leave, but Mary refuses to make him go, saying she cannot let him down. Angrily, Lonny leaves and goes ahead with divorce proccedings, not knowing that Mary is pregnant.

We next see Mary a year later playing with her son, Jackie, and refusing to share custody of the child with Lonny. Her career continues to be successful (she has even won an award for Best Actress) while Max Carey's sinks lower and lower. Carey is reduced to hanging around the set on Mary's pictures. Finally she gets word that he is in jail and immediately goes to bail him out. She takes him to her house, determined that this time she will persuade him to remain sober; but Carey has declined too far to be rehabilitated, and in self-disgust he shoots himself. In the ensuing scandal, Mary is questioned by the police, vilified by the public, and hounded by reporters; her films are even banned. Finally, she flees to France because she is afraid Lonny will try to get custody of their son. All of this is conveyed by a quick montage of newspaper headlines which give the impression that Mary is being crushed by relentless forces beyond her control. The film ends quickly and happily, however, as Mary is reunited with Lonny. He also delivers a message from

Saxe saying that he has a new story that will make a great comeback vehicle for Mary.

The film's major limitation is the divided focus of its second half. After establishing that Lonny and Mary live in two different worlds, the film, instead of concentrating on their marriage and its problems, concentrates on the declining career of Max Carey and his relationship with Mary. David O. Selznick, the producer of *What Price Hollywood?*, has said he wished he had been able to spend more time on the script. The shifting back and forth between Carey and Lonny leaves Lonny's character somewhat undeveloped, and his relationship to Mary is merely sketched in, although it is done cleverly and deftly. Despite this problem, director George Cukor handled the script's limitations and his actors so expertly that *What Price Hollywood?* became his first major screen success.

There are numerous clever touches in the way Cukor treats some significant scenes. In the first of these, we see Mary rehearsing over and over the line she has been given in Carey's picture until she finds the right note of brittle sophistication. Later, when Saxe and Carey are watching the daily rushes, Mary blunders into the projection room, is thrown out by Saxe, and watches her scene from the projectionist's booth. She is as amazed as Saxe at her image on the screen, and when he tells her he is going to make her a star, her dazed reaction is, "I'm in pictures." Quickly and adroitly it shows how this particular star is born.

Cukor nicely balances such lighter moments as these with the more dramatic scenes. The suicide of Max Carey is particularly well handled. In the hands of Cukor and actor Lowell Sherman, Carey is a sympathetic, witty alcoholic who never asks for pity, and especially not for Mary's pity. After Mary rescues him from jail and takes him to her house, he tells her he is dead inside, no longer the man she once knew, and that his career is finished. After she leaves the room, he accidently discovers a revolver in a desk drawer. He then sees his reflection in the mirror over the desk and flinches at the sight of his haggard, unshaven face. Underscoring the contrast with his former debonair, robust appearance is an old photograph of him on the desk below the mirror. As he stares at himself in the mirror with an expression of revulsion on his face, he hears a whirring sound like angry bees, and, his brain bursting, he shoots himself. As he falls, quick glimpses of his past life flash before his eyes.

The outstanding performance of the film is Lowell Sherman as Max Carey, but Constance Bennett as Mary Evans is also remarkable. As a waitress she is bright and vivacious and pretty enough to make her break in pictures credible. As a movie star she is the epitome of glamorous sophistication and elegant chic. She makes us believe that she does indeed have that certain "something."

Sometimes *What Price Hollywood?* is remembered merely as the inspiration for the original *A Star Is Born* (1937), and sometimes too much emphasis is given to the fact that the Max Carey character is supposedly based on the careers of silent film director Marshall "Mickey" Neilan and actor John Barrymore. While these are interesting sidelights, the film endures as a well-directed, well-acted work that stands on its own merits.

Julia Johnson

WHITE HEAT

Released: 1949
Production: Louis F. Edelman for Warner Bros.
Direction: Raoul Walsh
Screenplay: Ivan Goff and Ben Roberts; based on a story of the same name by Virginia Kellogg
Cinematography: Sid Hickox
Editing: Murray Cutter
Running time: 114 minutes

Principal characters:

Cody Jarrett	James Cagney
Verna Jarrett	Virginia Mayo
Hank Fallon/Vic Pardo	Edmond O'Brien
Ma Jarrett	Margaret Wycherly
Big Ed Somers	Steve Cochran

Cue magazine said of *White Heat*, "For two hours . . . you are subjected to an unending procession of what is probably the most gruesome aggregation of brutalities ever presented upon the motion picture screen. . . ." *Cue* obviously was not ready for the cinema's fresh trend of presenting the psychotic side of movie villains, a trend largely begun by Warner Bros. with *White Heat*. This classic gangster saga boasts James Cagney's chilling, fascinating screen work as the epileptic Mama's boy, Cody Jarrett. Indeed, the film remains a disturbing, unnerving experience today, even after a full troupe of drooling maniacs have troubled moviegoers' nightmares for the past three decades.

Cagney had departed from Warner Bros. after his Oscar-winning triumph in 1942's *Yankee Doodle Dandy* to form his own movie production company with his brother William. Even as he produced such films as *Johnny Come Lately* (1943), *Blood on the Sun* (1945), and *The Time of Your Life* (1948), starring in each as well, Warner Bros. never surrendered hopes of luring their prized attraction back to the Burbank lot. *White Heat*, based on a story by Virginia Kellogg (who also wrote the script of the 1950 asylum thriller *Caged* starring Eleanor Parker), proved to be the property that finally brought Cagney back. He was aware that the time was ripe for a return to the screen of full-blooded gangsters. Audiences were tiring of postwar musicals and romantic froth, and Edward G. Robinson's Johnny Rocco of Warners' 1948 *Key Largo* had scored so powerfully that a new parade of flamboyant hoodlums was certainly inevitable. Cagney signed a new contract with Warners, and *White Heat* went into production under the direction of Cagney's friend Raoul Walsh, who had earlier directed the star in Warners' 1939 hit *The Roaring Twenties*.

White Heat relates the tragedy of Cody Jarrett (James Cagney). He appears to have everything a thriving hoodlum could want: a successful hijacking/train robbery career; a shapely blonde girl friend named Verna (Virginia Mayo); and a streak of sadism that serves him well in his craft (when a captive he is carrying in his trunk complains that it is stuffy, for instance, Cody responds with "I'll give ya' a little air"—and fires bullet holes into the trunk). However, it is soon revealed that Cody also has two tragic problems: epilepsy, which plagues him with horrible fits, and a total emotional dependency on his mother (Margaret Wycherly). In one very famous scene, Cody says "Always thinking about your Cody, aren't ya'?" as he sits on his mother's lap, craving her solace and depending on her exhortation, "Top of the world, son!"

When Cody turns state's evidence in a minor hold-up in order to enjoy prison protection for a time, "T-Man" Hank Fallon (Edmond O'Brien) is placed in his cell to collect information about the murderer, and slowly manages to win Cody's trust. Then, one day in the commissary, Cody sees a freshly incarcerated hoodlum at his table. Thinking to get information about his mother's health, he passes the whispered question along the table. The word "dead" comes back. In a truly stunning piece of acting, Cody goes berserk, crying and bleating over the commisary table like a mad animal, taking on a number of guards before finally being subdued.

His sanity rapidly disintegrating, Cody soon effects a prison break; Hank joins him. Cody plots to hold up the payroll office of a chemical plant, and at this point, Hank informs his fellow T-Men of the gangster's latest scheme. The climax of the film was shot in Torrance, California, amidst monstrous gasoline tanks, and it provides one of the more thrilling episodes in cinema. Cody, taking sanctuary atop a tank, goes completely insane, giggling madly as the squad of T-Men scramble in the night in their efforts to apprehend him. "Made it, Ma!" screams the exultant Cody—"Top of the world!"—before a T-Man bullet explodes the tank into an inferno. "Cody Jarrett," eulogizes Hank. "Finally got to the top of the world—and it blew up right in his face."

A Max Steiner score starkly emphasizes the story's melodrama, and the entire cast is superb: Virginia Mayo, a sashaying delight as Verna, Edmond O'Brien, who generates a tense excitement as the undercover "T-Man," and Margaret Wycherly, grand as Cagney's mother. Director Walsh, ever a supreme craftsman, kept the film moving at a wild pace, speeding toward the now-classic climax.

However, *White Heat* owes its true power to Cagney. Fifty years old, heavier, jowlier, yet with all the fire of his *The Public Enemy* (1931), the star was at his peak of dramatic power, and his Cody Jarrett is one of the screen's most unforgettable characters. Only rarely had the cinema penetrated the leer of a villain to examine the psychological abnormalities responsible for his actions, and only a handful of incisive actors—Charles Laughton in *Mutiny on the Bounty* (1935), Robert Montgomery in *Night Must Fall* (1937), and Laird Cregar in *I Wake Up Screaming* (1941) and *The Lodger* (1944)—had succeeded in showing audiences a glimpse of the neuroses that can produce sadism. Here Cagney explodes as Jarrett, graphically conveying the character's assorted manias in a performance that never loses its power. Of all the heavies in Cagney's gallery of performances, from the wolfish Tom Powers of *The Public Enemy* to the pompous Captain of *Mister Roberts* (1955), none seem as at odds with the true, literate gentleman farmer Cagney as does *White Heat*'s manic Cody Jarrett.

While many ensuing films have emulated *White Heat*'s focus on the psychotic criminal mind, the film survives as unmatched melodrama. Considering the many Hollywood efforts that have sought to blame the wrath of criminals on the society that suffers at their expense, *White Heat* remains a refreshing, stark cinematic statement which proposes that society's most vicious public offenders are not created by their environments, but by the personal demons of their own minds.

Gregory William Mank

WHO'S AFRAID OF VIRGINIA WOOLF?

Released: 1966
Production: Ernest Lehman for Warner Bros.
Direction: Mike Nichols
Screenplay: Ernest Lehman; based on the play of the same name by Edward Albee
Cinematography: Haskell Wexler (AA) and Harry Stradling
Editing: Sam O'Steen
Art direction: Richard Sylbert (AA); set decoration, George James Hopkins (AA)
Costume design: Irene Sharaff (AA)
Running time: 130 minutes

Principal characters:
Martha .... Elizabeth Taylor (AA)
George .... Richard Burton
Nick .... George Segal
Honey .... Sandy Dennis (AA)

The excellence and popularity of *Who's Afraid of Virginia Woolf?* came from the fortunate combination of a great and justly famous modern American play, two highly publicized stars, and the film debut of a talented young theatrical director. Written by Edward Albee, the play won the New York Drama Critics Circle Award and the Tony Award for the 1962-1963 season. Besides its long Broadway run, it played all over the country, but many believed that it could not be made into a film because of the frankness of its language. Nevertheless, Jack Warner of Warner Bros. bought the play and signed Ernest Lehman, who had adapted *West Side Story* and *The Sound of Music* for the screen, to write the screenplay and produce the film.

Mike Nichols, who had first made his name as part of the comedy team of Nichols and May and then gone on to direct Broadway plays, was hired as the director, and Richard Burton and Elizabeth Taylor, whose romance had produced reams of publicity but no noteworthy films (*The V.I.P.'S*, 1963, and *The Sandpiper*, 1965, followed *Cleopatra*, 1963), were chosen to star in the film. Finally two other crucial decisions were made: to shoot the film in black-and-white and to make no significant changes in the play.

As the film opens, we see the moon above a college campus. Under the credits two figures walk through the deserted campus—George (Richard Burton), a history professor, and Martha (Elizabeth Taylor), his wife, returning home from a party given by her father, the president of the college. George is relieved that the party is over, but when they get home he finds that Martha has invited a couple over for drinks. What happens during the rest of the night is a shock to the guests, Nick and Honey, though it is all too familiar to George. Nick (George Segal), a good-looking new professor in the biology department, expects that a social visit with George and Martha will do his career no harm. Immediately, however, he and Honey (Sandy Dennis) find that it is not going to be an ordinary evening. As they enter, they find George and Martha in an argument. As the night progresses, they find themselves drawn into that fight—sometimes willingly, sometimes not—until at the end Nick and Honey have suffered more psychic damage than have George and Martha. The love-hate relationship of the older couple is manifested in games of verbal attack and humiliation which culminate in Martha's taking Nick to bed and then in George's destruction of the imaginary child he and Martha have used as a weapon throughout the night. From the very beginning of the film Martha and George have made strange references to their son. Finally we realize that he is imaginary and that he has been created long ago as a weapon in their continuing battle with each other. George destroys the son by announcing that he has died.

Who's Afraid of Virginia Woolf? is about truth and illusion. Nearly every statement, whether about matters of "fact" or of opinion, is suspect. We do not know whether the statements of George and Martha are meant to hide or reveal truth. When George talks about Martha's stepmother, Nick remarks that Martha has not mentioned a stepmother. "Maybe it isn't true," George replies matter-of-factly, and throughout the film he and Martha keep Nick and Honey guessing about matters both small and large in nature until Nick says in exasperation that he cannot tell when they are lying and when they are not. He is not supposed to be able to, they tell him, but even Martha, an expert at the games, finds herself caught when George announces that their imaginary son has been killed in an automobile accident. They had, as George says, been using the son as a bean bag, but Martha had not realized that she had left herself open for George to produce a new illusion (the automobile accident) to destroy the old one (the son).

The ambitious Nick finds himself in a world more complex than he can handle. Although the battle between George and Martha embarrasses him, at first he thinks he can keep out of it and remain in control since George is ineffectual and Martha is obviously attracted to Nick. He does not worry about sharing confidences with George, and he does not worry about enjoying Martha's humiliation of her husband. He discovers, however, that he is neither outside the battle nor in control; both Martha and George use him in their battle with each other, and when it suits them, they unite against him. What he has told George, he finds, is perfect ammunition for George to use against him when the game changes from "humiliate the host" to "get the guests." Throughout the evening he has failed to realize the significance of things until it is too late; therefore, when he finally understands, at the end of the night, that the son is imaginary, he seizes on the one bit of insight and says repeatedly, "I think I understand this."

The entire play is set in George and Martha's living room, but, as is usual in adaptations, more settings were used in the film, including several rooms in the house, the back and front yards, a car, and a roadhouse. Despite these changes in setting, the dialogue of the play is virtually unchanged. In one scene, for example, Honey says that she wants to dance, and George puts a record on the phonograph; in the film, however, the scene starts with the four in a car. When she sees a roadhouse, Honey says she wants to dance, so George suddenly stops the car, and they go in. The scene continues in the roadhouse and then outside in the parking lot with nearly the same dialogue that was used in the play. This sequence is probably the weakest part of the adaptation because it tries too hard to be cinematic, with the result that the close-ups of such things as the car's brake pedal, the overhead shot of Honey dancing, and the dramatic lighting in the parking lot get in the way of the material rather than enhance it.

Theatrical directors working in film are often expert at getting good performances from the actors and less expert at using such cinematic resources as effective camera position and editing. This is true to a great extent of Mike Nichols. Although he learned the techniques of cinematic directing quickly enough to win the Academy Award for *The Graduate* the next year, in *Who's Afraid of Virginia Woolf?* he shows an uncertainty in his use of close-ups. In the best scenes he has the actors moving and positioned well and keeps the camera far enough back to show more than one character or the character in his or her surroundings. In his worst scenes he uses close-ups pointlessly, such as showing a glass being filled, or to overemphasize something. He did, however, elicit from Elizabeth Taylor as Martha what is arguably the best acting performance of her career, and under his direction, Richard Burton gives a fine, modulated delineation of George. George Segal as Nick and Sandy Dennis as Honey do well in their less demanding roles. It is notable that Nichols presented two college professors without resorting in any way to the stereotype of the absent-minded "egghead."

The overall accomplishment of Mike Nichols and Ernest Lehman in transferring this shattering emotional drama to the screen is masterful. Despite the few visual lapses, the film is gripping, moving, and ultimately memorable for the power of its language and characterization realized in the fine performances of Richard Burton and Elizabeth Taylor, well supported by George Segal and Sandy Dennis. It is easy to see why Edward Albee, who wrote the play but had no hand in the film, was pleased with it and why it received five Academy Awards. Surely few playwrights have had their stage lines so closely adhered to in a film.

Timothy W. Johnson

THE WILD BUNCH

Released: 1969
Production: Phil Feldman for Minor-Seven Arts, Inc.; released by Warner Bros.
Direction: Sam Peckinpah
Screenplay: Walon Green and Sam Peckinpah; based on a story by Walon Green and Roy N. Sickner
Cinematography: Lucien Ballard
Editing: Louis Lombardo
Music: Jerry Fielding
Running time: 148 minutes

Principal characters:

Pike Bishop	William Holden
Deke Thornton	Robert Ryan
Dutch Engstrom	Ernest Borgnine
Sykes	Edmond O'Brien
Lyle Gorch	Warren Oates
Tector Gorch	Ben Johnson
Angel	Jaime Sanchez
Coffer	Strother Martin
T.C.	L. Q. Jones
Mapache	Emilio Fernandez
Pat Harrigan	Albert Dekker

In the late 1960's, the violence that had been implicit and muted in two of the classical genres of American movies—the gangster film and the Western—became for the first time graphic and visual. A decade later, it is easy to forget the controversy these films aroused at the time of their release. The mold of the classical gangster film cracked first, with the 1967 Arthur Penn/Warren Beatty production of *Bonnie and Clyde*. Two years later, *The Wild Bunch* not only accomplished for the Western what *Bonnie and Clyde* had done for the gangster genre, but it possibly exceeded the earlier film both in its claim to have rewritten the national epic and in the calculated sensationalism of its violence. Writer-director Sam Peckinpah was widely considered to have glorified all that the Western had to that time repressed. In the words of *New York Times* critic Vincent Canby, who called the film "the first truly interesting American-made western in years," Peckinpah had "turn[ed] the genre inside out." *The Wild Bunch* contains a theme which Peckinpah developed in his earlier, more traditional work and which is implicit in the genre: that of a way of life coming to an end, and of the Westerner dying with the frontier. Also evident is the director's fascination with the choreographed beauty of violence, which Peckinpah has gone on to develop in many of his subsequent films. The film examines the nature of heroism, which had not been attempted by the Western in any significant sense before. Furthermore, it depicts heroism as a quality rendered obsolete by an increasingly corrupt world, and made dangerous by the spread of technology.

The film begins with the Wild Bunch holding up a bank in a desert town while the railroad has its bounty hunters waiting in ambush. The gang spies the trap midway through the robbery, and as the town temperance union coincidentally marches unaware down the street, the bunch makes their break using them as a shield. The trap is sprung anyway. In the slow-motion blood ballet that follows, some gang members are killed and some are abandoned, as the decimated gang takes refuge in Mexico. The bounty hunters follow in pursuit. They are headed by Deke Thornton (Robert Ryan), once the closest friend of Wild Bunch leader Pike Bishop (William Holden), until Pike had abandoned him in the face of oncoming lawmen. Now, in order to win parole, Thornton must bring Pike back.

The gunfight's setting in the town is a harbinger of one of the prevailing themes of *The Wild Bunch*: the frontier is closed. It is, in fact, 1913, and in entering Mexico, the bunch knowingly is entering a three-sided conflict between Pancho Villa's rebels, the Mexican establishment embodied by a corrupt warlord named Mapache (Emilio Fernandez), and the United States government, which is calling out the army to defend the border against Villa's raids.

The gang chooses to work for Mapache. For $10,000, they will steal a shipment of arms from a United States Army supply train. Although Thornton is aboard, the raid is a success. The bunch stands off Mapache's troops who have come to kill them and then claim the arms without making payment. Afterwards, they trade the guns for money in a pre-arranged rendezvous. As a result, Mapache apprehends Angel (Jaime Sanchez), a young Mexican member of the Wild Bunch whose village Mapache has ravaged. Mapache accuses Angel, correctly, of having taken a portion of the shipment to arm the rebels. Meanwhile, still pursued by Thornton, the Bunch must seek refuge in Mapache's village. There, in drunken debauch, Mapache tortures Angel. This action Pike finally cannot abide. The four remaining gang members offer to return their money for Angel. The drunken Mapache produces Angel but slits his throat. Enraged, Pike and Dutch Engstrom (Ernest Borgnine) kill Mapache. In the ensuing climactic gunfight, the gang uses the stolen armaments—a machine gun, grenades, and explosives—to decimate the army and the village before they themselves finally succumb to gunfire. Thornton and the bounty hunters claim the bodies, but Thornton elects to stay and fight with the rebels, who have rescued Sykes (Edmund O'Brien).

Beginning with the freeze-frame credits which open the picture, Peckinpah's visual strategy is to present the bunch in a relentlessly heroic posture. Many of the longshots are stylized with the characters facing the camera as in formal nineteenth century photographs. Idealized, low-angle close-ups abound. In effect, Peckinpah's first three shots establish a child's point of view. At key moments at the beginning, at the first shootout, and at the gang's first rendezvous, reaction shots of children are intercut. Their hero-worshiping and their objective indifference (they are shown torturing a scorpion at the opening of the film) are both attitudes the audience is induced to share. The limits of this vision are underscored in the dialogue. "You have no eyes," Angel tells the Gorch Brothers (Warren Oates and Ben Johnson), two gang members. "I can't see, but I can ride," says a wounded gang member as he drops from his horse. He turns his face upward; it is covered with blood. He asks Pike to kill him; Pike complies.

The bunch is blinded by blood and Peckinpah's triumph is to manipulate the audience so that they share this viewpoint; his montage ranks with the classic Russian ones as among the most Manichaean in cinema, as he subtly makes the audience share in the experience of transforming humans into targets. During the first shootout, the camera is placed inside a store window as a gang member riding outside is shot and smashes through the glass, toppling three mannikins. Later, as one abandoned half-wit gang member lies dying inside a bank, he sees three townspeople gawking at him from outside the window. He curses and shoots them. The scene is made to be amusing in a macabre way; it is shot from the same angle as the earlier shot, and the subliminal association provides distance to the action. Similarly, the audience is asked to contemplate with equanimity and even enthusiasm the bodies that are sent flying by the machine gun in the final shootout. In an earlier scene, when the gun is presented to Mapache, his men fire it with no knowledge of how it works. Crockery shatters and people leap for cover. It is a comic scene that paves the way for the establishment of distance at the climax.

The absurdist heroics of *The Wild Bunch* provide settings for good performances. William Holden and Robert Ryan, in particular, played their first good roles in years, and make the most of them. In the area of character acting, the lowlife performances of Warren Oates, Ben Johnson, and Edmond O'Brien are particularly notable. Also significant is the whining depravity of Strother Martin in the role that established him as perhaps the last of the old-style character actors. The film is also distinguished by Lucien Ballard's cinematography and Jerry Fielding's tension-heightening score. The film's hero, however, remains Sam Peckinpah, whose subsequent films have demonstrated that he may possess the most comprehensive command of the resources of cinema of any American director since Orson Welles.

Harold Meyerson

WINCHESTER '73

Released: 1950
Production: Aaron Rosenberg for Universal-International
Direction: Anthony Mann
Screenplay: Borden Chase and Robert L. Richards; based on a story by Stuart N. Lake
Cinematography: William Daniels
Editing: Edward Curtiss
Art direction: Bernard Herzbrun and Nathan Juran
Running time: 92 minutes

Principal characters:

Lin McAdam	James Stewart
Dutch Henry Brown	Stephen McNally
Lola Manners	Shelley Winters
Waco Johnnie Dean	Dan Duryea
High Spade	Millard Mitchell
Steve Miller	Charles Drake
Joe Lamont	John McIntire
Wyatt Earp	Will Geer
Sergeant Wilkes	Jay C. Flippen
Young Bull	Rock Hudson

The title of this film, *Winchester '73*, refers to a rifle of unexcelled precision, nearly perfect in its workmanship. A rare weapon, it cannot be purchased but belongs rather to the man whose aim is truest. The story begins on a Fourth of July when scores of hopeful marksmen descend upon Dodge City for a rifle match. The contest eventually narrows down to two men who are arch-rivals—Lin McAdam (James Stewart) and Dutch Henry Brown (Stephen McNally). They match each other shot for shot until McAdam wins the prize rifle by shooting a stamp out of a coin in midair. Brown then steals the rifle, and from this point on a series of incidents describe its passage from one character to the next. A parallel thematic motif to the passage of the rifle from person to person is McAdam's obsessive search for Brown, but only at the end of the film is the deeper motive of this quest revealed: the two men are brothers and Brown had murdered their father. By chance the gun finally finds its way to Brown just before the two men act out their final battle, alone upon a barren escarpment.

The story moves in a circular pattern, with brother fighting brother at the film's beginning and end. Seemingly episodic, the remainder of the film is linked together by the rifle. More than a mere plot device, the rifle exists as a symbol through which a network of interweaving motifs emerge. In turn, each of these episodes suggests the film's central incident of the patricide and sibling rivalry. In addition to the narrative associations, which are both similar and yet varied, the film is rich in visual motifs which lend themselves to ambiguous interpretation.

The Western, particularly when it takes the form of the quest film, has often been likened to the tales of medieval romance. The Western hero is often guided in his actions by a sort of chivalric code, and *Winchester '73* is interesting to consider in this respect. The contest for the rifle is comparable to a knightly joust, with McAdam's victory almost magical in its vindication of virtue. The rifle itself is almost a mythical object, part Holy Grail and part Excalibur. Like some magical charm it can nearly be said to possess a life of its own, cursing each of its wrongful owners.

The rifle's central place in the film is demonstrated through the relationships between the two men and their father. Although the film begins *in media res*, much can be inferred from bits of dialogue and action, and from a pattern of relationships which mirror those of the two brothers and their father. The first reference to the father, purposely vague, comes during the shooting match when Lin explains that he and Dutch were both taught by the same man, who did not tell them what to shoot at. The father, as the provider of gun lore in the first half of the statement, is qualified in the second half by an implied irresponsibility. This is just one key to the film's ambiguity.

Three characters in the film figure as patriarchal substitutes. The first of these is Wyatt Earp (Will Geer), portrayed here as a much older man than usual. As much a figure of myth as history, Earp can be often understood as a personification of the establishment of civilized order in the frontier. In his role as marshal, Earp has authority over the two brothers since he controls events in Dodge City. He also presides over the contest and awards the rifle to McAdam. Ironically, he had earlier taken away the guns of all the people in town, including those of Lin and Dutch. The validity of his judgment is later proven when the two brothers first meet. Instinctively they both slap at their empty holsters in violent but impotent rage. In this scene, Earp occupies a central position between the two in the same manner that a family photograph later reveals the father to occupy. Yet, even Wyatt Earp is unable to prevent Dutch from stealing Lin's rifle within his own town, and this particular scene, as is typical with Anthony Mann's direction, is adept at conveying the brutality and pain of close physical violence.

The father-figure becomes even more ambiguous in the darker person of Joe Lamont (John McIntire). A renegade who sells whiskey and guns to the Indians, Joe cynically excuses his actions by saying they use his rifles for hunting game. He likens the Indians to children who would not betray their father, whom he sees as himself. He wins the Winchester from Dutch in a poker game and, in turn, loses it when he is killed by one of his "children," Young Bull (Rock Hudson). This action in itself is significant, but it is given added emphasis by having Dutch shoot the already dead Lamont in the back shortly after. It is as if Dutch were, symbolically, killing his own father a second time.

A third patriarch is Sergeant Wilkes (Jay C. Flippen), an authority figure similar to Earp whose command consists of a batch of young recruits over whom he rules with a genial but firm hand. In a battle with the Indians, McAdam saves the troop by killing their chief, Young Bull. The point is made that Wilkes's command would probably have been massacred without the repeating rifles, specifically Winchesters, of McAdam and his partner High Spade (Millard Mitchell). Young Bull epitomizes Dutch's anarchic impulses at a deep primeval level. His death, similar to that of Dutch, is implied to be necessary for the advancement of civilization, and the rifle plays a vital role here as well.

In the second half of the film, the idea of the rifle as a symbol of sexual potency emerges rather strongly. Included among the cavalry troop are two important characters—Steve Miller (Charles Drake) and Lola Manners (Shelley Winters), his fiancée. Earlier, Steve had lost his nerve during an Indian attack, abandoning Lola and running away. However, he does redeem himself somewhat during the battle, adding his repeating rifle, significantly an inferior Henry model, to those of Lin and High Spade. Lin leaves before the rifles are collected from among the slain, so Wilkes gives the Winchester to Steve as a reward for his help. Although Lola no longer loves Steve, she agrees to travel on with him; she has, in fact, begun to transfer her affections to Lin. They go to a farmhouse where Steve plans to meet with Waco Johnnie Dean (Dan Duryea) and his gang. Whether it is for Lola's sake or because of his newly found status as owner of the gun, Steve intends to measure up to the rifle by breaking with these outlaws. Unfortunately, he lacks the nerve to back up his new convictions, and Waco easily intimidates him.

The relationship between Waco and Steve mirrors that of the two brothers. Earlier in Dodge City, Dutch had taunted Lin by asking if he intended hunting squirrels with the rifle and ordering milk for him in the saloon. Similarly, Waco humiliates Steve by forcing him to serve coffee instead of Lola, even suggesting that he put on an apron. Waco also takes the Winchester away from Steve, forcing him to draw so that he can kill him. Essentially, Steve is unmanned, symbolically castrated by Waco; yet there is also something rather childish in all this behavior, similar to the older brother hurling the taunt of "sissy" at the younger. Not surprisingly, Waco takes Lola as well as the rifle with him.

Waco represents Dutch, only with an even more psychopathic streak. He is totally self-centered, watching his gang get gunned down as he sends them out the door, then leaving himself through another exit. Chased by a posse, when he gets to the farmhouse, his entrance is the most striking in the film. Gunfire can be heard from outside, and the camera makes a quick pan to the doorway, holding the shot for a moment as Waco enters, practically the physical incarnation of all the violence outside. His presence totally disrupts the uneasy domesticity of the house. When he joins Dutch and his gang, he passively gives the rifle to Dutch with every intent of getting it back at the first opportunity.

Dutch plans to rob a bank in a nearby town and sends Waco there to wait. Waco takes Lola with him, an action which proves to be his undoing since Lin and High Spade are there and become suspicious. The naked violence which Lin inflicts upon Waco is perhaps the most startling moment in the film. Usually easygoing and rational except where his brother is concerned, Lin's fierceness is unsettling, coming uncomfortably close to that of his brother. If Lin can be so easily provoked, one has to wonder if he is really all that different from Dutch. The manner in which the scene is staged recalls the earlier scene in which Dutch had stolen the rifle and beaten Lin.

After killing Waco, Lin chases after his brother alone. Up to this point, the terrain covered has been plains and gently rolling hills. Now, Lin and Dutch finally meet upon an almost sheer rock face, its jagged outlines reflecting their extreme mental states. Just as the landscape gives the feeling of a progressive bleakness, the situation is a return to the beginning, only this time their marksmanship is turned upon each other. McAdam's earlier comment about Brown's not being taught what to shoot at has ironically turned back upon itself—McAdam himself now hunting a man, his own brother, and killing him. With Brown's death, McAdam has placated his own personal Furies and has regained the rifle, although it has been at the expense of what family he has left. The ending infers that McAdam is now free to court and marry Lola, settling into civilized domesticity now that his quest is finished.

Within the Western genre it is often not difficult to detect personal conflicts as being symbolic of even broader social import. To a certain extent, the resolution of *Winchester '73* implies the bringing of civilization and order to an anarchic frontier. The film is ambiguous to the extent that the contrasting principles embodied in Lin and Dutch are seen as stemming from the same root—they both have the same "father." This conflict has an even deeper source that goes back in history to antecedents in Greek tragedy and the Bible. In this respect, the story of Cain and Abel would be relevant, the two sons—one good and one evil—relating back to the "original sin" of the father.

The themes found in *Winchester '73* can be found in the works of its two principal creators—writer Borden Chase and director Anthony Mann. Another film which Chase wrote, *Backlash* (1956), is very similar in its use of material. In that film the protagonist is pursuing the man who had murdered his father. His search leads him to the town which this same man and his gang are planning to raid. This man, in fact, turns out to be his own father, and the hero must choose between family loyalty or saving society from destruction. A relation between the two is earlier established in the similar way they both handle a gun. This film fails to the extent that its direction, by John

Sturges, has none of Mann's more forceful and epic style. Thus its interest remains primarily on the level of its script.

Two films which Mann made with other writers are particularly interesting for their reworking of similar material. *The Man from Laramie* (1955) is also a revenge story, the James Stewart character in that film searching for the man responsible for his brother's death. This leads him to two men who are also in a sense "brothers." The binding character in this film is a father. In *Man of the West* (1958), Link Jones can only reintegrate himself back into the social order after a series of trials which ends with him killing his evil adoptive father, Doc Tobin. This is by far Mann's masterpiece, the personal conflicts working themselves out against the visual text of a changing landscape. All of Mann's Westerns revolve around a central protagonist whose personal drives cast him in a role outside the social order.

Winchester '73 marked the first of five Westerns which Mann made with James Stewart. The relationship was mutually beneficial, Stewart's acting *persona* fitting in exceptionally well with the conceptions of the director. A good deal of the film's ambiguity relies upon previous expectations of Stewart as an actor, his basically good-natured character being tempered by a newfound toughness and hardness.

To some degree, *Winchester '73* can be criticized for a diffuseness dictated by its episodic framework. Although the central conflict can always be implied through other characters, it is less dramatically felt when McAdam and Brown are not present. Yet it is also, archetypally, the purest of the Mann Westerns. Lin has his faithful sidekick in High Spade, Waco Johnnie Dean's villainy is absolute, and the film itself covers a wide range of social conventions, from the conflict between Caucasian and Indian, to marauding outlaws. Although the themes found within this film would be worked out with even greater complexity and ambiguity later, *Winchester '73* is particularly significant in a study of the development of director Anthony Mann's work.

Mike Vanderlan

THE WINGS OF EAGLES

Released: 1957
Production: Charles Schnee for Metro-Goldwyn-Mayer
Direction: John Ford
Screenplay: Frank Fenton and William Wister Haines; based on the life and writings of Commander Frank W. Wead
Cinematography: Paul C. Vogel
Editing: Gene Ruggiero
Art direction: William A. Horning and Malcolm Brown
Costume design: Walter Plunkett
Music: Jeff Alexander
Running time: 111 minutes

Principal characters:

Frank W. "Spig" Wead	John Wayne
Carson	Dan Dailey
Minnie Wead	Maureen O'Hara
John Dodge	Ward Bond
John Dale Price	Ken Curtis
Admiral Moffett	Edmund Lowe
Herbert Allen Hazard	Kenneth Tobey
Lila Wead	Mimi Gibson
Doris Wead	Evelyn Rudie

The Wings of Eagles is one of John Ford's most enduring masterpieces. Although it is one of the most appreciated of the director's late works, it is one of the least understood. *The Wings of Eagles* is too often looked upon as simply an entertaining, moving, and brilliantly executed biography of the late naval commander, playwright, and screenwriter, Frank "Spig" Wead, yet the film is much more. Whatever its angle of vision, the film reveals with powerful insight and steady scrutiny the emotional but detached life of Spig Wead, who alternately personifies human frailties and strengths, failure and achievement. Credibility is established in the restraint, disarming poignancy, and mysterious reservoirs of strength captured by John Wayne. Wayne's role as Spig Wead is one of the best performances of his career.

The Wings of Eagles follows *The Searchers* (1956), filmed the previous year. To some extent, as in all the Ford-Wayne films, there are continuing patterns of themes, thoughts, and images which can be viewed simultaneously for their oneness and for their difference. The character of Spig in *The Wings of Eagles* can be related to that of Ethan in *The Searchers*; it is in obvious continuity and harmony with Ford's vision of the driven outsider. In *The Wings of Eagles*, Ford and Wayne move into a different realm in considering this archetype. Spig is seen as being both within and without the boundaries of society, belonging and yet ultimately not belonging to the Navy, to his comrades, to his beloved wife Min (Maureen O'Hara), or to his writing. Ethan is of the Old West and of the family tradition, although he is forever unsettled and apart, and there is a melancholy but satisfying conclusion to his odyssey. For Spig, however, there develops a constantly somber tone of immutability in his actions that culminates in an almost hopeless and heartbreaking feeling of alienation in the final scenes of the film.

What is truly masterful in *The Wings of Eagles* is the relatively simple execution of the story line. Ford is never heavy-handed, nor does he deliberately engage in a deep philosophical study that obscures the more immediately engaging qualities of the film. The mark of a master is to render the complex and universal into the simple and comprehensible. As in his previous films, Ford never sacrifices his first priority of being storyteller and entertainer. It is a film that engages both the wise and the unsophisticated viewer with levels of interest and methods of identification which strike a responsive chord in all who see it.

The narrative structure is classically direct and uncluttered. A young naval flier, Spig Wead, is impressively adventurous and happily married both to Min and to the Navy. He is reckless and fearless, coming through many mishaps without a scratch. But the death of his baby son scars him and haunts his marriage. He seeks escape from the heartache in greater service while Min waits. After five years of duty, he returns to his wife and two daughters as a more mature man who succeeds briefly in reconciling with Min, despite the feeling of estrangement his absence had created for both of them. Then, at the happiest of moments, tragedy strikes. Spig, who had piloted a plane solo before he could fly and emerged unscathed, trips on his daughter's skate and falls, breaking his neck.

The doctor's prognosis is grim, but the indomitable Spig finds another career in writing and learns to walk with crutches through determination and the support of his friend Carson (Dan Dailey), while Min keeps a distant, loyal vigil. Years after he was established himself as the successful playwright and screenwriter of such works as *Ceiling Zero*, the couple is about to reconcile for a second time when Pearl Harbor is attacked. Spig returns to duty at sea and works with jeep carriers in the Pacific; there, he throws himself into his work with such energy and passion that he brings on a heart condition. In the moment of his greatest naval success, the tragic paradox of the film is revealed: that Spig views his life as a personal failure. What he values most—Min and his daughters—may be lost to him, and he is incapacitated, unfit for duty, no longer able to serve. Alone in his cabin, he recalls through flashbacks the family and home he had scorned. Finally, he is transported by a high-wire cable chair to a vessel which will carry him to shore, and the film ends.

In the great Ford films, the balance between comedy and tragedy is a characteristically essential ingredient. In *The Wings of Eagles*, this balance is perfectly modulated, and the emotional reaction of the viewer is always in appropriate response to the action, even when a humorous moment is immediately replaced by a somber image. As the movie begins, for example, high-spirited Spig challenges his army rival Herbert Allen Hazard (Kenneth Tobey) to join him in a short solo flight. This incident begins a series of comic relief episodes of interservice rivalry between Navy and Army and permits the film to open in a daringly light mood. The irrepressible Spig climbs to the cockpit with daring bravado, neglecting to inform his passenger that he has never flown solo before. Pandemonium results. Spig's beautiful wife Min, dressed in becoming blue, pulls up in a red Stutz Bearcat as the plane lifts upward. She calls after him, running hip deep in the water and waving her blue parasol, her exhortations unheard. Moments later, the plane plunges into a pool at the Admiral's garden party, resulting in official reprimands.

In this hilarious opening sequence, we have learned of Spig's penchant for hell-raising and his seeming ability to escape mishap. Ford follows this sequence with one that stands in effective counterpoint. Finding their baby hot and feverish after a stroll, Min has summoned the doctor. Darkness is falling as Spig and a companion roar up the path in the Stutz Bearcat. The interior of the house is dimly lit, foreshadowing tragedy, and Min wears a white blouse and dark skirt which contribute to the fearful mood. A slightly intoxicated Spig slams the door and rushes to the infant, then paces the floor, shocked into sober reality. The gravity of his expression, his tender handling of the baby, and the suggestion of an unspoken prayer all prepare the audience for Min's anguished cry, "Spig!"

Ford has thus established the patterns with which he will tell Spig's story. That the death of the baby has a bitter effect on this marriage is implied in the images, but it is not explicitly stated. That home for Spig will always be a precarious place is already implicit. This separates the picture from the mainstream of Fordian thought in which home has been consistently depicted as a haven, as, for example, in *How Green Way My Valley* (1941) and *The Searchers*, and as a nostalgic cradle of happiness, removed from disharmony.

Ford also exercises a different direction in his treatment of women, a divergent track begun in *Rio Grande* (1950) and *The Quiet Man* (1952), both of which costarred Maureen O'Hara as the iron-willed but vulnerable woman whose onscreen chemistry with John Wayne is invaluable to the director. With a penetrating and compassionate eye, Ford enables us to predict the turbulent course this marriage will follow. As opposed to *Rio Grande*, in which the couple is separated more by the cavalry than by emotional conflict, it is Spig's own elusive nature as much as the Navy that deepens the gap in the relationship here. Min's emotions range from indulgence, patience, and devotion to skepticism, self-rejection, and despair. At the end she emerges with mature resignation and unconditional love.

After the death of the baby, Spig flees more intently into Navy service to compensate for his loss rather than staying close to Min. Ford follows him through a long tour of duty, intercut with uproarious peccadilloes between Navy and Army, one of which is an around-the-world flight. As Min and the girls sit in the semidarkness of a movie theater, the children recognize their father in a Movietone newsreel, where he is seen receiving a cup as leader of the winning Navy team. For Min, this image of Spig gives shattering insight into the emptiness of her life. She has gone through a period of living with images, interspersed with telephone calls and unkept promises. Spig's singleminded dedication to the Navy has forced her out and obliged her to live alone with their girls with only memories of the real Spig. It is at this moment of revelation, with a flickering projection on the screen, that she recognizes the lack of fulfillment in her life.

Ironically, it is after this scene that the maverick Spig returns home, but it is his two young daughters who welcome him, not Min. The children react with casual curiosity toward the father they do not know, but Spig rapidly disarms and charms them. There are empty liquor bottles in the house and it is clear that it has been unattended and the children left to their own devices. As Min enters through a softly diffused amber light, she epitomizes the self-neglect that has resulted from Spig's ambivalent attitude toward her. A cigarette dangles from her mouth as she pushes open the front door. She carries a bag of groceries, kicks off her shoes, massages her legs and walks to the kitchen with a slight stagger, suggesting that she has been drinking.

Spig has returned at a critical moment before the loneliness and rejection she has felt for so long have begun to change her irrevocably. Spig recognizes this and assumes the responsibility to change his priorities and perspectives. There is a romantic reconciliation which delights the children and steadies Spig and Min, affirming their love just before its greatest test. For in the tranquility of Spig's first night home, one of his children calls out. Spig dashes from the bed and trips on a roller skate that sends him crashing down the stairs. He lies stricken at the foot of the stairs, his neck broken, as the anguished Min calls the naval hospital. It is one of the greatest ironies in Ford's work that the reckless daredevil and hedonist is brought down not in a plane crash or a brawl, but by something as innocuous as a child's skate in the safe confines of his home.

Although Spig is not self-pitying in the hospital scenes, he is initially in a defeatist mood. Neither the doctors, the ever-vigilant Min, nor even his friend Carson can shake him into hope. In his most generous yet ruthless gesture, he endeavors to cast Min out of his life. "Take your turn, Min," he tells her. "I took mine." Only after he has faced the other side of himself, the shattered hero who has lost everything, can he begin to see things as they are. His ever-present and faithful buddy Carson helps him tap his reserves of inner strength and draw on the will to "move that toe." With total concentration which persists late into the night, as Ford shows in one of his most dramatic images,

Spig does the seemingly impossible: he moves his toe, and, in time, he graduates to crutches and a new vocation. Like a baby, Spig has learned to walk and to find a place in life. Unfortunately, his recovery is not complete, for he remains embittered, once again isolating himself in his work, an iconoclast who voluntarily locks himself out of any deep human relationship. His conquering of his physical handicap is admirable, but he cannot overcome his self-imposed alientation—a condition which is truly tragic.

Spig's writing career takes him to Hollywood to work with the noted movie director, John Dodge (Ward Bond), a thinly disguised version of Ford himself, for whom the real Commander Ward wrote *Air Mail* (1932) and *They Were Expendable* (1945). In his last role in a Ford film, Ward Bond plays the director as a down-to-earth man of keen insight, firmness, and ambiguity who enjoys a sip of whiskey hidden in his cane. His response to the handicapped Spig is sympathetic, but he makes no pretense that he expects anything less than perfection. Spig accepts his position with ease; he is accustomed to taking orders and following through. Thus, he relaxes into the role of high-paid screenwriter with an expansive house and the spoils of a successful Hollywood career.

It is at this time that Spig reasons he now has something tangible to offer Min at last, and he attempts a reconciliation. Although she has aged throughout the turbulent course of their relationship, there has never been another woman in Spig's life. There has been, however, his passion for the Navy. As Spig and Min meet at her San Francisco apartment, there is a mood of renewed hope and optimism. As Spig prepares for her homecoming, however, World War II intrudes and separates them once again. Spig goes to the Pacific where he throws himself tirelessly into his work. He is reunited with his friends Carson and John Price (Ken Curtis), whom he once more treats with initial warmth and then casual indifference. When Price visits him and innocently plants the thought that Spig will turn into the jeep carrier concept, Spig callously forgets the other's presence, only turning after Price has gone to call after him.

Ford's use both of Price and Carson measures the depth of Spig's responses to people and the carelessness with which he treats emotion. Carson has always been near when needed, a source of fun, loyalty, support, and motivation. Spig's recovery was, in part, attributable to Carson's upbraiding of him and the other's ingenuity, perseverance, and faith. Now, years later, Spig must again depend on him, for it is Carson who saves his life during a bombing. Although Carson is a good person and a true friend, gratitude and appreciation are not feelings Spig is able to express in words or in actions, and this relationship reveals Spig to be more sadly crippled emotionally that physically.

The end of the film shows Spig suspended on a wire between two ships. He is being taken, both metaphorically and actually, from a known past to an uncertain future. In a sense, the audience is left suspended as well. The real Spig Wead lived until 1947, but for dramatic purposes Ford wanted to end his story here, preferring to leave the impression of uncertainty with the audience to parallel the feelings of the protagonist.

Elizabeth McDermott

WINTERSET

Released: 1936
Production: Pandro S. Berman for RKO/Radio
Direction: Alfred Santell
Screenplay: Anthony Veiller; based on the play of the same name by Maxwell Anderson
Cinematography: Peverell Marley
Editing: William Hamilton
Running time: 78 minutes

Principal characters:

Mio	Burgess Meredith
Mariamne	Margo
Trock	Eduardo Ciannelli
Judge Gaunt	Edward Ellis
Garth	Paul Guilfoyle
Esdras	Maurice Moscovitch
Shadow	Stanley Ridges
Romagna	John Carradine
Policeman	Willard Robertson

Winterset, Maxwell Anderson's award-winning stage play, from which the 1936 film was adapted, was inspired by the famous murder-turned-political trials and subsequent executions of two Italian immigrant laborers, Nicola Sacco and Bartolomeo Vanzetti. In the spring of 1920, the two defendants were charged with the murders of a guard and a factory paymaster during a payroll robbery in South Braintree, Massachusetts. Sacco and Vanzetti were avowed anarchists who admittedly had left the country at one time to avoid the military draft. It became common knowledge that the prosecutor used this information to discredit the laborers, and they were found guilty of murder. Public protest erupted around the world because of the trial's political implications and because of new evidence obtained in 1925 which, it was felt, should have caused the case to have been reopened; a criminal, Celestino Madeiros, gave evidence that implicated the Morelli gang in the payroll killings. The presiding judge refused the motion for a new trial and handed down death sentences in April, 1927. Sacco and Vanzetti were executed that same month.

Maxwell Anderson's play was not an attempt to tell the Sacco and Vanzetti story, but rather to consider a projected consequence of that display of dubious justice. Anthony Veiller was responsible for the screenplay used for the Pandro S. Berman film production. Though the film does make significant changes in the original stage play, the story remains the same. The opening scenes of the film version, for example, are additions to Anderson's stage production, and they serve to rekindle a sense of the story's historical background. The audience witnesses a factory killing, after which the criminals stash the paymaster's bags in the car of an Italian radical. The man's innocence is unquestionable but he is quickly and unjustly tried, condemned, and executed. The thrust of the plot concerns the wronged man's son, Mio (Burgess Meredith), whose sole objective is to learn the real story underlying his father's conviction, hoping to exonerate him.

Trock (Eduardo Ciannelli), a gang leader, is another character with an intense, though intensely different, objective. Trock and his gangsters are responsible for the murder, and he fears that Garth (Paul Guilfoyle), a minor accomplice, may grow tired of hiding out and decide to turn state's evidence against them. Most of the later scenes occur in and around Garth's residence, a sublevel tenement apartment which he shares with his kindly father, Esdras (Maurice Moscovitch), and his young, romantic sister, Mariamne (Margo). Trock is especially worried because the half-crazed trial judge, Judge Gaunt (Edward Ellis), wanders through Garth's neighborhood trying to lay his burdened conscience to rest. Trock threatens the Garth household; Garth reassures the helpless judge; Mio and Mariamne fall in love (with very little provocation); and everyone, including the local policeman, dismantles Mio's lifelong hopefulness. In the film's only exciting scene, Trock is about to murder Mio and the judge when Shadow (Stanley Ridges), a gang member who has recently been gunned down and tossed into the river, appears at Garth's door dripping blood and mud. He points his gun at Trock, pale and twitching against the wall, nearly shooting him before he falls to the floor, blinded by death. Mio tricks the shaken gang leader into betraying himself when Trock, out of desperation, pins Shadow with the murder of the paymaster.

The film's ending is markedly different from that of the stage play. Both occur outside the tenement in a cavernous, ghetto-style *cul de sac*. In the stage play, Mio tries to leave by way of a dark, rocky path, but he is killed by Trock's strategically located sharpshooters. Bereft, Mariamne, who advised him to take the path route, darts up the same path to a similar, expected death. With Mio and Mariamne in the same predicament, the film concludes with Esdras being gunned down on that ill-fated pathway. Then, mistaking Esdras' death for that of Mio's, Trock walks out into the open and gives the signal his gunman was to look for when Mio got within his range. Trock, dying from the sharpshooter's bullet, then shoots his killer, leaving Mio and Mariamne to live happily ever after.

The ending proves to be the greatest flaw of the production, as directed by Alfred Santell. The option for implausibility, where justice must triumph unequivocally, undercuts the poetic, posthumous, tragic reality of Anderson's original stage play. The film achieves no higher status than the general gangster melodrama. The film's reductiveness also inhibits the possibility of developing strong, believable characters. The play's tonal posture, for example, is more suited to Mio bending toward verse when he periodically pleads with the gods in heaven.

The film's greatest achievements are to be found in its dramatic aspects. The viewer is treated to a fine display of character acting by Eduardo Ciannelli, who with Burgess Meredith, Margo, Edward Ellis, and Maurice Moscovitch, create a few engaging scenes.

Ralph Angel

WITNESS FOR THE PROSECUTION

Released: 1957
Production: Arthur Hornblow, Jr., for Theme Pictures; released by United Artists
Direction: Billy Wilder
Screenplay: Billy Wilder and Harry Kurnitz; based on Larry Marcus' adaptation of the story and the play of the same name by Agatha Christie
Cinematography: Russell Harlan
Editing: Daniel Mandell
Running time: 114 minutes

Principal characters:

Leonard Vole	Tyrone Power
Christine Vole	Marlene Dietrich
Sir Wilfrid Robarts	Charles Laughton
Miss Plimsoll	Elsa Lanchester
Brogan-Moore	John Williams
Mayhew	Henry Daniell
Janet McKenzie	Una O'Connor
Mrs. French	Norma Varden
Mr. Myers	Torin Thatcher
Diana	Ruta Lee

The witness for the prosecution, a surprise witness, is Christine Vole (Marlene Dietrich), presumably the wife of the man on trial for murder, Leonard Vole (Tyrone Power), a ne'er-do-well gadget peddler. She claims that she is not legally Leonard's wife, then refutes his alibi. The next day, however, Leonard's counsel, Sir Wilfrid Robarts (Charles Laughton), destroys Christine's testimony with a small bundle of letters that she had written to her "Beloved Max" in Germany, and consequently wins Leonard's acquittal. The trial over, Christine tells Sir Wilfrid that she knew Leonard to be guilty all along, that she, disguised, had tricked Sir Wilfrid into taking the phony letters the night before, perjuring herself in order for Leonard to be freed. When Leonard appears with a young, pretty blonde (Ruta Lee) and announces that he plans to go away with her, Christine, enraged, stabs Leonard there in the courtroom, using the knife presented in evidence as the murder weapon. Sir Wilfrid then makes plans to defend Christine against the charge of murder.

The multifaceted trick ending of Agatha Christie's original play made it highly popular in London's West End and on Broadway, where it ran for almost two years. Although the play was done as a straight mystery, Billy Wilder and Harry Kurnitz in their screenplay insert a good deal of humor and emphasis on character, their main addition being Miss Plimsoll (Elsa Lanchester), Sir Wilfrid's private nurse, the source of some of the finest comedy in the film. At the time of this film Wilder had earned considerable fame for a group of excellent *films noirs* that began with *Double Indemnity* in 1944; and in the 1950's and early 1960's he was highly regarded also for his dark comedies such as *Stalag 17* (1953) and misanthropic farces such as *The Apartment* (1960) and *Kiss Me, Stupid* (1964). *Witness for the Prosecution* combines the usual Wilder touches—masquerade, verbal wit, intimations of a corrupt environment—but emerges one of his lightest, least trenchant works, without denying in the end the reality of human baseness.

The film's effect depends upon misleading appearances, things turning out to be not what they originally seemed. The climax follows smoothly from the deceptions, not all of them malicious, that run throughout the various relationships within the story.

The humor in the film derives largely from the attempts of Sir Wilfrid, recovering from a coronary, to outwit Nurse Plimsoll, his "jailer" (he calls her) and the surrogate for his doctor, who has forbidden him a number of amenities, including participation in murder trials. Sir Wilfrid plays the naughty school boy to Miss Plimsoll's matron. He evades her naps, shots, pills, and, especially, injunctions against cigars and brandy. His antics extend to outright rebellion the night he receives the phone call from the mysterious cockney woman about the letters, as he rushes off to Euston Station after grabbing Miss Plimsoll's poised hypodermic and sticking it in the end of his cigar. Her browbeating and smothering attention, however, give way finally to pride and admiration at Leonard's trial: "Wilfrid the fox—that's what they call him" she proclaims to everyone in the balcony when Sir Wilfrid confronts Christine with the letters. She is also the one who orders the return of the luggage from the boat train, decisively announcing that Sir Wilfrid will appear for the defense of Christine. He has never really fooled her, anyway, as she makes clear when she reminds him that he has forgotten his brandy (his thermos of "hot cocoa"). Their growing camaraderie furnishes a healthy, innocent contrast to the treachery, both real and feigned, that marks the Voles's relationship.

Christine's deceptions underlie the major part of the film's climax. She bears out Sir Wilfrid's initial suspicion of her when she appears for the prosecutor Mr. Myers (Torin Thatcher), claiming that she was already married to a man named Helm when she went through a ceremony with Leonard in Hamburg while he was serving with the British occupation forces after World War II. Her testimony proves in fact no deception at all—Leonard did return home late on the night in question with blood on his clothes, admitting that he had murdered Mrs. French (Norma Varden)—although at the time it seems to be outright betrayal. She sounds convincing enough, particularly after Myers admonishes her in her own language about perjury, *Meineid*. In spite of Leonard's artless rebuttal, the jury members, as Brogan-Moore (John Williams) points out later, did not like Christine but believed her, whereas they liked Leonard but did not believe him.

Christine's *tour de force* of deception and disguise is her impersonation of a cockney trollop at Euston Station. She readily convinces both Sir Wilfrid and Mayhew (Henry Daniell) that they are interviewing a woman wronged by Christine Vole, who stole her lover and caused him to disfigure her right cheek. "Wanna kiss me, Ducky?" she asks Sir Wilfrid, pulling back her hair to show him her scar. In court the next day she continues her deception as Sir Wilfrid, with one of the bogus letters in hand, meticulously exposes her commitment to Max and her plan to give false testimony against Leonard. She follows through until after Leonard has been acquitted, even though some of the spectators physically abuse her as she tries to reach Leonard and Sir Wilfrid.

Leonard's masquerade is equally as expert as Christine's. Like his wife, he must hoodwink Sir Wilfrid at close quarters. In the initial conference Leonard wins Sir Wilfrid over, presenting himself as a sincere, talented young inventor, the victim of unfortunate circumstances. Sir Wilfrid decides to rescue him when Brogan-Moore as well as Christine show hesitation about his innocence. Already Leonard had convinced Mrs. French, a wealthy, middle-aged, lonely widow, that he would marry her, or convinced her of something that caused her to change her will and leave him eighty thousand pounds. Christine apparently knew little enough about the details of that relationship, and certainly nothing at all about his involvement with Diana, his blonde girl friend.

To give the story pace and to lead up to the action of the trial, Wilder uses flashbacks that fill in Leonard's relationship with the murdered woman and with his wife. Since the two episodes are narrated by Leonard, they lend credibility to his story. He tells how he happened to see Mrs. French from outside a milliner's shop, where he volunteered advice on a new hat, then in a cinema, and of their ensuing friendship and the encouragement she gave him for his inventions. He also tells of his first meeting with Christine, in the midst of a brawl, at the Hamburg cabaret where she performed. The fight had broken out when, after she sang a song, some of the patrons began to quarrel over her (presumably the sequence was thus staged in order to give the audience a glimpse of the famous Dietrich legs).

Wilder never lets the story become introspective: he mutes the tension between devotion and perfidy by keeping the audience entertained with various gimmicks. *Witness for the Prosecution* has an intelligent balance of courtroom drama, suspense, multilevel humor, and consummate acting. Wilder allows his actors a good deal of freedom. Power makes Leonard a sympathetic although basically shallow character. Just as Leonard seems incapable of stabbing a defenseless woman, his anguish and confusion during the trial appear symptomatic of an engaging naïveté. Yet he readily gives way to the smug callousness that his acquittal uncovers in him. Marlene Dietrich's Christine embodies the right amount of iciness, mystery, and, in the cockney interlude, low comedy. She does overact embarrassingly when Sir Wilfrid destroys her on the stand and when she finally avenges herself on Leonard. On the other hand, Elsa Lanchester performs at her best as the irritating but loyal Nurse Plimsoll. She shows excellent rapport with Laughton, whether coddling him, berating him, or admiring him.

Witness for the Prosecution nonetheless becomes Laughton's film: his Sir Wilfrid binds all together as he romps through each of his scenes. He bullies and cajoles, grimaces and smirks, assailing the veracity of witnesses by reflecting the glare from his monocle into their eyes. Surely the funniest episode in the film is his cross examination of Janet McKenzie (Una O'Connor), Mrs. French's testy, practically deaf Scottish housekeeper, who hates Leonard for working his way into her mistress' will and thus cheating her out of her share. Sir Wilfrid maintains his owlish dignity when he recognizes that Christine and Leonard alike have thoroughly duped him. Even though he suspected something because the solution turned out too pat, he admits that he never suspected Christine's masquerade. He is aghast after she asks him once again, in her cockney dialect, if he wants to kiss her. Yet he passes over defeat into a new challenge, Christine's defense, for she did not actually murder Leonard—"she executed him" he solemnly tells Miss Plimsoll.

Its surprise conclusion aside, *Witness for the Prosecution* appeals as a well-made, coherent melodrama whose performances engage at least as much as does the plot. It is a handsomely designed production, done almost entirely in interiors, the sets for the courtroom in the Old Bailey and for Euston Station, particularly, giving it a thoroughly London atmosphere. The film was Power's last; he died a year later at the age of forty-four while filming *Solomon and Sheba* (1959), and his scenes were reshot with Yul Brynner. Laughton would make three more films, but in none would he get the opportunity to exhibit the range he does here, not even portraying the wily Senator Cooley in Preminger's *Advise and Consent* (1962), his final role. As Sir Wilfrid, one reviewer noted, "the old ham has found the right platter." Sir Wilfrid plays off excellently against Leonard: he becomes defender, then antagonist, of a killer who has ingratiated himself into a tremendous amount of loyalty from two older women. Mrs. French leaves him her fortune, and Christine sets herself up for a perjury conviction and a prison term in order to ensure his freedom. "The wheels of justice grind slowly," Sir Wilfrid admonishes Leonard at the end, "but they grind finely."

Justice comes unexpectedly through the hand of a spurned woman. Leonard understands his acquittal as a piece of good luck and as the payment due for his bringing Christine out of Germany. Years of marriage have, however, failed to teach him an important thing about his wife, for if he accurately calculates the depth of her loyalty, he fails to reckon with the extent of her jealousy. All sympathy finally goes to Christine, whose acquittal seems assured with Sir Wilfrid by her side.

William H. Brown, Jr.

THE WIZARD OF OZ

Released: 1939
Production: Mervyn LeRoy for Metro-Goldwyn-Mayer
Direction: Victor Fleming
Screenplay: Florence Ryerson, Noel Langley, and Edgar Allan Woolf; based on Noel Langley's adaptation of the novel of the same name by L. Frank Baum
Cinematography: Harold Rosson
Editing: Blanche Sewell
Art direction: Cedric Gibbons
Special effects: Arnold Gillespie
Costume design: Adrian
Choreography: Bobby Connolly
Sound: Douglas Shearer
Music: Herbert Stothart (AA), Ken Darby, Murray Cutter, Paul Marquardt, and George Bassman
Song: Harold Arlen and E. Y. Harburg, "Over the Rainbow" (AA)
Running time: 101 minutes

Principal characters:
Dorothy .... Judy Garland (AA Special Award)
Professor Marvel/The Wizard .... Frank Morgan
Hunk/Scarecrow .... Ray Bolger
Zeke/Cowardly Lion .... Bert Lahr
Hickory/Tin Woodman ....Jack Haley
Glinda, The Good Witch .... Billie Burke
Miss Gulch/The Wicked Witch .... Margaret Hamilton
Uncle Henry .... Charley Grapewin
Aunt Em .... Clara Blandick

Among films that have been distinguished by the term "classic," few vintage ones have aged as gracefully as *The Wizard of Oz*. First released in 1939, it has found an ever-widening audience, not only in theatrical releases but in frequent television presentations. The most famous of musical fantasies, it is undoubtedly the best of the genre, enjoyed by succeeding generations of adults and children alike. The universal appeal of the film owes much to the fact that it represents an almost perfect integration of music and action, with every song either advancing the suspenseful plot or explaining the motivations of one of the intriguing characters.

The Wizard of Oz was not a new film idea in 1939. L. Frank Baum, author of the phenomenally popular children's book, *The Wizard of Oz*, published in 1900, and of thirteen other volumes in the *Oz* series, had formed his own movie company in 1914 and produced three five-reel *Oz* films based on his stories. Even before that, there had been some one-reel *Oz* movies, and a musical extravaganza on the Broadway stage. Popular comedian Larry Semon had appeared in his own *Oz* film interpretation in 1925. The 1939 M-G-M version, although more lavish and innovative than its predecessors, remains faithful to the concept and spirit of the L. Frank Baum book which traces the adventures of Dorothy, the little Kansas farm girl.

The Wizard of Oz begins in drab sepia tones as Dorothy (Judy Garland), an orphan, decides to run away from the farm where she lives with her Aunt Em (Clara Blandick), Uncle Henry (Charley Grapewin), and her three farm-hand friends. She intends to leave behind "unappreciative" relatives and escape from the nasty neighbor, Miss Gulch (Margaret Hamilton), who is determined to have her little dog Toto put away. Before she leaves the farm, Dorothy expresses her feelings of longing in the plaintive, haunting song, "Over the Rainbow." When Dorothy, on the advice of Professor Marvel (Frank Morgan), the carnival showman, tries to return to her family, she is caught up in a cyclone. Her modest house is tossed in the air, and she, Toto, and the audience look down on the black column of the Kansas "twister," as friends and neighbors go floating by her window. At last the house bumps to the ground. Opening the door, Dorothy looks out onto a strange place, vibrant in brilliant, garish, and exhilarating Technicolor. It is the Land of Oz, and some peculiar little people, the Munchkins, are happily singing, "Ding Dong/The Wicked Witch Is Dead." The Witch has been killed by the plummeting house.

The Witch's sister, the Wicked Witch of the West, whom the audience recognizes as Miss Gulch, threatens Dorothy, but Glinda (Billie Burke), the Good Witch, protects her and starts her on a journey to the Emerald City in order to consult with the omniscient Wizard of Oz about how to get home. On the way, Dorothy meets three unusual strangers who become her friends: the brainless Scarecrow (Ray Bolger), who resembles the farmhand, Hunk; the heartless Tin Woodman (Jack Haley), who looks like Handyman Hickory; and the Cowardly Lion (Bert Lahr), who is afraid of his own growl and whom we recognize as farmhand Zeke. As each newcomer is introduced, he sings of his problem in the lilting "If I Only Had a Brain/a Heart/the Nerve," and, as each one joins Dorothy in the quest for the Wizard, who they hope will also help them, they dance and sing the spirited "We're Off to See the Wizard."

The group is set upon by various evil characters, including winged monkeys, ferocious talking trees, and sleep-inducing flowers, all doing the bidding of the Wicked Witch. Yet so tastefully are the menacing elements presented that there are no extremes of horror to frighten very young filmgoers. There is even something reassuring about the dreamlike quality of the misadventures that convinces the audience that all problems will be solved—as indeed they eventually are.

When Dorothy is captured by the Wicked Witch, her companions help her escape and melt the Witch by dousing her with water. Then the four friends confront the Wizard, who resembles Professor Marvel, and unmask him as a well-meaning but bumbling old humbug who cannot really help the Scarecrow, Tin Woodman, and Lion; however, he convinces them that they already have the wisdom, compassion, and courage which each respectively has been seeking—qualities which have been revealed to us in the brave and clever rescue of Dorothy. He offers to take Dorothy back to Kansas in a hot-air balloon that he possesses, only to sail off without her as the cables are loosened too quickly. It is then that Dorothy learns from Glinda that she herself has the power to return home. All she has to do is say "There's no place like home," and she can go there. Dorothy, murmuring the phrase, awakens in her own bed, surrounded by her Aunt and Uncle and the three companions from Oz and the farm. She realizes that true happiness can be found in her own backyard—even though home is once again visible in the sepia tones of a dusty Kansas panorama.

The Wizard of Oz is an amalgam of many fine talents and is an example of the teamwork that was representative of the Hollywood studio system at its best. Director Victor Fleming carries the action forward at a never-flagging pace, which is no minor accomplishment in a musical movie with forty of its one hundred minutes' screening time devoted to songs. Especially admirable is his handling of the touching relationship between Dorothy and her three friends, a tender kinship that becomes neither romantic nor maudlin.

The screenplay, by Noel Langley, Florence Ryerson, and Edgar Allan Woolf, blends elements of the original novel with imaginative and amusing innovations such as the sight of the Wicked Witch skywriting, "Surrender, Dorothy!" as she rides through the air on her broom, or the Horse of a Different Color, who takes Dorothy and her companions through the streets of the Emerald City. No fantasy would be complete without special effects, and those in *The Wizard of Oz* are spectacular and refreshingly humorous rather than frightening in their creation of the illusions of the bizarre Land of Oz. They are heightened by the splendid artwork of scenic and costume designers and makeup artists.

However, the cast and the music are the most memorable features of the film. Each character is so well portrayed that it is difficult to believe that many members of the cast were not the first choices of the producers. W. C. Fields was replaced by Frank Morgan, as the Wizard; Buddy Ebsen by Jack Haley, as the Tin Woodman; and Shirley Temple by Judy Garland, as Dorothy. (At the time of its filming, Shirley Temple and W. C. Fields were unavailable and Buddy Ebsen became ill from the Tin Man's silvery makeup.) Judy

Garland, who was sixteen during the film's production, in no way resembled the famous W. W. Denslow drawings in the Baum book which portrayed Dorothy as a very young child with blond curls. Authors of books and articles have variously attributed the somewhat controversial casting of Garland to Arthur Freed, Mervyn LeRoy, or Roger Edens, among others. However, no matter who was responsible for the choice, it was a fortuitous one: Judy Garland is by turns wistful or spunky, but always a warm-hearted and perfect Dorothy. Her singing, particularly of the song "Over the Rainbow," helped make *The Wizard of Oz* her springboard to stardom as one of Hollywood's most important musical personalities of all time. Frank Morgan, Jack Haley, Ray Bolger, and Margaret Hamilton created characters in *The Wizard of Oz* with which they would be associated throughout their careers, and they helped demonstrate that fantasy on film could be presented as successfully with live actors as with animation.

All the music of *The Wizard of Oz*—the songs by Harold Arlen and E. Y. Harburg, the background music, and the arrangements—is exceptionally fine throughout the film. Similar to the casting of Judy Garland, the song "Over the Rainbow" was also controversial; M-G-M executives thought it slowed the action of the picture and tried to have it removed. Reprieved, however, it became so closely associated with the career of Judy Garland that it is difficult to imagine the film without the song. The melody is alternately complex and simple in its opening bars and bridge, respectively, and the words reflect a yearning that is ageless and timeless. In contrast, the other songs are all "upbeat"—rollicking, spirited, and humorous. The background music utilizes many of the themes of the songs, along with small recurring motifs that symbolize each character. The arrangements make use of audible effects which are as important as the visual ones: voices are speeded up or slowed down while the orchestral instruments sound normal. The overall talents of the cast as singing and dancing performers add much to the effectiveness of all the musical material.

When *The Wizard of Oz* opened in 1939, critics were almost unanimous in its praise, although there were a few dissenters, including the critic of the *New Yorker* who considered Bert Lahr out of place in the Land of Oz. Audiences generally enjoyed the film, but it did not become a consistent moneymaker until its theatrical revival in 1948. With its first (in 1956) and subsequent television broadcasts, *The Wizard of Oz* found a new audience and reaped great financial rewards.

In the 1939 Academy Awards competition, *Gone with the Wind* overshadowed most other productions, including *The Wizard of Oz*, winning eight awards and three additional nominations. Musical director Herbert Stothart won an Oscar for the score of *The Wizard of Oz*, however, and "Over the Rainbow" won the Award for Best Song. Judy Garland received a miniature statuette as the outstanding screen juvenile. The film was also nominated for its art direction and special effects. If director Victor Fleming was disappointed in not being nominated for *The Wizard of Oz*, he undoubtedly was able to find consolation in having won the Award for Best Direction for his other film, *Gone with the Wind*.

One other facet of *The Wizard of Oz* is significant: the contribution of Arthur Freed. He was a successful song writer who wanted to be a film producer, and he was given his chance as the uncredited assistant to the film's producer, Mervyn LeRoy. In this role, Freed's unerring judgment of talent and his ability to gather talented people around him proved invaluable. Having proved his capabilities, he went on to produce some of Hollywood's most prestigious and entertaining musicals, including *An American in Paris* (1951), *Gigi* (1958), *Meet Me in St. Louis* (1944), *The Band Wagon* (1953), *The Barkleys of Broadway* (1949), *Easter Parade* (1948), *On the Town* (1949), *Annie Get Your Gun* (1950), and *Singin' in the Rain* (1952). Those films were all an integral part of the golden age of the M-G-M musical, an era that was celebrated in that studio's compilation of film excerpts, *That's Entertainment* (1974), and which began with *The Wizard of Oz*.

Irene Kahn Atkins

THE WOMEN

Released: 1939
Production: Hunt Stromberg for Metro-Goldwyn-Mayer
Direction: George Cukor
Screenplay: Anita Loos and Jane Murfin; based on the play of the same name by Clare Boothe
Cinematography: Oliver T. Marsh and Joseph Ruttenberg
Editing: Robert J. Kern
Running time: 134 minutes

Principal characters:
Mary Haines .... Norma Shearer
Crystal Allen .... Joan Crawford
Sylvia Fowler .... Rosalind Russell
Miriam Aarons .... Paulette Goddard
Countess DeLave .... Mary Boland
Peggy Day .... Joan Fontaine
Mrs. Moorehead .... Lucile Watson

From the time of its first Broadway performance on December 26, 1936, Clare Boothe's comedy about the humors and manners of the female sex, *The Women*, was an enormous hit, but it still came as something of a surprise when Hollywood's top studio, M-G-M, acquired the film rights. It is a comedy with an acid wit; of the all-female cast, only one character, the lead, is sympathetic; she is a good although uninteresting woman. The rest of the women are stupid, idle, unscrupulous "bitches" who do nothing but gossip, talk dirty, and play bridge. Their preoccupation is men, although no man ever appears onstage. As movie material, it seems to have many strikes against it.

Producer Hunt Stromberg and director George Cukor, however, were not fazed in the least. They hired Anita Loos to give the play more bite as she wrote the screenplay, and they teamed her with Jane Murfin, who contributed warmth and humanity to several of the backbiting characters. Many of the lines in the play would never have passed the censor; others were markedly vulgar albeit truthful. The two screenwriters substituted dialogue which was far more witty and only verged on the naughty.

Stromberg and Cukor decided to cast the film, as the producers of the play had done, with an all-female cast. Norma Shearer, first lady of M-G-M, was cast in the lead of Mary Haines, the wife and mother who discovers that her world and her sex are predatory, and that she must be willing to fight for her happiness. Joan Crawford went to the studio's front office and asked to play the "other woman," Crystal Allen, an unsympathetic although glamorous role. Rosalind Russell was assigned to play Sylvia Fowler, the meanest woman in Manhattan.

A novel means of introducing the women was devised. As the cast credits were listed, a picture of each actress dissolved into a closeup of an animal whose nature is analogous to that of the character played by the actress. Thus the young and innocent Joan Fontaine, playing Peggy Day, is shown as a wistful, frightened sheep, and the other women become, in turn, tigers, cows, does, and other animals representative of each woman's character.

The ladies meeting for lunch at Mary Haines's well-appointed home are either married or about to be, or are separated and about to divorce. Their most exciting gossip is about their hostess, Mary Haines, for her husband is known to be philandering. Sylvia, who has been to her manicurist, got the information about Mary's husband because the manicurist knew the husband-stealing woman. Sylvia none too subtly suggests to Mary that she go to the new manicurist at Michael's salon named Olga, who gave her this gorgeous "Jungle Red" nail color. Mary divines that Sylvia is trying to tell her something about her marriage when Sylvia insists that "A woman's paradise is always a fool's paradise," and she decides to go to Michael's to get her nails done by Olga.

It does not take much time for Mary to hear the current gossip from Olga, who seems to be sharing it with every customer. The girl who is being kept by Stephen Haines calls herself Crystal Allen; she is a seductress who works behind the perfume counter at "Black's" Fifth Avenue.

Mary tells her mother, Mrs. Moorehead (Lucile Watson), of her husband's infidelity, and her mother gives her some wise advice: she should say nothing. It is something that happens to most wives, and it does not necessarily mean that her husband is tired of her. He may simply be tired of himself and wanting something new; everything would change if he realized that he already has what he wants and could lose it. Mary bides her time and only confronts Crystal when they occupy adjoining booths at a dress salon. Crystal tells Mary that she may be a saint but that she is a very dull woman, and that it is no wonder her husband is roaming.

Mary tries to maintain her calm with her husband, but although he does not want a separation, it is arranged, and Mary leaves for Reno to get a divorce. Meanwhile, others in Mary's circle are unhappy in their own marital lives. The divorce roundelay begins, and Mary meets some of her Manhattan friends in Reno — Sylvia, her archenemy, in particular, has been thrown out by her husband, who is even willing to make a large financial settlement in order to be rid of her. Sylvia learns that Miriam Aarons (Paulette Goddard) is the other woman in her husband's life, and the two women engage in a hair-pulling, kicking and screaming tussle.

The gentle Peggy Day (Joan Fontaine) has had a falling-out with her husband as well and has joined the women in Reno, where she discovers that she is pregnant. Mary advises her to phone her husband at once and acquaint him with the good news. This Peggy does, and there is a reconciliation over the phone, after which she leaves joyfully for Manhattan and her husband. Mary also gets a call from her husband, and for a moment allows herself to hope, but Stephen is only calling to see if the divorce has come through, because he has married Crystal that morning.

Mary sadly returns to New York a divorced woman. Although Crystal and Stephen are married, she is soon having an affair with a cowboy named Buck Winston, a Western radio star whom the silly Countess DeLave brought back from Reno as her new husband. Mary learns from her own young daughter that Stephen is disenchanted with Crystal and is really still in love with Mary; she also learns that Crystal is cheating on Stephen with Buck Winston. With that knowledge and a little bold faking, she blackmails Crystal. The last shot of Mary is when she goes to rejoin her husband, and his shadow appears on the stair wall as he comes to meet her. She has fought to regain the man she loves and won; there is a radiant, triumphant smile on her face.

As a movie, *The Women* enjoyed the same kind of success as the play. George Cukor, who had gained a reputation as a "woman's director," enjoyed working with his all-star cast. Norma Shearer probably had the most difficult role she ever played onscreen, in making a good woman interesting. *The Women* is one of her last outstanding features. The role of Crystal Allen was also one of Joan Crawford's final important films at M-G-M. She worked well with Cukor and respected him. She was to work with him twice again at M-G-M, in *Susan and God* (1940) and *A Woman's Face* (1941), both departures from the kind of glamour roles that had made her the shopgirl's delight. Rosalind Russell took a rare delight in throwing herself into the bitchy role of Sylvia, a prelude to the career woman comedies that were to be her specialty as a star.

Two younger actresses just beginning their careers as important players especially distinguished themselves in *The Women*. Joan Fontaine was charming, wistful, and appealing among all these cannibalistic females. Her next role after *The Women* was opposite Laurence Olivier in Hitchcock's first American film, *Rebecca* (1940), which made her a star. Similarly, Paulette Goddard, after Charles Chaplin's *Modern Times* (1936) and David O. Selznick's *The Young in Heart* (1939), shone with a luster in her wise-cracking role of Miriam, the girl who knows her way around and finally tangles with the wife whose husband she has stolen. After this film, Goddard went to Paramount, to whom Selznick sold the contract he held with her, and for the next six years she was a Paramount star, reaching her greatest popularity in the big Technicolor spectaculars of Cecil B. DeMille.

A fashion show staged in Technicolor with gowns by Adrian was another attraction of *The Women* and helped make it an unqualified box-office hit. It did not, however, gain a single Oscar nomination; 1939 was a year crowded with big hits, all potential Academy Award winners, such as *Gone with the Wind*; *Goodbye, Mr. Chips*; *Stagecoach*; *Wuthering Heights*; *Ninotchka*, and

The Wizard of Oz. In any other year *The Women* might have earned some Oscars. It was not an easy film to make, but good taste, wise showmanship, and stars in abundance supervised by a director in perfect control prevailed to make the film a hit.

Seventeen years later, in 1956, M-G-M remade *The Women* as *The Opposite Sex*, a Joe Pasternak production. The studio would have done better to reissue *The Women*, which was still remembered, liked, and considered definitive. As *The Opposite Sex*, it was no longer a stylish and scorching comedy but a tame, second-rate marital drama that featured musical numbers and men in the cast, neither of which helped. The actors were negligible, and among the actresses only Ann Sheridan and Joan Blondell managed to shine. As many times as *The Women* has been restaged as a play, only once did it have any of the glitter of its original Broadway production, and that was during World War II when it toured the European Army bases as an all-male USO production, with men in women's clothes playing the female characters. That, at least, was original and hilarious.

DeWitt Bodeen

WRITTEN ON THE WIND

Released: 1956
Production: Albert Zugsmith for Universal
Direction: Douglas Sirk
Screenplay: George Zuckerman; based on the novel of the same name by Robert Wilder
Cinematography: Russell Metty
Editing: Russell Schoengarth
Running time: 92 minutes

Principal characters:
Mitch Wayne .... Rock Hudson
Lucy Moore Hadley .... Lauren Bacall
Kyle Hadley .... Robert Stack
Marylee Hadley .... Dorothy Malone (AA)
Jasper Hadley .... Robert Keith

Simone de Beauvoir refers to middle-class bourgeois values and ideals as lacking in passion, love, or challenge. They offer women (and by natural extension, men as well) only a "gilded mediocrity," a beautiful cage, an alienated existence that not only is totally incapable of fulfilling the promises our culture makes for material success, money, and especially marriage, but which is so cut off from any perception about its real nature that the victim has only herself to blame for her malaise as she goes quietly mad. This syndrome was conclusively documented by Betty Friedan in her classic study, *The Feminine Mystique*.

Long before publication of that landmark book, and even before any notion of a women's movement which would at least give women the contact with other women that they so desperately needed in order to realize that their empty lives were not simply personal failures in the midst of what their culture and families defined as success, Douglas Sirk was making "women's weepies" which were somehow very different from the run-of-the-mill melodrama, and which were enormous box-office successes with female audiences. Sirk's 1950's melodramas are set in this "gilded mediocrity," the American upper middle class, and *Written on the Wind* is the best of these films which concern the breakdown and failure of the apparently successful bourgeois family.

The Hadleys are an oil-rich family living in Hadleyville, an ugly little town which they dominate. Marylee Hadley (Dorothy Malone, used here, as in *The Tarnished Angels*, 1958, to personify feminine sexuality in the extreme) is a spoiled nymphomaniac in love with Mitch Wayne (Rock Hudson), childhood playmate of the Hadley children and now the trusted right-hand man for the Hadley patriarch in his business empire. Kyle Hadley (Robert Stack) is an irresponsible playboy and alcoholic who cannot manage anything without

Mitch. Obviously, both Kyle and his father wish Kyle were Mitch, and the failure which Kyle seems hell-bent on achieving is a clear result of this constant comparison.

The introduction of a fourth character brings tensions to a head and leads to the almost total destruction of the family. She is Lucy (Lauren Bacall), a lovely, adult, responsible woman to whom both Kyle and Mitch are very attracted when they meet her in the course of business. When Kyle learns she cannot be bought (by insisting she fly to Florida with them, plying her with clothes, an expensive hotel room, and his own considerable charm), he falls in love with her, and, to his surprise, she marries him. Kyle cannot believe that Lucy loves him instead of Mitch, and therefore becomes a progressively dangerous drunk, proving his worst fears to himself and to everyone else. Kyle is terrified of impotence, a sexual metaphor of the sort that pervades this film. It symbolizes the insecurity that cripples him at every turn and leads him to believe that Lucy and Mitch are having an affair when she becomes pregnant after Kyle has been diagnosed as "the problem" in their childlessness. Assuming that the virile Mitch must be the father (the attraction between Mitch and Lucy has been growing as Kyle makes life nearly impossible for himself and Lucy), Kyle flies into a rage, knocks Lucy down causing her to miscarry, and finally attempts murder which results in his own death. His father has already died, and the apparently rich, powerful family is left as impotent as all were so ready to believe Kyle was. The comforts of money, advantages of every kind, beauty, sex, and alcohol are in reality nothing.

Sirk is able to make scathing attacks on the bourgeois ideals of romantic happiness, the family, and the corrupting effects of money for at least two reasons. One is that genre films (especially the lowly melodrama) have a certain degree of freedom with which to express opposing ideologies and thereby co-opt anger by allowing some of the pain to be expressed and shared. The notoriously tragic daytime soap operas on television are indictments of our social structures, but by making all failure a result of personal inadequacy, no real challenge is offered to those structures. Sirk makes it abundantly clear that the promises our culture offers to its members are impossible. Marriage does not provide freedom for a woman, any more than financial success at an oppressive job provides freedom for men.

Further, Sirk places a major part of his criticism in the *mise-en-scène* of his films where it is definitely felt, but not directly articulated. He creates a glittering, cold, flat milieu which perfectly expresses the "gilded cage" metaphor. He establishes a stylistic flatness, a two-dimensionality which distances the viewer and traps the characters in an inhuman environment. The lighting in his black-and-white films creates an artificial world of glittering surfaces, with objects dominating the foreground and sucking the life out of the characters much as the possessions of middle-class life displace the vitality and values of those families. His color films are garishly artificial, including worlds of icy blues, jarring reds and oranges, and other unnatural lighting colors. The flat, glittering surfaces are a transparent mask to the underlying horror permeating Sirk's view of bourgeois life, and the fragmented characters are unable to perceive the falsity of their desires because of the stifling cage made of the lies and material success which surrounds them.

Written on the Wind is particularly harsh and garish in its use of color, with neonlike shades bursting from the frame. Loud, chaotic music blares forth to emphasize the tawdriness of Marylee's cheap affairs in the dive-type bar where much of the film takes place. The boredom of middle-class life is emphasized by the ugly little town of Hadleyville, where there is nothing to do and nowhere to go; oil wells dominate the landscape. There is an undercurrent of throbbing, frustrated sexual energy whose most blatant expression is Marylee's masturbatory dance, which is intercut with her father's heart attack and fall down the magnificent staircase, which culminates in his death. The two events are linked in her dance of death, which expresses a frenzy of frustration. Sexual imagery abounds. At the end of the film, Marylee is left alone clutching a phallic model of an oil derrick—all that remains for her of the men in her life. Her father and brother are dead, and Mitch has left the Hadley mansion with Lucy for good.

Written on the Wind is full of mirror images which separate the characters from their own emotions by splitting them in two, graphically expressing the alienation and helplessness they feel. All of Sirk's characters are unaware of the false nature of their perceptions. Sirk creates worlds in which the illusion of happiness is never the reality of happiness, and that illusion is the sinking ship to which the metaphorically blind characters cling.

Sirk does not create sympathy for one character at the expense of another. We see each character in his or her worst moments of betrayal, self-doubt, and insensitivity to others. Yet there is never the possibility of forgetting that these people are driven by forces beyond their control. Marylee's nymphomania is an answer to Mitch's rejection, and her unrequited love for him is a deep desire to "go back to the river," symbolizing their shared childhood before the tensions of adulthood turned Marylee and Kyle into monsters. She taunts Mitch and Kyle and is somewhat responsible for her brother's death, but she is obviously the tormented victim of her own frustration.

Kyle is also an emotional child whose crippling insecurity was given to him by his father. His drunken rages and inability to accept Lucy's love are not chosen by him, but are the inevitable result of his family's feelings for him. Indeed, after a few viewings of *Written on the Wind*, the viewer cares at least as deeply for Marylee and Kyle, who retain their passion even when a deadly, distorted sense of their own worth drives them to self-destruction. Lucy and Mitch are much more sane, not having been born into the paralyzing prominence of the Hadleys, but they are powerless to save Marylee and Kyle. Mitch and Lucy leave together at the end of the film, their unconsummated love finally out in the open. The Hadley flame is extinguished.

Sirk takes material which would seem to support the *status quo* and, through his form, critiques it in a more scathing and far-reaching manner than do the so-called "women's pictures" of today. He presents a world in which a man's and a woman's options are limited and bleak, but instead of presenting easy targets or easy answers, he shows happiness and real meaning in life to be nearly impossible. Only the surfaces and mirror images, imitations of happiness, are within people's grasp.

Janey Place

THE WRONG MAN

Released: 1957
Production: Alfred Hitchcock for Warner Bros.
Direction: Alfred Hitchcock
Screenplay: Maxwell Anderson and Angus McPhail; based on a screen story by Maxwell Anderson and an actual criminal case
Cinematography: Robert Burks
Editing: George Tomasini
Sound: Earl Crain, Sr.
Music: Bernard Herrmann
Running time: 105 minutes

Principal characters:

Christopher Emmanuel (Manny) Balestrero	Henry Fonda
Rose Balestrero	Vera Miles
Frank O'Connor	Anthony Quayle
Lieutenant Bowers	Harold J. Stone
Detective Matthews	Charles Cooper

Christopher Emmanuel Balestrero (Henry Fonda), a New York bass player, works nights at the Stork Club and comes home to his wife Rose (Vera Miles) and their children in the early morning. Although he likes to chart the horses while riding the subway, perhaps because his family is never financially ahead, he seldom bets on his selections. He and Rose lead what might be described as a life of quiet desperation; soon, however, they find out what true desperation is. "Manny," as Balestrero is nicknamed, goes to borrow money on his wife's insurance policy and in the process is misidentified as a holdup man by one of the cashiers, whose fellow employees join in the error. Returning home, Manny is picked up by two detectives who take him in for questioning. In the course of interrogating him, they ask him to write the words of a note which had been used by the holdup man. The anxious Manny accidentally misspells a word and soon finds himself charged with robbery and spending the night in a Queens jail.

In the morning, he is freed on the bail raised by his family and proceeds to engage a lawyer, Frank O'Connor (Anthony Quayle), who believes in his innocence. O'Connor explains to Manny and Rose the importance of establishing an alibi, but the people he might have used as witnesses either have died or cannot be found. Rose begins to despair and finally has a nervous breakdown. After she is placed in a mental hospital, the saddened Manny stands trial, but a mistrial is declared and he must face the entire process once again. He prays; and at that very moment, the holdup man walks into a store to rob again but is subdued by the owners. One of the detectives who arrested Manny notices the resemblance between the two, and Manny is finally cleared of the charges and released. He goes to the mental hospital to tell Rose that the nightmare is over, but for her, it is not. "That's fine for you," she tells him, staring blankly into space.

Although this story sounds similar to the sort of nightmarish fabrication which might be expected from Alfred Hitchcock, the premise is not his own. *The Wrong Man* is singular among his works in that the story is a true one, a fact that he emphasizes in a personal appearance at the beginning of the film. It is sometimes said that Hitchcock needs very fanciful plots in order to make the kind of film associated with him, but it is impossible to believe this after seeing *The Wrong Man*, which is one of his most hypnotic and compelling films.

In *The Wrong Man*, we find both the themes and techniques closely associated with Hitchcock. He engages freely in the subjective shots for which he is celebrated, building up in the audience the same fear and claustrophobia which Manny feels when he is arrested and locked up. These sequences have a quiet intensity and concentration which reflect the director's masterful control over what may be his own anxiety; Hitchcock has stated many times that he has a dread of jails and the police as a result of a traumatic childhood experience. The mistaken identity theme is one which Hitchcock has favored often, but as a rule, it has appeared in films with considerably less sobriety of tone than *The Wrong Man*. *Saboteur* (1942) and *North by Northwest* (1959) are more appropriate works to display Hitchcock's rich sense of humor than the story of a man and his wife who actually suffered the tragedy described by the film. Regarding the theme of the transfer of guilt, one of Hitchcock's most striking and individual motifs, nowhere in the director's work is there a more dramatic example than that of the wife who goes mad by assuming the guilt she perceives to be part of the fabric of her life and her husband's even though he is completely innocent.

The exteriors and certain interiors of the film were shot on location in New York, and Robert Burks resourcefully varies the black and white tonality of the film without ever departing from the prevailing visual mood, delicately poised between realism and expressionism. Although Hitchcock and Burks had become enthusiasts of the expressive use of color long before this black-and-white film was made, they are no less inspired here in the use of the drab settings and downbeat images which dominate the story. Their imaginative re-creation of the cheerless environment into a visualization of an emotional nightmare is one of the finest aspects of the film. Hitchcock creates tension in the opening sequence as Manny leaves the nightclub simply by introducing the figures of two policemen who stroll along behind the musician for a few moments.

After Manny is arrested, the scene of his interrogation is handled with a restraint and matter-of-factness which generally characterizes the style of the film, but at a key moment, the suppleness of Hitchcock's technique enhances the presentation of the scene. Manny has been attempting to remain calm and cooperative, but when he is finally overcome by feelings of helplessness and frustration, the camera withdraws to a high angle, making him appear even more vulnerable than before despite the fact that he has become vocally assertive. Similar touches enhance other scenes, such as the one in the jail cell, in which Manny is overcome by a feeling of claustrophobia and the camera begins to move in a little circle around him, the movement becoming increasingly rapid so that the still man eventually seems to whirl helplessly in the space of the frame. The severity of Hitchcock's formal control results in the film's most ostentatious and stirring moment, which occurs late in the film. In the scene there is a slow dissolve from the face of the praying Manny to the face of the actual holdup man, a dissolve in which the faces of the men merge as if Manny's prayer is mysteriously being answered.

The filming of Rose's breakdown is characterized by a thoughtfulness and visual tension which make this sequence perhaps the most outstanding in the film. Most of it is directed with visual restraint, as Rose, initially calm but becoming increasingly disturbed, expresses her feeling of helplessness over their situation. When he perceives that she is becoming hysterical, Manny moves to touch her and she picks up a hairbrush and hits him on the head with it. Hitchcock breaks up this brief action within the long sequence into a series of short shots—close-ups of Rose and Manny, the raising of the brush, the smashing of the brush into a mirror after Manny has been hit, and Manny's face distorted by its reflection in the broken mirror. The sequence ends with Rose retreating into a trance and oppressively dominating the compostion as she stares blankly and virtually whispers that she is ill.

Although it is important to realize that each shot in a Hitchcock film is carefully prepared so that it will relate both visually and psychologically to the overall conception in Hitchcock's mind, it is also important to note that Hitchcock's interpreters play an essential part in this conception. It is possible that the very fact of having to follow direction so closely in terms of movement and gesture has a liberating effect on actors and actresses in a Hitchcock film. Whatever the reason, no director elicits better performances than Hitchcock, and Henry Fonda and Vera Miles are among the finest examples of this. Miles's restrained dialogue and her subtle changes of expression which culminate in the empty gaze she finally assumes for the remainder of the film produce one of the most credible and brilliantly realized nervous breakdown sequences in cinema. Similarly, Fonda expresses his subdued character remarkably, mostly through the ways in which Manny looks at the world around him.

The calmness of the film, a result of Hitchcock's understanding of the characters and his attitute toward the story, makes it more dramatic than if it were overwrought, and every aspect of the film contributes to this sense of calmness. The music of Bernard Herrmann, which appropriately emphasizes the bass, is discreetly somber, and the complex soundtrack is also subtle and restrained. The screenplay is admirably straightforward, and the relatively prosaic quality of the dialogue not only encourages identification with the characters, but also sets off the more poetic quality of Hitchcock's cinematic realization.

Although it is relentlessly bleak, *The Wrong Man* betrays no cynicism and makes no recourse to a facile pessimism. This apparent destruction of a man by a merciless stroke of fate, which becomes the actual destruction of his more fragile wife, describes a cruel and uncaring universe with great spiritual resonance. Perhaps this is because the characters are whole human beings, not choosing to suffer in the manner of crippled characters found in more neurotic films, but suffering nonetheless against their will, their limitations used against them by the caprices of circumstance. The gentle Manny journeys through hell with a childlike awe, but this same innocence prevents him from ever knowing of the inner hell of his wife, burning quietly until it blazes out of control to provide this masterpiece of the desolation of human existence with its final tragic irony.

There is something strangely consoling in Hitchcock's presentation. His subjective techniques are used to encourage identification with Manny, but we are not encouraged to the same extent of identification with Rose, at least not by the camera. With Manny, we find at last that we are overwhelmed with sadness for her assumption of his nonexistent guilt. Hitchcock's choices when determining the visual and psychological nature of each shot result in the possibility of feeling compassion, a consoling emotion. He makes *The Wrong Man* appear to be a detached and restrained film, even while reaching profound fears within the consciousness of the spectator, until the final meeting in the mental hospital between the heartbroken Manny and the insane Rose, which brings forth the feeling of catharsis which he has held in suspense.

Blake Lucas

WUTHERING HEIGHTS

Released: 1939
Production: Samuel Goldwyn for United Artists
Direction: William Wyler
Screenplay: Ben Hecht and Charles MacArthur; based on the novel of the same name by Emily Brontë
Cinematography: Gregg Toland (AA)
Editing: Daniel Mandell
Interior decoration: James Basevi
Running time: 102 minutes

Principal characters:

Cathy .... Merle Oberon
Heathcliff .... Laurence Olivier
Ellen Dean .... Flora Robson
Edgar Linton .... David Niven
Isabella .... Geraldine Fitzgerald
Earnshaw .... Cecil Kellaway
Hindley .... Hugh Williams
Dr. Kenneth .... Donald Crisp

It was during Laurence Olivier's third period in Hollywood that he played Heathcliff in *Wuthering Heights*. He had been on holiday with Vivien Leigh, driving through the south of France. It was the beginning of summer, 1938, and he had been working hard all the previous season at the Old Vic, and she had just finished her ninth film, *Sidewalks of London* (known in England as *St. Martin's Lane*), playing with Charles Laughton and Rex Harrison.

When they checked in at their hotel in Agay on the French coast, there was a cablegram awaiting Olivier, asking if he would be interested in a Goldwyn film of *Wuthering Heights* in which he, Vivien Leigh, and Merle Oberon would play the leading roles. Shortly thereafter, the screenplay arrived, written by Ben Hecht and Charles MacArthur. Hecht had suggested Olivier to director William Wyler as the only choice for the role of Heathcliff. Olivier admired the *Wuthering Heights* screenplay, but he had not been happy in either of his previous two adventures in Hollywood, and when he found out that Oberon was already cast for Cathy and Leigh was wanted for the secondary role of Isabella, he turned down the whole proposition.

William Wyler was in London when they returned from their holiday, and he did his best to persuade Olivier to accept the role; but Olivier seemed adamant. He still liked the script and he liked the role of Heathcliff enormously, but unless Leigh were part of the deal, he was not interested, and she had reaffirmed that she would accept only the role of Cathy. Olivier signed to do a melodramatic prewar film, *Q Planes*, and Wyler made a test of Robert Newton for Heathcliff; but the Newton test was no more favorable than a previous one with Douglas Fairbanks, Jr. Once again Olivier was approached by Wyler, and once again he declined. At this point, Leigh stepped in, realizing that they could not keep turning down offers on the grounds that there were not roles for both of them in the same picture, and she persuaded Olivier to reconsider; he did and signed a contract with Goldwyn to play Heathcliff.

Olivier's first days in Hollywood filming *Wuthering Heights* were a nightmare. He was not only homesick for London and Vivien Leigh, but also he had problems with Merle Oberon, with Goldwyn, and with Wyler himself, who had done everything to get him signed for the role. He muttered his way through rehearsals and sulked his way through scenes, but Heathcliff is a sulky man, and this behavior was decidedly in character. After tempers flared and there was a showdown, a turnabout slowly came; temperaments cooled, and personalities became more compatible. Relationships on the set actually became amiable.

Olivier and Leigh had parted in London with misgivings, knowing that their separation would last for a full three months at least. In spite of the fact that she was scheduled to begin rehearsals for a production of *A Midsummer Night's Dream*, she flew on an impulse to Hollywood for a few days to visit Olivier. During her visit, Leigh met David O. Selznick; he ordered a test of her to be made by George Cukor for Scarlett O'Hara in *Gone with the Wind*; and the ultimate result was that she got the most coveted role in Hollywood, one she had dreamed of playing. Thus Olivier and Leigh were able to work in Hollywood at the same time, if not in the same picture.

Wuthering Heights opened the pathway to stardom for Olivier and he earned a nomination as Best Actor at Academy Awards time, although the award went to another Englishman, Robert Donat, for *Goodbye, Mr. Chips*, over not only Olivier, but also Clark Gable for *Gone with the Wind*.

The story of the deathless romance of Cathy (Merle Oberon) and Heathcliff (Laurence Olivier) is told in retrospect, through the narration of Ellen Dean (Flora Robson), the housekeeper at Wuthering Heights. It is a bitter night on the Yorkshire moors, when a lone traveler, Dr. Kenneth (Donald Crisp), seeks refuge at the Heights. Grudgingly, he is given a room, and he prepares himself to spend the night. The wind is howling ferociously, but over it the traveler hears a woman's voice calling desperately, "Heathcliff! Heathcliff!" He goes to the window and peers out at the howling storm. There seems to be a movement in the wind, and the panes rattle as if someone were knocking on them. Impulsively, he puts his hand outside, and it is clutched almost immediately in an icy grasp. Startled, he flings himself backward with a cry. Ellen Dean hears his cry and takes him downstairs for a warm drink, and when she learns what has happened, she reluctantly begins to tell him the tale of stark passion, revenge, and terror that had taken place not so long ago in this same desolate house.

Earnshaw (Cecil Kellaway), who owned Wuthering Heights, was a widower with two children to rear, a daughter named Cathy, and a son, Hindley (Hugh Williams), who, although he was the favored young master, was thoroughly disliked by the household. One day Earnshaw returns from a visit to Liverpool, bringing with him a young gypsy boy, a waif who had attached himself to him in the wintry Liverpool streets. From the beginning, young Hindley loathes the intruder, calling him "gypsy scum," but young Cathy is fascinated by the young Heathcliff, which is the name given him by Earnshaw. The children mature, and the fascination between Heathcliff and Cathy grows into a fast, deeper emotion, even as the enmity of Hindley is fired by the sight of his sister's friendliness toward a dark stableboy from nowhere.

Even when they are grown, Cathy and Heathcliff have a royal time alone together on the moors, and one day they make their way to the nearest lodge, Thruschcross Grange, where a big party is being given. They climb the wall so that they may look upon the dancing couples, but Cathy has an accident and falls, arousing the dogs as well as the guests. Cathy is recognized and carried into the house, but Heathcliff is rudely dismissed and sent back to Wuthering Heights.

Cathy becomes fond of Edgar Linton (David Niven) and his sister Isabella (Geraldine Fitzgerald), the young heirs to the Grange, and she stays several weeks with them until her injuries are mended. She is brought home in style, wearing borrowed finery, a changed young lady. She has had a taste of society and worldly living and tries to goad Heathcliff into going away and making a gentleman of himself so that she might be seen in his company. Heathcliff overhears her deriding him, saying that it would degrade her to wed him, and in a rage he runs away. Edgar woos Cathy; she is flattered. Heathcliff has become only a memory, and Cathy and Edgar are wed.

The years pass, and then, with no warning, Heathcliff returns from America, which is where he says he has been. He has now returned with a considerable fortune. Hindley has turned into a brooding, ill-tempered drunkard, and Heathcliff wins the little fortune Hindley possesses, including Wuthering Heights. Hindley dies in bitterness. Heathcliff's helpless fury on finding that Cathy has become the wife of Edgar turns to nightmarish revenge when he uses Isabella as his pawn; he marries her and then treats her abominably, neglecting her entirely. Isabella knows no happiness in her marriage, nor has Cathy found any lasting pleasure in becoming the wife of Edgar. She knows that there is only one man for her—Heathcliff—and he has abandoned her out of revenge.

The moors become a scene of tumultuous, twisted passions, as the frustrated lovers yearn hopelessly for each other. Cathy sickens, and when Heathcliff learns that she is dying, he rushes to the Grange, forcing his way up to her room. The ensuing scene in which they plan an enduring love, and he carries her to the big window where she may look out on the moors she loves as if they were her sea and she a star-crossed maiden, is unforgettable.

With her death, the scene returns to Ellen Dean ending her narration. An embittered Heathcliff enters the room; he has aged and is half-mad. When he learns that the lonely, lovely ghost of his Cathy has come back to Wuthering Heights crying his name, a look of anguish crosses his face, and he rushes out into the wind and storm to claim her as his own.

Wuthering Heights became Goldwyn's favorite of all his personal productions, although during its shooting he often spoke of it with aggravation as "a doubtful picture." He withheld it for a long time from television release, preferring to reissue it for theatrical viewing in new prints. It remains one of the great love stories of all time.

Wuthering Heights remains Merle Oberon's finest piece of work in films. After playing Heathcliff, Laurence Olivier played several other moody heroes, such as Max de Winter in *Rebecca* (1940) and Lord Nelson in *That Hamilton Woman* (1941). He was a stunning Mr. Darcy in *Pride and Prejudice* (1940) before he went on to play the great Shakespearean roles that have made him the premier actor of our time. Geraldine Fitzgerald, a newcomer as Isabella, won a nomination as Best Supporting Actress for the year; Flora Robson was superb as Ellen Dean; and the whole production has sterling values in every category. *Wuthering Heights* was refilmed during the 1960's by American-International, but that production had none of the haunting beauty of this first dramatization of Emily Brontë's passionate love story.

DeWitt Bodeen

YANKEE DOODLE DANDY

Released: 1942
Production: Jack L. Warner and Hal B. Wallis for Warner Bros.
Direction: Michael Curtiz
Screenplay: Robert Buckner and Edmund Joseph; based on a story by Robert Buckner
Cinematography: James Wong Howe
Editing: George Amy
Sound: Nathan Levinson and Warner Bros. Studio Sound Department (AA)
Music: Ray Heindorf and Heinz Roemheld (AA)
Running time: 126 minutes

Principal characters:

George M. Cohan	James Cagney (AA)
Mary	Joan Leslie
Jerry Cohan	Walter Huston
Sam Harris	Richard Whorf
The President	Captain Jack Young
Schwab	S. Z. Sakall
Josie Cohan	Jeanne Cagney
Fay Templeton	Irene Manning

As America entered the 1940's, Warner Bros., a studio noted for its earlier biographies of men such as Pasteur (*The Story of Louis Pasteur*, 1935) and Émile Zola (*The Life of Émile Zola*, 1937), began a series of biographies of light composers such as George M. Cohan (*Yankee Doodle Dandy*), George Gershwin (*Rhapsody in Blue*, 1943), Irving Berlin (*This Is the Army,* 1943), and Cole Porter (*Night and Day*, 1946). Highly fictionalized, their emphasis was on music rather than drama. Nonetheless, among this group, *Yankee Doodle Dandy* stands apart as a tribute to both Cohan's music and the actor who portrayed him.

James Cagney had already demonstrated his versatility as an actor and song and dance man by the time he made *Yankee Doodle Dandy*, but few were prepared for the powerful performance which he delivered, and his energetic portrayal of one of America's foremost patriotic composers earned him a much-deserved Academy Award for Best Actor. The life of Cohan is told in a series of flashbacks generated by an invitation to the White House by President Franklin D. Roosevelt (Captain Jack Young). Not knowing the purpose of the visit, Cohan suspects it may be because he is impersonating the President in a Broadway musical, *I'd Rather Be Right*. Nevertheless, upon meeting the President, Cohan begins to reminisce with him. He tells about his birth on the Fourth of July, 1878, and a flashback begins.

George's father (Walter Huston) has just finished a theatrical performance when news comes of George's impending birth. Rushing into the street, which is filled with people celebrating the holiday, the elder Cohan commandeers a cavalry caisson to the hospital and upon George's birth, he signals to the men waiting below to fire a one-gun salute. Foreshadowed by this introduction to theatrics, the younger Cohan grows into a cocky young man whose performance in *Peck's Bad Boy* is a little too realistic. Nevertheless, he survives his adolescence to join his father, mother, and sister on stage in an act known as "The Four Cohans."

George does retain some of his cockiness into adulthood, however, as demonstrated by another flashback scene in which, dressed in the stage makeup of an old man, he cons an aspiring young actress named Mary (Joan Leslie). First wooing her with fatherly advice, he then shocks her by breaking into a highly energetic dance while peeling off his octogenerian disguise. Later, although he promotes and encourages her career, he succeeds only in getting her fired and himself blacklisted. Confident, however, that he can succeed, he sets out on a solo career. After failing to elicit much interest, he finally persuades a rich man, Schwab (S. Z. Sakall), into backing a show after promising to include in it a great many beautiful dancing girls, and in the process, he secures a partner, Sam Harris (Richard Whorf), who is also attempting to persuade Schwab into backing a production. Together, they produce *Little Johnnie Jones*, which becomes a smash hit. Armed with this success, Cohan and Harris now set out to lure a big Broadway star, Fay Templeton (Irene Manning), for their next show. Although initially uninterested, she is impressed when Cohan writes a song for her while she is onstage, and she is further impressed when Sam shows her a song entitled "Mary" which Cohan has written for his girl friend Mary. Since he has given away her song, Cohan attempts to soften the blow to Mary with candy and flowers; she has already guessed the truth, however, and settles for a marriage proposal instead, feeling that the star can have the song as long as she has the composer.

Cohan and Harris become very successful with Cohan's plays appearing on Broadway. However, with the outbreak of World War I, Cohan suffers two disappointments: he has his first theatrical flop when he attempts a dramatic play; and because of his age, he is rejected while attempting to enlist in the armed forces. He recuperates, nonetheless, and returns to that which he does best—entertaining. Together with his wife, he tours with the USO and is inspired to write a number of patriotic songs, including "Over There," the theme song of World War I. His play, "The Red, White and Blue," also demonstrates that no one, aside from John Philip Sousa, was more prolific a patriotic songwriter than Cohan.

As the film ends, we learn that President Roosevelt has called Cohan to the White House to present him with the Congressional Medal of Honor for his patriotic services to his country. Walking outside, the troops are marching off to yet another war singing "Over There"—a further reminder of Cohan's influence upon American music.

What saves *Yankee Doodle Dandy* from being dismissed as simple and sentimental is James Cagney's highly energetic yet earnest portrayal of Cohan. The film was in many ways a personal family project of the Cagneys since his brother William served as associate producer, and his sister Jeanne was cast as Cohan's younger sister, Josie. Director Michael Curtiz must also be credited for producing an entertaining vehicle in which to showcase Cohan's music. Like most of the screen biographies of the period, *Yankee Doodle Dandy* was made to entertain and honor the subject of the film rather than enlighten and inform, and the audience learns little about the man except that his ambition was the prime motivating factor in his life. In this cinematic presentation of Cohan's career, simplicity is of the essence. All details of that career are told in as entertaining and straightforward a way as possible. Whether events in the film are true is unimportant; they are entertaining and quickly serve the filmmaker's needs. One example of this is the meeting in the film between George M. Cohan and Eddie Foy. In their primes, they were two of the biggest names on Broadway; it is more than likely that they knew each other, or at least had met. However, for the purpose of entertainment, Curtiz has these two giants meet anonymously on the streets of Broadway where they trade jibes about each other's work. It is unlikely that this meeting ever took place as described in the film, but the audience does not care. The scene is entertaining, and the purpose of the film is to entertain.

Filmmakers in the 1940's were more interested in entertaining their audiences than in informing them; America was at war, and all of America was bound together by a patriotic fervor, which George M. Cohan symbolized. *Yankee Doodle Dandy* was a major success for Warner Bros. and James Cagney, and millions of Americans who never saw George M. Cohan onstage were given an opportunity to hear his music and appreciate for all time the contribution he made to the American theater.

James J. Desmarais

YOU CAN'T CHEAT AN HONEST MAN

Released: 1939
Production: Lester Cowan for Universal
Direction: George Marshall and Edward Cline
Screenplay: George Marion, Jr., Richard Mack, and Everett Freeman; based on a screen story by Charles Bogle (W. C. Fields)
Cinematography: Milton Krasner
Editing: Otto Ludwig
Running time: 76 minutes

Principal characters:

Larson E. Whipsnade	W. C. Fields
Vicki Whipsnade	Constance Moore
Phineas Whipsnade	John Arledge
Edgar Bergen	Himself
Mrs. Bel-Goodie	Mary Forbes
Roger Bel-Goodie	James Bush

You Can't Cheat an Honest Man, W. C. Fields's first film for Universal, teams the great comedian with one of the most popular radio comedy acts of the 1930's and 1940's—ventriloquist Edgar Bergen and his dummy, Charlie McCarthy. The film was, in many ways, a comeback for Fields. Absent from the screen for more than two years because of a serious illness exacerbated by his penchant for alcohol, Fields's career was, if not at its nadir, certainly in need of a boost. Indeed, only his appearances on Bergen's highly successful radio show, on which he engaged in a celebrated and hilarious feud with Charlie McCarthy, kept Fields in the public eye at all; and the ventriloquist and the redoubtable McCarthy were probably the primary reasons for the film's initial box-office success. Today, of course, Edgar Bergen and his dummies are regarded largely as a curiosity, and Fields's contributions, both as actor and as writer (under the pseudonym "Charles Bogle"), are the primary points of interest in the film.

Fields plays Larson E. Whipsnade, the larcenous owner of a broken-down traveling circus. Whipsnade has a son, Phineas (John Arledge), and a daughter, Vicki (Constance Moore). As the film opens, Phineas, who evidently inherited his father's avaricious streak, is pressing Vicki to marry Roger Bel-Goodie (James Bush), her callow but very rich suitor. Phineas is obviously willing to sacrifice his sister's happiness for a chance to live a life of ease as an in-law of the wealthy Bel-Goodies. When Vicki resists his pleas, Phineas urges her to think of their father, whose circus has recently fallen on hard times.

Eddie Cline, the director, then cuts to a shot of Whipsnade peering warily out of a horse-drawn coach which is speeding helter skelter for the state line, only yards ahead of pursuing lawmen. Whipsnade eludes capture, but he will continue to be fair game for every sheriff into whose jurisdiction he sets foot. Fields's role in this film has fewer redeeming social characteristics than the typical Fields protagonist. If Whipsnade has a heart of gold beneath his rough exterior, it is kept well-hidden from the audience. Instead, we are treated to Fields at his most unsentimental, unregenerate, and funniest. While selling tickets for his disreputable circus at the ticket window, Whipsnade has ample opportunity to hurl japes at his favorite targets. "You kids are disgusting, skulking around all day reeking of popcorn and lollipops," he whines. He also engages in some mildly racist banter with Eddie "Rochester" Anderson, and capitalizes on his famous propensity for strong drink: "Some weasel took the cork out of my lunch," he complains.

The only touch of class in Whipsnade's whole operation is the ventriloquist Edgar Bergen and his two dummies, Charlie McCarthy and Mortimer Snerd. They do a comical magic show in which Bergen's tricks are constantly being subverted by McCarthy's antics. When Vicki arrives at the circus to visit her father, she catches Bergen's act, and they immediately fall for each other. There is only one obstacle to their romance: McCarthy and Whipsnade despise each other.

The film continues the Fields-McCarthy feud in fine style. "Are you eating a tomato, or is that your nose," asks McCarthy innocently. "Quiet, or I'll throw a woodpecker on you," replies Whipsnade. In an elaborate plot to assassinate the dummy, Whipsnade contrives to have him swallowed by a crocodile, only to see him rescued by Bergen. Whipsnade spends much of the film dodging the local constabulary and attempting to break up the budding romance between Bergen and Vicki. He resorts to a number of disguises (including "Buffalo Bella" the bearded lady bareback rider) to elude the law, and finally gets rid of Bergen and McCarthy by sending them aloft in a balloon. The plot thickens when Vicki, upon learning that her father's legal difficulties are a result of his bad debts, resolves to marry Roger Bel-Goodie—and his fortune—despite her reservations about him. She is on her way to her engagement party at the Bel-Goodie estate when Bergen and Charlie McCarthy, having parachuted from their drifting balloon, crash-land on her car. Their parachute obscures Vicki's vision, and she wrecks the car; as a result, all three are thrown into jail.

Meanwhile, Whipsnade makes his way to Vicki's engagement party in a chariot, pursued, as usual, by a covey of law enforcement officers. Once he is safe inside the Bel-Goodie mansion, Whipsnade proceeds to make a shambles of the whole affair. The long party sequence that ends the film is one of the funniest that Fields ever filmed. "What a wickiup," he remarks as he saunters into the midst of the crowd. Amiably making conversation, he immediately launches into a long and apparently pointless anecdote about snakes. As it happens, Mrs. Bel-Goodie (Mary Forbes) has a horror of snakes that is so pronounced that she screams and faints every time she hears the word. "Probably drunk," remarks Whipsnade, relentlessly continuing his interminable story through many successive screams and faints.

Whipsnade is distracted from his anecdote by an interesting query from a matronly seductress: "How's your ping pong?" she asks. "Fine, how's yours," replies Whipsnade, momentarily taken aback. He soon recovers his composure, however, and, proclaiming himself the former ping pong champion "of the Tri-State League *and* the Lesser Antilles," launches into an epic table tennis battle with the woman. The combatants roam further and further from the table, as Whipsnade plays as though his life depends on victory. The scene is edited brilliantly, and even the most improbable twists and turns of the game do not disrupt its continuity.

Just as Whipsnade is about to be thrown out of the house by the Bel-Goodies, Vicki arrives. Furious at her prospective in-laws' treatment of her father, she calls off the wedding, and Whipsnade, with a distinguished flourish of his top hat, leads his children from the mansion. They board his chariot and take to the road, where Whipsnade leaves the film as he entered it—hotly pursued by the local sheriff.

The passage of time has diminished the comic impact of Edgar Bergen's ventriloquist act (oddly enough, however, Charlie McCarthy's repartee with Fields retains its bite—perhaps the dummy would have fared better had his master's personality been a bit less bland), although he and Constance Moore as Vicki handle the obligatory romantic scenes capably.

Nonetheless, Fields carries the film. His move to Universal effectively rescued his film career. After *You Can't Cheat an Honest Man*, he went on to make *My Little Chickadee* (1940), *The Bank Dick* (1940), and *Never Give a Sucker an Even Break* (1941), three of his finest films, for the studio. His comeback for Universal was not achieved without difficulties, however. Owing to the star's temperament, the filming apparently required the services of two directors. George Marshall handled the scenes involving Phineas, Vicki, or Bergen and his dummies, while Eddie Cline (who had worked with Fields on the 1932 classic, *Million Dollar Legs*, and who would direct all three of Fields's subsequent feature films) directed all of the scenes involving Fields. Somehow, their collaboration worked. *You Can't Cheat an Honest Man* is a Fields classic, which means that it is one of the classic comedies of the American cinema.

Robert Mitchell

YOU ONLY LIVE ONCE

Released: 1937
Production: Walter Wanger for Walter Productions; released by United Artists
Direction: Fritz Lang
Screenplay: Gene Towne and Graham Baker; based on their story of the same name
Cinematography: Leon Shamroy
Editing: Daniel Mandell
Running time: 87 minutes

Principal characters:

Joan Graham	Sylvia Sidney
Eddie Taylor	Henry Fonda
Stephen Whitney	Barton MacLane
Bonnie Graham	Jean Dixon
Father Dolan	William Gargan
Muggsy	Warren Hymer

Fritz Lang's narrative focus in *You Only Live Once* concerns the outrage of the unjustly punished. Compounding the melodrama in this production is the fact that its protagonist, Eddie Taylor (Henry Fonda), is not an average citizen but a "three-time loser."

As Eddie is released from his third term in prison, he is greeted at the gate by his fiancée, Jo Graham (Sylvia Sidney). Eddie promises her that he is through with crime and, he marries her, settles down, and takes a job as a truck driver. Yet after a local bank is robbed and an employee killed, Eddie becomes a prime suspect. Although innocent, he is arrested, convicted on circumstantial evidence, and, in view of his past record, sentenced to death.

Eddie Taylor is thus rapidly overwhelmed by the fateful forces of the film's narrative. Moreover, director Lang accents the harsh determinism of *You Only Live Once* with an accumulation of chance encounters and telling images, culminating when the truck used in the robbery, evidence which could prove Taylor's innocence, slips silently beneath the surface of the pool of quicksand. That image becomes a metaphor for the luckless Taylor, slowly and helplessly drowning under the weight of circumstantial events. Complicating the irony is the fact that Henry Fonda's interpretation of Taylor contains residues of hope and idealism which are almost incongruous in a man thrice-imprisoned by society for his acts.

Whereas Lang's earlier film, *Fury* (1936), to which *You Only Live Once* is often compared, concentrated on the question of mob psychology and recruited such stereotypes as the gruffly authoritarian sheriff, the politically motivated governor, and even the righteously liberal district attorney, rather than the victim Joe Wheeler, to probe that psychology, Lang does not elect to dramatize many of the possible parallel events in this film. As the title suggests, the individual and his one life is the major concern. Whereas Joe Wheeler's only significant narrative "act" was one of omission (failing to report his survival of the jailhouse fire), Eddie Taylor takes a far more active, if unwitting, part in the sequence of events which doom him.

On the date set for his execution, Eddie is sent a message that a gun has been hidden for him in the prison hospital. By the act of slitting his wrists, he has himself admitted to the hospital, finds the gun, and, holding the prison doctor as a hostage, demands his release. Both Eddie and the warden are unaware that the actual robber has been captured and that a pardon is being prepared for Eddie. When this word arrives and the warden announces it to him, Eddie assumes that it is merely a ruse. He refuses to give up and impulsively shoots the chaplain who bars his way.

You Only Live Once not only presents a more sustained treatment of a character's alienation at the personal level than did *Fury*, but also enjoys a more diverse visual style than the previous film. In *Fury*, Lang relied on montage and an occasional moment of overt symbolism to support his basically impersonal plot. As *You Only Live Once* is a more subjective film, so is its direction keyed to the emotions of Eddie and Jo.

In the opening sequences, a series of elegiac details establish Eddie and Jo's romantic dependence on each other, culminating as they stand in the evening by the frog pond of a small motel where Eddie explains to Jo that the frogs mate for life and always die together. Even as they feel secure in themselves, the motel manager is inside searching through his collection of pulp detective magazines under the harsh glare of his desk lamp. When he finds several photos and a story on Eddie's criminal past, Lang underscores the irony first with a shot of a frog jumping into the pond and diffracting Eddie's reflection in the water, and then of a dark, vaporous swamp—where the truck that could prove Eddie innocent of a crime of which he is not yet aware—sinks into the quicksand. Although the frog pond scene could have either ridiculed the naïveté of Lang's characters or awkwardly stressed their lowly social status, Lang's staging and cutting makes it a simple, evocative metaphor for the entire narrative.

For the trial scenes, the soft lighting and lyricism are replaced by high fill and oppressively harsh key lights. Lang even constructs a grim traveling shot which pulls back from a headline reading "Taylor Innocent" to reveal an alternate choice of "Taylor Guilty." Finally, for Eddie's escape, Lang fills the prison courtyard with fog, so that the searchlight beams reach out for him in the manner of white, spectral fingers; the whole, nightmarish array of mists, massive walls, blurred lights, hazy figures, and loudspeaker voices becomes an extension of Eddie's frightened and disoriented state of mind. In this visual context, Eddie's murder of the chaplain becomes, if not pardonable, at least understandable as a desperate response to a prolonged assault. It is an assault not merely on his life, but on his very conception of the world with its moral and physical realities of truth, justice, and love—an assault on the foundations of his sanity.

When Jo, now pregnant, joins Eddie after his escape, the audience must expect that for this couple, as it would be for numerous later fugitives in *film noir*, the only way to freedom is through death. After their baby is born and entrusted to Jo's sister, they drive toward the border to escape. At a roadblock, a flurry of gunfire forces them to abandon the car and flee on foot; a few yards from freedom, both are shot, Eddie falling last while he carries the already mortally wounded Jo in his arms.

Despite the inappropriate quasireligious conceit (reworked from his earlier *Der Müde Tod*, 1921) of having the dead chaplain cry out, "Open the gates," in voiceover, Lang's final shot of his couple, through the crosshairs of a police sniper's gunscope, is an image that is both characteristically *film noir* and surprisingly modern.

Alain Silver

YOUNG MR. LINCOLN

Released: 1939
Production: Darryl F. Zanuck and Kenneth Macgowan for Twentieth Century-Fox
Direction: John Ford
Screenplay: Lamar Trotti
Cinematography: Bert Glennon
Editing: Walter Thompson
Music: Alfred Newman

Principal characters:

Abraham Lincoln	Henry Fonda
Abigail Clay	Alice Brady
Mary Todd	Marjorie Weaver
Hannah Clay	Arleen Whelan
Ann Rutledge	Pauline Moore
Matt Clay	Richard Cromwell
Palmer Cass	Ward Bond
John Felder	Donald Meek
Stephan Douglas	Milburn Stone

Young Mr. Lincoln won no awards for 1939, the year in which John Ford's *Stagecoach* walked off with many. In recent years, however, *Young Mr. Lincoln* has been the subject of a wealth of serious film criticism. An example of "film-as-myth" par excellence, *Young Mr. Lincoln* weaves Lincoln's youth, loss of Ann Rutledge, choice of law profession, and early cases into a mythic tapestry that resonates in our knowledge of the rest of the Lincoln history/legend.

Young Mr. Lincoln begins with the legend. The film opens with the poem "Nancy Hanks" by Rosemary and Stephen Vincent Benét, in which questions to which we know the answers are posed by Lincoln's mother. We are thus alerted that a general *awareness* of the history (not simply the history itself) is going to be incorporated into the story. The film assumes and depends on audience awareness of the legend, yet at the same time, it rewrites it according to Ford's special vision of Lincoln, his role in America's history, and the forces that directed Lincoln. The poem sets up two dynamics: one is a series of either/or questons, and the other is a limiting function, establishing that the film will act out the Lincoln myth according to some principles while opposing others: it will be a rewriting, not a retelling. What is left out or repressed in such a rewriting becomes fully as important as what is included, especially in a process as self-conscious as the one employed in this film.

Three actions occuring from the film's beginning must be separated before they can be clearly seen. First is the rewriting of the Lincoln myth, second is the creation of new values (and the negative aspect—the leaving behind of values and history that are normally part of the myth) to be affirmed by this rewriting of the myth, and third is the complex function of critiquing the first two. This third function, carried out at a formal level of visual style, is what makes the best of Ford's films so much richer than most: it both affirms and critiques the values by which we live.

In the film's opening, Abraham Lincoln (Henry Fonda) decides to study law after being given a law book in trade by a family headed West. He discusses his decision at the gravesite of his beloved Ann Rutledge (Pauline Moore), who died the previous winter. Later, as a young lawyer, Lincoln handles cases with humor and fairness. During a county fair, a man is killed and the two sons of the woman who gave Lincoln the law books are accused. Lincoln takes the case and supports the mother (who witnessed the knifing) in her refusal to name which son is guilty. In an exciting courtroom drama, Lincoln forces the real killer—who has claimed to be an eyewitness—to admit that he actually killed the man after the two boys ran away from the site.

The poem and the backward-looking structure of the film are not the only indications that knowledge of the Lincoln legend on the part of the audience is assumed. In the first scene, in which Lincoln gives a speech (both to the audience and to the characters in the film), his first line is, "You all know who I am." The comment calls upon both knowledge of history and knowledge of film, thus setting the necessary self-awareness mechanisms in the audience into motion. The characterizations of Mary Todd (Marjorie Weaver) and Stephen Douglas (Milburn Stone) also rest on a knowledge of Lincoln *outside* the film, but necessary to it. Thus the film relies on external knowledge of the legend, but through Ford's choice of the determinants of the rewriting, the values of the legend are redefined. This retelling is experienced especially powerfully because it calls upon knowledge shared by the audience but external to the film. We become implicated in its reformulation as Ford directs us to supply knowledge selectively about the characters and their history.

The creation or recruitment of values is the ideological function of the film. Following the poem, this tends to be a series of binary oppositions, either/or choices, which immediately restrict the subtlety and nuance of the values represented. This is the usual ideological operation of myth: though the conventionalized, schematized representation of narrative, complexity and ambiguity are far less important than ritual. The narrative pattern of ritual must be constant, and must be schematized or abstracted from the complications of everyday experience. Thus they are nearly binary systems in which operation masks contradiction and function often as a repressive force in a culture—the Catholic Church in Latin America, for example. Ford treats the Lincoln myth in this manner in the narrative, then critiques its ideological function formally.

In *Young Mr. Lincoln*, this operation is represented graphically in the choices he makes: they are not masked but clearly represented, and all are immediately (because of our knowledge) recognizable as being determined, or operations of fate. The first is the acceptance of the law book from the mother (Alice Brady) in exchange for supplies, which not only is fated, but sets up determined, valued relationships: the mother is the giver of the law. The second determined choice is whether he will go into law: the spirit of Ann Rutledge and a stick "decide," but since we already know the outcome, this simply functions to further implicate Ann (and sexuality) in the decision. She then becomes another inscription in the Lincoln myth: a dead first love who influences important aspects of a mythic hero is often part of the legend.

Lincoln's role as mediator is insisted upon in a series of oppositions. His first law case is handled with intelligence and finally force ("Did you fellas ever hear 'bout the time I butted two heads together?"), and all parties are satisfied in the end. The money which changes hands is exactly right for Lincoln's fee, and his unifying function has been introduced. A somewhat irrational aspect of that function has also been introduced: the case is resolved not simply "by the law," but by Lincoln's threat and ability to carry it out. At the fair, this unifying function is again illustrated: he will not decide between the two pies he is "judging," and simply keeps taking a bite of one, then another, as the scene finally fades out.

Lincoln's force and irrational character are also demonstrated, however innocently: he wins the rail-splitting and he cheats by using a mule to win the tug of war for his side. In spite of his profession, unifying fairness and calm, he is even at this point shown to be not dependent upon logical, rational, knowable precepts. He is further the unifier in the main drama of the film: he refuses to consider one son guilty and split the family, and it is here that he demonstrates his greatest insight. He does not win the case with fancy legal maneuvers but with divine inspiration via the mother, who gives him the almanac. This element of irrationality is an important aspect in the myth, but relative to history, perhaps the expected metaphor of the family for the nation is of even greater value in terms of its absence. This film about the great unifier and mediator (in harmony with Ford's vision of Lincoln) does not even mention what the majority of the audience might most easily associate with Lincoln the President: the Civil War and the tearing apart of the nation. Only his unifying function is suggested in his "innocent" playing of "Dixie." The *repression* of this violent aspect in the reworking of the myth and the inscription of its opposite value—unification—describes exactly the repressive ideological function of myth, and it is reversed on the formal level in this film.

Another important aspect of the historical myth which is repressed in *Young Mr. Lincoln* is that of the work process. Not only do we see very little of the political in this film (one speech, after which we do not even know or care if he has won the election; Stephen Douglas; and a few references to his career, past and future), but also the process by which Lincoln becomes a lawyer and a politician is telescoped into the transition of a dissolve. The point is not that hours and years of hard work could have been shown, but that this repression leads to the second important variation of the myth. Lincoln is a mythological figure because of a special state of being, not a state of becoming. He is a passive, removed figure in the narrative from the first shot; he already *is* (in history, in the audience's knowledge, and in myth) at that moment and is very little different at the end. At one point in the trial he says, "I may not know much about the law, but I know what's right!"

This is the crux of the Lincoln myth: he *knows*, he *is*, he does not *learn*; that which he learns does him little good. What he *knows* on intuition, however, will take him to his fate. He has a special connection to God himself. In the Lamar Trotti screenplay (written with Ford) he actually talks with God as he walks off at the end of the film. Thus his value comes not from his culture, but from above. He is essentially a visitor, like most mythic heroes. Lincoln thus becomes less a historical myth and more a cultural one, in which the facts of history which root the character in "becoming" are repressed, characteristics of greatness are detached from their generation, and a mode of being unrelated to social processes is defined.

The narrative, then, is a standard one: the myth is rewritten to remove those problematic processes of work and failure; everything that does not affirm the values of the culture is repressed and the hero is removed from a historical context. The ideological operation offers knowledge as a divine gift, the repression of sexuality as a way to such divine gifts, mothers as handmaidens of God's word, and force as the right of those who *know*. It suppresses objection based on logic and work and teaches us that history is not a process of men and women but of larger-than-life *men* whom we can understand only on faith and acceptance. This is often the function of popular culture, to suppress and rework various myths and thereby to console, offer faith-based explanations, and repress those disruptive and sexual elements that would not fit well into a hierarchical society.

There are many reasons films fill this function, such as the huge amount of money required to make them, thus giving the power structure a real stake in their impact on people; and the ideological control exercised on both an implicit and an explicit level by the people and institutions who control the money. But there is room for protest, or subversion, and it exists at the level of the form. A director can question and critique and sometimes even condemn (as Douglas Sirk does in his melodramas of the 1950's) the values offered by the narrative of the film. In *Young Mr. Lincoln*, the critique functions through a process of abstraction which involves the audience in a constant process of "becoming aware" of the work of the narrative.

The character of Lincoln, through whom this process is carried out, is abstracted and removed from the narrative of the film first by our awareness of the myth and Lincoln's "real" place in history. Further, music, composition, focus, acting, movement within the frame, and chiaroscuro all function to remove Lincoln visually and emotionally and to create at least two levels (sometimes three) of which the audience is simultaneously aware. Lincoln seems to exist on a different level from that of the action of the film. He drops into the film to narrate his own story from time to time, but is rarely fully integrated into the narrative of the film. He illustrates and comments on the film from without, often merely "watching over" the stylized action taken from the events of his life, often "narrating" or walking through those events, but generally not belonging to the level of action.

The first view we have of Lincoln is accompanied by low music. It immediately removes what will follow from the preceding level of pompous, overacted, tongue-in-cheek speechmaking; we see Lincoln reclining in a chair carving a piece of wood. The shot is an introduction, a static shot acquainting the audience with the actor who will play the part. He rises slowly, moving with the thoughtful deliberateness which will continue to isolate him from the rest of the film by the necessary slowing down of action that his movement dictates. Throughout the film, most notably in the murder sequence and the trial scenes, Lincoln hangs nearly suspended on the side of the frame, watching the action, both to function as the determining influence which makes it possible and necessary, and to stand nearly motionless waiting for his cue. In the murder sequence he follows the crowd to the site without sharing their excitement, hangs back by the little family in his dark clothes and hat as the townspeople mill around in the background, and steps in at his cue to take his position in the narrative.

In the courtroom, Lincoln is often static, framing two sides of the shot by his dark outline. His foreground dominance is not part of the action, but determines it. In other shots, he moves restlessly on another level from the action of the trial, either above it (as when he goes up the stairs and leafs through some books with the trial going on around him, sitting down on the rail as though taking a rest from his role) or below it, sitting down on the little steps that lead up to the jury box while John Felder (Donald Meek) is giving an impassioned speech. This movement is in opposition to the general movements of the court, as well as to the expected movement of his character within the scene. There are shots which compose Lincoln to resemble a bust of himself, and one in which he is draped horizontally across the frame while questioning a witness. This deliberate failure to conform to expected visual composition calls attention to the difference in the elements of the frame. The contradiction between what the narrative would seem to demand—formal courtroom composition—and what Ford presents visually requires the audience to become aware (to varying degrees), and thus constitutes a critique.

From the day Lincoln rides into town on a mule to set himself up as a lawyer (the scene itself looking like a highly stylized reenactment) his clothes set him apart from the rest of the people through chiaroscuro: he is abstracted in black and white with no gray at all; others, even when dressed in black and white, contrast with his austerity. The costume itself is clearly a costume; the stovepipe hat no one else wears is a self-conscious prop in terms of the film. It is, however, primarily in the play of light and dark that his costume places Lincoln on a different level from the rest of the film: when he is first in his office settling a case, the white of his shirt seems to collect light and glow with it, while the black of his vest contrasts it. In the night with his coat on he is appropriately like a spirit belonging to another world.

Lincoln is played with a detachment unmatched by any other character. In the courtroom scenes this detachment is contrasted for humor (as well as for purposes of removing Lincoln from the level of action) with the overly enthusiastic and emotional investment in the case by the prosecuting lawyer. With Palmer Cass (Ward Bond), the trap is set and sprung in a manner that underscores the process of acting out that Lincoln demonstrates through most of the film. His detachment from the action of the film is a part of the scene: Lincoln already *knows*—both the answers to the questions and the entirety of the story of his life.

As the film draws to a close, Lincoln becomes totally abstracted to the level he has functioned on through most of the film, and the level of action falls away. When he walks out of the courtroom toward the door where the "people are waiting," he is already removed from the people around him, even while he speaks to them. Mary Todd cannot quite touch him, and Stephen Douglas refers to history: they will be opponents again, and he will not make the mistake of underestimating Lincoln again. As Lincoln walks on, the people do not exist. We experience them as the actor does, hearing only their cheers; but the cheers are reserved for the "real" Lincoln. They have no place on the level the film is moving toward. Only the family appears once more to take their leave of the man and the myth, and then Lincoln walks off into the storm and out of the film itself. Taking his place is a bust of himself, then the statue. The abstraction is total at this point; the "actor" Lincoln has returned to the level of statue and myth, having left it on one plane (but never moved from it on another) to narrate and illustrate this version of his story.

The constant split between Lincoln and the narrative is a self-conscious device which insists upon the necessity of becoming aware—of questioning both what is inscribed in the created myth and what is being repressed. Unlike Douglas Sirk, Ford is not clear in his denunciation of the ideology of the narrative (at least at this point in his career), but his insistence in visual terms that the viewer at least be aware of the process of mythmaking and the values affirmed and repressed is at least as powerful (if less easily articulated because it is visual) as those elements of the narrative which construct the myth. There is an unusual amount of freedom to perceive both functions simultaneously in Ford's films, and to experience them according to the subjectivity of the viewer.

Janey Place

ZORBA THE GREEK

Released: 1964
Production: Michael Cacoyannis for Rochley Productions; released by Twentieth Century-Fox
Direction: Michael Cacoyannis
Screenplay: Michael Cacoyannis; based on the novel of the same name by Nikos Kazantzakis
Cinematography: Walter Lassally
Editing: Michael Cacoyannis
Music: Mikos Theodorakis
Running time: 142 minutes

Principal characters:
Alexis Zorba .... Anthony Quinn
Basil .... Alan Bates
Widow .... Irene Papas
Madame Hortense .... Lila Kedrova

Zorba the Greek is Anthony Quinn's finest acting accomplishment. Virtually every film in which he has been involved has been compared in some way to the character of Zorba. Rarely has an actor so thoroughly dominated a film, but there is a reason for this: the script was written with Quinn in mind. At the same time, rarely has an actor enjoyed such supportive script, cinematography, photography, music, and setting for his skills. *Zorba the Greek* is an excellent example of an actor's film and an actor's triumph.

Zorba the Greek emerged from a fine story adapted from the monumental novel of Nikos Kazantzakis, the most talented Greek writer of modern times. The novel translates well onto the screen, and neither content nor intent of the story suffered at the hands of Michael Cacoyannis who authored the screenplay and knew Kazantzakis at the end of the novelist's life.

The story is powerfully simple. Basil (Alan Bates), an English author in his thirties, is in Pireaus, port city of Athens, awaiting passage to Crete. Having recently inherited a small cottage and long-defunct lignite mine there, he seeks the solitude of this rugged island for his writing. The audience learns that Basil, at work on a biography of Buddha, has been unable to convey the ascetic tranquility of this theologian and philosopher while trying to write in the hectic, modern urban atmosphere of England. While waiting for the ship in a crowded transit room, Alexis Zorba (Anthony Quinn) enters the room. He is quickly attracted to Basil, who is distinctive in his proper English attire; Zorba introduces himself and informs Basil that he, too, is bound for Crete. With this almost childlike introduction, the viewer becomes a party to one of the most impetuous, loving, and philosophically profound relationships to develop on film.

Zorba is in all ways the direct opposite of Basil: Basil is restrained, quiet, and silently dignified in manner and dress; Zorba is robust, unrestrained, and—as reflected in his attire—unconcerned about appearances. Although in his fifties, Zorba is still strong and tall, qualities which reiterate the sharp differences between the two men. Once in Crete, their differences continue to manifest themselves. Zorba is an ebullient yet gentlemanly pursuer of women; Basil is shy and retiring. When a handsome village widow calls Basil to her chamber, he goes only after Zorba implores him to go. Meanwhile, Basil's appearance begins to suggest Zorba's influence, as he ceases bothering to shave or change his clothes.

As the film progresses, Basil incorporates in himself unmistakable influences of Zorba. A cathartic incident at the end of the film reflects this evolution. Zorba has implored Basil to repair and begin operating the lignite mine which has remained dormant largely because of a lack of sturdy timbers to prop up sagging walls. Zorba claims experience in mining and proposes that Basil invest his inheritance in Zorba's elaborate sluice project. Basil agrees, and builds the sluice which is supposed to float logs to them from a nearby mountain. While a bevy of Orthodox priests christen Zorba's contraption and local townspeople excitedly watch the celebration, Zorba launches the initial log; then, all watch increduously as the sluice disintegrates under the weight of its speeding load. With the project a complete loss, Basil's monies are totally lost; his response is to ask that Zorba teach him to dance on the beach of Crete. It is the most hilarious scene in this film in which humor constantly vies with seriousness.

Basil's simple request testifies to a major expansion of his attitude, one inviting closer inspection since attitude and change are the main philosophical concerns of the novel as well as the film. The attitudes toward life embodied by Basil and Zorba were spawned from the ancient Greeks and enshrined in their religious belief in the gods Dionysus and Apollo. Dionysus was impetuous and passionate, unreflective and irrational; his passions were expressed in the strong emotional arts such as music and dance. There is little doubt that Zorba's spirit is aligned with that of Dionysus. Basil, on the other hand, represents Apollo. Rational and reflective, passive and restrained, the Apollonian world view is expressed in literature and sculpture, in the contemplative arts rather than the active ones. Apollo checked the emotions, Dionysus offered them free reign.

Although possessing opposite orientations in the world, Zorba and Basil are for a brief time coupled in harmony. Thus, when Zorba's sluice collapses, Basil opts for the Dionysian remedy of dance. He, too, has a choice of acting either rationally or emotionally. For the ancient Greeks, as well as for the modern Kazantzakis, this temporary union marks a rare peak of human experience, the material from which myths are made.

While the story leads toward this philosophic end, the entire film is a showcase for Quinn's brilliant acting; this role stands as his finest achievement. He is physically perfect as the wise, old, craggy and yet childlike Greek. He exudes both experience and visceral wisdom. So powerful and arresting was his performance that reviewers of his later films often refer to his subsequent roles as Zorba the pope or Zorba the politician. Zorba and Quinn, similar also to Dionysus and Apollo, had for a time become one. Alan Bates, too, is convincing as Zorba's shy, always reflective friend. Irene Papas is excellent as the brooding, quietly passionate widow who desires Basil, and the remaining cast, drawn from the people of Crete, lend unending credibility to the film.

The black-and-white cinematography of John Lassally is excellent, serving to reemphasize the almost dark and light philosophies which Zorba and Basil represent. The unforgettable musical score is carefully interwoven into the film, supporting the visuals rather than competing with them. Written by Mikos Theodorakis, the score effectively utilizes native Greek instruments.

The success of the film stems from many elements: the story rich with philosophic propositions of venerable heritage, the outstanding contribution of Michael Cacoyannis, the music, and the careful cinematography. In the end, however, it is the acting of Anthony Quinn which makes the abstract real, as he exudes his powerful presence in an uncommon screen triumph.

John G. Tomlinson, Jr.

DIRECTOR INDEX

DIRECTOR INDEX

DIRECTOR INDEX

SCREENWRITER INDEX

SCREENWRITER INDEX

SCREENWRITER INDEX

SCREENWRITER INDEX

CINEMATOGRAPHER INDEX

CINEMATOGRAPHER INDEX

EDITOR INDEX

EDITOR INDEX

EDITOR INDEX

EDITOR INDEX

PERFORMER INDEX

PERFORMER INDEX

PERFORMER INDEX

PERFORMER INDEX

PERFORMER INDEX

PERFORMER INDEX

PERFORMER INDEX

CHRONOLOGICAL LIST OF TITLES

1927

Jazz Singer, The

1929

Blackmail
Broadway Melody, The
Hallelujah!
Love Parade, The

1930

All Quiet on the Western Front
Animal Crackers
Hell's Angels
Min and Bill

1931

Cimarron
City Lights
Dracula
Frankenstein
Front Page, The
Monkey Business
Public Enemy, The
Struggle, The

1932

Dr. Jekyll and Mr. Hyde
Farewell to Arms, A
Grand Hotel
I Am a Fugitive from a Chain Gang
Love Me Tonight
Million Dollar Legs
One Hour with You
Rain
Rasputin and the Empress
Red Dust
Scarface: The Shame of the Nation
Tarzan, the Ape Man
What Price Hollywood?

1933

Bitter Tea of General Yen, The
Bombshell
Cavalcade
Death Takes a Holiday
Dinner at Eight
Flying Down to Rio
42nd Street
King Kong
Little Women
Morning Glory
Power and the Glory, The
Private Life of Henry VIII, The
Queen Christina
She Done Him Wrong

1934

Cleopatra
Gay Divorcee, The
It Happened One Night
Of Human Bondage
One Night of Love
Our Daily Bread
Scarlet Pimpernel, The
Sing as We Go
Thin Man, The
Twentieth Century

1935

Ah, Wilderness!
Alice Adams
Anna Karenina
Bride of Frankenstein, The
Informer, The
Littlest Rebel, The
Miserables, Les
Mutiny on the Bounty
Naughty Marietta
Night at the Opera, A
Tale of Two Cities, A
39 Steps, The
Top Hat

1936

Camille
Craig's Wife
Dodsworth
Follow the Fleet
Fury
Modern Times
My Man Godfrey
San Francisco
Show Boat
These Three
Things to Come
Winterset

1937

Awful Truth, The
Captains Courageous
Fire over England
Hurricane, The
Life of Émile Zola, The
Lost Horizon
Nothing Sacred
100 Men and a Girl
Plainsman, The
Prisoner of Zenda, The
Shall We Dance
Snow White and the Seven Dwarfs
Star Is Born, A
Stella Dallas
Topper
Way Out West
You Only Live Once

1938

Adventures of Robin Hood, The
Adventures of Tom Sawyer, The
Angels with Dirty Faces
Bringing Up Baby
Carefree
Citadel, The
Dawn Patrol
Holiday
In Old Chicago
Jezebel
Lady Vanishes, The
Love Finds Andy Hardy
Pygmalion
Three Comrades

1939

Beau Geste
Dark Victory
Destry Rides Again
Drums Along the Mohawk
Four Feathers
Golden Boy
Gone with the Wind
Goodbye, Mr. Chips
Hound of the Baskervilles, The
Hunchback of Notre Dame, The
In Name Only
Mr. Smith Goes to Washington
Ninotchka
Of Mice and Men
Only Angels Have Wings
Private Lives of Elizabeth and Essex, The
Roaring Twenties, The
Stagecoach
Wizard of Oz, The
Women, The
Wuthering Heights
You Can't Cheat an Honest Man
Young Mr. Lincoln

1940

Abe Lincoln in Illinois
Bank Dick, The
Broadway Melody of 1940
Dr. Ehrlich's Magic Bullet
Fantasia
Foreign Correspondent
Grapes of Wrath, The
Great Dictator, The
Great McGinty, The
His Girl Friday
Long Voyage Home, The
Mark of Zorro, The
My Favorite Wife
Philadelphia Story, The
Rebecca
Sea Hawk, The
Thief of Bagdad, The
Westerner, The

1941

Ball of Fire

Buck Privates
Citizen Kane
Dr. Jekyll and Mr. Hyde
Here Comes Mr. Jordan
High Sierra
How Green Was My Valley
Lady Eve, The
Little Foxes, The
Maltese Falcon, The
Meet John Doe
Never Give a Sucker an Even Break
Sergeant York
Sullivan's Travels
Suspicion
That Hamilton Woman

1942

Casablanca
Cat People
I Married a Witch
In Which We Serve
Magnificent Ambersons, The
Major and the Minor, The
Male Animal, The
Mrs. Miniver
Ox-Bow Incident, The
Road to Morocco
Talk of the Town, The
To Be or Not to Be
Yankee Doodle Dandy

1943

Cabin in the Sky
For Whom the Bell Tolls
Girl Crazy
Heaven Can Wait
Madame Curie
More the Merrier, The
Old Acquaintance
Phantom of the Opera, The
Shadow of a Doubt
Song of Bernadette, The
Watch on the Rhine

1944

Arsenic and Old Lace
Double Indemnity
Gaslight
Going My Way
Jane Eyre
Laura
Lifeboat
Meet Me in St. Louis
Miracle of Morgan's Creek, The
Mr. Skeffington
Murder, My Sweet
None but the Lonely Heart
To Have and Have Not
Uninvited, The

1945

And Then There Were None
Body Snatcher, The
Corn Is Green, The
Enchanted Cottage, The
Leave Her to Heaven
Lost Weekend, The
Mildred Pierce
Picture of Dorian Gray, The
Southerner, The
Spellbound
Story of G.I. Joe, The
They Were Expendable
Walk in the Sun, A

1946

Anna and the King of Siam
Best Years of Our Lives, The
Big Sleep, The
Blithe Spirit
Brief Encounter
Gilda
Humoresque
It's a Wonderful Life
Jolson Story, The
Postman Always Rings Twice, The
Razor's Edge, The
Seventh Veil, The
Spiral Staircase, The

1947

Black Narcissus
Body and Soul
Gentleman's Agreement
Great Expectations
I See a Dark Stranger
Nightmare Alley
Out of the Past

1948

Boy with Green Hair, The
Call Northside 777
Easter Parade
Hamlet
Key Largo
Letter from an Unknown Woman
Louisiana Story
Portrait of Jennie
Red Shoes, The
Search, The
Sitting Pretty
State of the Union
Three Godfathers
Treasure of the Sierra Madre, The

1949

Adam's Rib
Heiress, The
Kind Hearts and Coronets
On the Town
Passport to Pimlico
Pinky
Third Man, The
Tight Little Island
Twelve O'Clock High
White Heat

1950

All About Eve
Born Yesterday
Broken Arrow
Champagne for Caesar
Cyrano de Bergerac
Harvey
Rocking Horse Winner, The
Sunset Boulevard
Winchester '73

1951

African Queen, The
American in Paris, An
Bright Victory
Christmas Carol, A
No Highway in the Sky
Oliver Twist
Place in the Sun, A
Quo Vadis
Show Boat
Streetcar Named Desire, A
Thing, The

1952

Bad and the Beautiful, The
Come Back, Little Sheba
Death of a Salesman
Greatest Show on Earth, The
High Noon
Importance of Being Earnest, The
Lavender Hill Mob, The
Limelight
Man in the White Suit, The
Million Dollar Mermaid
Monkey Business
Moulin Rouge
Quiet Man, The
Singin' in the Rain
Viva Zapata!

1953

Band Wagon, The
From Here to Eternity
Gentlemen Prefer Blondes
House of Wax
Julius Caesar
Lawless Breed, The
Mogambo
Shane

1954

Bad Day at Black Rock
Caine Mutiny, The
Country Girl,The
Dial M for Murder
Hobson's Choice
Johnny Guitar
On the Waterfront
Riot in Cell Block 11
Sabrina
Seven Brides for Seven Brothers
Star Is Born, A
20,000 Leagues Under the Sea

1955

Big Knife, The
Daddy Long Legs

East of Eden
I Am a Camera
Marty
Mister Roberts
Night of the Hunter, The
Oklahoma!
Rose Tattoo, The
Seven Year Itch, The
To Catch a Thief
Trouble with Harry, The

1956

Around the World in 80 Days
Bus Stop
Carousel
Court Jester, The
Giant
Invasion of the Body Snatchers
King and I, The
Ladykillers, The
Patterns
Rainmaker, The
Searchers, The
Written on the Wind

1957

Bridge on the River Kwai, The
Incredible Shrinking Man, The
Love in the Afternoon
Peyton Place
Silk Stockings
Twelve Angry Men
Wings of Eagles, The
Witness for the Prosecution
Wrong Man, The

1958

Cat on a Hot Tin Roof
Gigi
Horror of Dracula
I Want to Live!
Last Hurrah, The
Night to Remember, A
Separate Tables
South Pacific
Teacher's Pet

1959

Ben-Hur
Compulsion
Mouse That Roared, The
Pillow Talk
Room at the Top
Some Like It Hot

1960

Apartment, The
Carry on Nurse
Elmer Gantry
Flaming Star
Magnificent Seven, The
Psycho

1961

Breakfast at Tiffany's
Children's Hour, The
Guns of Navarone, The
Hustler, The
Kind of Loving, A
King of Kings
Misfits, The
Parent Trap, The
Raisin in the Sun, A
West Side Story

1962

Advise and Consent
Billy Budd
Birdman of Alcatraz
Days of Wine and Roses
Lawrence of Arabia
Loneliness of the Long Distance Runner, The
Long Day's Journey into Night
Man Who Shot Liberty Valance, The
Phantom of the Opera, The
Requiem for a Heavyweight
Ride the High Country
To Kill a Mockingbird

1963

Charade
Great Escape, The
Hud
L-Shaped Room, The
Love with the Proper Stranger
Nutty Professor, The

This Sporting Life
Tom Jones

1964

Americanization of Emily, The
Becket
Dr. Strangelove
From Russia with Love
Hard Day's Night, A
Marnie
My Fair Lady
Pink Panther, The
Unsinkable Molly Brown, The
Zorba the Greek

1965

Darling
Dr. Zhivago
King Rat
Sound of Music, The
Spy Who Came in from the Cold, The
Thousand Clowns, A

1966

Alfie
Blow-Up
Fahrenheit 451
Film
Funny Thing Happened on the Way to the Forum, A
Man for All Seasons, A
Who's Afraid of Virginia Woolf?

1967

Bonnie and Clyde
Cool Hand Luke
Dirty Dozen, The
Far from the Madding Crowd
Graduate, The
In the Heat of the Night
King of Hearts

1968

Bullitt
Charly
Funny Girl
Odd Couple, The
Oliver!
Petulia
Planet of the Apes
Producers, The
Rosemary's Baby
2001: A Space Odyssey

1969

Butch Cassidy and the Sundance Kid
Easy Rider
Goodbye Columbus
Midnight Cowboy
Prime of Miss Jean Brodie, The
True Grit
Wild Bunch, The

1970

Five Easy Pieces
Little Big Man
M*A*S*H
Patton
Performance
Ryan's Daughter

1971

Beguiled, The
Carnal Knowledge
Dirty Harry
Fiddler on the Roof
French Connection, The
Go-Between, The
Harold and Maude
Hospital, The
Klute
Summer of '42

1972

Cabaret
Deliverance
Godfather, The
Poseidon Adventure, The
Sleuth
Super Fly

1973

American Graffiti

Exorcist, The
Last Detail, The
O Lucky Man!
Paper Chase, The
Serpico
Sting, The
Theatre of Blood

1974

Apprenticeship of Duddy Kravitz, The
Blazing Saddles
Chinatown
Godfather, Part II, The
Great Gatsby, The

1975

Barry Lyndon
Dog Day Afternoon
Farewell, My Lovely
Hester Street
Jaws
Man Who Would Be King, The
Nashville
One Flew Over the Cuckoo's Nest
Smile

1976

All the President's Men
Network
Rocky
Shootist, The
Taxi Driver

1977

Annie Hall
Close Encounters of the Third Kind
Spy Who Loved Me, The
Star Wars

1978

Coming Home
Deer Hunter, The
Heaven Can Wait
Interiors
Unmarried Woman, An

1979

Alien
All That Jazz
Apocalypse Now
Being There
Breaking Away
Kramer vs. Kramer
Manhattan
Norma Rae

1980

Coal Miner's Daughter